A JOURNEY THRO

A Journey
Through Illusions

KURT I. LEWIN

ες

Fithian Press

SANTA BARBARA • 1994

Design and typography by Jim Cook

Published by Fithian Press
A division of Daniel & Daniel Publishers, Inc.
Post Office Box 1525
Santa Barbara, California 93102

LIBRARY OF CONGRESS CATALOGING IN PUBLICATION DATA
Lewin, Kurt I.
    A journey through illusions / Kurt I. Lewin.
        p. cm.
    ISBN 1-564745-057-9 (cloth) 1-56474-211-3 (pbk.)
        1. Lewin, Kurt I., 1925– . 2. Jews—United States—Biography.
3. Holocaust, Jewish (1939–1945)—Poland—Personal narratives.
4. Sheptyts'kyĭ, Andriĭ, graf, 1865–1944. 5. Righteous Gentiles in the Holocaust.
6. Holocaust survivors—United States—Biography.
7. Investment advisers—United States—Biography. I. Title.
E184.J5L5743   1993
973'.04924'0092—dc20
    [B]   93-688
                                                 CIP

TABLE *of* CONTENTS

Preface / *7*

1. The Start of the Journey / *11*
2. The Order of St. Theodore the Studite / *51*
3. The Story of Colonel Torunczyk / *106*
4. The Story of La Spezia / *138*
5. The Clandestine Commanders School of the Haganah / *175*
6. The Story of Moshe Dayan / *206*
7. The Story of a Saint / *238*
8. The Story of Three Lives / *267*
9. The Discovery of America / *303*
10. The Warfare on Wall Street / *333*
11. The Discovery of Japan / *372*
12. The Rise of an Economic Power / *411*

Epilogue / *439*
Notes / *443*

PREFACE

T HIS BOOK tells the story of a rather unusual journey through Europe, the Middle East, the United States, and Asia. The core of the book consists of four groups of short stories describing actual events. Each story is self-contained and provides a glimpse of a situation or of people. The stories are linked by the narrator, who opens each vignette and closes it to provide a transition to the next one. They represent first-hand experiences and observations made on an extraordinary journey.

The first group of stories addresses the war years. The description of the Holocaust, as perceived by a teenager in Southern Poland, is followed by a portrait of life in the monasteries of the Order of St. Theodore the Studite. The story of Colonel Torunczyk introduces yet another facet of the war years as seen from the perspective of a soldier in the First Polish Army on the Eastern front.

The lot of some of the survivors of the Holocaust is described in the next group, which deals with the immediate postwar period preceding the creation of the State of Israel. High expectations are contrasted with the harsh reality and the brutal and bloody struggle for survival. The dream of a promised land was nonetheless fulfilled, and the new state withstood the concerted efforts of its enemies to destroy it. An insider's account of incidents, battles, and personalities provides insights into a little-known phase of the evolution of the new state.

The lot of the survivors touched on in the stories leads to the conclusion that, although the details were known, the magnitude of the Holocaust was not fully comprehended. The indifference and the disinterest encountered by the survivors after the war was the final tragedy of European Jewry. The survivors were left to their own devices in the struggle to rebuild their lives and at times were caught in yet another wave of turbulence.

The stories of the third group deal with the towering figure of the Metropolitan Andrew Graf Szeptycki, whose impact was widely felt in his church and beyond it. The process of his beatification and the descriptions of the individuals involved in it link back to the stories told in the chapters dealing with the war and the Studites. In a way, it represents the core of the book and provides a rare insight into unusual events and a ray of light and hope in this otherwise grim phase of European history.

The final group of stories deals with the experiences of a new immigrant after arrival in the United States. It charts the difficulties encountered and provides a view of the complex and changing society as seen from the perspective of a newcomer. It brings into focus the flexibility and dynamism of the United States, the opportunities it offers, and the limitations of a young and not yet fully formed society still in transition.

As I progressed in establishing myself in the new world, I observed from the vantage point of Wall Street the evolution of the United States and the impact on its society of extraordinary affluence. The position of the United States in the international environment has changed over the years, and major structural problems have emerged. This process of change is considered in the final stories of the book.

Encounters with Japan followed by thirty years of advising Japanese enterprises provided a unique view of that country's postwar evolution and its emergence as an economic superpower. A perspective appears on the problems and challenges facing the United States in the future as seen through the prism of Japan.

The book covers experiences on three continents and life in four distinctly different cultures. It describes a number of unique individuals encountered throughout the strange journey that was filled with adventures. Their friendship and support made it possible to meet the challenges and go on at times in tragic and difficult circumstances. The book was written as a tribute to those who saved my life during the Holocaust and made this journey possible.

Dr. Edmund A. Mennis, my friend, encouraged me to undertake this project. His advice and skillful editing helped to mold a complex collection of stories into a coherent chain. His support and assistance meant a great deal to me in carrying out a somewhat difficult undertaking in describing a long and arduous journey.

Schweizerhof, Grindelwald
July 1992.

CHAPTER 1.

The Start of the Journey

I WAS BORN in Poland in 1925. My father was a scion of an old rabbinical family whose members for many generations led the Jewish community first in Amsterdam and subsequently in the Commonwealth of Poland. He was a grandson of Isaac (Itzhak) Schmelkes, the rabbi of Lwów, an intellectual and spiritual giant revered to this day by orthodox Jewry. He was known as "Beit Itzhak," the title of his books that consist of a collection of responsa (briefs) still utilized in rabbinical courts. My grandfather, Nathan Lewin, originally the rabbi of Brody, later held the rabbinical chair of the old and important Jewish community of Rzeszow.

There my father was born in 1898, the youngest in a large family. He grew up in the relatively liberal atmosphere prevailing in southern Poland, which was then governed by Austro-Hungary. He simultaneously studied Talmud and attended a gymnasium, rather unusual for a rabbi's son in those times. After completing his studies, he was ordained. He remained throughout his life orthodox in his beliefs and practices (a mitnaged, or opponent, in contrast to the Hasidic movement), as did the great majority of Jews dwelling in Poland and Lithuania.

After graduation from the prestigious Jagiellon University in Krakow with a doctorate in philosophy, my father toyed with the idea of embarking on a political career. He ran for office in the elections for deputies to the newly created Sejm (parliament) and was active in the early days of the Zionist movement in southern Poland (Malopolska). The family frowned on all this and advised the young man to continue in the footsteps of his ancestors. Therefore, at twenty-six he changed his mind and accepted an invitation to become the rabbi of Katowice.[1] The Jewish community there was oriented toward German traditions different from the ones to which my father was accustomed. However, he served it well and was very popular, highly respected, and appreciated in a community consisting primarily of German speaking professionals and merchants.

My father was a tall, handsome man with interesting delicately carved features, a high forehead, accentuated by intelligent, smiling eyes. His black hair contrasted with a Venetian red beard that gave him a striking appearance.

In the 1920s a branch of the Nazi party already existed in Upper Silesia, where it was considered more of a nuisance than a political force. Its leader, invited to testify before the city council, spoke about the superiority of the Aryan race, which according to him was threatened with pollution by Semitic (read *Jewish*) blood. A councilman mockingly asked him to describe an Aryan. At that moment my father, who was an ex officio member of the city council, entered the hall. The Nazi leader pointed to him and stated that the man who has just entered was a splendid example of the Aryan race. My father let him finish and then courteously corrected him, stating that he was the rabbi of the Jewish community of Katowice.[2]

My first recollections are from my early childhood in Katowice. My parents, busy because my father's position involved a great deal of political and social activity, entrusted my upbringing to Lena, a young German nanny who was very kind and affectionate to me but rather strict. Consequently, as she was the dominant influence in the first six years of my life, I was brought up in the German tradition. German, which I spoke beautifully as a child, was my mother tongue. Lena was a daughter of a steel worker, and on weekends I used to travel with her to the nearby Konigshute-Krolewska Huta to visit her family. I still recall the coking plant near her parent's home, which fascinated and frightened me.

In 1928 my father, then thirty years old, was invited to submit his candidacy to the vacant rabbinical chair of Lwów.[3] He accepted the invitation, although it stirred considerable controversy in the orthodox community in Poland. The Jewish community of Lwów was essentially conservative (progressive), following the pattern of Judaism introduced in Germany and Austria after the Haskala[4] but rejected by the orthodox mainstream.

The Temple-Synagogue of the progressive movement in Lwów was completed in 1848. Its first rabbi, Abraham Kohn, a graduate of the theological seminary in Vienna, was poisoned by orthodox extremists. Nonetheless, the mostly emancipated Jewish community gravitated toward the temple, while the old orthodox synagogue in Lwów, whose rabbinical chair was once occupied by my great grand-father "Beit Itzhak," had a still powerful if much reduced following. It was frowned on in some orthodox circles to see the grandson of the illustrious Itzhak Schmelkes, the "Bait Itzhak," become a rabbi of the "progressive" temple. Vigorous attempts were made to dissuade my father from accepting the invitation. However, he dismissed the pressure exerted by a variety of quarters, concluding that he would have a better platform to lead and influence the spiritual renewal of the Jewish community in Poland from the pulpit of the temple in Lwów. He accepted the invitation of the "progressive" community under the condition that organ music would not be played on a Sabbath in the temple and the orthodox traditions would be adhered to. The community agreed to his terms, and my father was installed as the first ordained orthodox rabbi chosen to serve this interesting, varied, and vibrant community in a transition to modern times.

My father played an important role in the religious and political life of the Jewish community in Lwów, and, after he established himself there, his impact and influence spread throughout Southern Poland. He was a highly erudite man with a superb command of German, Hebrew, Polish, and Yiddish languages. He was a gifted orator and his sermons, usually in Polish, the language commonly spoken by Jews in Lwów, attracted many Jews and non-Jews alike. He spoke with ease without notes and invariably electrified his audience.

I can still distinctly recall the departure from Katowice to Lwów. The railroad station was packed with well-wishers who came to say farewell to my parents. The compartment of the train was filled with flowers for my mother—and chocolates for me. The trip to the unknown and the transition were made easier because Lena accompanied us to Lwów.

My new life in Lwów concentrated on my home and the nearby large Jesuit park where I played with other children. Gradually I became aware of tension at home. My mother, a few years younger than my father, and an intelligent and well-educated woman, was not suited to be the wife of a brilliant, inspired man, and a prominent leader of the community. Her interests concentrated on social life, fashion, and the fads of the roaring twenties that started to seep into Poland. The demands made on her by my father's position became an unbearable burden, leading eventually to a divorce. My father had the support of the community, which stood by him in those difficult days. My mother left for Italy where she eventually settled. As she had displayed little interest in me, I did not feel her absence too strongly.

Lena, my German nanny, found it difficult to adapt to life in a Polish city and returned to Silesia. She was replaced by a number of nannies who were hired to take care of me. They were mostly unsuited and unprepared for the task. Thus, a rather difficult phase of my childhood started, exacerbated by my frustration and inability to understand what was going on around me. This made me quarrelsome and difficult to deal with.

At the age of six the kindergarten I attended arranged a performance for parents and invited guests to display the achievements of the pupils. We were supposed to perform a little dance to the tune of Grieg's music, and the older children were to recite poems. As we marched on the stage in nice costumes made out of crêpe paper, a boy pushed me and tore my costume. I responded, tearing his costume to shreds. This started a free-for-all fight while the orchestra bravely continued to play and the parents, among them my father in the first row, and other invited guests watched the unfolding spectacle on the stage with amusement.

Not long after this episode my father remarried. Rachel, my new mother, was a daughter of a landowner whose rather large estate, Potoki, was near Rawa Ruska.[5] Her father did his best to provide her with an education and surroundings more appropriate than those available in the simple life on the estate. He set her up with her mother in Lwów in an elegant apartment furnished with genuine

Louis XV antiques and exquisite Persian carpets. Rachel, after graduation from a private gymnasium for girls, continued at the University of Jan Casimir in Lwów, studying psychology and specializing in treating children with emotional problems. She was working on her doctoral dissertation and was an assistant of a then-prominent professor of psychology, Stefan Balij. Her marriage ended all this as she had to undertake the many demanding responsibilities of a wife of a leader of the community.

I had some difficulty adjusting to these new circumstances and was not easy to deal with. However, my mother overcame my resistance with patience, kindness, and a firm hand. With time we became very close, and her influence made an important contribution to preparing me for the subsequent extraordinary events in my life.

At the age of seven, I was enrolled in the primary school named after a Polish poet, Adam Mickiewicz, a contemporary of Pushkin and Byron. I was very proud to wear a four-cornered cap with the colors of the school. The excellent system of local public schools followed a curriculum prescribed by the Ministry of Education in Warsaw. It consisted of an introduction to reading and writing, grammar, and then progressively composition, mathematics, geography, history, and science. The teachers were dedicated, well-prepared and respected by the community. The textbooks were interesting and entertaining. All this provided a sound basis for the continuation of schooling later either in a gymnasium or a vocational school.

The student body reflected the demographic composition of the population of the region and consisted of three equal components—Poles, Jews, and Ukrainians. At first the relationship among the students was harmonious and we visited each other's homes. In the second year when religious instruction was introduced, all this changed. The students were separated into three groups. A Roman Catholic priest taught the Poles, a Greek Catholic priest instructed the Ukrainians, and a teacher of religion introduced the Jews to their faith. Shortly after the start of religious instruction, Jewish children were attacked with insults and comments that they were Christ killers. The Roman Catholic priest, a pleasant and friendly man who taught the Polish boys, was a schoolmate of my father. He invariably asked to be remembered to him when he met me in the hall. Nonetheless, the misinterpretation of the teachings of Christianity introduced tension and made Jewish children a target of slurs and anti-Semitic outbursts.

One day at the age of eight or nine after leaving school I was chased by Polish boys on my way home. I ran as fast as I could and was stopped by a man. Looking up, out of breath and shivering, I had landed in the arms of my father who fortunately was passing by. Nothing was said. Holding on to my father's comforting hand, I continued on my way home.

It was my first encounter with such mindless hatred. With time I learned how to defend myself, and at the slightest provocation or anti-Semitic slur I attacked the offender. Eventually my mother was invited to meet the teacher in charge of my grade, who told her that while he sympathized with my knightly instincts, I nonetheless was given to spilling too much Christian blood in the school.

My mother's beneficial influence slowly redressed the damage caused by the divorce. I was much less unruly and became a reasonably good student. After administering a brutal beating to those who taunted me with epithets like "Christ killer" or "Dirty Jew," I was left in peace. This was probably the only normal phase in my childhood. I was turning into a teenager, somewhat sheltered from the world around me.

The labor riots in the otherwise calm and peaceful city and the occasional attacks on Jews by gangs of university students carrying walking sticks with razor blades imbedded in them were discussed at home and made me aware of growing tension. In the summer months while at our estate Potoki, I could observe the 14th Ulan regiment stationed at ours and neighboring estates carrying out the notorious "pacification"[6] of villages in the region that was predominantly populated by Ukrainians. I did not comprehend the full significance of these events. There was nonetheless a pervasive feeling of uneasiness, which was accentuated by the tenor of conversations with visitors and friends who frequented my parents' home.

The murder of a Jewish student at the University ended the complacency and the belief that the difficulties and the tension would eventually pass. Senior government officials took to attacking Jews, openly echoing Berlin. The Polish Catholic Church and its primate

Cardinal Hlond became quite vocal in attacking "the blight" of Jews. A Catholic priest by the name of Trzeciak, with the tacit support of his superiors, jointly with the wife of the then Polish prime minister, Mrs. Prystor, sued Jews, accusing them of systematic cruelty to animals through the practice of ritual slaughter. The objective of this accusation was to have the courts declare that ritual slaughter practiced by Jews (and Moslems) was inhumane and have it officially outlawed.

Anti-Semitism was by no means the central problem facing Poland in the 1930s. It was only one of the many symptoms indicating rapid deterioration of the environment and the approach of a cataclysm. However, in my universe, that of a schoolboy growing up in Lwów, it was the issue that affected me most directly. The "pacification" of the villages in the vicinity of Potoki, the poverty of the peasants whose villages were decimated by typhoid and other epidemics, and occasional acts of violence perpetrated against Jews were signs of danger ahead.

All this was not understood by Jews,[7] who deluded themselves that the Poles were a cultured and friendly nation and would protect Jews as they had in bygone years. I was aware of the tension and the occasional outbursts, but I could not understand all this. I was engrossed in my studies and my friends. The rest was of peripheral interest to me as I assumed that adults would somehow sort out all these matters.

In the early 1930s it was natural for me to attend a public primary school. After I graduated in 1936 it was decided that I had better continue at the Jewish gymnasium. Anti-Semitism in the otherwise excellent Polish gymnasiums had reached a pitch that could explode, endangering the safety of Jewish pupils.

After six years of attending a public school and mingling with Polish and Ukrainian boys, I landed in a school attended exclusively by Jews. It was a more gentle and civilized environment than the one I was used to, and I was not completely comfortable in it at the beginning. Somehow I preferred the no-nonsense, rough, and masculine environment of a public school. I was always alert and prepared for trouble and brought with me the habits and the customs acquired in the school of Adam Mickiewicz.

A boy from a higher grade, seeing a smaller freshman, pushed me and dirtied my new blue school uniform of which I was very proud. When he persisted, I administered a solid beating, as I was accustomed to do in similar circumstances in my old school. The bell rang and I returned to my class, thinking that this ended the incident. To my astonishment the director of the gymnasium, Dr. Salomon Igel, a distinguished educator, entered my class with the crying bully, who pointed me out saying that I beat him up. The incident was incomprehensible to me. In the old school a boy would never admit that he was beaten by a smaller one. Besides, it was unthinkable to snitch to a teacher and walk around with him crying and looking for the offender. Usually these matters were settled after school with the assistance of one's friends if required.

I was told that a nice Jewish boy did not behave like the gentiles do, and I was severely punished. I understood the punishment. However, I could not understand the argument that one should not resort to force to defend oneself. I became aware that there were two worlds with entirely different rules. I was not so sure that the code of behavior taught at the Jewish gymnasium was a realistic one. My experiences at the school of Adam Mickiewicz and in Potoki, our estate where I spent the summer months, taught me otherwise.

I started to understand my father, his activities, and the position he occupied in the community in the two years before the outbreak of the war in 1939. My mother explained our position to me, as we both were affected by it, albeit in different ways. She was forced to sit on boards of a variety of organizations. Some were interesting to her and others were a bore. The social pressures took a great deal of her time, which she would rather have dedicated to the upbringing of my brothers. She also dreamt about the possibility of returning to her studies. I was, on the other hand, constantly reprimanded because I did not behave like a rabbi's son. I could not have a fight with the boys in the park or walk with a girl without someone lifting the phone and informing my father. My mother and I once sneaked out to a delicatessen that introduced a novelty—kosher frankfurters. Naturally someone observed us, and rumors circulated that my mother and I frequented establishments that might not be sufficiently kosher for a rabbi's family. To be a wife or a son of a celebrity was not easy. My mother and I frequently discussed the restrictions imposed on the family, and I learned from her a great deal about the position and the work my father.

A rabbi's main function was to interpret the Law. The personality and the preparation of the individual determined his role in the community. After years of study of the Bible, the commentaries, the Talmud, and the vast religious literature governing every facet of life, three rabbis determined whether the candidate was qualified. A "smicha" (ordination) followed, entitling the individual to assume the duties of a rabbi. The position of a rabbi was not hereditary except in the Hasidic sects, and years of study were required before ordination. The "mitnagdim," the conservative non-Hasidic but strictly orthodox congregants, reflected the majority in the Jewish communities in Poland and Lithuania. The Hasidic sects with their dynasties of rabbis were at one end of the varied community and the assimilated Jews in reformed communities were at its other extreme. My father bridged the two worlds, the rich heritage of Scriptures and rabbinical literature with the secular studies of philosophy and classics.

The Jewish community in Lwów was divided into two camps that were drifting apart: the traditional orthodox core and the larger camp of those who gathered around the temple and the "progressive" movement. This gap in the community was growing as modern life introduced issues with which the orthodoxy, frozen in the rabbinical responsa, was no longer able to cope.

This split was present also in other communities, with the "progressive" movement embarking on the path of reformed Judaism. They were led by graduates of theological seminars in Leipzig and in Vienna, whom the orthodox did not recognize as ordained rabbis. In an increasingly hostile environment, poverty and lack of opportunities created a precarious and desperate situation for young people. My father, a relatively young rabbi of an important congregation in Poland, dedicated his life to leading a community in transition, bridging the gap between the orthodoxy and the "progressive" camp, and seeking untiringly a better future for the young. The pulpit provided a platform for the spiritual guidance of the community. The presidency of the Teachers Seminary provided him with the opportunity to influence and inspire its graduates, who spread to schools throughout Southeast Poland. Active participation in the executive committee of the Zionist Organization gave my father access to the political mainstream of Jewish life and the ability to curb the disruptive influence of the extreme, almost fascist, right and the communists who introduced discord and friction into an already divided community. After the demise of the chief editor of *Opinia,* an influential weekly, my father stepped in and guided it under a pen name (L). His editorial articles and a weekly column allowed him to reach yet another audience. Many young, inspired, and motivated men and women following his guidance exerted an ever-increasing influence in a community in transition. With time my father's impact spread, and he emerged as a spiritual leader of the community with his influence extending also to its political and economic life.

All this took its toll. He had little time for his family except in the summer when he spent a few weeks with us on the estate. Otherwise only on a Sabbath and on holidays did we have him to ourselves. My mother stood by him and supported him in his every endeavor. She did not necessarily share his vocation and the absolute dedication to his mission. Nonetheless, she was a pillar of strength and stability and knew how to curb my rebellious nature when the limitations imposed by being the son of a famous man were too much for me.

In 1935 Andrew Graf Szeptycki,[8] the Greek Catholic Archbishop of Lwów and the Metropolitan of Halicz, celebrated his seventieth birthday. He was a highly respected leader of the Ukrainian community whose impact was felt throughout the region. A scion of an old noble family with roots in Ruthenia, he was born a Roman Catholic and a Pole. He joined the Basilian Order as a young man since he had been invited by Pope Leo XIII to dedicate himself to the renewal of the Greek Catholic Church.

This task proved to be difficult and thankless, especially in the years after World War I. He showed considerable interest in the Jewish communities living side by side with the Greek Catholic population. During his frequent visitations to parishes in the diocese, he was invariably greeted by elders of the local Jewish community carrying Scrolls to show their respect and appreciation of the kindness and friendship shown to them. He knew Hebrew and had a great interest in Biblical studies.

After reading in the press that the Polish clergy and its leadership ignored the occasion of the Archbishop's birthday, my father decided to call on the Metropolitan and congratulate him in the name of the Jewish community. Accompanied by prominent leaders, he called at the residence of the Metropolitan adjacent to the baroque cathedral of St. George (*Jur* in Ukrainian). This was a gesture of respect in contrast with the rude behavior of the Polish Catholic clergy. It was also a form of a public protest against the intolerance and hostility of the Roman clergy shown to the Jews and the Greek Catholics alike.

This courtesy visit started a friendship that deepened with the years. The Metropolitan, crippled by arthritis, was rolled out on his wheelchair in good weather to the beautiful gardens on St. George hill behind his residence, which gave a splendid panorama of the city. There he and my father spent many an afternoon discussing the problems facing their communities. Sometimes I accompanied my father to the Jur and waited for him in the spacious courtyard.

The newspapers informed us about growing international tension. The Third Reich was rearming, arrogantly and openly ignoring the terms of the Treaty of Versailles. It intervened brutally with Italy in the civil war in Spain, annexed Austria, and started to exert pressure on Czechoslovakia. Refugees from Germany arrived in Poland telling stories of pogroms, humiliation, and horrors of concentration camps.

The ruling clique in Warsaw remained on its erratic path, oppressing Ukrainians and introducing ever-new measures directed against Jews. Although clouds were gathering on the political horizon, the Jews of Poland were passive and waited for the storm to blow over. My father, who travelled extensively and was well informed, warned the community repeatedly and encouraged emigration.

He was questioned why he stayed in Lwów if he considered it a volcano ready to explode. His answer invariably was that as a leader of the community he could not abandon his post. However, he urged anyone who was able to do so to escape. Regretfully, there were not too many avenues open. Emigration to Palestine, then administered by the British, was restricted.

I attended the Jewish gymnasium and enjoyed its liberal and calm atmosphere, sheltered from the violence and tension outside its gates. I liked the teachers and struck up friendships with boys my age. My summer and winter vacations were spent on the estate, enjoying working in the fields with the farm hands. I was paid like all the others and shared their life, starting the day at six in the morning and returning home in the evening very tired. I rode horses and enjoyed the freedom and the contact with nature, which prompted me to think of studying agriculture after finishing high school.

While in Potoki I lived simultaneously in two separate worlds. The estate owners, their families, the overseer, and the personnel working on the estate lived in a compound surrounding a spacious house on the hill in a large park. The farm hands lived in modest dwellings with thatched roofs, subsisting on the edge of poverty. I worked with them in the fields and frequently shared their simple lunch consisting of a piece of dark bread, cottage cheese, and water. Listening to their conversations I was introduced to their hard life, the poverty, the hopelessness, and the anger.

Riding one afternoon through the neighboring estate, I encountered its manager, who extended an invitation to a reception on the following Sunday. I had to scrub and change out of my working clothes, which smelled of horses and manure, and into a suit. After passing my mother's inspection we all left, driven in a carriage to the nearby estate and its impressive palace. There we were greeted by its owner, Martin Horowitz, whose father was a prominent jurist and parliamentarian who had been knighted by the Emperor Franz Joseph.

In the hall of the palace were assembled estate owners from the neighborhood. We were invited to proceed to a greenhouse (orangery) filled with rare subtropical and tropical plants and flowers. In the center of this impressive structure was a bronze bust of His Majesty the Emperor, the late Franz Joseph of Austria. It was August 18th, the Emperor's birthday. Butlers in white jackets served champagne, and a toast was raised by the host to celebrate the birthday of the Emperor of the defunct Austro-Hungarian Empire. We were in Poland and this was the year 1938. My father silently observed this extraordinary scene. I, then thirteen years old, did not believe my eyes. In a way this curious spectacle brought home the enormous gap between the reality surrounding us and the dream-world in which some existed, totally oblivious to the approaching catastrophe.

The shameful betrayal of Czechoslovakia in Munich by Neville Chamberlain was followed by Hitler's demands for revision of the Polish-German border and the elimination of the so-called corridor separating Pomerania from Germany. The newspapers daily brought more ominous news and the possibility of war was widely discussed in Lwów. However, nothing was done to get out of the rapidly closing trap.

On a sunny morning on the first day of September, we woke up learning from the news broadcast that at dawn German troops had crossed the Polish border. A few hours later dive bombers of the Luftwaffe attacked the defenseless city. The exploding German bombs signaled an end of an era, a way of life, and eventually the destruction of a community.

The news from the front was confused and contradictory, but within days it became clear that the Polish army was not able to stop the German onslaught and was withdrawing eastward. England and France, bound by a nonaggression treaty, were expected to declare war. We were certain that the nightmare would end once the Allies entered the war. Finally, the still-functioning radio station brought the eagerly expected news that, after the Germans rejected an ultimatum to withdraw from Poland, the Allies had declared war. We relaxed and assumed that now the situation would improve and the war would end within weeks. This illusion remained with us for a long time.

The daily attacks of the Stuka dive bombers kept us in cellars. It became dangerous to move around in the city, and supplies of stored food were quickly exhausted. Suddenly one morning German artillery shells exploded on the streets of the city. A siege started, with barricades erected by the population from stones paving the streets. The war came literally to our doors with the Polish state disintegrating before our eyes.

Finally news reached us that Soviet troops had crossed the Polish border. It was naively assumed at first that they were allies joining Poland in its struggle against fascism. We were quickly disabused of this, learning that the Soviets were disarming Polish units retreating eastward, and the German army was pulling out before the arriving Red Army and falling back to the so-called Curzon Line.[9] We were not aware of the details of the secret clauses of the cynical Molotov-Ribbentrop treaty dividing Poland between the Third Reich and Soviet Union. After more shelling of the city, the Germans withdrew and the Red Army marched into Lwów. I was standing with my father on a thoroughfare watching the arriving Soviet troops. Observing the troops representing every ethnic group living in the Soviet Union, like Uzbeks, Kazachs, Tadjiks, Bashkirs, and Ukrainians, my father remarked that we were overtaken by Asia.

Everyone was glad that the siege had ended. Lwów slowly returned to normal life, the barricades were removed, and municipal workers restored the flow of water and electricity. Stores were reopened for a day or two, to close again after the shelves were swiftly emptied and the quickly disappearing merchandise could not be replenished. Soviet army personnel were buying everything in sight, and with the arrival of the families of the officers a run started on the stocks of merchandise that had been on the shelves for years.

The population watched the passing Soviet troops wearing unfamiliar uniforms and armed with weapons entirely different from the World War I vintage equipment of the Polish army. Especially impressive to us were the Soviet tanks passing westward through the city. The troops were friendly, disciplined, kept to themselves, with an occasional politruk (political officer) answering questions of the curious on a street corner.

It did not require much time to recognize the chasm between propaganda and truth. Someone asked a politruk whether citrus fruit, a luxury in prewar Poland, was available in the Soviet Union. The answer was that there were factories producing an ample supply of this commodity. The fellow apparently had never seen an orange in his life. The wags started to ask similar questions, invariably getting the same answer. This started a barrage of jokes and anecdotes making fun of the arriving Soviet army and the equally curious civilian personnel.

The local communists, some jailed for years, emerged with the arrival of the Red army and took over the administration of the city. A "milicja" (militia) was organized wearing red arm bands and carrying old Mauser rifles discarded by retreating Polish soldiers. This regime lasted only a few days, because amazingly the communists were promptly arrested and the milicja disbanded and deported. Civilian personnel arriving from the Soviet Union took over the administration of the city, nationalizing factories, workshops, and stores. As there were no newspapers and the local radio station was not yet functioning, all this was learned from hearsay and from direct contact with the new rulers. The city was calm; there was no crime. However, there was hunger, and with the onset of the cold weather it was impossible to obtain coal or wood to heat our homes.

The only reliable information reaching us was from the Polish broadcasts of the BBC or Radio Free Poland in Toulouse. The generally accepted view was that the Soviet presence was temporary. It was expected that life would return to normal once the war was over.

At school I found my friends and teachers who had remained in the city. Its normal activities were resumed, classes were formed, and a new school year started following the usual program of studies. This illusion of normality lasted only a week or two. A Soviet director and a young woman from Kiev, a communist organizer, took over the school and started reshaping it into a Soviet "desiatiletka" (ten-year high school).

At a meeting of parents called in for a "consultation," the question was raised about what language the students should be taught. The matter was discussed at length and the majority of parents opted for the continuation of instruction in Polish. The Soviet director commented that this indicated the presence of suspicious political sympathies. The audience, which naively assumed that it had a choice, froze and waited for other suggestions.

The silence was finally broken when someone proposed to substitute Yiddish for Polish. The director responded that this was a splendid idea because under Stalin's constitution and following Lenin's guidelines every nationality had the right to self-expression. He informed the parents that after the revolution a Jewish Autonomous Republic had been established in Southern Siberia, called Birobidjan, on the border with China. He assured them that the authorities would be pleased to resettle there those who chose Yiddish as the language of instruction, the official language of Birobidjan. He followed the statement with a request that anyone who was interested in Yiddish as the language of instruction should stand up. There was silence and not surprisingly no one volunteered to resettle in Birobidjan.

Whereupon a resolution was introduced that Ukrainian probably was best suited, because the region would in any event be annexed to the Ukrainian Socialist Soviet Republic. A question was asked who in the audience was against this resolution. After short reflection, the parents unanimously accepted this recommendation. It was an interesting introduction to the practical functioning of the Soviet political system.

Comrade Rojfman, the komsorg (organizer of the komsomol, an organization of young communists), made every effort to ferret out socially undesirable students and, following the paranoia prevailing during the last phase of Stalin's terror, was looking for counterrevolutionaries among the students. The originally easygoing, friendly, and curious student body quickly realized that they were a target of a reeducation campaign, and those who did not cooperate would be persecuted and punished. The oppressive atmosphere triggered a reaction. In no time the students learned how to manipulate the system. The faculty was cowed and kept out of all this, concentrating on instructing in an unfamiliar language but following the Soviet program.

The communist cell consisted of students with leftist leanings, a minority in the generally Zionist oriented school, and was instrumental in curbing the komsorg and her informers. A number of students with their help enrolled in the civil defense program managed by military personnel. After a while the students active in these organizations were bold enough to harass the komsorg and systematically denounce her as incompetent to the all-powerful communist party committee.

The students had no particular interest in political games and only wished to be left alone. They resented bitterly the systematic encroachment on their freedom by an aggressive, primitive, and alien system. It did not take much time for them to learn to function in this environment and eventually to manipulate it. The komsorg, realizing it, left us alone while the director was preoccupied in fulfilling his "norm," namely showing that the performance of his school met the required standards. A modus vivendi developed with both sides recognizing that it was in the best interest of all concerned to keep out of trouble.

As the son of a rabbi I was a preferred target of the komsorg. Therefore, the communist cell found for me a spot in the Red Cross and Crescent organization. After a few courses I became an "expert" in first aid. At the age of sixteen I became an inspector for the Red Cross in the railroad district of the city. It was my function to supervise the first aid stations and the training in factories.

On one occasion while inspecting a factory I asked one of those present a question. The answer was given using Latin terms and was far more detailed than required. The woman answering my question was a physician. Only in the strange surrealistic world of the Soviet Union could a sixteen-year-old teenager be given power and responsibility over adults. Thus I found myself in the ridiculous situation in which I was determining the qualifications of a physician to administer first aid.

The city was decorated with "monuments" made from plaster and cardboard. Its walls were covered with placards showing smiling peasants, tractor drivers, children offering flowers to Stalin or to Nikita Khrushchev, the Chairman of the Ukrainian communist party. The barrage of propaganda was intensifying in preparation for the session of the "freely elected" general assembly of the representatives of the "toiling masses." No one knew the elected representatives or for that matter when these "elections" occurred. The meetings of the assembly took place in a beautiful theater built by the Austrians. As a precaution it was surrounded by NKVD troops with machine guns pointing at the passersby and also at the theater for good measure. All this activity was rather puzzling because it was clear that the Soviets were in a position to do whatever they wished. After two days of "deliberations," the assembly unanimously decided to incorporate Lwów and the region into the Ukrainian Soviet Socialist Republic. Shortly afterwards we were issued Soviet passports, which had to be presented at the local police station to obtain a permit to travel out of the city. At the same time systematic arrests were made, always in the middle of the night, of former politicians, newspapermen, owners of factories, and prominent merchants. Most of those arrested disappeared, never to be heard from again.

A variety of registrations took place, including Polish reserve officers, refugees from the part of Poland occupied by the Germans, those who wished to travel abroad, and so forth. The law-abiding and somewhat naïve complied with these requests to register. This eventually landed some in Katyn,[10] and others in labor camps or in Kazachstan.

The anniversary of the October Revolution was celebrated with a "spontaneous" demonstration of the "toiling masses" eager to express their gratitude and joy at being annexed to the Ukrainian Socialist Soviet Republic. All the schools were requested to participate to greet Nikita Khrushchev, who came to preside over this event. We were issued flags, banners with slogans like "Glory to The Red Army, the liberator of the oppressed!," and "Glory to the Socialist competition and the Stakhanov[11] movement." Uniformed political workers supervised the forming of columns and distributed sheets with similar "officially approved" slogans that we were supposed to call out on command. Finally we marched toward the reviewing stand on which Nikita Khrushchev stood with his entourage. It was astonishing to discover that Soviet soldiers were positioned on the street pointing automatic rifles at us, the ostensibly spontaneous and joyous demonstrators.

The Temple was reopened. It was filled every Friday and Saturday with worshipers and became more than ever a center around which the community gathered looking for guidance and solace. At first the Soviet authorities left my father alone and did not interfere in his activities. However, after the first wave of arrests of prominent citizens we were afraid that my father would be included in the lists. Whenever a Soviet army truck stopped on the street in the middle of the night, we were at the window observing from behind drawn curtains what was going on. A small valise packed with necessities was always prepared in case the NKVD arrived to arrest my father. We lived in constant fear as there was no way to find out what was in the mind of this shadowy organization that in those days dominated people's lives in the USSR. Even Soviet military personnel seemed to be nervous when encountering the officials of NKVD, easily recognizable because of the blue color of their military caps and the leather coats they wore. They were polite, even considerate and, when making an arrest, reassured the families stating that it probably was a mistake that would be cleared in a few hours at the milicja station. What went on inside their headquarters at Pelczynska Street and in the prison named after St. Brigitta, referred to in the local slang as Brygidki, was another matter.

We were aware of the purges that took place in the 1930s, the notorious Moscow trials, and the strange affair of Marshal Tukhachevsky, after which most of the general staff of the Soviet armed forces was executed in 1938. The horror perpetrated in the cellars of the Czeka (czerezwyczajna komisja—special commission), and its successors (first the GPU, and then the NKVD) was well known. Its troops and officials arrived with the Red Army and their presence was always dreaded. We were at the end of Stalin's terror, which started to subside as all the real or imagined opposition was executed or shipped to labor camps in Siberia. This process was carried out by selecting categories of "enemies." So far my father had not yet been included in one of them.

He was officiating as he did before the war at services in the Temple. Visitors called on him in his study at home asking for guidance and advice. He also acted as an arbitrator and judge in disputes. (Jews were reluctant to go to civil courts and preferred their rabbinical courts instead.) The Teachers Seminary was closed and so was the weekly *Opinia*. Nonetheless, the young people who worked with him there called on him to get his counsel. Obviously the authorities were aware of all these activities but chose for the time being not to interfere. So far the only sign of harassment was a horrendous real estate tax imposed on the Temple, which was promptly paid by the community to prevent its closing.

It was a precarious existence. For practical purposes my father dared to challenge the regime by continuing his duties as a spiritual leader of the community. He refrained meticulously from making any political comments and remained aloof, concentrating exclusively on religious matters. His sermons were carefully constructed and dealt with moral values and the interpretation of the Scriptures. Undoubtedly agents were reporting on his every move and on every sermon. With time we got used to it, but ever-present fear dominated our existence.

A few enterprising individuals tried to escape from Lwów and crossed to Lithuania before the Baltic States were annexed to the Soviet Union. From there, thanks to the assistance of the local Japanese consul who issued transit visas, they were able to leave the Soviet Union via Japan to Latin American countries. American consuls refused flatly to issue transit visas, providing the NKVD with a reason to refuse a permit to depart. (Only transit visas via Japan and the United States were recognized by the NKVD.) The soulless American bureaucrats could not be persuaded by guarantees (affidavits) that the applicants would not settle in the United States. The refusal of a transit visa by the American consuls active in the Baltic States caused the deaths of literally thousands who held valid Latin American passports and were stranded. There were among them many American citizens whose credentials U.S. State Department officials, oblivious to the circumstances, decided to send to Washington for verification. Most returned to Lwów, where the rest of the community was trapped waiting passively for developments to unfold.

The winter of 1939 was bitterly cold. As there was no coal or wood readily available, we were freezing and sat in our home wrapped in coats and blankets. The city was starving. Food was available only at exorbitant prices on a thriving black market. The Polish zloty became worthless overnight with rubles introduced instead, which made the situation worse. Epidemics spread without readily available medicines.

These hard and cruel days brought us closer together. We were all sitting in my father's study-library as the rest of the apartment was unheated. In a way we were compensated by the presence of my father. The quiet evenings were filled with interesting conversation discussing news reaching us from the London broadcasts and the bits of information brought by a stream of visitors.

The echoes of the far-away war occasionally reached us. We were filled with hope for spring and an Allied victory on the Western Front. The Royal Navy trapped the German cruiser *Graf Spee* in the river Rio Plata, and a strange battle was taking place in Narvik in Norway with the participation of Polish units formed as part of the British and French forces.

Spring arrived and brought some relief, which, however, was marred by the massive deportation of refugees from the part of Poland occupied by the Germans. A NKVD escort would arrive in the middle of the night, a few hours were given to pack, and the arrested were transported by an army truck to the railroad station to waiting freight trains that took them into the unknown. A few weeks later letters arrived from Kazachstan, Mordovian Autonomous Republic, Uzbekistan, and other places we never heard of. Literally thousands were deported in this fashion in accordance with meticu-lously prepared lists. They were left in the middle of forests or Siberian taiga to settle as best they could. They subsisted in primi-tive conditions working as lumberjacks or on collective farms (kol-choz). Starvation and diseases took their toll. Nonetheless, most sur-vived the ordeal.

The barrage of propaganda was unrelenting. Meetings were called to discuss the war between the USSR and Finland, to encour-age miners in the Donbas basin to increase the production of coal, and to glorify the heroic Stakhanov workers in the Kuznetzk basin. We were requested by the politruk to pass resolutions approving these appeals and congratulating the organs of the communist party and its glorious leader Joseph Stalin for doing so much for us. This meaningless farce was boring and tiresome. However, it was danger-ous not to attend these meetings as the block superintendent kept a record of the attendees. Probably the politruk and the superinten-dent also had to fulfill their quotas of resolutions assigned by the authorities.

Energetic preparations started for the celebration of May 1st—the workers' day. Massive demonstrations were planned in schools and factories, and floats with banners and slogans were provided for the festivities. The city was generously supplied with fur hats, thermometers, vodka, and canned and dried fish to celebrate the holiday. Ice cream stands sprouted everywhere. The May Day celebrations were a sort of watershed, as Lwów became, after Moscow, Leningrad, and Kiev, a show place, and life generally became somewhat more bearable.

The fall of France in May 1940 was a veritable shock, shattering the illusion that spring would bring an allied victory in the West and an end of this nightmare. We learned from the BBC broadcasts about Dunkirk, the occupation of Holland and Belgium, the bombing of Britain, and the submarine attacks unleashed on shipping in the Atlantic. The Soviet papers mentioned these events only casually and maintained a generally pro-German stance. We were getting accustomed to the drab life in the Soviet system, and delivery seem further away than ever.

I was attending school and became a low level "aparatchik" of the civil defense machinery. I was well paid and no one bothered me any longer as the "socially undesirable" son of the "reactionary" rabbi. Some sort of accommodation with the existing situation developed in the city, with the firm belief held that in the end the Allies would prevail and defeat the Third Reich. The shaded streets of the city with its many leafy chestnut trees in bloom were pleasant and clean, the parks were full of flowers, and one could harbor the illusion that not much had actually changed.

The martyrdom of my father started approximately at this time. Each Tuesday he had to report at the headquarters of the NKVD with a little valise ready for prison. There he was interrogated for hours and was not allowed to return home until late in the evening. We never knew whether he would return from these sessions, and waiting for him every Tuesday was a torment for my mother and me. My brothers were too small to understand the situation.

He was questioned about his political activities in his youth, he was confronted with anti-communist articles written by him in Katowice in the 1920s, and his views and other writings were discussed and analyzed by the NKVD interrogators. We were puzzled by this and pondered about its purpose. As seen from today's perspective, it was "brain washing" practiced widely in the Soviet

Union and in China. Its purpose was to break my father's spirit and make him to give up his activities, renounce his beliefs, and leave the city. He was offered a variety of academic posts in the field of his specialization at the Universities of Kiev, Leningrad, and Moscow. My father explained patiently again and again his point of view, stressed that he was interested exclusively in religious matters, and that Stalin's constitution guaranteed freedom of worship. He stated repeatedly that he wished to restrict his activities to what was permitted under Stalin's constitution. This was probably frustrating to the NKVD interrogators. Nevertheless, they too were patient and persisted, with a new team taking over from time to time.

My father, then forty-three years old, aged significantly in this year. His hair turned gray and only his eyes retained the old fire. He became detached and concentrated on his work on the manuscripts of the two books he was working on. The title of one was *Marcus Aurelius*. I do not recall the title of the other. My mother, a relatively young woman (thirty-five years old), remained serene and outwardly cheerful. However, a sadness could always be seen in her eyes.

Month after month of this existence passed with the gradual realization that the status quo would not change in the foreseeable future. We gathered fuel and food for the winter. When it came we were better prepared and enjoyed the long winter evenings in the study of my father, sharing our ideas and our hopes. We still believed staunchly that one day the war would end and life would return to normal.

From time to time mysterious visitors called on my father, who always received them alone in his study. By chance I learned that these were emissaries of Metropolitan Andrew Graf Szeptycki. The Greek Catholic Church was oppressed by the Soviets, monasteries and convents were closed, and priests, monks, and nuns were arrested. The Metropolitan and my father were comparing observations and were consulting how to deal with this complex situation. It was too dangerous for my father to visit Jur and, therefore, defensive measures were explored through emissaries. I eventually learned that the discussions concentrated on ways to deal with the heavy tax burden imposed on religious institutions and to understand the official policy toward religious institutions. All this took place in utmost secrecy because the position of Metropolitan Andrew was equally precarious in those days.

Nonetheless, both religious leaders retained great influence in their communities. Therefore, the ruthless regime found it more practical for the time being to leave both leaders alone. This was in contrast with the general and callous disregard of public opinion demonstrated elsewhere.

The political briefings of the civil defense personnel were more sophisticated than those at school or in the housing complex. The politruks were better prepared and were briefed directly by the political department of the Red Army in Moscow. Occasionally we were shown the briefing sheets. The Germans were initially referred to as "friendly neighbors," without ever mentioning the persecutions of communists and the atrocities committed in the concentration camps. Later, the tone of the briefings changed, and Germans were again described as fascists and a threat. It was stressed that the Soviet Union must be watchful because it was surrounded by capitalist enemies bent on its destruction. We were requested to dedicate our efforts to strengthening the civil defense system. A change, at first hardly perceived, but which became more pronounced with time, eventually hinted at the possibility of a military conflict with the Third Reich. Shelters were improved, first aid stations were organized throughout the city, and the training programs were intensified. Nonetheless, it was stressed that the great Joseph Stalin was watching the situation and would make every effort to avert war.

The spring was as always beautiful in the city, with its many parks and squares with manicured lawns and colorful flowers coming to life. This peaceful atmosphere was deceptive. The Soviet military personnel quite openly discussed the possibility of a military conflict. Transports of grain and petroleum continued to pass through Lwów, an important railroad junction, westward on their way to the demarcation line with the Germans.

On June 22, 1941, while trains loaded with grain and tank cars with petroleum were still crossing the border westward, German armored divisions moved swiftly eastward. "Operation Barbarossa," the invasion of the Soviet Union, had started. The by-now familiar German Stuka bombers drove us back into the cellars. The attacks were more brutal than in 1939, and the list of civilian casualties grew rapidly.

German armored pincers bypassed Lwów on their way into the Ukraine. The Soviets, calm in the first few days of the war, started to evacuate the city. Trucks loaded with their families passed through the streets headed East. The orderly withdrawal turned quickly into chaos, and we witnessed again disintegration of yet another regime. I was busy for a while in the civil defense system until it too disintegrated. We then waited in the cellars for the storm to blow over. Ukrainians, assisted by sabotage units dropped by parachute, sniped at retreating Soviet troops from the bell towers of churches and roofs of high buildings. This provoked a swift retaliation, and Soviet tanks passing through the city opened fire on places possibly manned by snipers. The huge complex of Brygidki was set on fire by the retreating NKVD troops. It was rather strange that no one escaped from there; indeed, it appeared that the prison was empty.

It became clear that the arrival of German troops would be a matter of days if not hours. The Jewish population was apprehensive, consoling itself with the idea that Germans were cultured people. Some excesses were to be expected, but by and large some modus vivendi would emerge. A nation that had produced Bach, Beethoven, Goethe, and great philosophers was expected to behave sensibly.

The last Soviet patrols passed the city on foot. An eerie quiet prevailed, with a red flag left fluttering on the tower of the city hall as the only memento of the Soviet regime.

The first units of young German soldiers in their field gray uniforms marched rhythmically through the city, followed by half-tracks pulling artillery. Self-assured, sunburnt, with rolled-up sleeves and with helmets attached to their knapsacks on a hot July morning, they gave the impression of invincibility. People on both sides of the thoroughfare were watching yet another army of conquerors passing by.

Early in the morning of the following day, visitors arrived at our home with the news that a Ukrainian mob was attacking Jews on the streets of the city. My father put on the garb worn by rabbis while officiating (ornat or cassock-like garment) and black gloves, asked me to translate a few sentences written in Polish into

36

Ukrainian, and accompanied by two elders of the community left for Jur to call on Metropolitan Andrew. He serenely said good-by to us with the same detachment and resignation we had regularly experienced before the Tuesday interrogation sessions at the NKVD.

He was received immediately by the Metropolitan. My father reminded the Metropolitan of the many occasions in which he had declared friendship for Jews dwelling in his diocese. My father stressed that now in this hour of mortal danger he was appealing for assistance in the name of the Lord. The Metropolitan was shocked to learn about the atrocities committed by his people. He promised to intervene at once with the German authorities and to send priests and monks into the streets to stop the pogrom. He invited my father to remain at the residence until the city returned to normal. My father replied that his place was with his community and left to return home.[12] At the entrance of our house he was caught by Ukrainians, beaten with rifle butts, and dragged with others to the Brygidki prison.

I had been waiting for the return of my father from Jur and was engrossed in reading a book. A group of young Ukrainians led by the superintendent of the building, also an Ukrainian, broke into the apartment. Before I knew what was happening I was dragged out onto the street where other Jews from adjacent buildings were assembled. On the sidewalks our Christian neighbors, Poles and Ukrainians, were yelling insults and goading the mob to beat "Christ killers and Jew communists." Beaten and kicked by our captors and bystanders who were enjoying the spectacle, we were then brought to the courtyard of the Brygidki prison.

This huge prison complex had been taken over in 1939 by the NKVD and was always filled with prisoners. These were primarily former Polish government officials, reserve officers, merchants, industrialists, newspapermen, and others arrested without a clearly defined reason. The inmates were primarily Poles and Jews, but there were also some Ukrainians among them. The prisoners were systematically executed in the spring of 1941, and the corpses were thrown into the cellars of the compound, which were then sealed. After the outbreak of the war with Germany, the prison was set on fire by the Soviets, and of the thousands of inmates (the estimates varied from 1,500 to

2,000) no one was left alive. The massacre of the prisoners was discovered by the Germans, who instructed Ukrainians to gather "Jew-communists" who had allegedly perpetrated this crime to remove the corpses from the cellars. Petrified Jews were gathered from the neighborhood by an inflamed mob and brought to the Brygidki prison to do this grisly job.[13]

The windows of the cellars were opened, and the decomposed bodies were pulled out by ropes and carried on stretchers to be laid out in rows in the courtyard for identification. The early arrivals like myself were assigned to this task while Ukrainians and German soldiers were beating and abusing us. After a while there was no need for additional workers, so that Jews brought in by the mob from the streets were driven into a far corner of the courtyard.

Suddenly I saw my father walking alone, beaten with rifle butts by German soldiers and driven to join others in the corner. He intoned "Shma Yisrael," in which other prisoners joined loudly. A merciful man working next to me grabbed me and covered my eyes when the machine guns opened fire. My father thus died in an attempt to protect and defend his community. At least he was spared the agony, the torment, the humiliation, and the horror of the systematic destruction of the Jewish communities in the gas chambers of the death camps.

We worked all day long removing the decomposed bodies from the cellars. The contorted faces in the last moment of agony, bodies dripping serum with a hand or a foot detached from the corpse as it was laid out on the stretcher, were a terrible sight. The brutal beating and killing of innocents by bloodthirsty German and Ukrainian sadists was equally grisly. All day long German officers and newspapermen passed by photographing the spectacle.[14] Late in the afternoon work was suspended, the tired tormentors left, and we were herded into the corner of the courtyard. In the evening we were chased out into the street with kicks and beating and instructed to return to work early in the morning.

Slowly we dragged ourselves home. There my mother and some neighbors were anxiously waiting for our return. They approached us at first but were driven back by the horribly sweet stench of decomposed bodies that emanated from us. After washing up and changing, I related what had happened. Our neighbor, a pharmacist who was with me in Brygidki, decided to commit suicide and offered me a cyanide capsule. He could not face another day of this horror.

The Ukrainian mob continued to attack Jews for another day or so. Then the influence of the priests and monks sent out by the Metropolitan Szeptycki quieted the crowds. In the first few days more than two thousand Jews were shot in the ruins of the Brygidki prison and many others perished during the pogrom.

Life under the Soviets seemed now idyllic by comparison. The city was decorated with blue and yellow flags, and Ukrainian nationalists proclaimed an independent state. After a few days the units of the Ukrainian special battalion Nachtigall[15] left the city. The leaders of the Ukrainian nationalists with Stepan Bandera were arrested, and the committee attempting to create an independent Ukraine was dissolved. Lwów and the region were proclaimed the District Galizien and annexed to the Generalgouvernement ruled from Krakow by Dr. Hans Frank, a war criminal later executed in Nuremberg.

There were sporadic acts of violence. However, from now on it was the prerogative of the Germans to deal with the Jewish question, and random violence was no longer tolerated. Jews were ordered to wear white arm bands with the Star of David on them. A Judenrat was organized to deal with administrative matters. Its first president was Dr. Joseph Parnas, a highly respected and trusted patrician, which instilled some hope. A demand was made by the military commander of the city for an outrageously large ransom. No one questioned it and the Jewish community surrendered its valuables in the hope of buying peace.

After a few weeks it became evident that those who qualified as Jews under the Nuremberg laws designed by Dr. Hans Globke, a subsequent advisor of Chancellor Konrad Adenauer, lost all civil rights. For practical purposes one-third of the population of the city was stripped of any protection of the law and was officially declared subhuman. This included converted Jews, Christian issues of mixed marriages, and Christians with one Jewish grandparent. All had to wear arm bands.

A special detachment of the SS (Sonderkommando) arrived in the city with prepared lists of prominent citizens. They arrested and executed a former Polish Prime Minister, Professor Bartel, writer Boy-Zelenski, a well-known surgeon Dr. Ostrowski and others. This was an operation premeditated and carefully planned in Berlin to destroy the political and intellectual leadership of Poland. Two officers of the SS came looking for my father, who was on the same list. Learning that he had disappeared, they slapped the face of my mother in front of the frightened children and left. An auxiliary Ukrainian police (Ukrainische Hilfspolizei) was organized by the German authorities, replacing the milicja. Their responsibility was to assist Germans in controlling the local population, and they were given a free hand in dealing with the Jews.

The formation of these units was celebrated with the so-called "Petlura days" in which a few thousand Jews perished. Simeon Petlura had commanded an army in the Ukraine in the postrevolutionary years (1918-19) and instigated massacres of Jews. He escaped to Paris after the collapse of the short-lived Ukrainian Republic and there was shot by Schwartzbart, a young Jew whose family was killed in a pogrom by Petlura's men. The Ukrainian police started its activities by arranging a pogrom, referred to officially as Petlura days, to avenge him on the Jews of Lwów, who had nothing to do with the assassination.

The summer of 1941 brought one shock after another to the tormented Jewish community. Dr. Joseph Parnas, the first president of the Judenrat, refused to deliver a quota of Jewish men required by the SS for the newly organized network of labor camps in Galizia. He stated that he was prepared to collaborate with the authorities in providing whatever was required with the exception of gathering Jews for delivery to the labor camps. The SS took him to a prison were he was executed with some of his aides. This seventy-year-old lawyer could not do much under the circumstances except stick to his principles. He was an assimilated Jew and not too interested in Jewish affairs. Nonetheless, when the test came he died rather than soil himself collaborating with the murderers. He was one of the long forgotten and unsung heroes who rose to challenge the mass murderers. Regretfully, the successors of Dr. Joseph Parnas had fewer scruples.

After the arrest of Dr. Parnas I was carted away to the Lacki prison together with other clerks working in the Judenrat. After a few days in prison squeezed into a cell with many others, we were taken to be executed in a sand quarry in the suburbs. I jumped out from a moving truck and succeeded in escaping. After Brygidki, it was the second close call. There were many more to come.

The shocking news of events constantly taking place did not permit the community to grasp the design of the Germans in dealing with the Jewish question. In the early days of German occupation, they goaded the local population to a pogrom. Random violence was tolerated for a while, culminating in the massacre of the "Petlura days." This diverted the attention of the Ukrainians from the dismantling of their administration and the arrest of the OUN (Organization of Ukrainian Nationalists) leaders in Vinnitza. An auxiliary police serving Germans and a puppet Ukrainian Committee staffed with Nazi collaborators were all that was left of the promises to create an independent Ukraine. A civilian administration supported by the German police, the SS, and a German military garrison established a firm control over the District Galizien.

The Judenrat was turned into an administrative body assisting the Germans in stripping Jews of their possessions, arranging relocation to an ever smaller but not clearly defined district, and providing a supply of free labor to meet the needs of German enterprises that sprouted up in Lwów to serve the army. Jews manufactured uniforms, underwear, shoes, and other necessities for the Wehrmacht, repaired roads, cleaned the streets, and performed every conceivable task required. A newly created Jewish police force, unarmed and issued only old Polish police caps, supervised all this on behalf of the Judenrat. Whoever did not possess a work permit could be carted away to the network of SS labor camps in the region, usually in the landed estates. No one ever emerged alive from these camps, with new quotas of inmates regularly required by the SS.

The decision to exterminate the Jewish population was taken later in the year in December 1941 in Wannsee, a suburb of Berlin. In the meantime, Jews were harassed and herded into ghettos. Jews representing one-third of the city's population were provided with only symbolic food rations and had to fend for themselves. As they were not allowed to travel, they could not barter for food with peasants in the neighboring villages. Therefore, they depended on Poles to act as intermediaries. Possessions were exchanged for food, with Polish traders like hyenas exploiting their tragic situation.

My mother was doing her best to take care of the three of us without ever complaining. We were starving, and at any time I could be caught on the street and sent to one of these dreaded camps. This prompted me to get out of the city in order not to be a burden to my mother. I was also toying with the idea of locating a possible shelter for the family. Rawa Ruska, a town near our estate Potoki, in a region which I knew well, was a logical choice.

My mother's cousin and I secured employment in an enterprise called Roh und Abfallstoffe, Filiale Victor Kremin Lemberg GMBH. This impressive name described a firm that had a franchise from the Göring Werke (industrial enterprises controlled by Hermann Göring) to collect rags, scraps of metal, paper, and anything else useful, sort it out and ship it to the factories in Germany. We were issued a document designating us as "Nutzjuden" (Useful Jews) and were issued a round aluminum plaque to be worn on the lapel. All this was supposed to protect us from persecution.[16] For a while indeed it did. For practical purposes we were appointed by a wholesaler as rag pickers for the Rawa Ruska district. On arrival there we obtained a barn on the road to the railroad station and organized professional rag pickers, poor Jews active in this field before the war. Together we bought rags and other scrap from peasants to fulfill the quotas required by the wholesaler.

Rawa Ruska, a service town for the region and a railroad hub, was predominantly Jewish, with a Ukrainian population relatively neutral and used to contact with Jews. There were a few Polish families that kept to themselves. The town was ruled by a Stadthauptmann (city administrator) and a detachment of German police (Schutzpolizei), headed by a former small town butcher from somewhere in Germany, to maintain "law and order." The Kreishauptmann (the administrator of the county) also resided there, and a small Gestapo detachment kept an eye on the region. After the arrival of the Germans, prominent Jewish and Polish citizens were executed by a SS Sonderkommando in the nearby forest.

Otherwise the Jews were left alone and only occasionally did the local Ukrainian police engage in any atrocities. The small number of German officials and policemen were bribed by the Judenrat and left Jews in relative peace. They even occasionally curbed the Ukrainian police. The Judenrat was headed by a former druggist, a well-meaning and an intelligent man, who was dedicated to protecting the community and organizing its life in these difficult circumstances. After the unrelenting horror of Lwów, life in Rawa Ruska was idyllic by comparison.

I took a job in the Judenrat because I could eat lunch there in the kitchen for the poor and homeless. This provided an interesting glimpse of how the system worked. A new Kreishauptmann arrived in town with his family. The Judenrat was given a list of all his requirements. It included everything from furniture, silver, china, and linen to toothbrushes and Nivea cream.

All this was meticulously assembled and delivered to his house, formerly occupied by a Polish judge. A few days later I was instructed to deliver to the wife of the Kreishauptmann a new Persian lamb fur coat. It was fascinating to see the house furnished with furniture and Oriental carpets collected from Jewish owners, with the family at lunch at a table covered with linen, using elegant china and silver. All this I had earlier seen prepared in the warehouse at the Judenrat.

In the vicinity of Rawa Ruska was a large former Soviet military installation where close to 40,000 prisoners of war were gathered. They were guarded by elderly Germans, probably a reserve unit. They were not given water or food, and on occasion emaciated Soviet prisoners were led through the town by an escort. They pleaded for bread, but if someone dared to throw a loaf of bread to these unfortunates, the friendly looking pipe-puffing middle-aged soldiers opened fire. After two months there was no one alive left in the compound. French, Dutch, and Belgian prisoners of war were brought into the compound, and they too disappeared after a while. Our peaceful existence in Rawa Ruska was very deceptive.

One winter afternoon a detachment of SS arrived in trucks, collected at random a few hundred Jews and drove away with them. They grabbed holders of "good" documents (working permits—

Arbeitskarte) and those who had none. The local peasants coming to town brought the news that in nearby Belzec the SS had erected a large compound and a railroad spur leading to it. No one knew what was going on inside. The Ukrainians guarding the compound told us that an installation was prepared there to electrocute Jews. It was a fantastic story that was met with incredulity.

As Germans and the Ukrainian police visited the Judenrat frequently, I decided to move out, remembering the events in Lwów. I preferred to work sorting rags. The warehouse was out of the way and we prepared a shelter under a heap of rags in case of trouble. From the warehouse adjacent to the railway tracks all winter long we could observe trains with boxcars filled with Jews and guarded by Germans arriving from Lwów on the way to Belzec. After a few hours empty trains returned on their way back to Lwów.

In Belzec, there was a refinery to which sugar beet from our estate were sent for processing. On several occasions I accompanied a shipment consisting of a number of horse-drawn wagons. As I was familiar with the town I was puzzled where all these people were accommodated. The rumors brought to Rawa Ruska by local peasants seemed increasingly plausible. Nonetheless, no details were known, and even the Germans in Rawa Ruska did not know much more than that in Belzec there was a camp where Jews were collected for processing. After the Wannsee conference in December 1941, German construction firms were given an assignment to construct gas chambers and crematoria. IG Farbenindustrie was given orders to deliver adequate quantities of Zyklon (a lethal gas used to kill Jews). In a special camp in Trawniki, further north, guards were trained for service in the death camps. There was a whole network of these camps erected, with the installations in Belzec and Majdanek intended for Jews from southeastern Poland. After these two camps were completed, they were tested by killing a few hundred Jews brought in from Rawa Ruska. After the tests were successful, regular transports from Lwów started delivering Jews for processing.

From the warehouse every day I could see twenty to thirty long trains filled with people steaming toward Belzec, to return later in the day empty. Occasionally a "paratrooper" succeeded in squeezing through a window of the boxcar closed with barbed wire and jumped from the moving train. Some "paratroopers" were shot by the guards sitting on the roofs of the boxcars, but a few succeeded in escaping and were brought to Rawa Ruska by the peasants. They told grisly stories of boxcars filled with people squeezed in there by guards with whips and German shepherd attack dogs.

This prompted me to travel to Lwów to warn my mother and the community about the death camp in Belzec. I obtained a permit countersigned by the Gestapo to travel by rail to Lwów to the head-quarters of the Roh und Abfallstoffe. Somehow I got through and arrived at our new home in the ghetto. My mother and my brothers were surprised and delighted to see me.

I related to my mother the story of Belzec, and we decided to see officials in the Judenrat to warn them. Accompanied by my mother I met with some officials who listened to my story and then asked me to leave the room. They told my mother that I was mentally sick and probably required psychiatric assistance because of my patholog-ical imagination.

I was not impressed by this reception, as by then I realized that age does not always make an individual wiser. My mother agreed with me that I should explore ways and means of escaping. I was blessed with what was then considered a "good look" (non-Semitic features) and spoke Slavic languages without a trace of an accent. It was not difficult to forge documents[16] and reappear somewhere as a Pole. The problem was that the Germans and the Ukrainians paid little attention to documents and checked whether a male was cir-cumcised. The Christian population by and large was on a lookout for strangers, who were immediately denounced to the authorities. There were a few who, endangering their lives, assisted escaping Jews and even sheltered them, but this was an insignificant minority.

After my return, the situation in Rawa Ruska deteriorated, and Jews from the neighboring villages and little towns were instructed to move to the still-open but crowded ghetto. In May a detachment of the SS assisted by the Ukrainian police collected a few hundred Jews who were led to the railroad station. We could see them from a distance from our shelter under the rags in the warehouse. They walked slowly, carrying valises, young and old, children and women guarded by Germans with shepherd dogs and the Ukrainian police. In a few hours after a short trip in crowded boxcars, they reached the death camp in Belzec.

In August half of the Jewish population of Lwów was gathered in a similar way and sent to Belzec. Whole districts of the city were emptied, with detachments of inmates of the Janowska concentration camp guarded by Ukrainian police systematically cleaning the emptied apartments. The possessions and the furniture of the deported Jews were sorted out and packed to be shipped to Germany. The noose was tightening and we were running out of time. The Judenrat of Lwów, including its president, were hung from balconies of an apartment building, their bodies dangling from ropes. A successor Judenrat appointed by the Germans was even more cooperative, assuming that in this way they would save themselves.

I was still able to shuttle between Lwów and Rawa Ruska, albeit at a great risk as documents were ignored. Each trip was a nerve-wracking experience. I suggested to my mother that I would like to call on Metropolitan Szeptycki to consult with him on ways to escape and also to place with him the manuscripts and documents of my father. She was somewhat skeptical but did not oppose my idea. The ghetto in Lwów was still open, and I reached Jur without difficulty. I pulled the chain of a bell at the door of the residence, a small elegant baroque palace facing the cathedral.

A Studite monk let me in and guided me upstairs to a large sunny room. There waiting for an audience were priests, monks, and nuns. No one paid attention to me sitting in a corner wearing the obligatory arm band with the Star of David. The doors to the study opened, and I was ushered into a large room with walls lined with bookshelves. In a corner next to a large old-fashioned desk in a wheelchair an old man sat or half reclined. Although he was reclining it was evident that the man was very tall. His legs, paralyzed by arthritis, were covered with a woolen blanket. A mane of white hair framed his lion-like large head and face. Deep-set penetrating blue eyes examined me carefully. He wore an old mended monk's habit (riasa) with a white collar and a leather belt. This was Andrew Graf Szeptycki, Metropolitan of Halicz and the Greek Catholic Archbishop of Lwów.

I greeted the Metropolitan and waited. I was apprehensive that I would be ushered out of the room. The old man in the wheelchair, with a hand deformed by arthritis, gestured for me to come closer and invited me to sit down on a chair next to him. He asked me who I was. Learning that I was the son of Rabbi Dr. Ezekiel Lewin, he put his arm around me and hugged me to his powerful chest. He gently stroked my hair and repeatedly whispered in German, "Poor child." (I addressed the Metropolitan in German because my Ukrainian was rather limited and I did not wish to speak Polish because of the antagonism prevailing between the two nations.)

I was very moved by this kind reception, but I collected myself and addressed the Metropolitan, mentioning the friendship linking him with my father. I briefly described the tragic situation of the dying Jewish community and the death camp in Belzec. The old man, looking like an Old Testament patriarch, listened carefully, tears streaming down his wrinkled cheeks. I concluded by asking for advice. When I finished, he again embraced me, reflected a while and suggested that I return in two days. "Son, your father was my friend. You can rest assured that I will do all I can. Bring with you the manuscripts and I will place them in a safe place. However, I have in mind to find a way to save you." The Metropolitan blessed me, embraced me, and I kissed his hand and uplifted left the residence.

I related to my mother the visit to the Metropolitan. She commented that he undoubtedly was a great and a noble man. However, she was of the opinion that the Metropolitan's entourage would talk him out of undertaking anything constructive.

I returned to Jur as instructed, bringing two briefcases with my father's manuscripts and other documents. Again I was very kindly received by the Metropolitan, who informed me that a place was prepared for my younger nine-year-old brother Nathan, and I was requested to return, bringing him and my mother to see him on the morning of the next day. My mother was reluctant, but I pointed out to my brother that with him away it would be easier to arrange something for my mother and for our six-year-old brother. Nathan agreed, and the next day the three of us went to Jur.

We waited for a while with others in the large room. My mother was ushered alone into the Metropolitan's study-library. After a while we joined her and there an old priest, Father Kyprian, was waiting. Nathan was introduced to him and was blessed by the Metropolitan and the two left the room. The Metropolitan reassured my mother that from now on Nathan was his ward and everything would be done to take care of him. We returned to the ghetto in silence, happy that Nathan was out of danger but heartbroken because of the circumstances.

A few days later I was invited to see Father Kotiw, a diocesan priest working in the administration of the Curia. I was introduced by him to Brother Ivan Makar, who took me to an orphanage in the outskirts of the city. Walking out of the Jur compound with the friendly but aloof Studite monk, I realized that I had left behind my mother and brother, a life, and familiar surroundings. It was a start of another dangerous journey into the unknown. It was a beautiful day in September, the equivalent of an Indian summer. Leaves turned yellow and red in the parks and streets of the city, which had become a Golgotha for its Jewish population.

Eintragungen des Unternehmers Нотатки (описи) підприємця Wypełnia przedsiębiorca			Nummernfolge (links) beachten Черговість нумерації (з лівої стор.) заховати Przestrzegać kolejności cyfr (z lewej strony)		
Name und Sitz des Betriebes (Unternehmers) Firmenstempel Назва і місце підприємства (підприємця), штемпель фірми Nazwa i siedziba przedsiębiorstwa (przedsiębiorcy). Pieczęć firmowa	Art des Betriebes, oder der Betriebsabteilung Рід підприємства або відділу підприємства Rodzaj przedsięb. wzgl. oddz. przeds.	Tag des Beginns der Beschäftigung День розпочаття праці Dzień rozpoczęcia pracy	Art der Beschäftigung (möglichst genau angeben) Рід заняття (подати докладно) Rodzaj zatrudnienia (podać możliwie dokładnie)	Tag der Beendigung der Beschäftigung День закінчення праці Dzień ukończenia pracy	Unterschrift des Unternehmers Підпис підприємця Podpis przedsiębiorcy
1	2	3	4	5	6
Alt- und Abfallstofferfassung Kreiskompoststelle Rawa-Ruska Sigmund Kamiński					
3					
4					
5					
6					
7					
8					

Arbeitsamt: ......ARBEITSAMT LEMBERG....

Nebenstelle: Nebenstelle Rawa-Ruska

Meldekarte für Juden
Nr. 7520

Der Jude _Lewin Kurt._

Die Jüdin

geboren am: _28. Februar 1925._

in _Lubatschow_ ledig, verh.

Rawa Ruska gesch., verw.

Wohnort _Grünwalde_ Str. Nr.: _49._

_256_

Berufsgruppe u. Art:

Auf Grund der Zweiten Durchführungsvorschrift zur Verordnung vom 26. Oktober 1939 über die Einführung des Arbeitszwanges für die jüdische Bevölkerung des Generalgouvernements vom 12. Dezember 1939 erfasst und steht dem Arbeitsamt zum Arbeitseinsatz zur Verfügung. Ein Auffangen auf der Straße ist nicht statthaft.

✠ ARBEITSAMT LEMBERG ✠

Nebenstelle Rawa-Ruska
(Stempel d. Arbeitsamts)

Grünwald, Reg.-Fre...

(Unterschrift)

Kontrollmeldung am

Jeder Woche, soweit kein Arbeitsverhältnis besteht.

Staatsdruckerei Warschau — Nr. 4779-41.

Zur Beachtung!

1. Die Meldekarte bleibt im Besitz des Inhabers. Sie ist bei Beginn und Beendigung jeder Tätigkeit dem Unternehmer zur Eintragung vorzulegen.

2. Die vorgeschriebenen Kontrollmeldungen müssen persönlich unter Vorlegung der Meldekarte zu der vorgeschriebenen Zeit bei der zuständigen Stelle des Arbeitsamts erfolgen.

3. Entlassung, Krankheit oder das Ausscheiden als Meldepflichtiger sind unter Angabe der Gründe dem Arbeitsamt sofort zu melden.

4. Beim behördlich genehmigten Umzug nach einem anderen Ort hat die Abmeldung beim Arbeitsamt persönlich zu erfolgen und die Anmeldung am Zuzugsort ist beim zuständigen Arbeitsamt innerhalb von 3 Tagen persönlich zu vollziehen.

5. Wer unbefugt Eintragungen, Streichungen, Radierungen oder andere Änderungen in der Meldekarte vornimmt, wird wegen Urkundenfälschung bestraft.

6. Wer der vorgeschriebenen Meldepflicht oder der Einberufung zur Ableistung des Arbeitszwanges nicht nachkommt, wird auf Grund der Verordnung vom 26. Oktober 1939 über die Einführung des Arbeitszwanges für die jüdische Bevölkerung des Generalgouvernements bestraft.

7. Bei Beschädigung und Verlust der Meldekarte wird eine Gebühr für die Ausstellung einer Ersatzmeldekarte erhoben.

Von Vorstehendem habe ich Kenntnis genommen

Lewin Kurt

(Unterschrift)

An identity card issued to every Jew from the age of 16 to 60 in the territories of Poland occupied by the Third Reich. This document stated where the holder was employed, and had to be approved by the SS (Sicherheits and SD) and renewed every two weeks. A Jew whose document was not stamped was deported to be gassed and cremated.

Generalgouvernement
DISTRIKT GALIZIEN
Der Kreishauptmann in Rawa Ruska
Arbeitsamt Lemberg
Nebenstelle Rawa Ruska

Rawa Ruska, d. 25.6. 1942.

Ausweis. N 169

Der Jude (in) Kurt Lewin ist bei(m) Alt -

geboren am 28.2.1925 in Lubeczow Rew. Ruck mit ~~besonderen~~ dringenden Arbeiten bis auf Weitere/s

und Abfallstofferfassung beschäftigt.

Zu seiner (ihrer) Familie gehören:

Klara Zimmermann, 1905, Schwägerin

Die vorstehenden Personen sind von Arbeitsamt listenmässig erfasst. Sie sind von der
Umsiedlungsaktion auszunehmen.

Leiter der Nebenstelle.

Gültig bis:
31.7.
1942.

---

*An identity card issued by the Generalgouvernement, District Galizien,
Department of Labor, to the Jew Kurt Lewin indicating that he is employed in
collecting and recycling materials important to the war effort. Therefore, the
document certifies that he is to be excluded from the resettlement (a euphemism
used by the Germans to describe deportation to death camps).
The document was valid until July 31, 1942; if not renewed,
the holder would be sent to a death camp.*

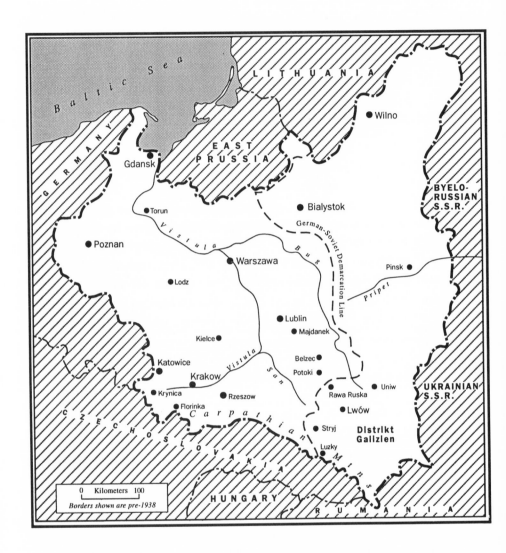

POLAND, 1918-39

CHAPTER 2.

The Order of St. Theodore the Studite

T HE SOUND of the bell filled the air. The monks gathered in the corridor of the monastery. At a signal given by the prior, a single line formed according to seniority, with the youngest member of the community leading the monks. They walked in silence toward the wooden church built in a style commonly found in the Hutzul, or Bojko villages in the Carpathian mountains.[1] Its intricate architecture had been brought by the Vikings, who long ago sailed down into the Ukraine on the Dnieper to become its rulers. The master builders echoed the work of shipwrights who built boats that navigated the seas and the rivers of Europe.

The church, built from cedar wood with small windows that provided little light, was almost dark. One could hardly discern the images of the icons making up the iconostas that concealed the altar. They were painted in bright colors in traditional Byzantine style. The monks entered the pews and knelt while the bell was still ringing, calling the monastic community to the evensong. Father Tyt stepped forward, was handed an *epitrachil* (a stole in Latin), kissed it, put it around his shoulders, crossed himself three times and started the service. The choir filled the church with the lively *Swite Tyxyj* (Serene Light) hymn signaling the end of the day.

Blended together were the singing, the solemn soothing melody, and the incense spread by Father Tyt. After bowing deeply, he approached the principal icons with the *kadylnycia* (censer). Then facing the monks he waved the censer toward the assembled community in a greeting and a blessing. The monks now divided into two choirs—*krylosa*—and chanted psalms. The ancient Hebrew verses, beautifully translated into the harmonious Old Slavonic language,[2] were recited, verse after verse, by alternating *krylosa*. The smell of the cedar wood, the incense, the chant of the monks, and the dimly lit icons created an atmosphere of peace and serenity, conducive to meditation and prayer. It was a deep spiritual experience that at the same time appealed to one's senses. The *Veczirnia*, the vespers, was like stepping into a different world, leaving horror and fear behind. This indeed was the Lord's sanctuary.

Father Tyt blessed the monks at the end of the service and in single file the monks started back on the path to the monastery. This first impression of the eastern monastic life was overwhelming as I entered an unknown, mysterious, and fascinating world.

We then assembled in the refectory. After a short prayer a monk, pronouncing every word carefully, read from a book describing the life and the martyrdom of long forgotten saints.

On a signal, *"Otche Nasz"* (Pater Noster) and *"Bohorodytze Divo"* (Ave Maria) recited in the Old Slavonic language completed the reading, and a simple dinner was brought from the kitchen by the serving monks in aprons. The food was simple and wholesome. As I had been starving for a year and a half, it represented a feast. I remained alert and on guard waiting for an indication of what would happen next. This was my introduction to the Studite Order.

I had been brought by Deacon Teofan Shevaha to the monastery of John the Baptist in Krywczyci, a suburb on the outskirts of Lwów, in a borough referred to as Lyczakiw. (Monks with seniority but without the required formal education were ordained deacons. They officiated at formal services with the priest, referred to by the Studites as Hieromonk.)

It was a pleasant afternoon in September. The autumn in 1942 was exceptionally beautiful with one sunny and warm day following another. This was referred to as *babie lato*, the equivalent of an Indian summer. Deacon Teofan and I walked briskly through a meadow toward the wooden church and the monastery visible on the horizon. I carried a little bag with my few belongings, as I was informed that I was being transferred to a new location.

Nathan, my younger brother, was already in Pidmichajliwci, a

village south of Lwów, in the mother house of the Basilian nuns.
There he was taught the language and the customs of the Ukrainians. The arrangements to place him there were made by Metropolitan Andrew. There he lived with Father Kyprian, a Studite priest
and a chaplain of the convent of the Basilian nuns.

I had been placed originally in an orphanage administered by
Deacon Teofan, also a Studite. It was assumed by Ihumen Clement,
the Superior or the Archimandrite, and Father Kotiw, a secular priest
who was entrusted with a variety of administrative matters, that
there I would be safe and relatively inconspicuous and that Deacon
Teofan could be relied on. I arrived at Jur, a hill overlooking the city,
where the baroque cathedral, the residence of the Metropolitan, was
located, from the ghetto then in Zamarstynow, a suburb of the city.
Although the ghetto was not closed yet, it was nevertheless a dangerous undertaking. Patrols of the Ukrainian police were everywhere,
and a Jew found on the streets of the city outside the ghetto was
delivered to the Janowska concentration camp.

On arrival at Jur, in the office of Ihumen Clement I was introduced to Brother Ivan Makar, then a student in the seminary, the
first of the many Studite monks whom I subsequently met. We took
our leave and left Jur for the orphanage in Lyczakiw on a rickety
streetcar that had seen better days. There, I was introduced to
Deacon Teofan as a ward of Ihumen Clement. Brother Makar told
me not worry, that all was arranged, and I was in good hands. The
friendly but reserved monk, after reassuring me, left for Jur.

After a day or two at the orphanage, Deacon Teofan asked for my
personal documents. I had none as I had escaped from the ghetto
and the ongoing deportation to Belzec. On learning that I had none,
he suggested that I should go to the Ukrainian Committee, which
would undoubtedly issue new documents.

This institution, organized by the Germans but run by collaborators, existed for the sole purpose of controlling the Ukrainian population. Appearing there without any identification, I would be
apprehended and delivered to the notorious Ukrainian police.
Therefore, the next morning I risked the trip back to the Jur
through the city, which was constantly combed by patrols looking
for Jews who, like me, tried desperately to escape from the ghetto.

Ihumen Clement was surprised to see me at the Metropolitan's palace. Astonished to learn about the suggestion made to me by Deacon Teofan, he decided to move me at once to another and safer location.

Brother Makar was entrusted again with the task of accompanying me back to the orphanage. We crossed the city on the rickety streetcar and from its last station walked to the orphanage. There, after a short conversation with Deacon Teofan, he told me to collect my belongings, and we walked to the nearby monastery of John the Baptist. We rang the bell, and after a while the door was opened by a tall monk with sharply chiseled slavic features. The somewhat somber appearance of the monk in the black riasa and the klobuk was softened by the blue friendly and smiling eyes that put one at ease at once. This was my first encounter with Father Marko Stek, the superior of the monastery, and start of a two-year stay in the Studite monastic community disguised as a monk.

The Studite's day was divided into three parts. Eight hours were dedicated to prayer, eight hours to work, and eight hours to rest. The cycle of the year was divided into holy days and religious feasts, with Christmas and Easter the focus of the cycle. Frequent fasts and penance completed the rhythm of the Studite existence in prayer and in service for the community.

The day in the monastery started at six o'clock in the morning. A monk passed through the corridor with a wooden clapper chanting *"Pinia wremia, molytvy czas."* He was in charge of waking up the community. He remained in front of the door of each monk's cell until he heard the answer "Amin." After fifteen minutes a single file formed in the dark corridor, and when the monks were assembled they proceeded to the church. Its interior was dark, with the only light provided by a flickering flame in an oil lamp in front of the iconostas.[3]

The monks knelt motionless and silent. After a few minutes an oil lamp on the reader's pulpit was lit, outlining the images on the iconostas and the silhouettes of the kneeling monks. The priest read a sentence from the Gospels. Then the light was dimmed and the motionless monks were meditating. This was repeated three times. The morning light brightened the church and *utrenia*, the morning service, commenced. The opening prayers were intoned by a priest. They collectively recited *"Otche Nasz"* (Pater Noster) and *"Viruju"* (Nicean Credo), which were followed by the alternate chanting of psalms from the *"Czasoslov"* (Breviary). Then came the *ektenias* (litanies) intoned by the priest, followed by the *tropars* and *kondaks* (hymns in the daily cycle) dedicated to the saint of the day; these were found in the *"Horologion"* (a huge book with hymns for everyday translated from Greek into Old Slavonic probably in the ninth century) and sung in the *hlas* (weekly melody or tone of the liturgical cycle). The beautiful and serene service was completed. At seven o'clock the ringing of the bell announced the beginning of the liturgy, calling the brothers who were busy in the kitchen, in the stables, and milking cows to join. The choir completed the Utrenia with a melodious hymn to the Virgin *"Czestnijshuju Cheruvim i slawnijshuje bez sravnenia Serafim"* (more honorable than the Cherubim, beyond compare and more glorious than the Seraphim) that mingled with the solemn deep sound of the ringing bell calling to prayer. A few brothers having completed their morning chores walked in and joined the community. It was time for the liturgy.

Father Marko, dressed in simple Byzantine vestments, identical to those seen on old icons, with the *felon* (chasuble) beautifully embroidered with Ukrainian motifs, started the liturgy standing in front of the altar. The *tsarskie wrata* (the royal doors), the central part of the iconostas, were opened and the church was brightly lit. Father Marko's pleasant tenor intoned the opening ektenia. The choir responded to each phrase with the somewhat mournful *"hospody pomyluj"* (Lord have mercy on us). Then the tropar and kondak dedicated to the saint of the day were sung. Then the *prokimen* (a sentence from the Psalms) opened the reading of the *"Apostol"* (Epistles-letters of St. Paul) and the Gospels. The "Apostol" was read by a deacon endowed with a deep resonant voice. The choir concluded this part of the service singing alleluia. At the end of the reading of the "Apostol" Father Marko entered the nave through a side door of the iconostas, carrying the Gospels and preceded by a deacon waving an incense burner. He stopped before the tsarskie wrata, rested the book on the head of one of the monks who held it open with his lifted hands, and read the Gospel of the day.

Father Marko returned the Gospel book to the main altar and picked up the chalice with wine and the *diskos* with the cut *prosphora* (unleavened bread used in the Eastern Rite), both covered with silk, from the side altar in the sanctuary, the *proskomidnik* (a table for the preparation of the bread and wine to be consecrated). Preceded by a deacon waving an incense burner, he entered the nave through the side door of the iconostas. This symbolized the entry of Christ with the Apostles into Jerusalem on Palm Sunday. The choir sang the hymn *"Izhe Cheruvymy"* (the Cherubic hymn) while the celebrant returned to the main altar through the other side door of the iconostas. After depositing the chalice and the patina (diskos) on the altar, he returned to the nave, this time through the open tsarskie wrata, and blessed the assembled community, which recited the *"Viruju"* (credo) and sang Sanctus. The tsarskie wrata were closed, the curtain drawn, and the consecration commenced.

The monks knelt and only the sound of the birds in the garden interrupted the silence. The tsarskie wrata were opened again, the public confession was said, and the celebrant entered the nave with the sacraments. A few monks approached to receive it and, with bowed head and hands crossed on their chests, returned to their places.

The celebrant, after blessing the monks with the sacraments, returned to the sanctuary to complete the liturgy while the monks were singing thanksgiving hymns. The ceremony was at its end, and Father Marko reemerged and blessed the community before dismissing it. The single file formed again and the monks returned to the monastery.

The monks dispersed to their cells, changed into working clothes, and returned to the refectory for a quick breakfast consisting of bread and tea. After breakfast the monks went to the workshops or the fields, or left for their jobs in the city. This was a silent order and no one spoke unless it was absolutely necessary.

The Studite monastic community in which I was privileged to live for two years was and remains little known. The monastic communities established in the early days of Christianity were originally a refuge for individuals who dedicated themselves to prayer and meditation. With time, some of the monasteries and convents addressed the needs of the community. Monks and nuns took care of the sick, disabled, and old. They taught in schools, while others assisted the poor. Their communities became guardians of knowledge almost forgotten after the collapse of the Roman Empire.

The rules governing monastic life were fashioned in the west by St. Benedict and in the east by St. Theodore the Studite. The Studite order was revived by Metropolitan Andrew at the turn of the century to fill a need in the Ukrainian community and to become a bridge between Latin and Eastern (Orthodox) Christianity. The other orders in the Ukrainian Orthodox Church united with Rome while constructive, did not accept the almost illiterate peasants who had a vocation to religious life. In addition, these monastic orders were Latinized, which did not facilitate communication with the mostly Orthodox population in the Ukraine, which was accustomed to the Byzantine (or Eastern) Rite.

The Basilians, an old monastic order of the Uniate Church, were for a long time moribund. After their revival and reformation by the Jesuits in the second half of the nineteenth century, they acquired some of the characteristics of their mentors. They recruited young Ukrainians into their excellent schools run on the Jesuit model. However, they were selective, and their doors remained closed to the poorly educated or illiterate sons of peasants.

The Redemptorists of the Eastern Rite were organized by the Belgian province of this order on the invitation and the initiative of Metropolitan Andrew. He felt that its rule was exceptionally well suited to serve the spiritual needs of the Ukrainian villages by providing missionaries in the positive sense, namely, preachers dedicated to spiritual revival of the community rather than hunting for converts. However, this community in a way also was elitist.

By contrast, the Studites were a working and praying order with doors open to everyone. A small community was formed at the turn of the century (1901-02) in Sknilow near Lwów. They lived simply on the verge of poverty and experimented with eastern monasticism. Casimir Graf Szeptycki, the brother of Metropolitan Andrew, probably joined the small community at his behest in 1912. Ihumen Clement (his monastic name) gave direction to the newly established community and was responsible for its remarkable expansion. I met a number of the old timers like Father Nikon, Father Josaphat, Brother Gervazij, and others. However, the monks were not given to idle conversation. Therefore, there was little to learn about the early days from the snippets of information collected here and there.

A dynamic group of monks emerged in the 1930s whose activities were increasingly felt in the Ukrainian community. The monks were forbidden to beg and had to be self-supporting. Every monk was trained in a skill or a profession according to his ability and interests. Father Rafail, and Brothers Filotej, Christophor and Juvenalij were encouraged to study painting. Brothers Ambrozij and Patrikij were trained master printers. Father Marko and Brother Teodozij specialized in tanning hides. Brother Laurentij, who had lost three fingers of his right hand in an accident while working a saw mill, was trained as an apiarist and a *diak* (cantor). Brothers Damian and Isidor were tailors. Father Herman and Szmahlo, a layman who observed the rules without taking vows, were chartered accountants.

Following Eastern monastic tradition, the individual characteristics of a monk were respected, and he could live in the community without efforts made to regiment him. In the two years of staying in Studite monasteries, I met most members of this remarkable order. They represented an interesting and impressive group of highly motivated individuals who tried hard to follow the teachings of the Gospels.

Their example and attitudes made a powerful impact on their surroundings. The doors of their monasteries were always open to those in need of shelter or food. They provided spiritual services in areas where there were no priests or churches. They ran orphanages and workshops in which they trained young peasant boys in a variety of crafts. Their impact on the Ukrainian community in the villages, in little towns, and in the city increased with time.

In the years 1939-41 the monks were dispersed during the Soviet occupation of Western Ukraine. Some were arrested, to return after the arrival of the Germans; others perished without a trace. They reassembled and resumed the routine of monastic existence. They were a remarkable and dedicated group of men led by ascetic

Ihumen Clement and ready to carry out any task given to them, including even sheltering Jews at the risk of their lives.

My status was defined as that of a novice, and I was required to participate in all the prayers and exercises with the exception of the sacraments.

After breakfast I joined Father Tyt, an ascetic looking monk in his mid-thirties from Volyn, who taught me Ukrainian, and old Slavonic, and introduced me to customs and manners observed in the monastery and among the Ukrainians.

At twelve o'clock the monks who were in the monastery joined Father Tyt in the church for the sixth hour, consisting of psalms, invocations and a blessing. Following it we assembled in the refectory for lunch, the main meal of the day. The monks were silent, and only the voice of the reader reciting the life of the saints from the *Hagiography* (a book consisting of descriptions of the life of saints translated from Greek) could be heard. The simple meal consisted of potatoes and cabbage, or beans followed by an apple or a piece of *malaj* (maize bread sweetened with honey) and tea. A knock on the table by the superior ended the meal and after a prayer to St. Joseph the monks moved to a conference room. There again a knock on the table announced the start of the "recreation" during which the monks were permitted to speak, exchange ideas, or play a game of chess or dominoes. Some read, others walked in the garden. After twenty minutes the recreation was over and the monks resumed their usual activities.

At six o'clock the working day was over, with the monks changing into riasas and assembling for the even song. A simple meal in the refectory was followed by the *Povecheria*, a short night service, consisting of reading psalms and ektenias, one that I always found especially moving. It beseeched the Lord to take care of travellers on sea or land, to heal the sick, to console the dying in their hour of agony, to protect the oppressed and imprisoned, the soldiers on the battlefield, all people suffering and in mourning, to protect everyone everywhere. The priest pronounced the pleading sentences of the ektenia and the community answered *"Hospody podaj i pomyluj"* (O Lord, grant it and have mercy on all). Then the monks approached the superior one by one to be blessed. Each monk approached him, kissed an extended cross, and left in silence for the monastery and his cell.

At midnight the old monk with a wooden clapper walked through the dark corridor, stopping at each and every cell chanting *"Pinia wremia, molytvy czas."* After a few minutes the single file formed again, and the monks with the klobuks over their heads proceeded to the church for the midnight service *Polunosznycia.* The priest initiated the prayers and the monks, divided into two choirs, alternated chanting the verses of the psalms. "I shall lift my eyes unto the hills"—my favorite psalm—as well as the *"Yoshev be Seter eljon"* (sitting at the foot of the throne—in Hebrew)—the favorite of my father—were recited. The Polunosznycia concluded, and the monks returned to the cells for a short rest before the start of another day.

The routine of the monastic life was extremely oppressive to me as I was not accustomed to kneel for hours, listen to chants in an unknown language, and meditate. The first few days were very difficult, but then slowly I submitted to the rhythm of the monastic life, learned how to sing in the choir, and recite psalms in old Slavonic. One day when I was asked by a monk to recite the psalms at the midnight service I realized that I had been accepted by the community at the St. John the Baptist monastery in Lyczakiw.

Gradually, I was emboldened to explore the monastery, the farm, the fields, and the nearby vicinity. The main three-story high brick building was rather simple and neat. The window frames painted white gave the utilitarian structure some character. The cells were on the upper floor, each simply and identically furnished. The whitewashed walls were bare, with only a crucifix over the plain bed covered with a blanket. A chair, a table, and a wash basin with running water were the only concession to creature comfort in these austere quarters (only in the newly renovated building in the monastery in Lyczakiw). The view from my cell was on a vineyard, an experiment in the unsuitable climate for viticulture, tended by an old monk from Croatia. Every year, disappointed that his efforts did not produce results, he persevered and, claimed that the following year the vineyard would present the community with a drinkable wine.

The dairy farm was tended by Brother Dorotej, assisted by Brother Vinkentij and a novice. The cows were well cared for and provided milk and cottage cheese for the neighborhood and the monasteries and convents in the starving city. The monks taking care of the cows were generally cheerful and pleasant although somewhat self-conscious. They washed carefully and changed their clothes before joining others. Regardless of the effort they always smelled of cows and manure. Their neighbors at the church or in the refectory never complained. Nevertheless, inconspicuous efforts were made to keep a distance from these brothers.

On the second floor was a part of the house mysterious to me. In a large room a number of monks were working on a project. A glimpse inside gave the impression that this was a sophisticated carpenter's workshop. Gathering courage I walked in.

I greeted the busy monks, *"Slava Isusu Chrystu"* (Glory be to Jesus Christ), to which they replied, *"Na vik i vikiw amin"* (For ever and ever, amen). No other conversation was permitted in the monastery.

Brother Filotej was polishing a wooden plank and treating it with a variety of materials. Brother Christophor was outlining an image of the Virgin with child on a prepared surface of a square wooden plank treated with a whitish substance. In a corner Father Rafail Chomyshyn, a tall, slim, and elegant looking monk, was painting, or, as it was described by the Studites following the Eastern Rite custom, "writing" an icon. Father Juvenalij was gilding a surface to provide a background for his design. Some were preparing the carefully chosen wooden planks for the icons, others were painting, or better "writing." I was pleased to be allowed to observe their work.

This was the Studite studio dedicated to the revival of a neglected and little known art of painting icons. Metropolitan Andrew, a spiritual leader of the Uniate or Greek Catholic Church, was dedicated to promoting the social welfare of the community and its cultural activities. The restoration of the original Eastern Rite to the Latinized Uniate Church was one of his manifold interests, as he realized that only by returning to its origin would the Uniate Church be in a position to act as a bridge between Western and Eastern Christianity.

The painting school of the Studites was one of the many projects he promoted. Gifted monks or students were sent at his expense to Vienna and Munich, there to learn the art of restoration and painting in museums and art institutes. On their return a workshop was created for them at the monastery of St. John the Baptist in Lyczakiw. There they developed their own style and produced beautiful icons that can be found in Eastern Rite churches all over the world.

On the ground floor there was a carpenter's workshop where Brother Modest and others were repairing furniture and making new furniture for the community. A tailor shop prepared riasas, hoods, mantias, and other items of the monk's clothing. The cobbler's shop was closed as Brothers Teodozij and Lazar were managing a factory in town, producing shoes for the German army.

The kitchen was of special interest to me in those days. After starving in the ghetto, I was fascinated by the preparation of food for such a large community.

The spacious and well-equipped kitchen was presided over by monks Inokentij and Pantalejmon. The simple food was cooked there, and preparations were made for the long winter when the markets no longer provided vegetables and occasional fruit. Heaps of cabbage were cleaned and chopped for fermenting in large barrels into sauerkraut. Cucumbers were selected, washed, and placed in other wooden barrels to be pickled. Bread was baked in a huge old-fashioned oven fired with wood. The kitchen was a busy place, with pots steaming on the large steel plate covering the cheerfully burning fire underneath. Sacks of potatoes for the next meal were carried in to be peeled by novices sitting in a corner.

The mornings were spent in lessons with Father Tyt. The rest of the days were free because I was not given a specific task beyond sweeping corridors and washing the wooden floors in the refectory, the chapel, and the conference room with Brother Laurentij. One day I ventured to climb the hill behind the monastery, from which a panorama of the south-east part of the city could be seen. I recognized the Zamarstynow railroad station, with a plume of white steam from an engine of a train arriving from somewhere obscuring the view from time to time.

The railroad tracks were the border of the last ghetto where, after the deportation in August 1942 of 60,000 Jews to be gassed in

Belzec, the remnant of the population was squeezed into a small area. There they were starving, dying of rapidly spreading typhoid and other infectious diseases, and waiting for the final journey to the death camps. My mother and my little brother were among them.

I approached Father Marko and asked his permission to return to the still-open ghetto to see whether there was anything I could do to help my mother. He suggested that we go to the city together. The next morning after the services Father Marko, dressed in a business suit, and I took off for the city. We cautiously approached the present ghetto, walking through a district from which Jews were already deported. The previously crowded streets were empty. Only working parties of inmates of the Janowska Road concentration camp, guarded by the Ukrainian police, were emptying apartment houses of the possessions of the inhabitants earlier deported to Belzec. These were sorted out at the Janowska Road camp and shipped to Germany.

We strolled through the depopulated district giving the impression that we, like many others, came to loot the abandoned Jewish apartments. In this fashion we approached the entrance to the ghetto, a railway underpass.

We parted company and agreed to meet in an hour in a doorway of a house. I put on the white armband with the Star of David, which every Jew under penalty of death had to wear, and entering the ghetto I became again a part of the community condemned to death.

The farmhouse in which my mother lived with four other families was not far from the entrance. My arrival surprised her, and the joy was mixed with fear that I was risking my life for a pointless visit. I urged my mother to escape and pleaded with her to allow me to approach Metropolitan Andrew and ask for assistance. My mother explained that this could endanger me and my brother, that there was a limit to the kindness of these people, and that my youngest brother was nervous and disturbed by witnessing the horror around him and would not be able to cope.

I was aware that this was my mother's last opportunity to save herself. However, I could not find the right arguments to convince her. She walked back with me to the entrance of the ghetto. As we approached the railroad underpass, she asked me to promise that I would take care of my brother Nathan, then ten years old, who was placed with Father Kyprian in Pidmichajliwci. I replied that there was not much that I could do as I was only seventeen years old.

She nevertheless insisted that I promise to do my best and that the knowledge I would take care of Nathan would help her die in peace. In this short last meeting all that had to be said was said. We kissed, and I left the ghetto. When I turned and looked back, my mother was still standing on the other side of the underpass.

My stepmother, Rachel Reiss Lewin, was then a thirty-six-year old widow. Shortly after my brief visit to the ghetto, my six-year-old brother was shot by a German SS officer by the name of Grzymek in her presence on the street of the ghetto. She and others died six months later in the women's compound of the Janowska camp, deliberately set on fire by the Germans and their Ukrainian assistants.

Father Marko was waiting for me in the doorway. There I took off the white armband with the Star of David and became again a Studite monk. We checked the street and discovered that no one was around. We walked out of the doorway and turned toward the city. Suddenly I became aware of the sound of the measured steps of hobnailed heavy boots and realized that we were being followed. I looked backward from the corner of my eye and saw two Ukrainian policemen approaching us. Most probably someone saw me leaving the ghetto and pointed me out to the police, a common occurrence in those days.

I took out a cigarette, turned, and calmly asked the policemen in Ukrainian to allow me to light it from his (matches were precious in those days and it was a common thing to do). One of the policemen offered me his cigarette. I lit mine from it, thanked him politely, and returned to Father Marko. We continued to the corner of the street, and when we turned it we took off running for our lives through the empty streets of the former ghetto. I knew every nook and corner of this district. Walking through yards and passages in the back of abandoned buildings, we finally emerged on a thoroughfare and mingled with the crowd.

We returned to the monastery and Father Marko, after changing into a riasa, went to the church to thank the Lord for getting us safely out of this predicament. If I had been arrested, the Ukrainian policemen would have shot me on the spot and handed Father Marko over to the Germans to be executed publicly for assisting Jews. This was a rather common occurrence in those days when life was snuffed out without much thought. I forgot this incident, and it was Father Marko who years later reminded me of it during one of his visits in New York.

On arrival at St. John the Baptist monastery I was still rather conspicuous. However, after a few weeks under Father's Tyt tutelage, I spoke reasonably fluent Ukrainian, sang in the choir, and was practically indistinguishable from the rest of the community. I was given a Ukrainian peasant's linen shirt without a collar, richly embroidered with multicolored thread, a pair of heavy boots, and a *Mazepynka*. This was a cap fashioned to resemble a Cossack headgear with a small Tryzub (trident)—a symbol brought to the Ukraine by the Vikings[4] and adapted by the Ukrainians as their coat of arms— attached to it, which was worn by the Ukrainian police. It was a very popular headgear with young people.

My stay at the monastery of St. John the Baptist, arranged to prepare me for life among Studites, came to an end. Father Tyt reached the conclusion that I was sufficiently ready to be moved to a new location. Too many had observed my arrival at the monastery at a time when I could not yet blend into the community. Therefore, it was safer to move me to a location where no one knew me.

Father Marko and Father Tyt were satisfied that I looked like a Ukrainian peasant's son. The slightly slanted eyes, the somewhat Asiatic features acquired long ago by someone in the Herzberg family in Lubaczow, the route of the Tartar invasions, had a great deal to do with it. It was observed by acquaintances in the ghetto that I was endowed with a "good look," namely, I did not look like a Jew. Roman Pavlo Mytka, a novice in the Studite Order (my new identity), was transferred to the monastery of St. Josaphat on Petra Skarhy in the vicinity of the Jur.

I arrived at the St. Josaphat monastery. Namistnyk (administrator) Isidor Livyj assigned a cell to me, I was given a riasa and fell into the routine of Studite life to which I had been accustomed at the St. John the Baptist monastery. After morning services and breakfast, the monks left for their jobs at the Jur or in the city. Only the Namistnyk Livyj, the superior, Father Nikanor, an occasional visiting out-of-town priest, and myself remained in the monastery. Downstairs, outside the *clausura* (closure, living quarters out of bounds to outsiders) in the kitchen an elderly nun was preparing meals for the community. Namistnyk Livyj in his workshop was sawing. Father Nikanor was in his cell studying or writing.

With the monks gone, the house was silent and lacked the purposeful activity of the Lyczakiw monastery. My responsibility was to sweep the corridors, the stairway, and the chapel. I was a novice, which was all that interested the monks. The services during the day were attended by those who were in the house. Occasionally they were joined by Brothers Antonij, Vissarion, and Ierotej, who worked at the church compound at the Jur.

In the evening the monastery came to life. The monks changed into habits and assembled in the chapel. It was time for the evensong—Veczirnia. The interesting frescos, reproductions of Byzantine icons representing the Nativity, the Transfiguration, and other biblical themes that were painted on the walls, were brought to life in the brightly lit chapel and transported one into a different world. The dark hues of colors employed to paint them gave the frescos an appearance of pictures by Tintoretto. The *pravylo,* the service, presided over by Father Nikanor and Deacon Livyj, was beautifully sung by the monks. The old icons of an iconostas acquired by the Metropolitan and installed at St. Josaphat, the smell of the incense—all created an atmosphere of peace and refuge from the horrors occurring around us. St. Josaphat in the evening became a community not much different from the ones found in the other monasteries of the Studites.

A mysterious German dressed in a well-tailored expensive suit occasionally joined the monks at meals and in the chapel. As at St. Josaphat, the rules of canonic silence were interpreted more liberally at breakfasts. I asked my neighbor Brother Vissarion, the *diak* (cantor) of the cathedral at Jur, who this guest was. He replied that this was Father Peters, a German member of the order. I did not pursue the topic because a display of curiosity was not appreciated in the community.

The peaceful existence of the Studite monks was an illusion. Horrors were perpetrated in the city daily. The killing of Jews on the streets, columns of emaciated Janowska concentration camp inmates passing escorted by the Ukrainian police on their way to work, the killing of Ukrainians by Poles and Poles by Ukrainians—all were a constant reminder that a disaster might strike at any time.

A discovery of a Jew in the monastery during the frequent searches could bring death to all at St. Josaphat. Although the monks were aware of who I was, they accepted my presence among them. Some objected to exposing a whole community to the risk of being wiped out by sheltering one individual. This position was taken by Father Rafail and was supported by other monks. They expressed this view to Ihumen Clement and their superiors, Hieromonks Marko and Nikanor. Nevertheless, nothing was ever done either to exert pressure to remove me, or to betray my identity.

A German raid on Jur and St. Josaphat brought this danger into sharp focus. I was on my way to the refectory in the basement of the building after cleaning the corridors and the chapel. On the stairway I encountered SS men racing upstairs. I dashed to the basement, ran out into the yard, and through passages carefully explored before-hand emerged in a nearby thoroughfare. There I mingled with the people on the street and took a streetcar to Lyczakiw and St. John the Baptist.

I informed Father Marko that Jur was surrounded by Germans troops and SS men were searching St. Josaphat. Alerted that the Germans might arrive at any time, the monks prepared for their arrival. In those days one could be shot for sheltering a Jew, but equally so for hiding an unregistered pig or a cow. Livestock was strictly controlled and was the property of the Third Reich, as signi-fied by a metal band attached to pierced ears of the animals. Brothers Dorotej and Vinkentij raced to the pigsty and the stables to remove the unregistered animals. I was hidden by Father Marko in an abandoned half-ruined house in a field and was instructed to stay there until his return.

Late in the evening I was released from my shelter by Father Marko and learned that Fathers Peters and Nikanor had been arrested. The Germans departed without searching Jur or other monasteries in town.

I returned to St. Josaphat and resumed my daily routine. The community was tense, and we lived in anticipation of further searches and arrests. Father Marko took over the responsibilities of Father Nikanor and commuted between the two houses.

The front was far away in the heart of the Soviet Union. We had only a vague idea of the developments, as the press controlled by collaborators published only official communiques. An occasional German and Italian visitor calling on the Metropolitan brought news from the distant battlefields. The movement of German and Italian troops through the city, an important railroad center to the eastern front, intensified. The battle for Stalingrad was in its early stage.

Ihumen Clement decided that it would be better if I were moved to a quiet monastery and out of the way. The choice was a small Studite community in the *skyt* (retreat) of St. Andrew, high in the Carpathian mountains near the Hungarian border. A monk from there was expected in town any day and it was decided that I would travel with him to the skyt in Luzky.

Father Marko recommended that I be given a birth certificate. At one of my frequent visits to Ihumen Clement I approached the subject. He was in his office in the palace sitting at his enormous old-fashioned roll-top desk. Ihumen was a very tall and thin man, probably in his mid-seventies. The finely chiseled aristocratic features and ascetic appearance of this man, made even taller by the conic Eastern Rite monk's headgear he usually wore, made him look rather forbidding. This was misleading as he was a warm-hearted, kind, and considerate individual.

Ihumen Clement agreed with Marko's suggestion. Reflecting a minute, he took out a blank baptismal certificate, filled it in with my name, birth date, and the name of my parents, signed it and applied a seal of the parish of Szistka, in far-away Pidlasha, a district of north-east Poland with a large Ukrainian minority. Before the war the Studites had been sent to far-away parishes too poor to support a priest and his family. (Eastern Rite Catholic priests were permitted to marry.) After 1939 a number of these outposts had to be abandoned and Szistka was one of them. Ihumen Clement, while filling out the form and forging the name of the parish priest, Father Horoshka, was grumbling that the war forced him in his old age, a lawyer and a monk, to forge documents. He handed me the "birth certificate," put his hand on my head, blessed me and sent me away. The "birth certificate" of Roman Paul Mytka, the son of Anna and Nicholas, is still in my possession.

The *schimnyk* (a monk after taking final vows) Volodymyr Poberejko from the skyt of St. Andrew in Luzky finally arrived. He was a pleasant and cheerful monk with an excellent sense of humor, and he and I hit it off well at once. He indirectly indicated to me that he was aware of who I was and he would do his best to arrange for me to stay in the skyt. He mentioned that the major obstacle would be the superior, Father Nikon, an old monk of Polish origin, who had joined the small Studite community with Ihumen Clement in their first house in Sknilow. According to Brother Volodymyr, Father Nikon carefully listened to arguments. However, once he made up his mind no one could sway him. I left St. Josaphat with some misgivings. I had felt secure with Ihumen Clement and Father Marko within reach. However, Brother Volodymyr projected confidence, and I had little choice in the matter anyway.

At dawn we left the monastery for the railroad station. All the arriving travellers were scrutinized by the Ukrainian police. Germans were not able to distinguish a Jew from a Ukrainian or a Pole and therefore relied on local collaborators to point out escaping Jews disguised as Aryans. Brother Volodymyr, relaxed and smiling, approached a patrol of Ukrainian police asking for directions. The policemen volunteered to show us the way and, chatting and joking, we proceeded to the platform. Brother Volodymyr offered the policemen a holy picture, thanked them, and told them that he was proud to encounter representatives of the future Ukrainian armed forces. The policemen, flattered and pleased, returned to the main hall to continue to look for Jews.

Our train arrived and, after making numerous stops to let military transports through, we arrived in the evening in Broshniw, after travelling a whole day a distance of little more than one hundred miles. The narrow-gauge mountain train heading for the mountains had left long ago, and we were compelled to stay in this little town until morning. There were no restaurants or hotels there in those days.

Brother Volodymyr, as always enterprising, declared that to sleep at the railroad station was not desirable, and we had better call on the local parish priest. We were cordially greeted at the parish house by the priest and his diak (cantor) and we were asked to join them in the simple meal prepared by the housekeeper.

Brother Volodymyr took from his bag a bottle of honey and offered it to the host. After the usual ceremonial refusal, the gift was accepted with great appreciation. This was honey from the Luzky apiary high in the Carpathian mountains. The almost-transparent honey had an aroma of mountain flowers and wild raspberries with which the slopes of the Carpathians were covered. The Studite honey was well known and highly valued, and it was rumored that it had medicinal properties. To reciprocate, the host offered a tiny glass of vodka and a sliver of sausage, equally precious in those times.

The conversation at the table turned to events in the region. Germans were confiscating livestock, grain, and potatoes, leaving the peasants barely enough food to survive the winter. Peasants objecting and complaining were unceremoniously shot. The diak described the brutal deportation of Jews, herded into cattle cars and transported north.

The conversation shifted to church matters, and its tenor indicated the deep differences existing within the Uniate Church. The Metropolitan was its titular head. The comments of the parish priest pointed out that the policy of revival of the Eastern Rite was not popular in the diocese of Bishop Chomyshyn. Although the parish priest spoke with utmost respect about the Metropolitan and the Jur, the implied disagreement with his policies was apparent. I was too young to understand the problem and besides I was preoccupied with other matters. Later over the years I learned more about the issues involved in the difficult and tragic life of the Metropolitan.

It was getting late, and we were invited, as expected by Brother Volodymyr, to stay overnight. Early in the morning we left for the station to board the little mountain train for Perehinsko, a Bojko village in the mountains, and Pidlute, the summer residence of the Metropolitan. Before the final stop in Czorna Rika, near the crest of the Carpathians, on the old border between Poland and Hungary, was Luzky.

The narrow gauge train, consisting of a scaled-down engine puffing steam, flat cars for transporting logs, and a caboose with a chimney, slowly climbed the hills before entering the mountain valleys. Similar trains, relics of the past, can be still be seen in amusements parks. It played a critical role in the life of the skyt in Luzky, as it was the only link with the outside world.

Brother Volodymyr attached to the caboose a little wooden platform on four wheels, identical to those on the flat cars. He explained that he came on it all the way from Luzky, a fifty-mile distance. The little carriage could travel at considerable speed all the way from the mountains to Broshniw because of the large differential in elevation. In only a few areas crossing a valley did the carriage have to be pushed to the next decline, after which gravity took over again.

The carriage was capable of accelerating to a considerable speed, which had to be controlled by a lever made of hard wood inserted through a hole in the platform and applied to a wheel if required. If properly employed, the lever acted as a rather efficient if primitive braking device. On the return trip up the mountains the carriage was attached to the little train, and on arrival at Luzky it was pushed back to the monastery on a siding.

The train left the valley and slowly made its way toward the Carpathian peaks visible on the horizon. The landscape changed as it left the lowlands and became increasingly rugged. The train travelled on the narrow tracks along the swiftly flowing Limnitza, crossing the river and its tributaries from time to time on steel bridges. The trip took a whole day, but the caboose, with a cast iron stove fired by logs and discharging sap and the aroma of burning dry pine wood, was warm and cozy. Occasionally, mountain peasants embarked at one of the stops with their sheep and gathered at the stove. The sight of the snow-covered mountains, the enormous forests on both sides of the river, the puffing of the train, and the crackling fire in the stove made one sleepy.

We arrived in Luzky in late afternoon. The monastery was on a plateau, the only inhabited structure in a radius of ten miles. A large Alpine chalet-like building, reddish because it was built entirely from cedar, with a gracious porch, its window frames painted white, from a distance gave the impression of a hotel in the Bernese Oberland. On the same plateau a short distance from the monastery was a church built from cedar wood, similar to the one in Lyczakiw.

I was led to a guest room outside the clausura. There after a while a young friendly monk brought dinner. Sniffing the air he suggested that I stop smoking as Father Nikon, the superior, could not stand the smell of tobacco.

I waited for Brother Volodymyr to explain what was going on. It was winter and the church was snowed in. The services were therefore conducted in a chapel in the house. I could hear the now-familiar singing of the monks and was somewhat worried that I was left in the guest room. After services Brother Volodymyr came to greet me and related that he had not told Father Nikon anything yet, leaving it for the morning. He implored me to be patient and not to worry. I fell asleep listening to a pack of wolves assembled somewhere on the plateau howling at the moon.

In the morning Brother Matkowski brought hot tea and a milk soup. Again I could hear the Utrenia and Liturgy sung in the chapel. I had no choice but to wait. I reflected that the trip back to Lwów alone would be a dangerous one and the chances of making it were slim. Late in the morning there was a knock on the door of the guest room and Father Nikon came in.

He was of middle height, apparently an army officer in his youth, held himself ramrod straight, and the closely cropped white hair and a full beard framed a pleasant calm face. The penetrating deep blue eyes examined me carefully. Finally, in his strangely accented Ukrainian Father Nikon stated that I was going to stay in the skyt, that my status was that of novice, and I would work as everybody else in the monastery under the direction of Namistnyk Sergei. I thanked him for the hospitality and the kindness. Little else was said.

Later Brother Volodymyr related that he called on Father Nikon after services, apprised him of the situation and the suggestion of Ihumen Clement to allow me to join the monastic community in Luzky. Father Nikon reflected for a while and without much ado agreed to my presence at the skyt. We both were much relieved that Father Nikon had accepted me. Sometime later Brother Volodymyr confessed that he had been not at all sure of the outcome of his meeting with Father Nikon.

Half a century has passed since my first encounter with Father Nikon. I still vividly remember the serene monk, always neatly dressed in a freshly pressed spotless habit with a monk's hood over which he always wore a black thick hand-knitted woolen sweater, and the only luxury—meticulously polished elegant boots. Every day in the afternoon, summer and winter, he used to go behind the house to a nearby flowing stream to soak his feet in the icy water. Soft-spoken and a man of few words, he firmly but unobtrusively managed the small monastic community.

The escape from the ghetto and the immediate daily danger of existence in Lwów in constant fear of discovery were over. However, in the wilderness of the Carpathian mountains, in the quiet environment of a monastic community, another struggle started. It was not easy to sort out the events of the past two years and to maintain a psychological balance under the circumstances. Observing me, Father Nikon was probably aware of the inner turmoil. From time to time he gave me a new task in the house, or an additional responsibility. Today I understand that he was trying to keep me busy to take my mind off fear and worry.

I developed a high fever after working outdoors chopping wood. Father Nikon accompanied by Brother Matkowsky came to my cell after vespers carrying a bottle of "Onysymka." This was a special vodka with herbs distilled annually with the permission of the Ihumen Clement for the feast of the Assumption, the great event in the Lawra (the mother house) in Uniw. Brother Onysym in charge of the kitchen was known in the order as a master cook. His fame spread because of this special brew, which was sent to all the Studite houses. A bottle of it was kept in the superior's cell and a drink of this "medicine" was administered when a monk was ill. Otherwise only at Christmas and Easter after mass was a tiny glass offered each monk in the refectory. A combination of a stiff drink of "Onysymka" and the concoction of herbs prepared by Brother Matkowsky restored my health.

The adjustment to the daily life among the Studites was over. I got accustomed to the rhythm of the daily monastic routine. Nevertheless, the fear of discovery and death was always with me. Germans were in Czorna Rika, and the Ukrainian police had an outpost in Perehinsko. The occasional visitor to the monastery always presented the threat of recognizing me as a Jew, followed by a denunciation to the authorities. The inner peace of the monks, their conviction that we all are in the Lord's hand, and that our souls cannot be destroyed were gradually transmitted to me. Days and then weeks passed, and eventually I accepted the notion that the skyt of St. Andrew was my home. There I could observe the ways and the rhythm of Eastern monastic life at close quarters.

The order was governed by the *Typikon,* a rule written by Metropolitan Andrew and Ihumen Clement after years of research of monastic life as it was practiced in Byzantium and in Kiev. This constitution or rule was submitted to Rome in 1938 by a delegation of Studites led by Ihumen Clement. It was finally approved only in the 1960s, thanks to the efforts of Father Michel de Lattre, a knowledgeable canonic lawyer and vice postulator of the cause of beatification of the Metropolitan Andrew Szeptycki.

The governing body of the order was *Rada Starciw* (Council of Elders), an assembly of "old" monks who had taken the *obity* (final vows). They were referred to as *"schimnyky."* (*Schima* was the ritual of taking the final vows.) The second group of the community was the *"riasophory"* (wearer of habits). These were monks who after a successful novitiate were permitted to wear a habit and a wide leather belt. After securing permission from the Rada, they were allowed to make a one-year vow to observe the Studite rule and live in poverty, obedience, and chastity; this could be renewed annually in a special ceremony. Generally only after seven to ten years was a riasophore permitted by the Rada to take the schima, the final vows. Newly arrived prospective monks were referred to as "candidates," or guests contemplating joining the community. They wore secular clothing, were subject to the rules of the order, and worked as everyone else. It was the Rada that decided whether a guest after a trial period was allowed to progress to the status of a novice. The official novitiate lasted twelve months under the tutelage and supervision of a magister, a senior monk. At the end of the novitiate, *postryzhyny* (a ritual cutting of the hair) transferred the novice to the status of a monk.

From then on he was permitted to wear a belted habit and without taking vows for at least three years had to follow the rule. At the end of this period the Rada decided whether to grant him the privilege to take the schima, or let him continue as a riasophore and only renew the annual vow. My status was officially that of a novice, and at this stage I was indistinguishable from any other monk.

Hieromonks—ordained priests—had no special status in the community. Their function was to officiate at services, say the liturgy, and administer the sacraments. The selection of the monks sent to a seminary was determined by their suitability for priesthood and their level of education. Superiors were usually recruited from the ranks of Hieromonks.

However, effectively the administration of the monasteries was entrusted to the *namistnyk*, a monk with organizational and administrative ability. Brother Garvolinski was the namistnyk of St. John the Baptist in Lyczakiw, Brother Isidor Livyj at St. Josaphat, and Brother Sergei in Luzky. The mother house in Uniw, the Lawra (Old Slavonic for monastery) of Assumption with its large community and variety of workshops, had a number of administrators. Deacon Danylo was in charge of the novitiate and the orphanage, Brother Kohut was in charge of the workshops, Father Ilarion controlled the purse and the relations with the outside world. Brother Onysym presided over the household, the stores, and the kitchen. Father Joseph was the superior and the spiritual leader of the community.

The monks lived as a closely knit group with clearly defined tasks. They were rotated from time to time between monasteries. Generally a monk stayed in a community for two or three years. This practice was not always rigidly observed, and some lived for many years in one monastery.

The Studites represented a dynamic and a vibrant monastic order growing and expanding rapidly in Western Ukraine. This could be attributed to the way of life that suited well the dedicated but not necessarily well-educated men whose roots were in the Ukrainian villages. The monasteries filled a need in the region, acting as centers of spiritual life, managing workshops in which villagers or their sons were trained in a wide range of skills. The Studites were strictly forbidden to beg and the rule required them to be self-supporting. Thus they contributed by their presence and were not a burden to their surroundings as church institutions frequently are. Thanks to the leadership and the inspiration of Ihumen Clement, the Studites in a relatively short time became an integral part of the Ukrainian life in Halyczyna.[5]

The monks in Luzky lived in very close quarters. There were usually seven to ten Studites in residence at the skyt. The winter was long and cold with temperatures frequently below -30 degrees centigrade. The frequent snow storms, the cold, and roaming packs of wolves kept us mostly indoors, venturing only to the stream to fetch water and to the stables to take care of the animals. The short spring, the summer, and autumn had to be utilized to prepare for the winter. A sufficient supply of hay had to be accumulated to feed the animals during the long winter months, trees had to be cut and sawn into logs to provide fuel, the buildings exposed to a harsh climate had to be repaired and kept in good condition.

Survival near the tree line high in the Carpathian mountains was a difficult but nevertheless a rewarding task. We lived in close contact with nature. Wolves assembled in the winter months on the plateau near the house and the church, singing to the moon throughout the night. Our neighbor, a bear, used to visit regularly in the summer, attracted by the excellent wild raspberries on the slope behind the monastery. In the summer deer grazed frequently near the church. Down in the valley on the other side of the railroad tracks, Limnitza, a mountain river, laboriously worked its way through the enormous boulders strewn in its path. Its constant hum was especially pronounced in the silence of the night.

The monks were an interesting and highly individualistic group presided over by Father Nikon. Namistnyk Sergei was a reserved, private individual who spoke only when it was absolutely necessary. The conversation with him was limited to discussing the detail of a task, or a request to assist another monk. Brother Matkowsky, a riasophore, was a jovial somewhat rotund young man with a ready smile and a joke, always wearing an apron and a conic monastic hat. When not at the services, he presided over the kitchen. His day started at 5:30 in the morning laboriously kindling a fire in the stove, not an easy task as matches were precious and in short supply. His day ended late at night after the dishes were washed and butter was made for delivery to the authorities.

Brother Damian, a tailor, was busy sewing uniforms for the German Grenzschutz (border police). The first time I visited his cell, which also served as his workshop, I was startled to see a German uniform. Brother Damian smiled and explained that this was a finished uniform for one of the Germans in Czorna Rika. He knew some German, and occasionally when stopping by for a fitting his customers told him what was going on at the Eastern front. The comments made were different from the usual communiques appearing in the newspaper that arrived from time to time in Luzky with the mail.

Brother Ihnatij Stasyshyn, a monk then in his late twenties, pleasant and kind, was treated with condescension by the others. He was given to making strange statements and experimenting with the tasks given to him. Brother Ihnatij was in charge of the four cows and the few sheep and was responsible for the laundry. He had a strange gift for predicting events, and I am unable to this day to explain this phenomenon. On several occasions he told monks about coming changes in their lives. He had no way in the isolation of Luzky to have contact with sources of information that could provide these insights. Nowadays he probably would be described as a psychic. Frequently, I assisted him either with the laundry or with the animals. On these occasions his remarks were startling indeed and his predictions proved to be accurate.

Brother Modest Voronczak, a carpenter, was probably in his late twenties. A friendly, kind and considerate individual, he was generally to be found in his workshop preparing cedar wood for cabinetry, or building beehives. Occasionally, I used to stop there for a chat and learned about his family and shared views on current events. After Brother Ihnatij injured his hand, I was given the task of milking cows. As I had never done it before, my hands were soon swollen and hurt. Arriving early in the morning in the kitchen to pick up the vessels for the morning milking, to my surprise I discovered the milk was already on the table in the kitchen. This was repeated daily. Intrigued, I got up early and in the stable I discovered Brother Modest milking a cow. He smiled and remarked that as I was not used to it he took over the morning milking to enable me to rest my hands.

Brother Laurentij was in charge of the apiary. The bees were of critical importance because their honey provided livelihood not only for the community in Luzky, but also supported other houses. The honey was precious because there was no sugar. The skillfully managed apiary produced between 800 and 900 kilograms of honey annually. The honey was stored in tightly made boxes of well-dried cedar wood that were built by Brother Modest, the carpenter. The honey taken in the late spring was derived from pollen collected by bees from the early mountain flowers. Honey taken in the summer was derived from the pollen of raspberries covering the mountain slopes. The last honey collected in the late autumn had a characteristic and different aroma. This was the most appreciated quality and it was colorless with an overpowering aroma of wild flowers. A kilogram of honey could be exchanged for seven kilograms of grain, twelve kilograms of potatoes, or bartered for beans, bacon, cucumbers, or cabbage. In charge of the barter was the ever-enterprising Brother Volodymyr Poberejko, who used to disappear for a few days with a box or two of honey to return with a supply of treasures in those times of famine.

At the end of the corridor in a spacious cell was the workshop of Brother Volodymyr Poberejko. There in a corner were his tools, a cobbler's table, and a supply of leather. He used to sit in a corner and repair footwear. The precious leather was obtained from the factory "Solid" in Lwów, organized by Father Peters for the Studites, which manufactured boots and shoes for the Wehrmacht (German armed forces). His workshop was my favorite place to visit.

Time permitting, Brother Poberejko made new boots for the monks. It was a slow and laborious process, as he was the link between the skyt and the outside world and was frequently away. My shoes had disintegrated a long time ago. The monks fashioned for me a sort of moccasin made of two shaved-down pieces of an old tire kept together by hand-made copper rivets. As leather was not available, this was the common footwear of the Bojkos who cut trees on the slopes high up in the mountains. Brother Poberejko during one of my brief visits to his cell declared that he would make me a pair of boots.

The boots were finished after I had returned to Lwów and lived at St. Josaphat. They were brought by Brother Poberejko, who stopped briefly in Lwów on his way to Uniw in the winter of 1943-44. He never reached the mother house. On his way from the rail-road station in Peremyshlany to the monastery in Uniw he was killed by Polish partisans not far from the monastery.

I walked around in these boots in Lwów until the liberation of the city by the Red Army. I marched in them while serving in the Polish army, and they survived wandering through Poland, Czechoslovakia, and Germany. I crisscrossed Italy in them and embarked on an illegal trip to Eretz Israel from La Spezia. They were finally discarded in the kibbutz Tel Itzhak when they could no longer be repaired.

The small community in Luzky was not without frictions and tensions present in every human society. However, an effort was made not to carry grudges and to try to be understanding. The monastic rule and the spiritual life of the monks had a great deal to do with the ability of this small group of individuals, despite their limitations and idiosyncrasies, to function peacefully together. The sound common sense of peasants, frequently absent in modern sophisticated society, equally contributed to the harmony generally prevailing at Luzky. The wise and experienced guidance of Father Nikon was also an important factor.

It was December 1942 and Luzky was snowed in. The mountain train could not get through for days because it was impossible to keep the tracks clean during the snowstorms. Only the rolling of an avalanche high above us near the Carpathian peaks occasionally broke the silence on the plateau. The valley and the mountains were covered with an impeccable coat of snow glittering like diamonds in the rays of the sun that occasionally broke through the low ceiling of gray clouds.

The snow crackled with every step made on the way to the

stream to bring water, or to the stables to tend the animals. On clear nights the eerie light provided by the moon outlined the snow-covered peaks around us, with the extraordinary blinking bright stars creating the illusion that they were not too far away.

Christmas was approaching and the preparations for it were felt throughout the monastery. While Brother Laurentij and I were washing the wooden floors with hot water and lye and Brother Volodymyr Matkowskij was baking and cooking, Brother Poberejko travelled to Perehinsko to get supplies and hopefully some sausage or ham in exchange for the famous Studite honey. Father Nikon held a religious conference every evening before Vespers. Services in the winter were generally held in the chapel within the house. However, in anticipation of visitors for the Midnight Mass, the snow had to be cleared in front of the church and passages were made to the monastery. A new hlas, the fourth one in the liturgical cycle, was introduced, a more tuneful and cheerful one.

Brother Ihnatij, Brother Damian, and I went in the morning before Christmas eve to locate a small, nicely shaped pine tree in the nearby forest that we cut, brought home, and placed in the refectory. The table was first covered with hay, over which a linen tablecloth embroidered with Ukrainian motifs was placed and set nicely with the best dishes and cutlery. Hay was also spread on the floor in com-memoration of Christ's birth in a stable. Brother Matkowskij, Brother Damian, and I prepared *kutya,* a dish offered to the gods in the pre-Christian times consisting of scaled grain soaked for hours in water; after draining it was mixed with liberally added poppy seeds and honey. The mixture had to be stirred for a long time in earthen-ware deep dishes to achieve the right consistency. Somehow, long ago it became a traditional dish on Christmas eve. Finally everyone warmly dressed in his best clothes assembled on the porch to wait for the appearance of the first star.

The sun had already set, and it was bitterly cold. The sky was cloudless, and the view from the porch on the snow-covered moun-tains was breathtaking. The first star was spotted, and we returned to the chapel. After singing the Christmas tropar and kondak, we continued the Vespers. (Tropars and kondaks are hymns appropriate for the occasion composed in Byzantium and then translated into Old Slavonic.)

After the service we assembled in the refectory. Father Nikon greeted everyone, offering a slice of the prosphora, the leavened little bread used in the Liturgy. After exchanging Christmas greetings and wishes *"Chrystos razhdajetsia, Slavite Yoho"* (Christ is born! Glory to Him!), we sang a few carols. They were actually lullabies with the Christmas message, old folk songs with simple rhythmic texts and melodies sung for centuries in Ukrainian villages while rocking a child to sleep. Brother Matkowskij had outdone himself producing the meatless Christmas dinner consisting of twelve traditional dishes to commemorate the Apostles. After each dish the monks sang a carol or two. As canonic silence was suspended, stories were told about bygone Christmas eves, folk legends, and customs. Some went back to pagan times, like the one that called for pouring melted bees-wax into cold water and predicting the future from the shapes formed. It was a leisurely meal with the dishes served in small quantities throughout the evening and the best honey of Luzky providing the desert.

It was getting late, and I was sent to open the church and prepare coal for the silver incense burner suspended on four chains from its handle. Arriving at the church I was surprised to find a group of people waiting, all bundled up. The air exhaled from their nostrils turned into vapor or froze on the mustaches of the men. These were the few neighbors from Mszana, Osmoloda, and from the *kolybas* (shelters) of lumberjacks in the nearby forest.

It was time for the Midnight Mass. The monks arrived and gathered at their usual pew with the Czasoslov, Psalter, the Horolgion, and Book of Canons on it. The visitors filled the small cedar church and stood because in Eastern Rite churches there were no chairs or benches. Father Nikon, dressed in the vestments appropriate for the holy day, took the incense burner from me and placed on the glowing coals a spoonful of aromatic herbs taken from a silver dish and mixed according to an old formula. He crossed himself and bowed three times to the altar and waved the *Kadylnycia* (incense burner) toward the altar, then toward the icons on the iconostas, and finally facing the monks and worshipers he blessed the assembly. The usually empty church was filled to capacity, with the delicate aroma of incense mixed with cedar wood permeating the air. The Midnight Mass had started, with everybody joining in singing the responses to the ektenias pronounced by Father Nikon.

After the service, large earthenware platters decorated with the traditional embroidered towels were placed in front of the congregation. Eggs, sausages, cakes, cookies, kutya, and whatever else a family could gather for this occasion were nicely laid out on the platters.

The monks sang thanksgiving hymns while Father Nikon passed by and blessed each family assembled next to its platter, sprinkling the colorful arrangement with holy water. After the service was over the monks returned to the clausura (premises closed to outsiders) and their cells. The visitors settled for the short night, women and children in the guest rooms covered with blankets while men went to the stable, climbed to the loft and buried themselves deeply in hay to keep warm. In the morning Brother Matkowskij served hot milk and malaj (corn bread sweetened with honey), and the guests then drifted away to their homes.

It was a unique experience and a privilege to observe the careful and long preparation for the celebration of Christmas. The solemnity of the occasion was certainly felt in the monastery. It was equally reflected on the faces and the behavior of the visitors, who, despite the cold and danger, came to celebrate it with us.

Christmas started another liturgical cycle, followed by the New Year, and Jordan (the baptism of Christ) celebrated according to the Julian calendar (the old style calendar used before the introduction of the Gregorian calendar). The deceptively quiet world around Luzky isolated by the winter was dreamlike, with days following one another in the orderly measured routine of the monastic life. The news of the destruction of a German army in Stalingrad eventually reached Luzky. The reports were rather vague and told about events taking place far away. We in Luzky did not realize that Germany was losing the war.

The rivulets of water coming down the slopes swelling the stream next to the house were the first signs of the arrival of spring. The snow started to melt, and with time the first patches of grass appeared on the meadow. An occasional storm brought a wave of high winds and a blast of cold air, as if winter was fighting not to give up its icy grip on nature that was waking to life. The days were longer and frequently the sky was cloudless, with the sun shining brightly. The spring brought Lent with its spiritual exercises, fast, and long services. We worked harder than ever to repair the damage caused by the winter storms.

Brother Matkowski, the jovial good-natured cook, developed an ulcer and was shipped for treatment to the lowlands. Brother Joseph Miskiw, his replacement, arrived. A good-natured man in his thirties, he was always positive and tried to calm his confratres if irritated by something. He took over the responsibilities of Brother Sergei the namistnyk, who was transferred to another house.

The Studite family in Luzky shrank somewhat and only Brothers Poberejko, Damian, Ihnatij, Modest, Joseph, and Laurentij and I remained. The services at midday were mostly attended, in addition to Father Nikon, by only Brother Laurentij and myself as everyone else was busy.

I became fluent in Old Slavonic and started to understand the meaning of the text of the hymns (the tropary and kondaky) to the saints of the Eastern Church. At the midnight service we sang long paeans composed in honor of St. Theodora, whose history and morals were somewhat controversial. I learned that I, a Jew, belonged to the old Jerusalem that had betrayed the Lord. Its mission was taken over from the arrogant traitors by the new Jerusalem. I was reciting passages describing the life of St. John Chrysostom and praising him for his hatred of the perfidious Jews. These were ancient texts compiled between the eighth and eleventh centuries that reflected old intrigues, hostilities, and long-forgotten conflicts. There was little time or inclination in those days to reflect and philosophize on these matters.

All this was of little consequence to the monks. They sang and worshiped to be closer to the Creator. I doubt whether these long-forgotten stories had much meaning for them except for the rhythm of the language and the melody of the right hlas in the cycle. On the eve of feast days there was in addition to vespers a special service called Lytia, at which verses from the Old Testament were read from the Prophets, Kings, and occasionally the Pentateuch. On a little altar in front of the iconostas, grain, oil, wine, prosphoras, and candles were laid out. Lytia had a special meaning for me because of its relationship to the Old Testament and the harmony and the beauty of this service.

During Lent, Bojkos used to appear at our door. They were Ukrainian mountaineers dwelling in the central Carpathian range, who, isolated, maintained their local customs, some of which could be traced to Doric roots through the music and the patterns employed in decorating pottery and in the colorful embroidery. They came from afar, sometimes walking for miles to spend a day in the monastery, to confess, and the next day to receive the sacraments. It was interesting to observe the spiritual preparation and the reverence with which they approached the exercise. We shared with them our meager food, while they reciprocated with gifts. Sometimes they brought a piece of bacon wrapped in linen, a loaf of bread, or an embroidered towel for the altar. Later in the spring they brought children to be baptized. The men volunteered to help with cutting wood, working on the house, washing the animals. After a day or two they wandered off into the mountains. These were lumberjacks, shepherds, and mountaineers. These simple and illiterate people carried themselves with dignity and treated the monks with respect.

They brought with them the disturbing news of partisan activity in the mountains. There were Ukrainian partisans of the UPA (Ukrainian Insurgent Army), Polish partisans of the AK (Armia Krajowa) and the NSZ (Narodowe Siły Zbrojne), and roaming bands of German deserters. In the late spring of 1943 the famous partisan raid commanded by Major General Kowpak, which originated in the forest of Byelorussia, penetrated deep behind the German lines into Poland and Western Ukraine. They marched hundreds of miles fighting German garrisons, cutting supply and communication lines of the German army, and eventually reached the Carpathian mountains on their way to Hungary.[6]

The visitors told stories of whole villages burnt and the population killed for withholding grain or keeping unregistered animals. Polish families living in the region were killed by Ukrainian partisans. In turn Polish partisans retaliated against innocents. The horror perpetrated throughout Western Ukraine in the mindless fratricidal struggle encouraged by the Germans reached the region in the spring.

We realized that we were defenseless in the wilderness and that a disaster could strike at any time. Nevertheless, the monks went about their daily tasks and prayed as prescribed by the cycle of the season. Every evening before retiring we were reminded by Father Nikon that this might be our last night, and we had better be prepared for the worst.

Jews were deported to death camps and whole districts were officially declared *"Judenrein"* (clean of Jews) with a board announcing it placed at the entrance to the towns. Occasionally the Grenzschutz (the German border police) patrol stopped for a glass of milk and told us that they encountered Jews escaping to Hungary and shot them. We were admonished to report to them the presence of any suspicious individual.

Our only other contact with the German authorities was in Perehinsko, a village thirty-five miles from Luzky. The monastery had four registered cows and it was required to deliver an assigned quota of butter. Once a month one of us traveled to this village. We had at times to barter honey for butter to meet the quota when the cows did not produce enough milk. We took care and fed the cows throughout the long winter for the privilege of keeping the skimmed milk.

This typified the attitude of the German master race to the local population, which was stripped of most of what it produced and was starving. There was a well-camouflaged dugout in the forest behind the stable, and there we secretly kept an unregistered pig to be slaughtered before Christmas. This provided fat and a little meat for the rest of the year. The presence in the monastery of the unregistered pig, or for that matter my presence if discovered, would have identical fatal consequences for the monks in those unusual times.

Lent and its lengthy services sung in a mournful hlas culminated in the celebration of Easter. On Good Friday a *plaszczanycia* (a piece of silk on which the body of Christ was painted in the style of an icon) was placed on the *tetrapod* (little altar) before the iconostas. Final prayers were sung and the church was closed with a nail ham-

mered in the door, turning it symbolically into a grave. All day
Saturday guests arrived from different directions. Some came over
the mountain on little-known paths. Others arrived on the little
train.

At midnight the monks, led by Father Nikon dressed in vestments and carrying the incense burner, walked to the church. A procession formed, with the assembled people following the monks led
by Father Nikon and a monk carrying an icon depicting the resur-
rection. The procession circled the church three times and stopped
before the closed church. The nail was removed, the door opened,
and the congregation holding lit candles walked in singing the resur-
rection tropar and kondak. The Liturgy started and was sung with
everybody joining the monks in the responses.

After the service, as at Christmas, the beautifully decorated earthenware platters were brought forward to be blessed by Father Nikon.
One platter was prepared from small donations and offered to the
monks—a few eggs, a *pascha* (Easter bread), a sausage, a goat cheese,
some bacon. It was not much, but it was presented with affection,
sharing with us the little that these people had.

After the service Brother Joseph brought from the kitchen a large
pot of hot milk, malaj, and some honey, which was served by the
monks to the guests. Hard-boiled eggs were sliced into small pieces
and placed on a plate. Father Nikon approached first the monks and
then the guests, offering all a slice of egg and wishing them a Happy
Easter. In the morning the guests dispersed, and we returned to our
cells for a well-deserved rest.

The snow melted, the meadows were green again, and the winter
was forgotten. Every morning after services and breakfast I picked a
piece of bread, a little salt, and occasionally an onion or a pickle from
the kitchen and went to the stable. I left with a flock of sheep and
followed the cows with bells attached to their necks. For a while I
continued on the dirt road meandering along the Limnitza and then
turned into the mountains and meadows high above the monastery.
On occasions this little procession encountered the German
Grenzschutz patrol. Greetings were exchanged and we proceeded on
our way. On the meadows the cows and the sheep grazed while I read
a book taken from the monastery's library, daydreamed observing the

clouds passing overhead, or took a nap. In the late afternoon the same procession returned slowly to the monastery, stopping on the way for a drink of refreshing, cold water at a swiftly flowing, gurgling mountain stream.

During the spring and the summer, visitors arrived from other monasteries for a short vacation and a spiritual retreat in the skyt. The first to arrive was Brother Onysym. He brought with him a bottle of his famous brew as a gift to the community. It was locked up in a cabinet in Father Nikon's office waiting for a special occasion. Then his assistant Brother Simeon arrived, a cantankerous middle-aged man who suffered from insomnia and disturbed the monks' rest. After a hard day's work and long services followed by the midnight vigil, the monks were not pleased to have the few hours of sleep disturbed by the rumblings of Brother Simeon. However, no one complained, as he was a kind if somewhat disturbed individual. Nevertheless, we were all relieved when he departed for the mother house in Uniw.

Brother Gabriel was an elderly monk, cheerful and easygoing. However, it was Lent when the good brother came from the lowlands. This was the time of the year when he imagined that he was developing stigmata. Again we had a problem on our hands as nightly the loud prayers of the good brother interfered with our rest.

Father Martyn, a young and dynamic hieromonk with an excellent sense of humor and a repertoire of stories and anecdotes, was a welcome change. His visit was followed by schimnyk (honorific title given to monks who were permitted to take final vows) Poberejko's brother, a secular priest, who brought news from the outside world. He was an intelligent, thoughtful, and very kind individual. On several occasions he accompanied me to the meadows, and while I kept an eye on the grazing livestock we spent pleasant hours chatting. The guidance and advice offered by Father Poberejko was much appreciated and it helped me to maintain the inner equilibrium essential for survival in my circumstances.

Shortly before Easter Father Marko arrived for a few days. I was delighted to see him and learn about Ihumen Clement, the Metropolitan, and the monks at St. John the Baptist and St. Josaphat. He brought news from my younger brother, who was

presently back in Lwów, lived at Jur, and worked with Brother
Antonij. My brother seemed to be well-adjusted and in good health.
Father Marko told me about other Jewish children sheltered by the
Studite monks and by the Studite nuns. He found me, guided by
the sound of the bells of the grazing cows, on a meadow in the
mountains. It was a lovely afternoon with bees busily collecting
pollen from the flowers that turned the grass into a richly textured
and colorful carpet.

Father Marko mentioned that he was in contact with my mother
in the ghetto. He related that she had tried to escape but it was too
late and nothing could be done any longer to help her. He took a
scrap of paper addressed to me from his wallet. It was my mother's
last message. She wrote: "Leon (my seven-year-old brother) is no
longer alive. Forget us and cherish life. Love." We remained silent as
there was nothing more to say. Next morning Father Marko celebrated the Liturgy with Father Nikon. He was in black vestments
worn usually at a memorial Mass, or a *Panachida*. Our paths crossed
many a time during and after the war, but we never mentioned the
afternoon on the meadow on the Carpathian mountains.

Days passed uneventfully with only the frequent visits of guests
breaking the routine of life in Luzky. The guests came to rest and to
refresh their spirits at the skyt of St. Andrew, which was the original
mission of this beautiful retreat. The news they brought with them
was distressing, telling of violence spreading throughout the land. At
the outset it had been directed primarily against the Jews. Now it
encompassed everybody. Young men and women were arrested and
deported to Germany to work in munitions factories. People disappeared without a trace. The partisans were more aggressive, provok-
ing ruthless retaliation by the Germans.

After Pentecost Deacon Teofan Shevaha arrived from Lwów and
replaced Father Nikon, who went to Zarvanycia in the Podilia, a
Studite monastery and a pilgrimage place. Father Josaphat, an old
half-blind monk from the original Sknilow community, took over
the spiritual guidance of the community. His hair and beard were
always untidy, his riasa spotted and torn, and his boots never
cleaned. It was rather difficult to communicate with him. Deacon
Teofan smiled pleasantly, and made little compliments; the pair were

the antithesis of the leadership provided by Father Nikon. The monks occasionally grumbled that Father Nikon was sometimes too strict. Now the community was genuinely sorry to see him go. The rule of the order and the inner discipline of the monks guided the community and the changed style of leadership had little impact. We knew our responsibilities, and Deacon Teofan left us alone while Father Josaphat administered the sacraments.

The question of my documents was again brought up by Deacon Teofan. Brother Poberejko suggested that he would take me to Dolyna, and there the Ukrainian Committee would issue an identification card. We left in our little carriage, which rolled swiftly down from valley to valley. In the late afternoon we reached Dolyna. The parish priest received us cordially and we settled in the barn for the night. The next morning I had my picture taken and Brother Poberejko disappeared with it. He returned in the evening with an identification card stating that I was a monk and a member of the Studite Order. This document is still in my possession, a memento of Brother Poberejko. I never learned how he managed to obtain it without presenting me at the Ukrainian Committee's office. The next morning we attached the carriage to the little train, which, puffing laboriously, made its way up the mountains, eventually reaching Luzky in the late afternoon.

The summer passed quickly, the days became shorter, and the monks were busy preparing the monastery for the winter. Logs were sawn, split with an ax into firewood, and stored neatly adjacent to the wall of the building. There protected by the roof they dried and were easily accessible; a comforting sight in view of the winter months to come. On the slopes high on the mountain, grass was cut with a scythe and left to dry in the sun. After a few days the hay was ready to be transported to the monastery and stored in the loft. A large stack of it was placed on a piece of burlap suspended between two poles and dragged all the way down to the plateau of the monastery to the stable.

Brother Laurentij was busy preparing the apiary for the winter. Frames with honeycomb were removed from the beehives, the wax seal was cut away, honey was separated in a centrifuge operated by hand and placed in cedarwood boxes to be stored in the attic of the house. The apiary was my favorite place. It was peaceful there, at the end of the plateau on which the church and the monastery were built, and only the hum of the bees returning from the meadows to the hives and singing of the birds could be heard.

Autumn was in the air. At daybreak on the way to church for the Utrenia it was necessary to wear an overcoat to keep warm. The morning frost turned the drops of dew on the grass into ice, providing an illusion of snow for a short while. Then the warm sun melted the sparkling crystals. Down in the valley leaves started to turn, first yellow and then red. The bellowing of deer could be heard with the echo repeating their mating call throughout the valley. In the afternoons Brother Laurentij, Brother Ihnatij, and I gathered mushrooms in the forest behind the stables. They were brought to Brother Joseph to be dried on the stove in the kitchen.

One day I was assisting Brother Ihnatij with the laundry. With his usual somewhat shy smile he remarked that very soon I would leave Luzky and return to Lwów. Puzzled, I inquired whether he heard something from Deacon Teofan, or possibly from anyone else. He replied that no one had told him anything and that this was only a feeling. Deacon Teofan had been in Luzky by now for some time and could not have had direct contact with Ihumen Clement. Lately no one came to visit us because travelling became very dangerous. Our only link with the outside world was the train arriving every afternoon from the lowlands, stopping to deliver mail at the siding. A few days after the conversation with Brother Ihnatij an unopened letter from Ihumen Clement addressed to me was given to me by Deacon Teofan. In it was a short note instructing me to return to Lwów. I recalled the strange remark of Brother Ihnatij, who could not have known about the letter and its contents.

I packed my few belongings and accompanied by Brother Joseph left the next day for Broshniw. I said goodbye to the brothers, to Deacon Teofan and Father Josaphat, and to newly arrived Brothers Filotej and Christophor, both painters of icons whom I had met at the St. John the Baptist monastery in Lyczakiw. From the siding before placing the carriage on the tracks I looked at the monastery, at the church, at the stable and the workshops.

Almost a year had passed since I arrived, accompanied by Brother

Poberejko, at the skyt of St. Andrew in Luzky. Here I had lived a life of a monk in a closely knit community that I had learned to respect and cherish. These were difficult days and life in the austere monastery high in the mountains was hard and demanding. Nevertheless, we lived in peace with ourselves, and with each other while madness was all around us.

Brother Joseph was braking the carriage to slow it before it reached the main tracks. I was looking backward at the plateau on which the vision of Metropolitan Andrew had created this beautiful retreat. I sensed that I would never see it again. A few months later retreating German and Hungarian units evacuated the monks and the skyt of St. Andrew was burnt to the ground. All that remains are memories I can share with the old Brother Laurentij, the apiarist presently living in a Studite monastery in Canada.

I threw the switch, allowing the carriage to enter the railroad tracks, then turned it back to the previous position and we took off at an accelerating pace downhill. Brother Joseph and I changed places, working the primitive brake to slow down the considerable speed of the carriage, particularly before it reached a curve. In the afternoon we arrived in Broshniw, left the carriage there to be attached to the next train going up the mountains, and were fortunate to find a connection to Stryj and Lwów. Waiting at the railroad stations with other travellers, we were constantly inspected by agents of the Ukrainian police looking for Jews. From time to time Brother Joseph took out his rosary, a sign that he was as scared as I.

We arrived in Lwów late in the evening and walked through the deserted streets from the main railroad station to St. Josaphat near the Jur. The curfew was on and we had to sneak through little-frequented passages not to be arrested. With a sigh of relief we reached the doorway of the monastery, rang the bell, and after a while Namistnyk Isidor Livyj let us in. In the kitchen he offered us hot tea and a piece of bread. We slept wrapped in our coats in his workshop on the huge tailor's table, delighted to be under a friendly roof. The next morning cells were assigned to us, and we could recover from the ordeal.

St. Josaphat was more tense than when I had left it for Luzky. Father Nikanor, its superior, was still in prison and Father Peters, a

German citizen, had been sentenced to death for treason and shipped to Germany to be executed.

The city was combed every day for young people who were sent to Germany to work in munitions factories. They could find themselves in a street suddenly surrounded by German and Ukrainian police. Trucks were waiting to transport the herded young people to the railroad station, where they were unceremoniously loaded into boxcars and sent westward. Some ended in Auschwitz and Birkenau at the IG Farben installations. Others, perhaps more fortunate, ended in the Ruhr. Occasionally a hiding Jew was found, denounced to police, and shot.

This was the time when Jur was requested to support the newly forming SS Division Galizien, which was assembled from the ranks of the Ukrainian Hilfspolizei and young Ukrainians who preferred to join the SS rather than be shipped to Germany to work in the munitions factories. A large number of young Ukrainians involved in the atrocities committed during the German occupation joined to escape retribution. When the Metropolitan refused to give his blessing to this dubious venture, the relations of the Uniate Church with the authorities became tense.

Life in Luzky was spartan. However, by comparison to the conditions prevailing at St. Josaphat, it seemed now a luxurious refuge. The city was starving. Meager supplies were provided by the monastery in Lyczakiw and by an occasional delivery of flour, potatoes, and cabbage from the nearby villages if the monks succeeded in smuggling it through the barriers at the entrance of the city. However, these supplies were hardly sufficient to feed the community.

The monks left for work early in the morning after services. They worked in the compound of the Jur tending the large garden. Brother Atanazij took care of the Metropolitan, crippled by arthritis. Brothers Vissarion and Ierotej were diaks of the cathedral, Brothers Patrikij and Ambrosij worked in the administration of the Ordinariat (curia), Brothers Teodozij and Lazar supervised the workers at the factory Solid where shoes were produced for the German army. I was assigned to the library Studion, where I assisted Father Tyt Prociuk, my mentor from St. John the Baptist, and Dr. David

Kahane, a teacher of religion and a rabbi of a small congregation on Szajnochy street in Lwów who used to visit my father.

Dr. Kahane was rescued by the Metropolitan Andrew from the notorious Janowska Road camp and was hidden at St. Josaphat in the Studion and the library adjacent to it. Later I found out that one of the reasons I was brought back from Luzky was to take care of Dr. David Kahane.

Part of the private archives of the Metropolitan were placed in a vault at the Studion. Every morning I walked over to the palace-residence at Jur, bringing books for the Metropolitan Andrew and picking up envelopes with documents and books to return to the Studion.

Priests, arriving in Lwów to attend the synodal sessions or to take care of administrative matters, stayed at the monastery. At breakfast they related what was happening in the world. A major battle had been fought in the Ukraine and Byelorussia, and the Red Army was approaching the prewar border with Poland. The German army was retreating, and only occasionally a counterattack was launched to slow the progress of the Soviet troops. We learned about the landing of the Allies in Africa, and from letters of the deported we knew about the systematic bombing of Germany by the allies.

The Christmas season arrived. The preparations for it did not differ much from those I had observed in Luzky. We followed meticulously the same rituals and customs and the spirit of the holiday lightened up the atmosphere at St. Josaphat. Guests joined to celebrate Christmas, and among them were Brother Poberejko and Brother Modest, recently transferred to Lwów. Brother Poberejko brought the promised pair of boots he had made for me and a bottle of honey, a gift from Brother Laurentij. On Christmas eve we all gathered in the refectory for dinner and sang carols until the time arrived for the Midnight Mass.

I led a double life. At the library with Dr. David Kahane I was again Kurt Lewin; once I left it I became a novice of the Studite Order, Roman Mytka. Staying mostly in the monastery except for the daily walk to the nearby Jur to bring books and documents, I lost my self-confidence. Father Herman, a newly arrived hieromonk, after observing me for a while remarked to me in the refectory that I began to look like a Jew and behave like one. He explained that one can sense that I was afraid and suggested that he had a cure. The following Sunday I was requested to accompany Father Herman and act as his diak.

This started a weekly expedition walking through the city to remote parishes in the suburbs. Father Herman said Mass, I served him and read the antiphone, prokimen, and the *Apostol.* The rest was sung by the congregation. These Sunday excursions restored my courage and confidence, and Father Herman and I became good friends. He was formerly a bank official in a town in Volyn (a district of Poland annexed to Russia after the partition and populated by Ukrainians) and was married. After his wife and child died, the widower joined the Studites and eventually became a priest. He was in his late thirties, bald with a red beard framing an intelligent, smiling, and open face. His green eyes carefully observed everything but he did not readily share his thoughts.

Father Herman was arrested in 1947 by the KGB. After years in prisons and Gulag camps, he was released after the speech made by Khrushchev at the Twentieth Congress of the Communist Party exposing Stalin's crimes. In 1964 I received a letter from him asking for assistance. He had been sentenced by a Soviet court to prison for collaborating with the Germans in the destruction of the Jews in Lwów. He asked that I confirm that he assisted me during the time of persecution. Such a statement was required from him by the Soviet authorities in Lwów to grant him an old age pension.

Those were days of the cold war. I prepared a carefully worded affidavit stating that Father Herman had sheltered me from the Germans. I omitted to mention that he was a priest and we lived in the same monastery. The affidavit was submitted to the State Department for authentication with a request to forward it to the Soviet authorities.

To my amazement I received a copy of a letter of the then-Secretary of State Dean Rusk addressed to the U.S. Ambassador in Moscow, requesting him to forward the enclosed affidavit authenticated by him personally to the proper authorities. Father Herman eventually did receive his pension. He is still active in Lwów, highly respected. During a visit to him by a mutual friend, he recalled our expeditions during the war and our friendship.

The Soviet Air Force attacked the city with increasing frequency, usually in the middle of the night. First flares were released on parachutes, which lit the city with an eerie, extraordinarily bright light. Then wave after wave of low flying bombers passed overhead releasing bombs that fell from the sky with a piercing hissing sound, culminating in a terrifying explosion. Practically every night we were compelled to go to the cellar as the vicinity of the main railroad station made the neighborhood a preferred target. Dr. Kahane had to remain in the library, and on occasions I stayed with him to keep him company.

A bomb hit St. Josaphat, destroying three upper floors. Fortunately no one was hurt as the monks were in the cellar. The library and the archives in the adjacent Studion were intact, but the chapel and the monk's quarters were gone. The community was attached to the beautiful chapel. There in the middle of the horror and madness they could gather and worship in peace. We salvaged whatever we could from the destroyed chapel. The nuns managing the nearby hospital offered vestments and liturgical vessels. The brothers prepared a new chapel and resumed their usual routine. Their strength was derived not from premises or forms but from their vocation, their rule, sense of purpose, and spiritual guidance of Ihumen Clement, who came early in the morning after the air raid to ascertain that we were well.

The news brought to the community or to Jur was frightening. Monks arriving from the mother house related the details of the death of Brother Poberejko, shot by Polish partisans. We learned that Luzky was taken over for a while by Soviet partisans belonging to the raid led by the legendary Major General Kowpak. Occasionally a Jew sheltered by friends was denounced to the Ukrainian police and was shot on the street.

The deep antagonism existing between Poles and Ukrainians blinded by mutual hatred added yet another dimension to the horror. Poles left an explosive device at the entrance to the wooden church in Lyczakiw, my first home during the stay with the Studites. It went off while the monks were leaving the church after Mass on a spring Sunday, killing a monk and blinding Namistnyk Garvolinskij. From the upper floor of the library that survived the bombing of St. Josaphat, we could see at night the flashes of artillery fire. The front was approaching, and with it, if we survived, a liberation for Dr. David Kahane and the many other Jews sheltered by the Studites in their monasteries. The return of the Soviet regime signified for the Studites a renewal of persecution and perhaps martyrdom. The tense community waited and prayed.

German troops were retreating westward. At first their convoys were orderly, then it was an escape using every conceivable vehicle or horse-drawn carriage, passing three abreast on the thoroughfare near the bombed-out monastery. All this could be observed from the upper floor of the library.

After a few weeks of this activity, the nightly flashes of artillery duels taking place somewhere in the east stopped. The city was quiet, the streets deserted, and only an occasional German patrol in full battle gear passed by. The well-dressed and well-fed beefy members of the German Schutzpolizei who usually strolled in pairs on the streets of the city in their shining helmets with swastikas painted on them were nowhere to be seen. The Ukrainian Hilfspolizei disappeared, as most of them were incorporated into the SS Division Galizien.

The snow melted, and the old chestnut trees planted on most streets of Lwów were green again. One morning on a path leading up the hill to Jur I unexpectedly encountered a camouflaged sniper in a Soviet uniform. It was a woman soldier aiming her rifle with a telescopic sight toward Grodecka Street, a thoroughfare leading to the railroad station and westward. She ignored me and I proceeded on my way. The city was in Soviet hands and the nightmare that had commenced with the German entry into Lwów on June 1941 was over.

The Red Army bypassed the city and for a while no one was in charge. Then gradually the Soviet civilian administration took over, behaving with restraint. The Soviets were primarily preoccupied with disarming Polish partisan units, which proliferated after the departure of the Germans. The Poles were particularly aggressive, assuming that they would take over the city. Their command post was in the Polytechnic, and from there armed militia units roamed the city, killing Ukrainians and the few remaining Jews who emerged from their hiding places, assuming that they were safe. Among them was Dr. Bartfeld, a young and promising rabbi, who was shot by Poles on the street a few days after the liberation of Lwów by Soviet troops.

It was Sunday and Father Herman and I left St. Josaphat for Batoriwka, a remote suburb. It was a long walk along Janowska Street where the notorious camp was located. We decided to stop there on the way back home. In Batoriwka we learned that after the Liturgy there would be a funeral for a leading Ukrainian who was shot by Poles.

The usual Sunday Mass was followed by a Panachida, a memorial service with the coffin placed in front of the altar. A carriage was brought to the entrance of the church, the coffin was placed on it, and the small congregation led by Father Herman proceeded to the nearby cemetery. The final services were said, the coffin was lowered into the grave, and one by one those present approached the site and threw a shovelful of earth into the grave. To my surprise the widow invited everybody for a *stypa,* a meal in her home. There food was served with vodka, with everybody joining in lively conversation. This was a custom from pre-Christian times. Rather than mourn, the family and the congregation were taking leave of the departed, sharing a moment of togetherness and support for the bereaved relatives.

On our way home we entered the Janowska Road camp. There was no one there. Not far from the entrance there was a large pit filled with a thin layer of sand through which human hands were sticking out. Apparently in their haste the Germans and their Ukrainian henchman had killed some of the remaining inmates and only wounded others. The wounded and the dead were covered with a layer of sand through which the suffocating wounded had tried to get out. Horrified we stood in silence and after saying a prayer we left this site of torture and martyrdom where thousands had died.

The nightmare of German occupation was over. The Red Army swiftly restored law and order and it was relatively safe to walk the streets of the city. It was apparent that the Soviet Union was settling permanently in Western Ukraine and it was most unlikely that Lwów would revert to Poland. The Uniate Church was so far left alone.

The Allies landed in Normandy, and in Italy the Germans were retreating toward the Alps. The Red Army was consolidating its position and preparing for the final thrust into Germany. It was tempting to stay with the monks and wait for developments to unfold. After all, the war was still on and I was among friends. Nevertheless, I understood that sooner or later I would have to get out of the Soviet Union and explore the newly forming Poland under the leadership of the PKWN (Polish Committee of National Liberation). In those days I harbored the illusion that somewhere assistance was waiting for the survivors of the Holocaust, which would be provided by humanity at large once the story of the genocide was told and documented.

I asked Ihumen Clement for advice, and he too was of the opinion that I should move on to Lublin where the PKWN was active. I started preparations for my departure. Father Herman issued a document stating that Roman Pavlo Mytka was indeed a monk of the Studite Order residing at the monastery of St. Josaphat. Namistnyk Isidor checked my belongings and procured a civilian suit, shirts, and sundries. This was a time when a cake of soap was a precious commodity and a new shirt was treasured, as one could barter food for any textile. I started to say goodbye to my many friends at Jur, at Lyczakiw, and called on Ihumen Clement asking for his blessing and his guidance.

On the eve of my departure I was asked to go to the palace-residence to say goodbye to the Metropolitan Andrew, ailing since the onset of winter. Ihumen Clement led me to his private chamber where the giant (both brothers were well over six feet tall) old man, breathing with great effort, was resting. When we entered Brother Atanazij lifted him, and he put his good arm around my head and blessed me. I bowed, kissed the hand of the dying man, and accompanied by Ihumen Clement left the room.

We went upstairs to the chapel of the palace. Ihumen Clement said a short prayer, blessed me, and again I bowed, kissed the hand of my benefactor and left for St. Josaphat.

All evening long monks came to my cell to say goodbye. Namistnyk Isidor brought a bottle of wine, Brother Joseph Michajluk arrived with a shirt, Brother Patrikij with a pair of socks, Father Herman with rubles that he had taken from the monastery cash box. Others came in saying farewell, as is the custom of Eastern Rite monks, touching lightly each other's shoulder with lips and bringing holy pictures for me. I was leaving a cherished family of friends with whom I had shared danger and an important chunk of life. Not much was said; however, the feelings were clearly expressed. The next morning I left with a knapsack and the little valise that was given to me by my mother when I left the ghetto. At the outskirts of the city I stopped a Soviet army truck, the soldiers helped me to climb into it, and I left Lwów.

ℭℭ

Altogether I lived almost two years among the Studites. I got to know well the mother house in Uniw, St. John the Baptist monastery in Lyczakiw, St. Andrew skyt in Luzky, and St. Josaphat obytel-monastery in Lwów. I lived with quite a number of monks at very close quarters. Never did I encounter anything that upset me or scandalized me. Their world and mine were very different. Nevertheless, as long as I was prepared to make an effort and adjust to their ways, I was received after a while with open arms. No effort was ever made to proselytize.

The Studites were not perfect, nor were they saints. Some were well educated and intelligent, others were primitive and illiterate. Some were friendly and kind, others were abrasive and grouchy. In short, they represented the full spectrum of individuals found in every society. They were primarily sons of peasants and grew up in the villages of Western Ukraine. Most of them were without schooling because their parents could not afford it.

I once asked Brother Modest what brought him to the monastery. He smiled and replied that this was a private matter never to be discussed. Based on my observations, the monks joined the community in order to lead a life of prayer and work, dedicate themselves to the Lord, and save their souls. In the materialistic world in which we live, this sounds somewhat trite. It made perfect sense to the Studites who chose this path to leave the world behind and focus on spiritual life. Those who came in search of an easy way left after a short trial. The life of a Studite was spartan and full of trials. They worked hard to improve themselves and to lead a life as taught in the Gospels. They knew what the ideal is and realized that it cannot be attained.

Nevertheless, they tried hard, testing the limitations of their personalities and their ability. They accepted every task entrusted to them by Metropolitan Andrew, including sheltering Jews at the risk of their lives. They did it voluntarily, for the love of Christ, without expecting thanks or a reward. Like most Ukrainians, they were not particularly friendly toward Jews, or interested in them. Nevertheless, a large number of Jews (over two hundred) were saved in extraordinary circumstances, considering the size of the order.

This description might seem over-idealized. The two years of daily life with these people provided an insight into their motivation and ways. The perspective of time and varied experience acquired over the years have not changed my view of the Studites. There was in this community an element of the spirit of St. Francis and his simplicity before the Franciscan Order over centuries modified and distorted it.

The monastic community of the Studites was formed, developed, and guided by Ihumen Clement. A small group of pious peasants by no stretch of imagination would have been able to develop the order and give it a sense of direction. Its growth and expansion started only after Ihumen Clement joined it. I heard it again and again from the old timers how he influenced the young community by his example. One of them commented that when he arrived in Sknilow and a Polish count joined him, a poor peasant's son, in cleaning a latrine, he realized that he was in a very special place. After so many years I also retain the impression that I was indeed privileged to live in a very special place.

The Metropolitan Andrew and Ihumen Clement defined the task of the Order and gave it direction. It was a refuge for young peasants' sons who wished to test and follow their vocation and to whom the doors of other more illustrious orders were closed unless they wanted to dedicate themselves to the service of the better educated members of the monastic communities. Its strength was derived from the Ukrainian villages and its mission was to function in them as an example, a spiritual center, and to contribute to their development.

The Ukrainians are Slavs and their roots are in the Eastern Rite of Christianity. The Greek Catholic Church, a splinter of the Orthodox Church, united with Rome following an agreement signed in Brest Litovsk in 1595-96, and became Latinized with time. This precluded the undertaking of the mission that was a life-long dream of Metropolitan Andrew, to build a bridge between these two interpretations of Christianity, torn apart because of political and theological disagreements.

Therefore, the Metropolitan selected the Studites to cultivate the Eastern Rite in its original Slavic form. This endeavor was reflected in the services of the Studites, in the superb collection of Byzantica in the Studion library of which they were custodians, and in the school of painting dedicated to creating traditional icons. It was their special mission to become custodian of this heritage, following the vision of the farsighted Metropolitan Andrew. The progress made in advancing this design was achieved thanks to the guidance of the former lawyer Ihumen Clement. The Typikon (rule) regulating the behavior of the monks and their daily life was developed, tried, and defined by him. The practices and the spirit of Eastern monasticism were brilliantly transplanted and adapted by him to serve the needs of a primarily agricultural Ukrainian society. He resided in the mother house in Uniw and supervised the affairs of the order and the novitiate. The then-young, dynamic, and dedicated men, Father Marko, Father Peters, Father Nikanor, Father Herman, Father Martyn—strong, intelligent, and not easily led— were all his pupils. Shortly before the war a new generation joined the Studites like Ivan Makar, Sebastian Ben, Tyt Prociuk, Modest Voronczak, Bojarski. All these were inspired and guided by this great man. He had time for everyone and even during my stay at the skyt of St. Andrew in Luzky I regularly received short notes inquiring about my activities and asking how I was.

It was only much later through Father Marko and Father Peters that I could understand better this ascetic and self-effacing man. It became apparent to me through the years of research undertaken for the process of beatification that Metropolitan Andrew could not have accomplished as much as he did without the support of his brother. This support became even more critical after the Metropolitan Andrew was crippled by arthritis. Ihumen Clement moved to the palace-residence and discreetly assisted the Metropolitan in guiding the diocese, navigating between the extreme nationalistic leaders and the Uniate bishops, generally defiant and critical of the policies of his brother the Metropolitan Andrew. Ihumen Clement by design left very few traces of his contribution. He was content to live and work in the shadow of his brother.

The Studites started on a very modest scale before the first world war. The real expansion of the Order took place in the years before the outbreak of hostilities in 1939. The Studites spread throughout Western Ukraine and beyond. Their mother house in Uniw became a major spiritual center for the region.

The two houses in Lwów were engaged in a variety of activities including publishing religious books, managing an orphanage, and providing a base for the monks who were studying in the seminary or learned trades. Zarwanycia was an important pilgrimage center for Ukrainians, similar to Czestochowa in Poland. The Studites served this parish and took care of the continuous flow of pilgrims. In the Carpathian mountains there were three separate ethnic groups with their own dialect and folklore. In the East there were the Hutzuls, in the center the Bojkos, and in the West the Lemkos. These mountaineers were poor and neglected, and their livelihood consisted of migrating north to the lowlands for seasonal labor in the summer and working in lumberjack camps in the winter. Three Studite monasteries were established to serve these communities. Dora in the East, Luzky in the center, and Florinka in the West provided priests with field altars, moving from one lumberjack camp to another offering spiritual guidance and liturgy for workers who were away from their families for months. In Szistka, far north in Pidlasha, there was another parish dedicated to serving the forgotten Uniate communities abandoned by the church in the nineteenth century after the Russification of the region.

All this was brought to a standstill after the arrival of the Red Army in 1939.[7] The persecution of the Studites was limited to the arrest of individuals and to general harassment. The arrival of the Germans in 1941 permitted the Studites to regroup and prepare for martyrdom, which was openly discussed and anticipated. The Uniate Church was driven underground by the Soviets in 1946 after refusing to repudiate the Union with Rome. The monks were dispersed, many were arrested, and many perished in the labor camps in Siberia. Among them was Ihumen Clement, who according to witnesses who were released after the thaw, died in one of those camps on May 1, 1951.

The Studites in Ukraine survived the ordeal. The community reassembled in Lwów and in Uniw in monasteries, which were returned to them. There are very few friends of mine alive today, with Father Herman and Father Modest Voronczak among them. There is a small community of Studites in Canada, which was assembled from the survivors of the Order by Father Marko in Germany. This community and its evolution are another story.

The next chapter of the history of this remarkable Order will have to be written by the next generation of monks in Western Ukraine. Hopefully, it will be equally remarkable as the brief snippet of their life I had the privilege to watch and participate in as a young man.

Gültig im Reich!
(VO - RSHA - v. 20. 10. 42. - IV. D. 3a - 1066 39)

Name / Прізвище: *Mytka*
Vorname / Імя: *Roman-Paul*
Beruf / Звання: *der Mönch*
Geburtsdatum / Народжений дня: *28. III. 1925*
Geburtsort / Місце народження: *Prіstka*
Bekenntnis / Віроісповідання: *gr-kath.*
Familienstand / Родинний стан: *ledig*
Heimatanschrift / Сталий побут (адреса): *Osmoloda - gr-kath. Studiten kloster - Luzky*

Der Inhaber dieses Ausweises ist ukrainischer Volkszehöriger.
Посідач цієї виказки є українцем.

Dolina den *3. August* 1943
ДНЯ
in DOLINA

Sekretär / Секретар
Siegel / Печатка
Obmann / Голова

Бр. Митка Роман

Unterschrift des Inhabers
Підпис посідача виказки

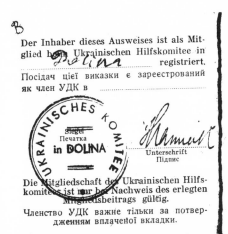

Der Inhaber dieses Ausweises ist als Mitglied beim Ukrainischen Hilfskomitee in *Dolina* registriert.
Посідач цієї виказки є зареєстрований як член УДК в ....

Siegel / Печатка
in DOLINA

Unterschrift
Підпис

Die Mitgliedschaft des Ukrainischen Hilfskomitees ist nur bei Nachweis des erlegten Mitgliedsbeitrags gültig.
Членство УДК важне тільки за потвердженням вплаченої вкладки.

Der Ausweis bleibt Eigentum des Ukrainischen Hauptausschusses und ist auf jederzeitige Aufforderung zurückzugeben.
Виказка є власністю Українського Центрального Комітету і на кожне домагання треба її звернути.

UKRAINISCHER HAUPTAUSSCHUSS IM GENERALGOUVERNEMENT
Український Центральний Комітет у Г. Губернаторстві

UKRAINISCHES HILFSKOMITEE
Український Допомоговий Комітет
in *Dolina*
y

Ausweis - Виказка

Nr. 312597
Ч. 1587

Herausgegeben im Einvernehmen mit der Regierung des Generalgouvernements
Видано в порозумінню з Правлінням Генерального Губернаторства.

An identity card issued by the Ukrainian Committee in Dolina, District Galizien, to Roman Paul Mytka, a Greek Catholic, residing in the Studite monastery in Luzy (Osmoloda).

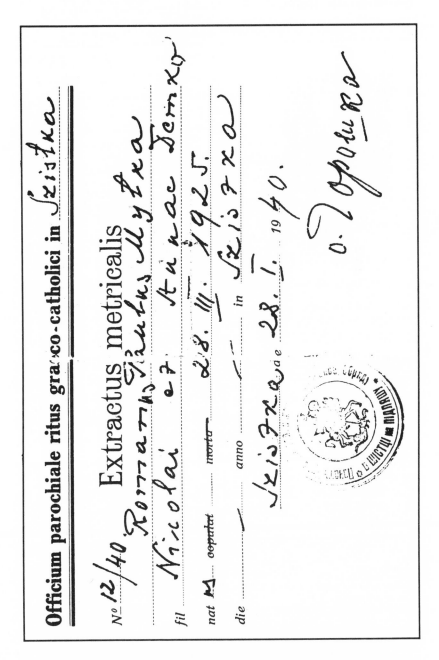

A birth certificate issued to Roman Paulus Mytka (Kurt Lewin), the son of Nicolas and Anna Demko, by the parish in Szistka, in Pidlasha. (The document was issued by Ihumen Clement Szeptycki.)

CHAPTER 3.

The Story of Colonel Torunczyk

I N 1982 THE regime of General Jaruzelski declared martial law
in Poland. Solidarity gained broad public support and challenged the communist establishment that had ruled the country
since the end of the war. These developments could easily have
invoked the Brezhnev Doctrine and resulted in the invasion of
Poland by the Soviet Army. Access to Soviet bases in East Germany,
Czechoslovakia, and Hungary depended on control of the railroad
hubs, roads, and airports of Poland. After the disintegration of the
Soviet Union in 1991 all this became immaterial. However, in 1982
a repetition of events that had taken place in Czechoslovakia in
1968 was a real possibility.

Reading *The New York Times*, I found in it an article describing
events taking place in Warsaw. Included was a brief comment on the
arrest of the wife of one the key leaders of the Solidarity movement,
the daughter of Colonel Henryk Torunczyk, a vice minister in the
Polish communist government shortly after the war. This article
triggered memories of long-forgotten events. It reminded me of a
lunch with Colonel Torunczyk and his wife Roma in Warsaw before
I left Poland for Germany and Italy.

It was September 1945, a few days after my discharge from the
Polish Army. I called on the Torunczyks to thank them for the assistance they had extended after my arrival in Lublin from Lwów in
1944. In the dining room there was a few-months-old baby in a carriage. This was the daughter whose arrest was described many years
later in the article in *The New York Times*.

The Torunczyks were living in a housing complex in the center of Warsaw, one of the few left intact after the systematic and vicious destruction of the city and its historical monuments by the General der SS Bach-Zelewski. Following the defeat of the heroic but futile Polish uprising in the autumn of 1944, German troops, assisted by Lithuanian and Russian Liberation Army units, demolished the city block by block. The comfortable apartment, an extraordinary luxury in a city virtually leveled to the ground, was furnished in a tasteful fashion generally found in the homes of the middle class in prewar Poland.

Roma, or Captain Roma Pawlowska *(nom de guerre)*, Torunczyk's wife, was a tiny dark-haired woman radiating charm and poise. She probably was then in her thirties. She was very intelligent, a journalist by profession. It was rather strange to see her as a mother, lady of the house, and no longer in uniform. In September 1945 one had to get used to the notion that the war was over and life was returning at least for some to a semblance of normality.

The Torunczyks inquired about my plans after my discharge from the army. They were aware that I was a survivor of the Holocaust and that the name under I which I had served in the Polish Army, Roman Matkowski, was an assumed one. The reason for this metamorphosis from a Ukrainian into a Pole was dictated by expediency. On arrival in Lublin from Lwów, I realized that the virulent anti-Semitism of the Poles remained intact even though the Germans were gone. Jewish survivors were referred to as *"niedopalki"* (pieces of wood left unburnt in a fire place), or were asked with malice, "How come the Germans did not gas you, Jew!" Interestingly enough, to live among Poles as Roman Mytka, a Ukrainian and a Greek Catholic, was equally fraught with danger. Therefore, I borrowed the Polish-sounding name of the good Studite Brother Matkowski from Luzky, and while in Poland that was how I was known.

At the leisurely lunch, interrupted occasionally by the crying of the baby, we spoke about the new Poland, the social changes, and the scars left by the war. I commented that Poland was no place for me and that I planned to go to Palestine (the name in use during the British Mandate). The Torunczyks were taken aback by the directness of my statement, as in those days personal information was not readily divulged. They inquired how I proposed to get there. I replied that I planned first to cross the border illegally to Czechoslovakia and from there slip into the American zone in Germany. There I expected to be assisted by Zionist organizations.

Henryk Torunczyk commented jokingly, "Matkowski, we tried to make a decent man out of you and we failed!" He remarked that the Arabs would give the Zionists a hard time. The years he spent in North Africa had provided him with first-hand experience with the Moslem world. He had been interned there by the French with other survivors of the International Brigades after the fall of Republican Spain.

It was a pleasant and relaxed lunch, one of the few occasions when we could engage in an open exchange of ideas. Torunczyk was an idealist, a communist, and totally dedicated to fighting fascism. He sincerely believed then that a new and a better world would emerge under the leadership of the Soviet Union. After experiencing life under Stalin's regime in Lwów from 1939 to 1941, I did not share his opinion. We did not argue, but we represented diametrically opposed points of view. Torunczyk and his wife probably were assimilated Jews and felt that their place was in Poland. After observing the glee of the Polish population during the "resettlement" of the Jews, a term used euphemistically by the Germans when referring to the Holocaust, I believed that there was no place for a Jew among Poles.

Before I left their home Henryk Torunczyk told me, "Well, Matkowski, I hope you manage to get out. If you are caught crossing the border, remember that I am in Warsaw. If you really insist and cannot manage to cross to Czechoslovakia, I will get you a passport and a permit to travel."

Henryk Torunczyk, before accepting the assignment of managing the new territories carved arbitrarily out of Germany for Poland by the Soviet Union (referred to euphemistically as the "recovered western provinces"), was for a while a Vice Minister of Internal Affairs in postwar Poland. This ministry had direct links to the NKVD in Moscow, the dreaded Commissariat of Internal Affairs subsequently renamed KGB. It was comforting to know that in a pinch I could rely on my friend, whose influence at that time was still at the zenith.

Our paths had crossed first in 1944, shortly after my arrival in Lublin from Lwów. Lublin was an old city fortress made famous by the union between Poland and Lithuania signed at the end of the sixteenth century. It was an important administrative and trading center until the partition of the Commonwealth of Poland by its neighbors at the end of the eighteenth century.

The sleepy provincial town was brought to the world's attention by the notorious General of the SS and Police, the Austrian Odilo Globocnik, originally a Slovenian.[1] He chose Majdanek, a suburb of Lublin, as the site of one the six death camps in the General-gouvernement created by the Third Reich in 1939 from the territories of prewar Poland. In these camps the program was executed of permanently "resettling" the Jews of Poland through gas chambers and the chimneys of the crematoria.

Thousands of Poles and Ukrainians also perished there, among them the Greek Catholic parish priest of Peremyshlany near Uniw, Father Kowch, who was betrayed to the Germans by the Ukrainian police for sheltering Jews. The terrible smell of burnt human flesh still permeated this suburb when I arrived in Lublin.

The First Byelorussian Front,[2] with the First Polish Army attached to it, liberated this rather obscure provincial town, the first in the former territory of Poland. There Stalin decided to form the PKWN (Polish Committee of National Liberation), an experiment and subsequently a model for similar "liberation" committees active elsewhere.

This committee was the nucleus of the government of postwar Poland, and at this stage had the misleading appearance of a coalition of all parties united in the determination to liberate the country from the Germans. A well-known writer in prewar Poland, Wanda Wasilewska, chaired this committee. Its other members were Soviet agents like Boleslaw Bierut and Osobka Morawski, Boleslaw Drobner from Krakow (a socialist leader active in prewar Poland), and Dr. Emil Sommerstein.

Dr. Emil Sommerstein, a prominent lawyer and Zionist leader in Lwów before the war, had been a good friend of my father. He was

arrested in 1940 by the NKVD, but after the German attack on the
Soviet Union he was released from prison in Moscow and trotted
out with others to join the PKWN. The news of his appointment as
a minister in the newly formed "government" of Poland reached me
in Lwów a few weeks after the liberation of the city. Knowing that a
friend of my father and someone I knew from childhood was a minister in the new Polish government in Lublin motivated me to go
there. I assumed that all my and my brother's problems would be
resolved once I reached Dr. Sommerstein. It was another shattered
illusion in a chain of many more to come in the years ahead.

I had left the Studites in Lwów with some reluctance and took
off for Lublin. The distance was not too great, probably 150 miles.
However, it was a dangerous undertaking because I had to cross the
demarcation line between the USSR and the former Generalgouvernement through forests full of partisans. Fortunately I was assisted
in crossing the Soviet checkpoints by Greek Catholic priests in the
region.

I stayed a few days at the home of the Uniate parish priest in
Rawa Ruska while ways were explored to get me across the demarcation line. The occasion arose when a peasant died in a nearby village. I accompanied the parish priest from Rawa Ruska to the
funeral and performed the function of the diak. A priest from
Hrebenne, a village on the Polish side of the demarcation line,
joined the funeral procession. Thanks to the training of the Studites,
I was able to assist in the service and in singing and reciting the
appropriate prayers. Following the coffin, I crossed into the Polish
side where the cemetery was located. After the burial I returned with
the parish priest from Hrebenne to his village.

From there through the forest, which I knew well from my childhood because it was a part of my grandfather's estate Potoki located
nearby, I walked to the highway leading to Lublin. Emerging from
the forest I was accosted by a Soviet patrol. Father Herman's certificate stating that I was a monk and a member of the community of
St. Josaphat saved me from being inducted there and then into the
Red Army by the soldiers who were looking for "volunteers." Priests
and monks were for the time being exempted from military service.
A Soviet sergeant who checked my papers commented, "Well, you

fool (*durak* in Russian), go and pray for our victory." I assured him that I would do my best, happy that I did not end up in a Soviet uniform. I then could proceed to the "promised land" of Lublin.

Lublin in September 1944 was a busy place with military convoys passing on the way to the front. The town was humming with activity, with new arrivals like myself from parts of the country liberated from the Germans hastening to join the army or the PKWN.

The PKWN was located in a spacious modern building probably completed shortly before the war. I located Dr. Sommerstein, who received me graciously. He said how very pleased he was that I had survived the German occupation of Lwów. He shook my hand, led me to the door of his office, and that was the end of the meeting.

Somewhat bewildered, I left his office pondering what to do next. Dr. Sommerstein's daughter, who was acting as his secretary, suggested that I get in touch with the widow of Rabbi Dr. Levi Freund, a colleague of my father. I found her working in one of the offices of the PKWN. With her assistance I secured a place to sleep and was given meal tickets for the dining hall that were issued to the personnel of PKWN. This was a fortunate encounter indeed as it provided me with a roof over my head and a meal. I decided to stay on in Lublin because there was no point in my returning to Lwów.

The personnel department of the PKWN, after learning that I had some experience as a librarian, directed me to Captain Roma Pawlowska in the Department of Public Relations and Information. After a short interview I was hired as a librarian, so that my immediate problems were resolved for the time being.

I was now employed by the PKWN. I then rented a sofa in an apartment of a judge who, mobilized in 1939, was serving in the First Polish Corps fighting in Italy as a part of the British Eighth Army. The wife of the judge had sheltered her Jewish boyfriend in the apartment during the German occupation. She supported herself renting rooms in the apartment to individuals who, like me, worked at the PKWN. It was one of the many instances of lives messed up by the war, strange relations, and resulting tragedies when a semblance of normality returned.

Two of her tenants were a Vice Minister of Transportation and his wife, who ran the secretariat of the ministry. Another was organizing the office of the Ministry of Commerce. In the evenings, as there was a curfew and a blackout, we gathered in the living room and drank tea and compared observations and experiences.

I was nineteen years old, and the war was still on, with occasional vicious German counterattacks launched to slow the advance of the Red Army. I was happy to have a roof over my head and food to eat. The future at this juncture was not really an issue preoccupying me or anyone else. We dealt with the problems of daily life and waited for the end of the war.

The office of Captain Pawlowska was pleasant and quiet. There was not much to do there as the library consisted of a few propaganda pamphlets ground out by the newly formed Ministry of Information. I was sent by Captain Pawlowska to a school for political officers, which was a requirement for the personnel of this Ministry. There I was exposed to the usual indoctrination with which I was familiar from the days in 1939-41 when I attended a Soviet school in Lwów.

Occasionally, I had to run errands for Captain Pawlowska, which brought me into a variety of interesting offices, among them those of the then Soviet Ambassador to Poland, Major General Nikolai Bulganin, an urbane, gracious, and elegant individual. Although I was carrying only personal communications from the PKWN, he always received me with courtesy and invariably offered me an excellent Kazbek cigarette—a brand generally reserved for the Soviet elite.

The appointment of Bulganin to this post indicated the importance Stalin attached to the PKWN. Bulganin was one of the key officials in the Kremlin. He emerged after the death of Stalin in 1953 together with Kosygin and Khruschev as a member of the triumvirate ruling the Soviet Union. While observing the activity at PKWN from Captain Pawlowska's office, it became quickly apparent to me that many threads from it led directly to Moscow.

Poland in 1944 in the last phase of the war had two governments. One functioned in London with some legitimacy, as the prewar government of Poland was for practical purpose a military dictatorship. The other one, the PKWN, was formed under the protection of the USSR in Lublin. It was called a committee in

order not to challenge openly the Polish government in London officially recognized by the Allies.[3]

Some members of the PKWN took themselves very seriously,
harboring the silly illusion that they really mattered. Among these
was Boleslaw Drobner, a former leader of the Polish Socialist Party
in prewar Poland. A middle-aged, pompous individual with an
impressive drooping mustache, dressed in meticulously tailored
worker's overalls, he regularly pontificated in the corridors to whoever was prepared to listen to his vision of the future socialist
Poland.

Wanda Wasilewska, a writer of some consequence in prewar
Poland, a socialist, was married to Kornijczuk, a Soviet playwright
popular with the Stalinists. She was chosen by the Kremlin to head
the PKWN because of her outspoken criticism of the prewar Polish
ruling clique. It was a signal given to the Allies that a "new" Poland
was being created dedicated to "social justice and progress." Wanda
Wasilewska showed up at the official ceremony announcing the formation of the PKWN. After the opening ceremony of the PKWN in
June 1944, she disappeared never to be heard of again. The mystery
that surrounded her was never cleared.

The other members of the committee had been well known in
prewar Poland. They were used as a front at the PKWN to give it
the image of a free and independent group representing all factions
of public opinion in Poland. One of them was Dr. Emil
Sommerstein, the Minister of Social Welfare. He was usually in his
office, which no one bothered to visit. A prominent lawyer before
the war and an active Zionist leader, he was a man broken by prison.
He did not know what hit him, why he was arrested, and why he
was suddenly plucked out of the notorious NKVD Lubyanka prison
and presented to Stalin as a promising Polish political leader.

The real power was in the hands of Colonels Torunczyk, Szyr,
Zawadzki, the gray eminence General Swierczewski, Minister of
Propaganda Matuszewski, Vice Minister of Internal Affairs and
Security Romkowski, the architect of the centrally planned eco-
nomic mess Hilary Mintz, and other rather mysterious personalities.
The appearance of complete sovereignty and independence from
Moscow was carefully cultivated, and an illusion was created that

after the war was over Poland would emerge as an independent, democratic, and free country.

After hours I usually stayed in the pleasant and quiet office at the PKWN, as I was not particularly eager to return to the cramped apartment with the lack of privacy. One day a tall man in uniform walked in and asked where Captain Pawlowska was. I suggested that he wait as she was expected back shortly. We chatted for a while and the visitor left.

When Captain Pawlowska returned I mentioned that a man in a uniform had inquired about her. As I was not too familiar with ranks, I related that the visitor could be a sergeant or perhaps a junior officer. Captain Pawlowska smiled and said that this was her husband, Colonel Henryk Torunczyk. Subsequently on several occasions while he was waiting for his wife he engaged me in conversation on a variety of subjects. Eventually he suggested that I join the unit he commanded, as in any event within weeks I would be mobilized.

Henryk Torunczyk had been a young journalist, probably from Lodz. He escaped from Poland in 1936 and joined the International Brigades formed by the Republican Spanish government to fight the Falangists of General Franco. He served in the brigade that consisted of Polish volunteers and was named after Jaroslaw Dabrowski, a prominent Socialist leader at the turn of the century. This unit was similar to the Abraham Lincoln Brigade formed from American volunteers. Eventually he became Chief of Staff of General Walter, a *nom de guerre* of General Karol Swierczewski, the commander of all International Brigades in Spain. The Republican cause was probably lost at the outset of the struggle, because General Franco enjoyed the support of the landowners and the church, and was assisted by Hitler and Mussolini with arms and "volunteers." Soviet "assistance" to the Republicans included agents of the GPU, who introduced purges and mass executions.

The gold reserve of the Spanish Republican government was shipped to the USSR. The infighting among the different factions, the intrigues, and the discord prevailing in the Republicans ranks did the rest. The fiery speeches of La Passionaria, the communist Dolores Ibarruri, the idealism and sacrifice of the Spaniards and the international dreamers and idealists who joined them could not overcome the ruthless professionalism of the Falangists, assisted by German and Italian expeditionary forces. The bombing of the civilian population by the German and Italian air forces spread terror and was expressed vividly in the painting "Guernica" by Picasso.

In 1939 the uneven struggle was over. The remnants of the International Brigades crossed into France to be interned and shipped to camps in North Africa. The start of the Second World War in September 1939 did not change the status of the interned survivors of the Spanish Civil War, and the French colonial authorities in North Africa continued to hold the internees. The arrival in 1941 of the German Africa Corps opened the possibility of a transfer to Nazi concentration camps of the internees, among them many German and Austrian Socialists. Fortunately the battle of El Alamein and Operation Torch decided their fate.

The allies shipped them through the Middle East to the Soviet Union, as they represented a controversial group of individuals and probably were thoroughly infiltrated by communists. There most of them ended in the SBS (Samodzielny Battalion Specjalny—Battalion for Special Assignments). Their leaders were Karol Swierczewski (General Walter, who was killed by Ukrainian partisans near Lubacziw, in Western Ukraine, in 1946) and Henryk Torunczyk. Torunczyk was a pseudonym and to this day I am not certain whether or not he was a Jew, where he came from, or what his real name was. I remember him as a tall, handsome man unobtrusively projecting strength and authority, who was highly regarded by anyone who came in contact with him.

After discussing with Captain Pawlowska the suggestion that I join her husband's unit, I decided to accept this rather tempting offer. Colonel Torunczyk sent an officer from his unit, who accompanied me to the mobilization office. Following a perfunctory medical examination I was led to the recruiting office, and after the formalities were completed I was issued a uniform and became a soldier in the Polish Independent Special Battalion, part of the First Polish Army.

The First Polish Army was formed in the Soviet Union after the Polish Corps, organized by the Polish government in London, departed for the Middle East to join the British Eighth Army. The First Polish Army was a part of Marshal Zhukov's First Byelorussian Front. Originally, it was commanded by a Pole, General Berling, who was replaced after he extended on his own initiative assistance to the beleaguered insurgents in Warsaw. His replacement, General Rola Zymierski, a rather passive and easily manipulated man, was more to Moscow's liking.

Thus I embarked on another adventure that thrust me into an interesting if somewhat dangerous world. I was sent to Jastkow, a landed estate near Lublin, where Torunczyk's unit was stationed. There, after a few hard weeks in an accelerated officers school, I was graduated as a second lieutenant and was transferred to Piotrowice Wielkie, another landed estate nearby, where the headquarters of the unit was located.

Gradually I became familiar with the new environment in which I found myself. The special battalion was formed in the Soviet Union on the river Oka in 1943. It was referred to in a variety of ways. The most common was the Partisan Headquarters (Sztab Partyzancki).[4] Its officers were a rather unusual group of individuals, mostly survivors of the former international brigades in Spain, including Spaniards and Frenchmen. There were among them Jews serving as such, and there were also a number of Jews serving under assumed names. A large percentage of the personnel was trained as paratroopers. The unit served originally as a command and logistic center for partisan operations behind the German lines in Byelorussia and Poland. The last teams to act as a liaison with the partisans were dropped behind German lines shortly after I joined the battalion.

This was undoubtedly an elite unit. Its officers were carefully picked according to their political orientation. The soldiers were former partisans, veterans of many a campaign behind German lines. The large number of survivors of the International Brigades fighting the Franco regime gave it a special character. Everyone was very friendly, and in the course of my duties I had access to all the activities that were going on. However, the inner circle was closely knit and kept to itself. I was very young, spoke excellent Polish with a heavy Ukrainian accent, and was guarded in expressing my ideas. All this served to erect a barrier between the old-timers and myself.

After all, to most of them I was just a kid. Interestingly, past experiences were rarely brought up, and it was an unwritten rule that one did not discuss personal matters. Occasional snippets of comments provided a glimpse of life on the river Oka, behind the enemy lines; Spain was never mentioned. Some old-timers were communists, among them Torunczyk and Pawlowska. Others had joined the unit in the USSR, where they had been deported from other European countries or where they had fled ahead of the invading German armies. Nevertheless, they either were or pretended to be attracted to communist ideology. The USSR provided an opportunity to fight fascism and a framework for the vague dream of a better future after the war. Stalin's terror and purges were suspended for the duration of the war, and appearances pointed to a more flexible and liberal policy to be pursued in the future.

There was little time to reflect on all I saw and experienced. It was December 1944, and the final westward thrust of the Soviet-led military machine commenced with the crossing of the Vistula river. The First Polish Army entered Warsaw, which presented an extraordinary sight. In Germany I later saw cities destroyed by carpet bombing. Warsaw was altogether another matter. The city had been systematically demolished block by block by German combat engineers in a cold, well-planned, and concerted effort to break the will of the Poles ever again to challenge the Third Reich. Special attention was given to national monuments, which were carefully obliterated. The civilian population was evacuated. Only a few individuals occasionally could be seen moving carefully through the rubble as yet another ruined building threatened to collapse at any moment. It was an eerie sight even for the battle-hardened Polish and Soviet troops rolling westward in American-made trucks, command cars, and jeeps.

A veritable human wave consisting of Slavs, Kazakhs, Uzbeks, Kalmyks, and Tadjiks was united in the determination to destroy the German invader. The treatment of POWs, the massacres of civilians, and the horror stories told by the local population after the German retreat made a much stronger impact on the soldiers marching westward than all the official Soviet propaganda. This was a powerful, highly motivated human wave stirred into action by the German attitude and behavior in the eastern territories formerly occupied by them. The soldiers knew that they fought for survival, for their families, for their homes. A war song of the artillery units popular throughout the front expressed this sentiment best: "From a thousand batteries, for the tears of our mothers—fire! fire!" *("Iz tysiacz baterej za sliozy naszych materej! Ogon! Ogon!")* During my service I encountered many Soviet soldiers and officers who had been away from their homes for years, some since the outbreak of hostilities in 1941. No one complained, and no one questioned the necessity of fighting the Germans.

The enormous mass of humanity, materiel, and equipment rolled westward and did not stop until the German border was reached. In the west the Allies broke out of Normandy and in pursuit of the fleeing German troops reached Belgium and the Ardennes. The last offensive of Field Marshall Rundstedt started and the Battle of the Bulge was on. The slow progress of the Allies in Italy from south to north finally accelerated after Monte Cassino was taken by the Polish Corps of the British Eighth Army. The defeat of Germany was in sight, and I was glad to have a part, albeit a minor one, in the struggle to wipe out the nightmare of the Third Reich. Daily survival during the winter of 1944-45 again became an all-consuming task. It was not so much the danger as the effort required to keep warm and find the next meal, which the simple Soviet logistic support on which the Polish First Army depended was not always able to provide.

The Soviet authorities were cautious in dealing with the population in the liberated territories. Looting, rape, and violence were punishable by death, with offenders summarily shot. In Poland every effort was made to preserve the appearance that a representative government, the PKWN, was in control. The Soviet authorities were present only as allies and invited guests. The First Polish Army and the Second Polish Army subsequently formed in the liberated territories were led by Soviet military personnel in Polish uniforms, with the explanation that there was no senior Polish command available. As soon as Polish graduates of higher military schools arrived, the Soviet personnel would be replaced. There were even Catholic chaplains, and field masses were said regularly every Sunday on a battalion level.

The Allies were lauded by the Soviet Union as comrades in arms in the task of defeating the Third Reich and Japan, both menaces to humanity. The Polish government in London was referred to as colleagues, sharing with PKWN the responsibility of rebuilding a democratic Poland after the end of the war.

However, shortly after Yalta the propaganda machinery changed its tune. It now distinguished between Americans, the staunch and reliable allies, and the British, who could not be trusted. The Polish government in London was from now on referred to as lackeys of British imperialism and a relic of the corrupt and incompetent clique that had run Poland before 1939. The first symptoms of Stalin's design for Central Europe started to appear. All this was visible only to experienced observers, well attuned to the machinations and perfidy of the Kremlin.

The battles fought on the Eastern front in the winter of 1945 were no less difficult than those fought near Kursk and Belgorod. The collapsing Wehrmacht and the SS units were still capable of launching vicious counterattacks and inflicted serious casualties. No one paid much attention to the political maneuvers taking place that would decide the future of Europe for years to come. Marshal Zhukov launched the final attack on Berlin, referred to as "the beast's lair." Marshal Rokossovski marched through Prussia and Northern Germany, protecting the flank of Marshal Zhukov's thrust. Marshal Konev, in whose theater the Second Polish Army served, marched through Silesia, protecting the southern flank of the thrust toward Berlin. These were hectic and difficult days, with Germans making desperate efforts to stem the Soviet tide to allow the Allies to move deeper into Germany.

The collapse of the Third Reich was not at all like the *Götterdämmerung* in the Wagner opera. It was reflected in bombed-out cities, in long lines of bedraggled, unshaven Germans full of lice, and in the discovery of the extensive network of concentration camps with a few emaciated inmates left alive by their torturers. The German civilian population was scrounging for food and cigarettes, was servile, full of self-pity, and afraid. The years of enthusiastic support of the policies of the Third Reich were forgotten. No one had been a Nazi, most had opposed Hitler and his policies, etc. It was extraordinary to observe the sudden change that had taken place in the mentality of the *Herrenvolk* (master race) after the collapse of the Third Reich.

It was May 1945 and the war was over. My unit returned to Warsaw, and we were stationed in a lovely suburb called Boernerowo that had escaped destruction.

Nearby was a former military base, a sort of a showpiece, of an anti-aircraft regiment of the prewar Polish Army. The barracks housing the personnel were spacious and clean and had been used by a German headquarters unit and thus escaped destruction. Our unit quickly made itself at home in the new quarters. The officers were quartered in private homes in Boernerowo. It was a pleasant and welcome change after the variety of bivouacs occupied during the march westward. The war was finally over.

I was attached to the headquarters of the unit as an aide to Colonel Torunczyk. Actually my responsibilities were those of a glorified clerk who supervised incoming and outgoing mail. The content of it was another matter. I had always realized the somewhat special position the battalion enjoyed. My new assignment demonstrated the extraordinary relationship of Colonel Torunczyk with the key personalities in the Provisional government (as the PKWN was renamed) and with the Soviet Ambassador. It became apparent to me reading the incoming and outgoing correspondence that preparations were on their way for a communist takeover of Poland.

My responsibilities required a few hours in the morning and while interesting were not very strenuous. There was an accredited gymnasium (a high school and a junior college combined) in Boernerowo. I called on its headmistress and asked for assistance in completing my high school studies. I explained that I would soon be discharged and would like to enroll at a university. She suggested that in a few weeks the final examination (baccalaureate) would be administered, which I could be allowed to take. If I passed I would be issued a "matura"—a graduation certificate entitling one to entry into a university. The school was symphatetic and the faculty extended all reasonable assistance. The teachers tutored me in preparation for the final examination administered by a commission of the Ministry of Education at the end of June.

In all fairness, the two years at a Soviet school *"desiatiletka"* attended in the years 1939-41 provided an excellent basis. This and extensive tutoring allowed me to pass successfully the final examinations which admitted me as a special external student. My grades were reasonably respectable. Not surprisingly, I passed the religion and theology examination with distinction. Poland, a Catholic country, combined religion, theology, and philosophy as a discipline. However, I passed the examination under my assumed name and subsequently had a problem proving that Kurt I. Lewin and Roman Matkowski were the same person.

The month of May in Poland is exceptionally beautiful. The weather is generally excellent, the days are long and sunny, and the countryside is lusciously green. Flowers blossom everywhere and their aroma permeates the air. On a sleepy Sunday afternoon, one of the few moments of respite in the generally hectic schedule, a young officer from another unit and I were staying in a private home assigned to us by the quartermaster. He was studying calculus in preparation for entry to a university, and I was reading a book and daydreaming.

Two Soviet officers barged in and told us to get out of the house as the area had been requisitioned for a Soviet regiment. An attempt to explain that our unit was stationed in Boernerowo met with ridicule, juicy language, and some nasty comments about Poles in general. All this occurred in front of the owner of the house, a Polish woman with two teen-age children whose husband was in military service and had not yet returned from Germany. The incident was humiliating, and the brutality and rudeness displayed by Soviet soldiers were experiences we had not encountered before. I ran to the residence of Colonel Torunczyk down the street to report the incident. There I found assembled other officers of the unit who came with the same complaint. The nearby base was contacted, an alarm sounded, and within minutes units in full combat gear were assembled from those who were not away on Sunday leave.

The Soviets were requested to leave the area. When they refused

a skirmish started, first using rifles, finally employing PPS, a predecessor of the Kalashnikow, a rather efficient weapon with an impressive fire power, and light Tokarev machine guns. The pleasant and
generally peaceful suburb was turned into a battlefield. Small patrols
in full battle gear were moving along the hedges, opening fire in
short bursts from the PPS. Eventually the Soviet troops were chased
out. There was a lot of shooting, a lot of noise. Fortunately the incident ended without casualties. The outcome of this affair was that
our unit was moved to large military barracks on the outskirts of
Warsaw, which had served the German troops demolishing Warsaw
and therefore escaped destruction.

The short euphoria following the end of the war ended quickly as
the magnitude of the devastation of the country became apparent.
The brutal occupation left marks everywhere in the form of little
plaques or crosses, indicating where someone had been shot by the
Germans. There was a shortage of everything. The Warsaw government was in control only of large cities, while the countryside was
still a battleground. The pro-London government AK (Armia
Krajowa) was fighting the Nazi-spawned fascistic NSZ (Narodowe
Sily Zbrojne); and in Eastern Poland the Ukrainian UPA (Ukrainian
Insurgent Army) was fighting Polish government troops, the AK,
the NSZ, and the Red Army. Occasional attacks on government
installations and frequent assassinations of those suspected of collab-
oration with the Soviets added a dimension of tension and uncer-
tainty. The Soviet units returning from Germany were stationed in
Poland as "guests" and strengthened the Warsaw provisional government. Gradually control of the countryside was established with the
partisan units retreating into the forests and into the Carpathian
mountains.

The Jewish population of Poland was gone. The Holocaust had
left a void and the elimination of Jews dismantled a commercial and
financial infrastructure. Virulent anti-Semitism did not abate, and in
the churches Catholic priests were referring in their sermons to the
Holocaust as a punishment for rejecting Christ. Living as Roman
Matkowski, a Pole, provided me with a unique insight into the mentality of Poles, in which anti-Semitism is deeply ingrained in their
culture and folklore. The few survivors meeting in the newly orga-

nized so-called Jewish committees looked for guidance and assistance. There was little to offer and there was no leadership to give this pitiful handful of survivors any direction.

PKWN, referred to as the Provisional government, moved to bombed-out Warsaw. Its offices spread to the suburbs because there were few buildings left intact after the insurrection in 1944. The city was coming alive, with numerous government officials arriving from Lublin and settling as well as they could in the huge heap of rubble into which the German combat engineers had transformed Warsaw. The demand for housing for the returning survivors of the insurrection and the newly arrived officials of the Provisional government resulted in hectic construction activity, repairing and salvaging what was possible, literally with shovels and hands as no building materials and no equipment were available. There was a relief that the horrible war was at last over and life was returning to some normality with a hope for a better tomorrow. There was a degree of idealism and elation with regained independence.

Convoys of victorious Soviet troops were passing through returning from Germany to the USSR, carrying with them as "trophies" every imaginable object—furniture, sofas, pots and pans. Anything that could be moved was taken. All this resembled a gigantic travelling flea market, amazing the Poles in this part of the country who were for the first time in direct contact with the Soviets. Soviet Army engineers systematically dismantled industrial installations in Germany, loaded the equipment on flatcars, and shipped them by rail eastward.

The returning Soviet soldiers were by and large friendly, did not molest the population, and kept to themselves. In Poland the strictest discipline was maintained, and any transgression was swiftly and brutally punished. The Soviet authorities were invisible, and it seem likely that Poland had regained independence. Negotiations were conducted between the Provisional government backed by the USSR and the Polish government recognized by the Allies in London. Soviet moles, burrowing deeply into key positions within the Warsaw regime, were invisible but to a few.

One morning I was called to the personnel department where I was told that our unit had been allocated three places at a sanatorium–vacation home in Krynica, a well-known spa in the Carpathian mountains, and that I had been selected to be sent there. This was another kind gesture of Colonel Torunczyk, who, realizing that the years in the ghetto had undermined my health, had secured for me one of the three places normally allotted to high-ranking officers. At the personnel department I learned that Colonel Torunczyk had been transferred to the Provisional government, and the Polish Special Battalion would be absorbed into the Fourth Infantry Division of the First Polish Army that was expected to arrive any day from Germany.

I tried to see Colonel Torunczyk before my departure to the spa to thank him for the kindness shown to me since we met. However, he was no longer available. Shortly afterwards it was announced that he had become Vice Minister in charge of the "recovered territories," a euphemism for the lands between the prewar Polish border and the Oder Neisse line arbitrarily selected by Stalin and agreed to in Yalta as the new border of "democratic" Poland. This involved the resettlement of millions of Poles forcibly removed from their homes in eastern Poland, which had been annexed to the Soviet Union, to lands arbitrarily carved out of Germany by Stalin after the war. Millions of Germans were expelled from the "recovered territories" to make place for the displaced Poles.

In effect Stalin moved Poland westward with a total disregard for the millions uprooted from lands on which generations of Poles had dwelled for centuries. Lwów became Lvov, a Soviet city, and Breslau became Wroclaw, a Polish city. The administration of the regions newly acquired by Poland was entrusted to Colonel Henryk Torunczyk.

The real reason for his transfer was, as I found out later, that he was not a Stalinist. He vigorously protested whenever he became aware of an abuse of power by the Moscow-installed agents. As a protégé of General Walter-Swierczewski and a number of high communist officials of the former Comintern in the Kremlin, he could get away with it. However, when he started to interfere with the plans laid out in the Kremlin for the takeover of Poland, he was "promoted" and removed from the center of activity. All this became apparent after the Polish Corps of Internal Security (*Korpus*

Bezpieczenstwa Wewnetrznego) was formed from the combined Polish Special Battalion and the Fourth Infantry Division.

In the midst of this reorganization I left for Krynica and two weeks of mind-boggling luxury. It was an unusual experience and provided a rare insight into the workings of the socialist system. Krynica is in the western part of the Carpathian mountains. It is a pleasant mountain resort in the lower part of the mountain ridge. Its climate is mild and the surrounding forests and meadows make it an ideal place for a vacation.

The sanatorium–rest home in Krynica was in a complex built by Polish singer Jan Kiepura, who had been discovered by Hollywood in the late 1930s and had become a popular film star in the United States. After the occupation of Poland in 1939, it had been used by the German elite, and it remained completely intact with all the original furnishings. The sanatorium now catered to Polish and Soviet officers of high rank. Thanks to Colonel Torunczyk, I, a lowly lieutenant, found myself in this august company.

The two years in a territory administered by the Soviet Union was an excellent introduction to the working of the socialist system and prepared me for a variety of things. The hypocrisy of it was demonstrated daily, and its distorted patterns became an accepted part of our lives.

The stratification of the society in the "workers' paradise" was equally complex and as unfair as it had been in prewar Poland. The only difference was in the shift within the society of yardsticks, symbols, status, and the concept of wealth. Access to textiles, leather, medicines, and food created new upper classes overnight. A whole society was suddenly destabilized and its long-established patterns became irrelevant. Nevertheless, Krynica was a novel experience, as it introduced me to a standard of life of the communist elite, for which, despite previous experiences, I was not prepared.

After registering on arrival, I was assigned with two other officers to a spacious room with a balcony and a view of the mountains. The real surprise was the elegant restaurant with silver and white tablecloths. The impeccable service was provided by waiters in meticulously pressed white jackets and black pants. The daily menu included meat, fresh fruit, wine, and other specialties I had not seen since 1939. After a day or two of this life of luxury, I asked the quartermaster to explain the arrangements.

The logistic support in the Soviet Army called for several "norms" (allocation standards), which regulated the quality and the quantity of food supplied. A unit active within a range of 100 kilometers from the front line was considered "in combat" and was entitled to norm 1. After being pulled out for rest the norm switched to 4. The norm provided in military hospitals was 7. The difference between these norms was in the quantity of meat, bread, and pork belly provided. The Red Army did not starve, neither was it supplied as lavishly as the U.S. Army, nor did it follow the more modest standards found in the British or German armies. It was a bare minimum necessary to survive, with occasional extras offered if a unit was in combat. The quartermaster explained that I was now on norm 12—the generals' ration. He apologized that the supplies of caviar and champagne had not arrived yet. Therefore, we were issued instead extra rations of vodka and canned crab meat "Snatka"—Alaska King crab legs.

A few miles away in another mountain valley, in the heart of the Lemko country, was Florinka. There a small Studite outpost was serving the poor Lemko communities. The superior of the community, Father Marko Stek, had been sent there from Lwów before the arrival of the Soviet troops by Ihumen Clement to have one of the senior and capable members of the Studite community located in the west.

The Lemkos, an isolated group of mountaineers ethnically Ukrainian and Greek Catholic dwelling in the western part of the Carpathian range, were in a way related to the Bojkos in central Carpathy, where Luzky was located. Because of their isolation, they maintained a distinct pattern of life and customs going back to prehistoric times. They wore a characteristic garb consisting of an embroidered linen shirt, worn with its tails outside the pants, which were made from a coarse heavy material woven from hemp (konopie). Its fiber was utilized for weaving a thread used to make sacks and some items of clothing worn by the poor. A sleeveless sheepskin vest with the fur on the outside, a headgear made of leather folded around the crown and cut open in the form of a V in the front, and moccasins made from shaven down old tires completed this outfit. Their feet were wrapped in strips of linen up to the knee. It was an outfit not much different from the one I had worn in Luzky.

Lemkos could be found wandering in the Krynica village. I approached one of them and greeted him with the customary, *"Slava Isusu Chrystu"* (Praised be Jesus Christ), to which he answered, *"Na vik i vikiw"* (forever and ever). Then I inquired, "Uncle, how are things?" He answered ceremonially as is the custom among Ukrainian peasants. The Lemko, seeing the Polish uniform, first froze and was suspicious. However, being greeted properly according to custom he relaxed, recognizing another Ukrainian stuck in the hated Polish uniform. Then I approached the subject, telling him that I was a Greek Catholic (a Uniate-Catholic of the Eastern rite) and I would like to attend a mass on Sunday in my rite. The Lemko examined me carefully, reflected for a while, and then said, "I am an ignorant mountaineer and I came to Krynica to get some salt and tobacco. I think that the Basilian nuns in the convent nearby can provide you with the information." I thanked him politely and departed looking for the convent.

Indeed nearby I found the convent and rang the bell. A rather frightened nun opened the door and asked what I required. I requested to see the mother superior on a private matter. I was invited to the guest room outside the clausura, and a few minutes later the nun in charge of the house came in. I addressed her in Polish and stated that I was aware that the Studite Father Marko Stek lived in nearby Florinka. I requested that he show up at their convent the next day at three o'clock in the afternoon.

The nuns replied that they didn't know Father Stek, that their life was dedicated to prayer and to teaching children, that they were poor and ignorant. In short, the nuns were frightened out of their wits by seeing a Polish officer looking for a Uniate priest. I told the nuns that they were charged with the responsibility of producing the Studite and I would return the next afternoon.

It was not a nice thing to do. However, I had no choice as I too had to be careful. Those were strange days. Ukrainian partisans were active in the mountains, there were still armed German stragglers around, and Polish partisans were killing Ukrainians and collaborators with the Soviets and the Provisional government. My presence in the sanatorium classified me as one of the collaborators.

At three o'clock the next day I rang the bell of the convent. A nun opened the door and ushered me to the guest room. There the mother superior and Father Marko were waiting. We exchanged greetings in the customary Studite fashion, embracing and placing a symbolic kiss on each other's shoulders and switched into Ukrainian. The surprised nun tactfully left us alone. A few minutes later she arrived with another nun carrying a tray with tea and cookies.

I had not seen Father Marko since Luzky. He had been transferred from Lwów to Florinka shortly before my arrival at St. Josaphat from Luzky, and a year had already passed since I had left Lwów and the Studites. A great deal had happened to both of us and we exchanged stories of our experiences since we had met last.

It was a pleasant afternoon. The guest room of the convent reminded both of us of the days in the Studite monasteries in Lwów. In a place of honor in the room was a nicely framed excellent photo of Metropolitan Andrew. He was in a wheelchair and the photo was taken in the garden of Jur with the cathedral in the background. The man who had made an indelible impact on our lives was facing us from the opposite wall.

I informed Father Marko that the deportation of Ukrainians from Poland to the Soviet Union was only matter of time. Therefore, I suggested that he join me on my return to Warsaw. From there a way possibly could be found to cross the borders westward. Father Marko responded that he would have to contact Ihumen Clement to get his views and his blessing (permission in a monk's term). We parted, returning to resume our respective lives in two different worlds. The meeting in Krynica had far-reaching consequences for both of us. However, that is another story.

The stay at the sanatorium came to an end and it was like a dream. Krynica was the first opportunity to take stock of my and my brother's situations and our future. Our parents, relatives, and friends were gone, and the nagging question of what to do next had no clear answers. This was the first time I realized the full impact of the tragedy and the void it left. In the meantime I, Roman

Matkowski, was an officer serving in the Polish Army and there was little time for reflection and speculation. I had to make decisions and act before the onset of winter.

On the return to my unit I learned that it was no longer stationed in Boernerowo. It had been absorbed into the Fourth Infantry Division of the First Polish Army and was stationed in the huge prison-like prewar army barracks in a suburb of Warsaw, Mokotow. The Fourth Division was commanded by General Kieniewicz, a Russian who did not speak a word of Polish. We were told that he was a descendant of revolutionaries who, after the failed Polish uprising against Tsarist Russia in 1863, were deported to Siberia. The key staff positions were filled by Russians in Polish army uniforms referred to in jest as "POP" (performing the function of a Pole).

The combined units were renamed first WW (Internal Forces) and subsequently KBW (Corps of Internal Security). I was still sitting in an office shuffling papers and observing the swiftly changing environment. Under pressure from the United States and the new British Labor government, the Polish government in exile in London was forced to negotiate with the Soviet-controlled Provisional government in Warsaw. The rather naïve idea in the West was to combine both Polish governments into one government of national unity. It was one of the simplistic solutions that surrendered Eastern Europe to Stalin. An agreement was eventually forged in London and in Moscow.

It was conveniently overlooked that the general staff of the Polish underground (Armia Krajowa) was invited to go to Moscow to negotiate its incorporation into the Polish Army. On arrival there they were arrested and disappeared. Prime Minister Mikolajczyk arrived in Warsaw with the propaganda machinery in full force, touting the benefits of a new, united, and democratic Poland.

In my office I could observe preparations for the takeover of the country. A stream of NKVD officers in well-tailored uniforms, in contrast with the Soviet combat personnel wearing generally faded and ill-fitting standard issue uniforms, was arriving from the Soviet Union. I was attached as a translator and an aide to one of them. My first duty was to find him a tailor to make a Polish uniform.

Colonel Czerniach was an urbane, pleasant, and cultivated Russian, and we got along rather well. Remembering always his affiliation with NKVD,[5] I was on guard. My last military duty was to accompany Colonel Czerniach on an inspection trip to Krakow and Rzeszow.

We travelled to Krakow all night long by car without an escort. We arrived there Sunday morning and were informed that Major Welker, his staff, and the units of the Second Brigade of the KBW were assembled in the Sukiennice Square in the center of Krakow attending a field mass.

Colonel Czerniach was curious about what was going on, so we proceeded to the old historic square, Sukiennice. There a mass was celebrated with all the military ritual so beloved by the Poles. Loud orders were issued when to kneel, when to take caps off, and during the consecration sergeants bellowed orders to present weapons. Colonel Czerniach was fascinated by all this activity and asked for detailed explanations. The mass was approaching its end and, when the priest turned from the altar to those present and pronounced *"Ite missa est,"* a runner approached Major Welker with an urgent message. Orders were issued and platoon after platoon marched from the square in different directions.

We approached Major Welker and inquired what had happened. The answer was that a pogrom was taking place in the ghetto where a few surviving Jews lived; they had returned from concentration camps or had come out from hiding. Units of the brigade went into action and stopped the pogrom, which ended with a few survivors hospitalized.

Colonel Czerniach asked me who these people were and who had instigated the pogrom. Regretfully, I could not be of much help as these episodes were a result of deep-seated anti-Semitism, an inseparable part of Polish culture. Besides I found it prudent to limit myself to the duties of a translator.

We proceeded from Krakow to Rzeszow, a city where my grandfather had been the rabbi of the large and well-established Jewish community and where my father grew up. It was an interesting experience to see the city about which I had heard a great deal in my childhood. My uncle and his family had lived there before the war.

They all died in the death camp of Auschwitz. There were no Jews left in Rzeszow.

We visited a battalion of the corps stationed in the city. Colonel Czerniach studied its disposition and its plans to fight the different partisan groups still active in the countryside. The battalion commander, a charming and jovial Russian probably in his late fifties or early sixties, was a veteran of all the campaigns starting in 1941 with the attack of the Third Reich on the Soviet Union. In 1943 he had been transferred to the First Polish Army and came with it from Lenino near Smolensk in Byelorussia (the first battle in which the Polish units were employed) all the way to Poland.

After inspecting the battalion, the three of us had dinner, and the old Russian soldier told interesting tales about his rich combat experience. He looked at his battalion as a farmer looks at his farm. He took pride in the fact that they were not only well trained but well cared for. He kept referring to me as *"malchik"* (kid). Jokingly he suggested that a transfer could be arranged, and he would make a real soldier out of me. I enjoyed meeting the old veteran; however, the offer did not tempt me. The next day we left for Warsaw.

I still could not understand why a senior officer of the NKVD undertook such a long trip to inspect a battalion. We passed through Krakow without stopping. At the outskirts of Kielce, the next city on the way to Warsaw, we were stopped by one of Major Welker's roadblocks and were told to return to Krakow, as AK partisans had taken over Kielce and were killing Jews. (Forty-one Holocaust survivors died in this pogrom.) We turned back, and I suggested to Colonel Czerniach that I had friends in Krakow and it would be better if we stayed in their home overnight.

We spent the night at my friend's home, and the next morning, this time with an escort provided by the brigade, we took off for Kielce. The city was quiet and military units were everywhere arresting individuals found without documents. The AK "military" operation ended with the killing of the few surviving Jews. It was a foretaste of what to expect. In the map room of the KBW (Corps of Internal Security), little flags indicated more instances of such partisan activity.

A struggle was on in Poland with the returning Soviet troops employed jointly with the KBW to destroy the partisan units still operating. The regular Polish units were not trusted as a number of them, including a company of the Polish Special Battalion, joined the partisans, taking their weapons with them. Colonel Czerniach was apparently inspecting a field unit of the future KBW in preparation for planning operations to eliminate the partisan threat to the new Polish regime.

The arrival of the NKVD "advisors" prompted me to look for ways to disengage from this unit as fast as I could. The opening came with the announcement of demobilization, which started in early September. I was discharged without difficulty as I had seen combat service and had volunteered before my age group was called.

Before leaving the corps I prepared a duplicate set of personal documents, a pistol, and food stamps that entitled me to draw rations *(sukhoy payok)* from military depots at the railroad stations while travelling. I also provided myself with a supply of stamped blank forms that permitted me to produce orders identifying me as an officer travelling on duty, thus giving me free use of the railroad system or any other army transportation. Therefore, although demobilized, I retained all the privileges and freedom of movement of an army officer on active duty.

My next project was to contact Father Marko and induce him to leave Poland with me. I had written to him and explained the situation, hinting that this might be his last chance to get out.

In the meantime a new complication developed. I was invited to visit the Central Committee of the Polish Workers Party (a code name for the Polish Communist Party). There in the personnel department a party official informed me that I had been observed for some time, and an offer was made that might influence my future. I was told that I seemed to be politically "progressive" and my military record was impeccable. Therefore the party had decided to take care of my education.

I was offered an opportunity either to go to the School of Diplomats (a recruiting area for future spies), or if I preferred they would send me to the Jagiellon University in Krakow where I could study whatever I was interested in. This way, the official suggested, a brilliant career was ahead of me combined with the challenge and the satisfaction of building a new democratic Poland. I thanked him for the offer and the interest in my future, and I asked for time to reflect. We agreed that I would return the next day with an answer. Although I am not sure, most probably the interview was arranged by Colonel Torunczyk to help me settle after demobilization.

It was dangerous to decline such an offer. On the other hand I had no desire to get involved more deeply in the communist infra-structure. I returned the next day to the personnel department and informed the official that I had decided to pursue my academic studies at the Jagiellon University in Krakow. I was provided with a letter of introduction and funds to travel to Krakow to register at the University.

I went to Krakow, enrolled at the Jagiellon University as a regular student, and was informed that I had to report at the beginning of the academic year in October. This left me three weeks to get out of Poland.

From Krakow I travelled by railroad to Grzybow, which was in a territory infested with partisans. In the compartment of the railroad car were three Polish armed partisans also going to Grzybow. They boasted that they would make mincemeat of the Soviets and their Polish lackeys who had assembled in Krakow and Rzeszow to fight them. They inquired in which unit I was serving. I replied that I was from the Fourth Infantry Division, which recently had returned from Germany to be demobilized. This was the equivalent of being a harmless "dogface." This satisfied the partisans and I was invited to share with them a sip of *"bimber"* (home brewed vodka), sausage, and bread. On arrival in Grzybow we parted company.

From there I walked alone at night to Florinka, a distance of ten miles from the railroad station, through a forest with a cocked pistol in my hand. It was a frightening experience. To the Polish partisans I was an officer of the hated regime, to the Ukrainian partisans I was a Pole, to the German deserters I represented a pistol, ammunition, hand grenades, a coat, and boots. I was thinking while walking to Florinka about Brother Poberejko. This was the way he died after encountering Polish partisans in the forest on his way to the Studite mother house in Uniw.

I arrived in Florinka late at night and immediately started to discuss my plans to escape with Father Marko. Father Marko was reluctant to leave the monastic community. My counterargument was that it was his duty to escape because a spiritual leader of his people was needed in the "free" world. There would be so much more he could do to convey the ideas of Metropolitan Andrew than being locked up in a Soviet camp. Finally he agreed to call a *"rada"* (conference, or council of elders held customarily in Eastern Rite monasteries if confronted with an important decision) of the monks to sound out their views. The monks suggested that he leave Florinka as the deportations had already started in the nearby villages. Besides, other priests were available to take care of the needs of the community.

The debate dragged on until late at night. Father Marko finally agreed to accompany me under the condition that I take with us a diocesan priest, Anton Ryzak, who was staying in Florinka after having escaped from Lwów. I agreed to it and the rest of the night was spent packing and preparing for the journey into the unknown. In the morning Brother Inokentij drove us to the railroad station in Grzybow. In daylight the road to Grzybow through the forest looked less frightening than it had the night before. There we took a train to Krakow on the first leg of our escape to the West. The curious trip westward is a subject of another story to be told later.

The article in *The New York Times* in 1982 was in a way an epitaph for a whole generation of dreamers who embarked on an effort to repair the world. Henryk Torunczyk, a decent and kind man, was among them. It was sad to learn that his daughter and her husband, who contributed to the dismantling of the communist regime, were persecuted because of their possibly Jewish origin in a Poland they helped to liberate from Moscow.

The article reminded me of the days in Lublin in 1944, the formation of the PKWN, and Colonel Henryk Torunczyk, who played a key role for a while in the postwar evolution of Poland. This is a story of one of the well-meaning idealists who dedicated themselves to a cause. However, having followed false prophets they found themselves disillusioned and eventually sidetracked by their masters. Torunczyk, who dared to protest the brutal measures introduced in preparation for the communist takeover of Poland, was swiftly removed from positions of power and influence. Idealism and decency were not necessarily an asset in those days.

Reflecting on the story of Henryk Torunczyk and the forgotten events that took place in Lublin and in Warsaw in the years 1944-45 brought into focus the impact they had on the direction of my life. The distance of a half a century and subsequent experiences permit a detached assessment of these strange gyrations of historical events on "God's Playground." This is a description of Poland coined by the author Norman Davies and the title of the comprehensive history of Poland written by him. The events that took place in Lublin and in Warsaw in 1944-45 are nowadays mentioned at best on half a page in history books.

The story illustrated the dilemma of young people who emerged from universities without a future and no direction to follow. They were attracted to a broad variety of radical causes, expecting to contribute to creating a better world. It was an expression of a desperate search for answers to the questions that the then-existing political, social, and economic structure was unable to provide.

The dreamers, idealists, communists, and socialists who came from a variety of quarters died in bloody battles. The survivors like Torunczyk ended dispersed throughout the world, their efforts, sacrifice, and idealism forgotten. The legacy of their efforts in the final analysis was not reconstruction of Poland and other countries of Central Europe but a social, economic, and an ecological disaster. Some of the survivors of the International Brigades were executed, like Slansky in Czechoslovakia and Rajk in Hungary, some were jailed; a few ended in obscurity after the various purges.

Half a century later the Soviet Union disintegrated, as most empires do, from within. Europe is again dominated by the reunited Germany with neo-nazism raising its ugly head. Its expressions can be found in Austria, Germany, France, Belgium, and in the Balkans. Ethnic conflicts, dormant for a long while, erupted with unexpected virulence. The threat of Soviet expansion into Western Europe has evaporated, to be replaced by other uncertainties and fears. The irony of history is that Leningrad, now renamed St. Petersburg, is starving again and Germans are shipping emergency food supplies to relieve the threat of starvation.

The struggle, the hecatomb of victims of the war and the death camps, and the hunger and disease caused by the devastation of war are forgotten. So are the sacrifices, the idealism, and the hopes and yearnings of the participants in this gigantic encounter. Were they in vain and a consequence of a caprice of history in "God's Playground?"

WOJSKO POLSKIE
Naczelne Dowództwo
Główny Rabinat
Nr. 132/45
"2" października 1945 r.

ZAŚWIADCZENIE.

Stwierdzam niniejszym, iż osobiście znany mi ob. Matkowski Roman ur. we Lwowie dnia 28.II.1925 r. jest identyczny z Lewinem Kurtem ur.28 lutego 1925 w Lubaczowie synem rabina lwowskiego Dr. Jecheskiela Lewina.

Nazwisko Matkowski przyjął za czasow okupacji niemieckiej celem uratowania zycia.

Upraszam wszystkie Instytucje Żydowskie o udzielenie wyżej wymienionemu, pomocy materialnej i moralnej.

Główny Rabin W. P.

(-) Dr. Kahane Dawid
ppłk.

A document issued by the Chief Rabbinate of the General Staff of the Polish Army on demobilization attesting that Roman Matkowski and Kurt Lewin, the son of the Rabbi of Lwów Dr. Ezekiel Lewin, are the same person.

CHAPTER 4.

The Story of La Spezia

C INQUE TERRE in Liguria is a cluster of villages clinging to a slope of a mountain range facing the sea. Every tiny nook and corner of the slope is utilized to plant vines. The vineyards, although difficult to access, produce an excellent white wine. The five villages were isolated until recently, when roads were built providing a limited access to this charming corner of Italy.

The sea provides livelihood for the inhabitants. At night one can see in the bay the bright carbide lights on the fishing boats that are used to attract fish. The tired fishermen return to the tiny sheltered harbors early in the morning. The women wait to assist with the catch and the cleaning of the boats and the gear. Later in the day they stretch the nets to dry and repair the damage.

The generally calm sea can turn suddenly rough and angry. Many a seaman has perished in it, as can be seen in the small chapels in the harbors, where tablets display the names of those who did not come back. The poet Shelley, caught in a sudden storm while on a sailing excursion, drowned in the gulf. Since then the locals refer to the Gulf of Cinque Terre as *"Golfo dei Poeti."*

The tiny villages of Cinque Terre cling to the steep drop of the mountain. They are protected by huge boulders, which serve as breakers and a base for the little piers to which fishermen's boats and occasionally a private yacht are moored. The violent winter storms buffet the villages and wash out all the beaches. Monteroso del Mare is an exception, as it is the only village with a small protected harbor and a beach.

In the spring of 1946 a strange set of circumstances brought me to La Spezia. From the deck of the small wooden bark *Fede,* on which I was imprisoned with many other DPs (displaced persons) trying to reach Israel, I could see in the distance across the bay the slopes of hills covered with vineyards. The *Fede* was docked at an Italian Navy pier located on the outskirts of La Spezia on the road leading to Lerici. Sitting on the pier looking at the hills shimmering in the distance, I dreamt that one day I would explore this charming countryside. The memory of the dream and the excellent white wine of Cinque Terre prompted me to spend a summer vacation in Monteroso del Mare in 1990. From there on a sunny morning in July I drove to nearby La Spezia.

The city had grown and changed. However, the center, with its buildings in the style of architecture popular in Italy during the days of Mussolini, remained as I remembered it. The harbor had expanded and was bustling with activity. The area, once quiet and isolated on the fringe of a restricted military sector, was now a terminal for container ships. I drove slowly toward Lerici looking for the pier at which the *Fede* was tied with 1,014 displaced persons imprisoned on it for almost three months.

After reaching Lerici I turned back. I gave up the search for the pier, assuming that it had disappeared to make room for the huge modern container terminals. Suddenly driving along the harbor I recognized the familiar iron gate—indeed this was the pier. It was still an installation of the Italian Navy, squeezed between two large and modern container harbors.

I parked the car and went to the little guardhouse at the gate, still where it had been in 1946. No one was in it, but an old black-and-white television set was turned on. The cluttered office was empty, as the occupants probably had left for lunch at a nearby tavern. I entered the pier, following the tracks of a spur of a railroad built long ago and then forgotten. The massive cast-iron mushroom-like posts used to tie the heavy ropes from the docked ships were still there as I remembered them. At the end of the otherwise empty pier a small oiler of the Italian Navy, painted gray, was docked. The breeze brought the pungent smell of cooking emanating from its galley. After a while a sailor wearing jeans and an old and faded sweatshirt came out of the galley, looked around, yawned, and went back into the bowels of the ship, ignoring me altogether. A little mongrel, probably belonging to the ship's crew, wandered around in the midday heat and inspected me with some interest. He then too trotted away, looking for a shaded spot in which to take his afternoon nap. I wandered slowly on the pier, rediscovering nooks and corners so well remembered from the days of the La Spezia affair.

Memories of long forgotten events from almost half a century ago were revived as if they had happened only yesterday. The nearly abandoned pier, a property of the Italian Navy, was in those days humming with activity. I remember the pier, a speck of land made available in hospitable Italy, with a makeshift flagpole flying the blue and white flag with the Star of David. There we were permitted to play out a political drama in which we were chosen by its architects to be the main actors.

In the spring of 1946 the pier was full of life. Men and women, mostly in their twenties, were milling around or resting in the shade with hardly an empty space left. The *Fede*, a large wooden fishing bark, was docked at the pier, attached to two mushroom-like iron posts with thick ropes still new and smelling of hemp. The motor bark was also new, its woodwork gleaming and its hull freshly painted in dark blue. Its masts and beams had neatly folded sails attached with steel rings. It displaced 650 tons and was built as a fishing and coastal cargo vessel.

At the end of the pier was a tent-like installation serving as a washroom and a toilet, with raw sewage pouring into the sea. This installation made it possible for the DPs to remain on the pier in defiance of the British authorities.[1] A makeshift kitchen, distributing only cold food consisting of portions of sausage cut from gigantic mortadellas, chunks from huge wheels of cheese, cans of sardines, bread, and fruit, was located near the guard house at the gate. A large pipeline, quickly constructed by the city of La Spezia from a main line on the road, provided fresh water along the pier and to the washroom tent.[2] For practical purposes on the pier there was a little town humming with activity, lively conversation, and a collection of colorful individuals assembled there to challenge the British Empire.

The La Spezia affair was a turning point in the relationship of the *Yishuv* (the Jews living in Eretz Israel or Palestine) and the Labor Government in London. The British Empire was a guarantor and protector of the Jewish National Home, as stated in the declaration by Lord Balfour made on behalf of His Majesty's Government during World War I. The relationship with London, while not always smooth and harmonious, was nevertheless correct. Zionism had many friends and admirers in the UK. Among them was General Charles Orde Wingate,[3] referred to to this day in Israel as the Friend (*Yedid* in Hebrew), who was in a way one of the founders of the Haganah, the self-defense organization organized by the Jewish Agency, the elected governing body of the Yishuv. In 1947 it had approximately sixty thousand members, in contrast to the Irgun Tzvai Leumi led by Menachem Begin with two to three thousand members, and the Stern Group with two to three hundred members.[4]

Palestinian Jews had fought in the British forces in Africa, in the Middle East, and in Europe. Moshe Dayan had lost an eye acting as a scout for the British forces fighting the Vichy French in Syria. A Jewish Brigade had been formed as a part of the Eighth British Army and had fought with distinction in Italy. The Palestinian Jews felt a part of the British Empire and condemned the terrorist acts of the Stern Group, such as the assassination of Lord Moyne. Nevertheless, the Foreign and Colonial Office, populated with a large contingent of Philbys, MacLeans, Burgesses, Blunts, and other "Arabists," were determined to appease the Arabs at the expense of the Yishuv.

The horror of the Holocaust was well known during World War II in London, in Washington, and in Jerusalem. However, the gory details were disclosed to the world by the Allied troops after they entered Germany and inspected the concentration camps. A practical aspect of the tragedy was the question of the resettlement of the survivors. Italian, French, Dutch, Belgian, and Greek Jews who survived the "final solution" had a country to return to. This was not the case for the Lithuanian, Latvian, Polish, Hungarian, and Rumanian Jews. After the end of the war quite a few remained who had survived the concentration camps in Germany. They were placed in DP camps throughout Europe, waiting for an opportunity to immigrate while subsisting on the handouts of the United Nations Relief and Rehabilitation Administration.

Their number was swollen by those who, like myself, had escaped from Poland and other Eastern European countries. The total number of survivors of the Holocaust was not that great. Altogether it approached only a hundred thousand because the "final solution," with the active cooperation of the population in some European nations, had been quite effective.

The possibilities of emigrating to the United States, Canada, or Australia were limited, and the formalities could take years. Life in the camps was intolerable and despondency set in. The yearning to get away from Europe and its anti-Semitism prompted the survivors to pursue the dream carried into Diaspora since the destruction of the Second Temple—a return to Zion. All that was asked of the British government was the issuance of a hundred thousand certificates (visas) to the survivors. The Labor Government, guided by its Foreign Secretary Bevin, refused to grant these certificates and stuck obstinately to the annual quota of two thousand immigrants established in one of the White Papers issued before World War II. The pleading of British friends, the call for understanding and compassion for the survivors from a variety of quarters, fell on deaf ears in London.

The patience of the leaders of the Yishuv was exhausted, in particular by the open hostility displayed by Bevin and his undersecretary. Even the generally moderate members of the Jewish Agency were calling for action. The extremists and hotheads led by Menachem Begin declared war on the British Empire, a seemingly ridiculous act in those days, but others followed their example. The Jewish Agency, the elected body of the Yishuv, and the Haganah, its military arm, took a more circumspect attitude and challenged the British by organizing an extraordinarily effective illegal immigration, sending ships with survivors from Italy, France, and even Greece to Eretz Israel. A strange assortment of not always seaworthy ships was collected in a variety of harbors and plowed the Mediterranean, carrying a human cargo in their holds.

The survivors were organized in groups in Poland, in Hungary, and in Rumania. From there they were assisted in crossing the borders into Italy by representatives of the Haganah and frequently by Palestinian units of the British Army. There at an auspicious moment they were transferred to waiting ships like the *Fede*, and, when they could evade British surveillance, left for Eretz Israel. The British navy, the radar stations, and the British Intelligence service active in the harbors were increasingly successful in stemming this flow of immigrants, and ships were intercepted as they approached the shores of Eretz Israel.

Yehuda Arazi, a former officer in the British Police of the Palestinian Mandate, a brilliant and highly cultivated man originally from Krakow, took over the orchestration of the La Spezia affair. The newly acquired ship, the *Fede,* waited in La Spezia harbor, manned by a trusted and dedicated Italian crew whose captain later became a legend with poems and songs written about him. The ship was under the observation of British Intelligence agents, and it became clear to Yehuda Arazi and his assistants that a secret departure with a contingent of survivors was impossible. He decided to play an interesting and bold chess game to out-maneuver the British, and we were the pawns on the chessboard. Although, there were many variations of this incident, the La Spezia encounter was one of the more dramatic.

My journey to La Spezia started when I left Poland for the West with Father Marko and another priest, both disguised as Jews. In Katowice we joined a transport of Jews determined to escape from Poland. After weeks of adventures and close escapes we reached Munich. There I stayed for a few days to recover from the hardship of the journey and to explore the environment that was new for me. Winter was approaching and I decided to continue to Italy.

I left Father Marko in Munich and proceeded to Mittenwald, on the border of Austria, where I was told that one could cross into Italy by joining a transport of Italian prisoners of war repatriated from the USSR. These were survivors of Stalingrad and other battles who were repatriated by the Soviet government to Italy as a gesture to Togliatti, who then headed the powerful Italian Communist Party.[5]

At the railroad station of Mittenwald we found a large transport of boxcars in which the half-starved and mostly sick Italian POWs were travelling. They were standing on the platform waiting to be sprayed with DDT powder. We joined one of the queues and were too sprayed with the white powder. We then climbed into a boxcar with the others. The train left Mittenwald for Innsbruck, Austria, then in the French zone. There the train was inspected by French soldiers who discovered the few DPs who had joined the transport, beat them up, and robbed them of the few possessions they carried. I was covered with the white DDT powder and huddled in a dark corner of a boxcar car to keep warm, so I escaped their attention.

From Innsbruck the train proceeded to the Brenner Pass where the POWs were greeted by a reception committee. The POWs jumped out of the railroad boxcars, yelling "Viva Italia!" Some cried, some were numb. Bread and wine were distributed. It was a moving and unforgettable scene.

The train left Brenner and reached Bolzano in the middle of the night. There I decided to get off and continue on my own. At the station, a Jew whom I recognized because of his semitic features advised me that travelling in Italy was a rather simple matter. One entered a first-class compartment reserved for Italian officers, and when the conductor arrived and asked for a ticket one answered *"Polacco."* The conductor would salute and goes away. I decided to try out this method because I had nothing to lose.

A passenger train arrived at the Bolzano railroad station going to Bologna. I found the first-class compartment and in it joined an Italian major and a captain. A conductor opened the door and asked for the ticket, *"Biglieto per favore!"* I answered, *"Polacco!"* He saluted and closed the door of the compartment. Thus I discovered an efficient and, more important, a costless way to travel in Italy, which I utilized fully during my stay in this beautiful country. (Families of Poles serving in the Second Corps of General Anders stationed in Italy were arriving from Poland, and the railroad officials were instructed to assist them. This was the reason for this helpful arrangement.)

After a few adventures I finally reached Rome. I was penniless and hungry. At the office of the "Joint" (American Joint Distribution Committee), the much-touted Jewish charitable agency, I was angrily turned away by a good-looking blonde woman who shouted that I should not bother her as it was lunch time. (I met her socially years later in New York and had the good manners not to remind her of the encounter in Rome.)

After leaving the office of the "Joint," I wandered through the streets of Rome in search of a contact or information. I was desperate, because in Rome everybody looked Jewish to me. In those days I spoke Polish, Ukrainian, Russian, and German. When I addressed someone in German, his or her face hardened and turned away. Finally another DP, recognizing my predicament, approached me and guided me to the office of the Zionist Committee. My problems were over, at least for a while. I did not realize it then, but this launched me on the La Spezia affair.

At the Zionist Committee, located in an apartment house near the railroad station, I was received by a busy and brisk individual who inquired who I was and where I came from. Without much ado he assigned me to a kibbutz in Marino near Castel Gandolfo. Actually these were not kibbutzim in the classical sense. These were DPs who had arrived from Eastern Europe and were organized in groups that drew rations from UNRRA and were somewhat assisted by the "Joint." They lived together and shared meager resources. I was introduced to a young man my age, and we left for a kibbutz called "Bemachane" ("in the camp" in Hebrew). Most members of this group were young Hungarian Jews with strong leftist leanings. Among them I was like a fish out of water. After two days with them I thanked them for the kind hospitality and took off for Rome.

There at the committee I asked the official to find another group for me. He suggested Lido di Roma, where most of the DPs were from Poland and Rumania. He offered me three choices: "Beitar" (the name of a fortress of the Bar Kochba uprising in the days of Emperor Hadrian in A.D. 121—a favorite name of the extremist movement), a kibbutz consisting mostly of followers of Menachem Begin; "Bachazit" ("on the front"), consisting of followers of Hashomer Hatzair, a leftist group believing in world revolution; or "Shaar Yashuv" ("the remnant will return"), a strictly orthodox religious community, I opted for the latter one.

Shaar Yashuv was the right environment for me. Its members were survivors of various concentration camps. Most of them came from Western and Southern Poland. These were young men and women who had survived by an accident of fate. Either the German tormentors had no time to execute them, or they worked in factories and therefore were not under direct control of their SS guards. Their backgrounds varied greatly.

Some came from poor families whose breadwinners eked out a living as craftsmen, shopkeepers, or traders. Others were from somewhat assimilated families living in larger towns. Among them were Hasidic Jews from the Gerer and Belzer sects. These too somehow survived the hell of Mauthausen, Gussen 1 and 2, Buchenwald, and a whole slew of smaller camps in Silesia.

The Hungarian group was somewhat different. There were those who came from concentration camps in Germany. Others survived in isolated mountain valleys. There was among them a Hasidic Jew from the Satmar sect. The Rumanian group again was different. These were children of Jews from Bucharest, Transylvania, Bukovina, and Bessarabia sent by their parents to Italy and hopefully to Eretz Israel.

There were among them assimilated Polish Jews who had survived either hidden by Christians, or had lived under assumed names and assumed identities, as I had. There were also battle-hardened partisans from the forests of Byelorussia and Lithuania who came to Italy as a unit. These too were survivors of ghettos and years of skirmishes with Germans and Lithuanians.

It was an eclectic gathering of individuals thrown together from varied backgrounds by an extraordinary hurricane that had shattered their lives, leaving them bewildered and alone. The extraordinary characteristic common to all was the zest for life, optimism, and a determination to rebuild their lives. They were on neither drugs nor alcohol, nor full of self-pity, and only occasionally related their hair-raising experiences. They reflected an assortment of individuals representing every nook and corner of Jewish life in Eastern Europe. They were by and large friendly. Their views clashed occasionally but without the antagonism and the bitterness frequently found in an ill-assorted group of people thrown together.

The more than 120 members of Shaar Yashuv were squeezed into a three-floor villa requisitioned from a fascist accused of war crimes. The basement served as a dining room and a kitchen. On the first floor was a synagogue, with charming if somewhat naïve murals painted on its walls by Ketzale (a little cat in Yiddish, a nickname), a gifted Rumanian boy. These were symbols of Jewish religious art painted in a style similar to that of Grandma Moses. Women lived on the first floor and men on the second and third. British army cots and military blankets supplied by the Jewish Brigade provided the sleeping arrangements for the inhabitants, thirty to a room.

Regular services were conducted in the morning and in the evening. Chanina W., a Hasidic Jew well versed in religious matters, supervised the liturgy. The congregation rotated in leading the daily prayers. The deep faith and the fervor of these people were remarkable in view of their experiences.

Sara, a middle-aged Rumanian widow, a good cook with an excellent sense of humor, presided over the kitchen and the service in the dining room. From the rather limited supplies she invariably managed to provide decent and reasonably varied meals. The carefully selected Hungarian and Rumanian girls whom she considered competent assisted her in cooking, setting the tables, and serving the meals. The less-bright ones were relegated to washing dishes and laundry. However, this was never stated directly, as Sara tactfully stressed the importance of every task. The cleaning of the house was the responsibility of Malka, who bullied not only her younger brother but everyone else in the house, demanding neatness in the rooms of the men. Each floor had a rotating detachment responsible for all the chores.

It was cold at Shaar Yashuv, as winters in Lido di Roma near the sea can be unpleasant, and the villa was built as a summer home. Somehow we managed to keep warm and to live on the monthly UNRRA rations, which were sufficient for three weeks. The "Joint" helped somewhat. Shaar Yishuv organized those who knew how to sew and opened a small workshop, with sewing machines provided by a Polish Jew who had settled in Italy before the war. Mr. Kichelmacher, a manufacturer of lenses, and his wife adopted Shaar Yashuv and visited it frequently, offering assistance if needed. We were proud that we did not resort to begging and were able to support ourselves. UNRRA provided the basics, while the Italians generously provided food rations that, although meager, were an important addition.

The rations to foreigners were issued by the police, who were also in control of the so-called "soggiorno" (temporary residence permit). When the time arrived to renew the permits and obtain rations at the police station, the commandante, an impressive looking man in his blue uniform with red piping and silver buttons, asked me, "How many of you are there at Luigi Borsari (the name of the street where the villa was located)?" I replied, "A hundred and twenty." "No," said the commandante, "there are a hundred and fifty." Seeing my surprise he stated that there were one hundred and fifty of us because this was the number of rations he was going to issue. He smiled and said the rations were so meager that we needed a few more.

The community could function because of the high degree of cooperation and consideration shown to others. The place was spotlessly clean, the inhabitants reasonably neat in their worn-out, carefully mended and frequently washed clothing. This is the way daily life at the Shaar Yashuv went on, with the community waiting for the opportunity to depart for Eretz Israel.

Every Friday morning hectic activity started in the house in preparation for greeting the Sabbath. Sara presided in the kitchen to prepare special dishes for the Friday night dinner and for Saturday, as in strict observance of the ritual no cooking was permitted on a Sabbath. A special schedule was worked out for the use of the four bathrooms in the house to permit everyone to take a shower. The cleaning went on through the day to make the villa spotless. In the late afternoon everyone, dressed in his or her best clothes, was assembled for the start of the services. After the services, we assembled in the basement dining room. The tables were covered with sheets that acted as tablecloths. Candles burned at the head of the table, and we all greeted the arrival of the Queen Sabbath with songs led by Ketzale, who had an excellent voice and hoped one day to be a cantor. Chanine or another senior said kiddush and Sara and her assistants presented the first dish, usually a surprise. Then led by Ketzale we sang *zmirot* songs (Saturday hymns), psalms, and poems composed centuries ago in honor of the Queen Sabbath. After the second dish was served it was customary for one of us to address the congregation. On one of the Fridays it was my turn. (This proved to be a mistake because a few weeks later I was elected to lead Shaar

Yashuv, creating many a problem for me during the La Spezia affair.) After the dessert and tea, a thanksgiving prayer concluded the gathering to celebrate the Sabbath.

Saturday was a day of rest. After the morning prayers and lunch, weather permitting we walked along the seashore. There we met friends and acquaintances from other kibbutzim in Lido di Roma. Sometimes guided by Chanine we went in the afternoon to call on the kibbutz "Bnot" (daughters). This was a strictly orthodox community of women, who, unmarried, would not live with men under the same roof. It was a bit of an exaggerated concern, as not much could go on in a villa with twenty to thirty inhabitants to a room. These were rather formal occasions, and Chanine always had his handkerchief tied around his neck to demonstrate that he did not carry things in observance of the law on Saturday. These visits actually were for searching out and courting a suitable orthodox-observing wife.

All this might appear as an anachronism and an exaggeration. But, the observance of rituals and customs, some introduced three thousand years ago, provided a structure and a basis for this community to keep its sanity and a sense of balance and purpose. It performed this function also at La Spezia, where Shaar Yashuv provided a responsible and reliable team to assist Yehuda Arazi in his difficult task.

The winter in Lido di Roma brought an introduction to an extraordinary politicization of the survivors. A few months after the end of the war, individuals who survived the Holocaust by the skin of their teeth were involved in complex political arguments. One might assume that the recently experienced horror would reduce the differences and bring this remnant of European Jewry together. Regretfully, this was not the case. The origin of the malaise was in Eretz Israel. The complex political structure of the Yishuv was introduced into the refugee camps by the *shlichim* (messengers) who aggressively recruited new members among the survivors.

All the political parties from the extreme right to the extreme left were represented in the Jewish units of the British Army stationed in Italy.[6] The well-meaning servicemen regularly visited the kibbutzim, telling about their lives and answering questions posed by the curious survivors. These visits were greatly appreciated and provided an introduction to the life that awaited us in Eretz Israel. Their concern was in contrast to the indifference encountered otherwise. Invariably the discussions reflected the views of parties represented in the Yishuv.

The messengers, however, had the task to speak about the life in Eretz Israel, the joy of building one's own national home, and what to expect on arrival in the new land. Regretfully, they also introduced political bickering and in-fighting in which the ill-informed and confused survivors were inclined to join. They were hungry for attention, interest in their future, guidance, and approval. The messengers offered it, sometimes making unrealistic promises to lure them to a specific political path.

There was a practice in Italy during the annual migration of birds from the North to the warm South in the late autumn to catch one and blind it. Then it was tied to stretched nets and with its singing lured birds into the hunter's nets to provide a tasty dish prepared from the trapped, tired travellers. The comparison is not exactly an accurate description of the cynical task of the messengers, which was to lure survivors to join a specific political party.

Nonetheless, only a handful of the individuals representing political parties were interested in the survivors or their lot. One group of these political messengers travelled through Jewish communities in the Diaspora, making rousing speeches and collecting large sums of money for the settlement of the survivors of the Holocaust. In reality only a little of it trickled to the survivors. These funds were employed for a broad variety of objectives, ranging from financing public relations campaigns to providing kosher food and prayer shawls. The survivors of the Holocaust had no leadership and no representation, and only some of these activities brought direct benefits to them.

Other messengers arriving from Eretz Israel described it in glowing terms, and the promise of building one's own home was a very attractive proposition to the survivors. The future, once the promised land was reached, was painted in unrealistic bright colors. The only obstacle in the way of a solution seemed to be the refusal of the British to issue entry permits to the survivors.

The messengers succeeded in recruiting a number of followers among the survivors. These in turn broadened the agitation by spreading the pedantic and frequently pointless arguments so beloved by the otherwise well-meaning and dedicated political leaders of the Yishuv. These followers performed the function of the blinded birds attached to the nets of the hunters. Each newly arrived group of survivors was approached by the DPs representing political parties of the Yishuv. After a short while political arguments were in full swing, resulting in discord and confusion.

I was reminded of one of these professional messengers sent from Jerusalem to recruit immigrants and mobilize financial support who had shown up in Lwów sometime in 1938. His name was Nathan Bystrycki. A handsome man in his forties, with a deep vibrant voice, prematurely gray, his features were accentuated by a net of wrinkles. He was always tieless and in a white shirt with an open collar, as was the fashion popular with leftist Zionist leaders.

He was lionized by the strong and dynamic community. He was invited to our home on a Friday night for a dinner given in his honor. He told about the drying of swamps, building of roads, the life on the land in *moshavim* (agricultural settlements consisting of individual farms), and he sang the latest Hebrew songs beautifully. The ladies were mesmerized by him. They whispered that this was a true pioneer. He was already prematurely aged, as evidenced by the gray hair and the wrinkled face, both a consequence of the hard work in a difficult climate toiling in the land of Israel.

After arrival in Eretz Israel in 1946, I called Nathan Bystrycki and was invited to his home somewhere in Talbiye, then an elegant quarter of Jerusalem, for an afternoon tea. I was received in a spacious villa surrounded by a beautifully manicured garden. I was met by Mrs. Bystrycki, who assumed wrongly that I was someone of importance; she appeared all dressed up and bejewelled. The house was elegantly furnished with splendid oriental carpets on the floor of the spacious living room. Nathan Bystrycki showed up in an elegant tropical suit wearing a tie, a rarity in Eretz Israel in those days, charming as ever. An Arab served coffee from a finjan, or offered tea English style. The contrast was striking between the image of a pioneer projected in Lwów and the elegant Anglicized gentleman

receiving me in his opulent home. The fellow was a brilliant show-
man who probably had never dirtied his hands working on the land.
Over the years I encountered quite a number of similar professional
messengers peddling a large and varied collection of ideologies to
gullible audiences.

Probably the majority of messengers were well-meaning and
motivated individuals. However, the fruits of their activity, in addition to introducing Eretz Israel and the life awaiting us there, were
bitter and pointless arguments among the survivors. Kibbutz Beitar,
a rather untidy affair, was on the extreme right and quite bellicose
about it. Bechazit ("on the front") was on the extreme left with its
membership primarily from Poland; it was well organized and
equally aggressive in presenting its arguments. The messengers kept
coming; confusion and discord were on an increase. Only a few of
the visitors like Benjamin Mintz, representing the Poalei Agudat
Israel and travelling with Rabbi Myszkowski, offered consolation
and practical assistance.

Rabbi Herzog, the Chief Rabbi of Eretz Israel, visited Shaar
Yashuv and left an impression of an elegant, eloquent, cold, and
detached man. Each visit of a prominent leader was a let-down.
Reflecting on the issues faced then from the perspective of time, it
appears that the magnitude of the tragedy of the Holocaust and its
consequences was not fully comprehended. Therefore, no one knew
how to deal with the problem at hand.

One Friday evening at the end of February 1946 events started to
unfold with an extraordinary speed. The aimless and vague waiting
was over. A sergeant of the Jewish Brigade joined us for the Sabbath.
Sergeant Meir Davidson, in his British uniform with the patch of the
Jewish Brigade with the Star of David on the sleeve of his battle dress
and with campaign ribbons on his chest, was an impressive sight. He
was not the first soldier of the Jewish Brigade who had come to visit
us. Therefore, we received him like all others. The kitchen on that
occasion baked little traditional *hallas*. The usual services and dinner
followed, with the guest joining in the singing. Meir was sitting on
my right and while chatting I found out that he was originally from
Rzeszow and knew my family. He had emigrated to Eretz Israel before
the war and joined the Kibbutz Chanita on the Lebanese border.

After the thanksgiving prayer Meir got up and in Yiddish, the common language to all, announced that from this moment on Shaar Yashuv was under the command of the Haganah.[7] I was ordered to lock all exits from the villa and to make sure that no one entered or left the house. Meir stated that the trip to Eretz Israel had commenced and orders had to be obeyed to make the journey successful.

This was an electrifying moment. The silence was broken by my request for everyone to return to his or her room and wait for instructions. I asked a few senior members of the community to remain and assist me in making the necessary preparations. Meir Davidson left, probably to alert other kibbutzim. That was a memorable and sleepless night. Shaar Yashuv had to be divided into two, as only half of it was chosen to participate in this venture. The decision of who would go and who would remain was a difficult one to make. Meir told me to expect hardship and difficulties. Therefore, I decided to include only young and physically fit individuals. I was also determined not to separate families.

There was among us a man named Zalman, a kind, quiet, and thoughtful widower from Rumania, a teacher by profession, who had a teenage son. I needed Zalman's counsel and support. Therefore, I included the youngster in the list, although the guideline given was not to take minors. There were two young women from Lwów, one my age and her somewhat younger sister accompanied by their father, a frail man of nondescript age. The mother had perished in the Holocaust. They too were included. Sara was indispensable for the adventure. The leaders of the group that would remain objected to having her on the list, as she was considered essential for the running of Shaar Yashuv. However, I needed a leader who could take care of the girls. Sara was respected and listened to as she was genuinely concerned with the welfare of the teenage girls from Rumania and Hungary.

There also were two married couples who had gotten engaged and married at Shaar Yashuv. Their marriages were celebrated according to the rite of Moses and Israel, with orthodox weddings arranged according to the custom. Apartments were rented for them in town. Fortunately, they were at the kibbutz for the Sabbath.

Others included were Mala from Krakow (the Polish equivalent of Sara), and a Hungarian couple important because the husband, assimilated to a point no one suspected he was a Jew, had served with the Hungarian Honveds (infantry) on the Russian front; he was enterprising and could be relied on. His wife was one of the chief assistants of Sara.[8] Compiling the list of the participants was a complicated and difficult task that took a good part of the night.

The leadership of the remaining group was taken over by a trio consisting of Munczik, Chanina, and another man whose name I no longer recall. The books of Shaar Yashuv were closed, an accounting was made, and the available cash was transferred to the new leadership. Then Shlomo, a Gerer Hasid and a graduate of Buchenwald who was the quartermaster in charge of the supplies, and Sara were called. Their job was to prepare the departing group for the journey. Each person was allowed to take only a knapsack. Shlomo had to make sure that the men had sufficient underwear, socks, soap, a toothbrush, and toothpaste. Sara had to attend to the requirements of the women.

A stupid and callous order had been given to destroy all personal documents. I instructed the group to ignore it and to make sure that either they were sewn into the lining of the clothing, or a pouch was prepared to carry them on one's body. I opted for this, as in addition to my personal documents I had to carry the manuscript of a book I had written while in Lido di Roma. The book was written using a pencil and cheap school copy books. A Hungarian boy, a book binder, bound the manuscript for me with available materials and the girls prepared a pouch with a strong ribbon attached to wear about my neck. What I did not know was that Father Marko's personal documents and his celebret (document issued by the Church permitting him to say the Liturgy) were sewn into the lining of my winter coat in Florinka before our departure. He had forgotten to retrieve them in Munich, so they still were travelling in my coat without my being aware of it. It would have been amusing indeed to have been unmasked by Haganah officials as a Uniate priest pretending to be a Jew.

After the Sabbath morning service we started to pack and prepare for the trip. My Hungarian friend, the former Honved, was in charge of security, making sure that no one left the house and started gossip in the other kibbutzim. Meir Davidson disappeared, and we did not hear from him during the day. I was somewhat worried, but we continued preparations. After the Sabbath Sara and the women quickly served a cold dinner and prepared sandwiches and supplies for the trip. They even succeeded in baking sponge cakes to be taken with us. Late in the evening a soldier of the Jewish Brigade showed up bringing instructions from Meir Davidson. The message was to be ready to be picked up at 7 A.M. sharp. The remaining members of the kibbutz were moved to the second and third floors and instructed not to come down until we had left. We settled for the night on the floor of the synagogue and the living room, using the knapsacks as pillows. We were apprehensive and somewhat wistful.

It was a short and tense night. We started the day early, washed, and the men assembled for the morning service. At the end a *cohen* (a priest descendant of the tribe of Aaron) pronounced the traditional blessing: "The Lord bless thee and keep thee. The Lord make His countenance shine upon thee and be gracious unto thee. The Lord lift up His countenance towards thee and give thee peace." It was a turning point in our lives. We had survived the Holocaust but we had lost our families and our friends; now we were departing for the unknown. Some were quietly crying, others prayed silently. We had anticipated this moment for many months. Yet we were sorry to leave the temporary home we had created and the closely knit community which had to be divided.

After breakfast we assembled again in the makeshift synagogue on the first floor and were ready to take off. At 7 A.M. sharp the bell of the door rang and a British army truck backed up to it. A soldier ordered the first group to enter the truck. I sent Zalman, the Rumanian teacher, with the Hungarian in the first party. The soldiers secured the canvas cover and the truck left. Immediately a second truck backed to the door and the second party was ordered to climb into it. I was the last one to leave the house on Luigi Borsari and observed that the soldiers in British uniforms were not from the Jewish Brigade. I did not share my reservations with anyone but took my knife and cut the heavy canvas to make an opening to permit me to look out.

The two army trucks with the canvas tightly tied left Lido di
Roma for Rome. A few minutes later another two army trucks
joined in, and before entering Rome we were travelling in a convoy
of eight trucks. After leaving Rome on the way to Arezzo, other military trucks joined in following the convoy that travelled north.
Dispatch riders on motorcycles in helmets with MP arm bands
shepherded the convoy. At this point I lost count, as more than
thirty trucks were travelling with ours. A jeep with a British major
and captain occasionally passed by inspecting the convoy.

Somewhere near Arezzo we were stopped at a British checkpoint.
Documents were checked and the convoy continued north. After an
hour or so, the convoy stopped and we were ordered into the field to
relieve ourselves. It was an unbelievable sight. Nobody spoke, as
strict silence was ordered. There were literally hundreds of men and
women disembarking from the army trucks; men were directed to
one side of the road and women to the other.

After a short rest the convoy took off again. It was dark and little
could be seen, but I could smell the sea. We were slowly cruising
and stopping for a while and then continuing, clearly approaching a
harbor. Suddenly the convoy accelerated and started to travel at
great speed on twisting mountain roads. Apparently we were escaping from someone or were chased by somebody. It was evident that
something had gone wrong. The convoy again stopped for a while
letting us out for a few minutes, and we were again on our way. We
arrived at dawn on a farm somewhere in the country and were
ordered to disembark from the trucks as quickly as we could.

Meir Davidson was there waiting for us. We assembled in front
of a barn and were told that we were being driven to a ship that was
supposed to take us to Eretz Israel. The British had gotten wind of it
and were watching the ship. As they could not be shaken off, the
Haganah decided to bring us to its secret camp (in Tradate near
Milano). Here we would rest and wait for further developments and
instructions. We were advised not to mention that we were brought
here by British army trucks. Haganah crews served breakfast, and we
were assigned a barn. Finally we could stretch our legs, sleep a little,
and take stock of what was going on.

It became obvious that we were a part of a large operation carried out with precision by the Haganah. In Tradate we met travellers from all the kibbutzim in Lido di Roma, Grotta Ferrata, Marino, Rocca di Papa, Aqua Santa, and other places in the region of Rome. The kibbutzim were divided just like Shaar Yashuv, leaving a skeleton group to receive the DP transports newly arrived from Eastern Europe. As a wave of *maapilim* (travellers in Hebrew) departed, a new one was brought from the staging stations in Germany and Austria.

Our sailing was no longer feasible because the ship had been taken from the embarkation point to an Italian naval installation in La Spezia. The task was to bring us to the ship and then allow the British army transport units to escape. Yehuda Arazi decided to turn the failure to embark the illegal immigrants into a carefully orchestrated drama to embarrass the British, and we were destined to play a role in it.

We were asked not to leave the barn unless it was absolutely necessary. Apparently British spotter planes were flying over, looking for unusual concentrations of people and hoping to discover the camps of the Haganah. The tension, the preparations, the long hours of being locked in the back of a truck and driven around on treacherous mountain roads had taken its toll. Our group was tired and tried to rest, leaning against the walls. The older members (probably in their late forties or early fifties) Sara, Zalman, and Mr. Fisch, the father of the young women from Lwów, caused concern as they were visibly exhausted and not up to such wear and tear. The logistics were barely adequate and all we could do was wait.

On the second day in the late afternoon the trucks arrived and we were ordered to embark. We were driven again in a convoy toward the sea. As we approached a harbor, the convoy slowed and, stopping from time to time, cautiously approached its destination. Around midnight the convoy started to move at high speed on the difficult and twisting roads of Liguria. Some of us got carsick. Suddenly the convoy drove into a trap set by the Italian army in Chiavari. The convoy was let into a piazza and there it was stopped by armored cars that closed all the exits except the one we had come in.

British military intelligence somehow had been informed about the outfitting the *Fede*. They decided the best way to act would be to employ Italians to catch the transport in order not to act directly and involve themselves into a potentially messy affair. They informed Italian military authorities that a group of SS men planned to escape to Spain on the *Fede*. This prompted the Italian navy to impound the *Fede* and take it to the naval installation near La Spezia. All this happened while we were already on our way in the military convoy travelling north. Yehuda Arazi knew that under the circumstances the transport could not sail. He decided to convince the Italians to let the passengers embark on the *Fede*. Once they were on board he expected to negotiate with the British authorities or provoke a showdown.

The drivers were lined up against a wall and covered by a light machine gun. Two drivers passing by spoke in Yiddish saying in effect, "We have had it!" I relaxed, realizing that these were Palestinian units of the Eighth Army that for practical purposes were controlled clandestinely by the Haganah. Italian soldiers opened all the canvas to check who was in the trucks and were taken aback to discover just tired and frightened people. We were grateful to be able to breathe fresh air again. The sight puzzled them, and a lively discussion ensued to determine the meaning of all this. I understand Italian and could get the general idea of the conversations. The Italians seemed to be embarrassed by this affair and where not eager to get involved with a British military unit. After a while the Italian soldiers guarding the drivers and the British soldiers exchanged cigarettes and everybody seemed to relax. Around twilight orders were given, the drivers returned to the truck cabins, and the convoy moved again, this time escorted by Italian armored cars to the harbor.

We crossed La Spezia and stopped at the military pier. There tied to one of the mushroom-like iron posts was the new and gleaming *Fede*. We were ordered to leave the trucks and assemble in front of the ship, which was guarded by Italian carabinieri. I looked at the thick hemp ropes with which the ship was tied and told my neighbor that if we were desperate we could climb on them to board the ship. We assumed naively that once on the ship we would be able sail to Eretz Israel. In front of the pier was an Italian corvette with guns trained on the *Fede*, blocking the way to the open sea. The La Spezia affair had started.

The *Fede* had been purchased by the Haganah and was outfitted to carry a thousand passengers in its hold. The term "passengers" is an exaggeration. Actually the hold was fitted with pipes used to construct scaffolds into a rather sturdy structure on which canvas was stretched and attached firmly in order to accommodate one individual. For practical purposes, to this firmly anchored scaffolding were attached a thousand hammocks in twelve layers from the bottom of the hold to the top, leaving corridors and a space at the ceiling for air to circulate. The construction was basically sound and rather imaginative. We, with a somewhat tasteless sense of humor, referred to the hold as either the gas chamber or the crematorium. However, the *Fede* was hardly fit to transport a thousand people for twelve to fourteen days, the time required to sail from La Spezia to Haifa. Food and water were stored and plans were made to sail either from Portovenere, Lerici, or some other little fishing harbor.

The plan called for the transportation companies of the RASC (Royal Army Service Corps) of the Eighth Army to collect the DPs and transport them to the ship. Its officers (Palestinian Jews) were requested by the Haganah to go on leave in order not be involved in this affair, and papers were issued indicating that the trucks were being dismantled for routine servicing.

The convoy travelling from Rome approached the *Fede* on the first night and, after discovering a trap near La Spezia, drove all night long to Tradate near Milano. The second attempt to reach the *Fede* in La Spezia resulted in the convoy's being intercepted by the Italians in Cagliari and Lavagna. The problem facing Yehuda Arazi was a complicated one. The Jewish Agency could not be found directly manipulating British military units. Therefore, it was essential for the two transport companies to return to their respective bases in Modena and near Naples without being discovered. The Italians had to be persuaded that we were not escaping SS men but survivors of the concentration camps trying to sail to Palestine. Arazi eventually had to face the response of the British. Finally this rather complicated maneuver required our full cooperation as we were in for hard times and possibly danger.

After the trap set by the British was sprung by the Italians, negotiations commenced with the Italian authorities about how to disentangle from the net woven by the British Military Intelligence. The human cargo on the trucks was examined and the Italians while still puzzled realized that these were not SS men. The Italian military authorities, in effect under British command, were reluctant to take responsibility for further developments.

Therefore, during the night a compromise was hammered out between Yehuda Arazi and the Italian commander of the operation. The convoy was allowed to proceed to La Spezia and the *Fede*. There, after discharging their human cargo, the trucks could leave. Three sergeants, Meir Davidson, Israel Lubartowsky, and, if I remember correctly, Shalhevet Freier, had to remain in La Spezia to meet the British and take responsibility. The DPs were allowed to embark on the *Fede*, but an Italian corvette would block its way out of the harbor until instructions were given to let it sail. The terms of the compromise were sensible, were accepted, and the game was on.

The transportation companies of the RASC, after quickly discharging their human cargo, were guided by Italians to their bases. After being told about the plight of the DPs and the potential predicament of the drivers, the Italian authorities extended all the assistance required. The route taken was on little-travelled country roads, which allowed them to avoid all the road blocks set up by the British. They drove the whole day and reached their camps in time to dismantle the engines and engage in servicing activities. The officers returned from leave and found the units diligently working on the trucks.

The British team investigating the whereabouts of the two companies in the past few days determined, after studying the documents, that they had not left their camps and were engaged in repairs of their equipment. The three sergeants left behind in La Spezia were picked up by the British military police and were court-martialed. They did not offer any explanations and were jailed for six months and then released and discharged.

We were assembled in front of the *Fede*, and Yehuda Arazi addressed us in Yiddish. He introduced himself, stating that he represented the Haganah; however, for the purpose of this exercise he was a Polish Jew, a survivor of the Holocaust, and his name was Moshe Feldman. He informed us that the *Fede* had been purchased by the Haganah and was prepared for the voyage to Eretz Israel. Because the surveillance of the British had intensified, we had been selected for this voyage because we represented a disciplined, young, and motivated group that could manage the challenge. Regretfully, the convoy had been stopped by the Italian army because of the perfidy of the British, who informed the Italians that we were escaping SS men trying to reach Spain. The Italians regretted the involvement in the incident but had now no choice but to comply with orders given by the British. Nevertheless, they would extend all assistance possible under the circumstances. However, the decision whether to fight or to walk peacefully away back to where we came from was ours. All that would be lost in such circumstance was the ship, which would be confiscated by the British. He invited us to join him and the Palyam members of the crew on board in the struggle.

He reiterated that the decision was left to us. The Shaar Yashuv group decided to join and others reacted in the same fashion. He thanked us for the confidence shown and the support. He turned to the officer in charge of the carabinieri, who issued an order to permit embarking. It took some time to climb the walkway and descend into the hold of the *Fede*, as after all there were over one thousand men and women. Each kibbutz was assigned an area on board, and the operation was completed smoothly. From then on we were imprisoned on the *Fede*.

Yehuda Arazi was then probably in his mid-forties, of middle height, always meticulously dressed, usually in a gray well-tailored suit, well-starched white shirt, and an elegant tie. His gray hair was carefully trimmed and brushed upward, accentuating a high forehead and blue-gray eyes. His features where almost Slavic and the total impression was that of an elegant Polish nobleman. He spoke a beautiful Hebrew with a slight Polish accent. He was precise and soft-spoken, projecting authority and strength tempered with kindness and courtesy. He listened carefully and attentively before replying. He was a born leader of men, decisive, tough, and correct.

He was usually in a little cabin in the bulkhead, which was his command post. Next to it was another one with the wireless equipment, which also served as quarters for the Palestinian crew, consisting of Moshe Feldman, the real one (Arazi had assumed his identity to confuse the British), his deputy, and a young woman operating the wireless set. They all were from the Palyam (an abbreviation, literally "Companies of the Sea," a unit similar to U.S. Navy Seals)—a unit of the Haganah.

The Italian crew, consisting of middle-aged sailors, friendly and pleasant, were busy with the usual chores, making repairs or painting. The captain, a man in his forties in slacks and a navy blue crewneck sweater, was generally around supervising the activities on the ship. It was an arrangement similar to the one found on sailing ships in the days of the clippers, where there was a captain and a master. Yehuda Arazi was the master of the ship, which in turn was commanded by the Italian.

An announcement made on the loudspeaker system requested all men to report immediately on deck. An Italian commission was waiting there, consisting of three men and a high police officer. We were asked to take off our shirts and line up for inspection. Originally I thought that we were to be vaccinated. However, this was not the case. The commission had come to be certain that we were not members of the SS, whose practice had been to tattoo recruits with the SS under the armpit. The tattoo could not be removed without a complicated operation leaving a scar. The purpose of the examination was to make sure that the men of the *Fede* were not tattooed. This deception of the British Intelligence proved to be quite effective.

After examining fifty or sixty men they left, satisfied and angry at the British authorities. While this examination was in progress, construction crews sent by the municipality were extending the water main to the pier. The mayor of the city came to greet us, and an invitation was extended to use the municipal bathhouse, with transportation provided courtesy of the city. It was obvious that a well-synchronized and planned operation was in a full swing. Later in the morning the representative of the Jewish Agency in Rome arrived. An Italian, a middle-aged man dressed nattily and always wearing an impressive Borsalino hat, came to act as liaison between the *Fede* and the authorities. The British had not shown up as yet.

In the afternoon buses started to shuttle between the municipal bathhouse and the *Fede*, and at last we were able to shower and feel human again. The whole thing was beginning to appear interesting and promising. We returned to the ship in a good mood. Friends and acquaintances met on the pier and exchanged news and experiences. The whole affair started to appear like a huge social outing.

This impression was quickly dispelled when the British arrived the next morning. First two officers showed up with a patch "Intelligence" on their sleeves. This was strange, because neither in the Soviet nor in the Polish army was an association with an intelligence service advertised. They tried to engage the crew and the DPs in a conversation. It was futile because neither the sailors nor we spoke English. Finally they asked to meet the leader.

Yehuda Arazi accompanied by the leaders of some of the kibbutzim on board received the officers on the deck. He informed them that we came from Austria, and on our way to La Spezia, as was customary then, we had stopped passing military trucks. Kind and considerate British soldiers permitted us to climb into the trucks and brought us to the pier. The story told was not believed by the British officers. However, neither could they disprove it.

The officers gave up. They knew who Arazi was and surmised where we came from and who brought us to the *Fede*. However, nothing could be proved. They stated that they had to seal the food and water supplies stored on the ship. Arazi informed them that they were dealing with desperate survivors of concentration camps, and if they insisted on sealing the food and water supplies he had to decline any responsibility for their safety. He approached the microphone and requested men only to assemble on deck immediately. The British officers, seeing the men emerging from the hold, decided that it was time to leave the ship.

In the late afternoon a detachment of marines in full battle gear drove in and disembarked from command cars onto the pier. Their commander informed Yehuda Arazi that they had come to take the ship with the passengers to a British naval installation in Genoa, where our request to sail would be studied and replied to. While this was discussed with Yehuda Arazi on the pier, the DPs started spontaneously dancing the Hora. First one ring of dancers formed around the British marines, then another, and behind it yet another one, and so on. Finally most of us joined in the Hora with new rings formed around the ones circling the marines. One ring danced in one direction while another danced in the opposite one. They only danced and sang and no harm was meant. However the spectacle of a few hundred people dancing the Hora seven or eight rings deep was too much for the marines. The commander ordered the marines to form a column and march out. The rings opened to let the detachment of marines out and then closed again with the dancers continuing the spirited Hora. The marines climbed into command cars and left.

So did the Italian captain and his crew, taking with them essential parts of the engine, thus crippling the ship. The British intended to convince Arazi and the captain to sail the ship to a British naval installation in Genoa. The British promised that there matters would be sorted out and any instructions given by London would be followed. The captain by immobilizing the ship compelled the British, if they wished to take the *Fede* to Genoa, to board the ship, use force, and then tow it to the harbor in Genoa. The captain and the mayor of La Spezia were jailed by the British for obstructing the troops attempting to discharge their responsibility to maintain law and order. The legality of such an arrest and the reasons given were questionable. The two men nevertheless were placed in jail by the enraged British.

The international press started to show interest in the affair. Newsreel crews were daily rowed by fishermen around the *Fede*, filming the ship and the DPs. The story of the plight of the *Fede* was told by emissaries of Arazi in press conferences in Rome, Paris, London, and New York. It was a good story and the battle was on.

Arazi assembled the DPs and addressed them, explaining the situation and his plans. He stressed that we were locked in a hopeless situation because the British Labor government would not give an inch as long as Bevin was its Foreign Secretary. Therefore, we had two alternatives. One was to walk away from the ship. The other one was to declare a hunger strike, which would shake public opinion. He asked the DPs to make a choice. We opted for the continuation of the struggle, as we had already a considerable investment in hardship suffered and were not prepared to turn back in defeat.

Arazi announced that the Italian authorities had agreed to lease the pier to the Jewish Agency for the duration of our presence there and from now on it was renamed Shaar Zion (the Gate to Zion). A flag with the Star of David was hoisted on a pole especially prepared for the occasion. We sang "Hatikva" (the Zionist and later Israeli anthem) and dispersed. The gate was locked and a guard was posted. A sign stating that this was a hunger strike of desperate survivors of the Holocaust was displayed on the wrought-iron gate, with a separate sign changed hourly showing how many hours had passed since the start of the strike.

Arazi's penchant for publicity and public relations was extraordinary. A commission of Italian physicians was appointed to supervise that the strike was strictly observed. Food supplies were officially sealed in the presence of the press and specially appointed witnesses. A first aid station was set up near the gate for the public to see. It was indeed a bona fide hunger strike without cutting any corners. We were allowed to drink as much water as we pleased. The first day was difficult as the pangs of hunger were felt by all. On the second day they started to subside. On the third day we were numb and apathetic. On the fourth day we could hardly move.

At that time Harold Lasky, a prominent British Labor leader and economist, was attending an international congress of labor unions in Florence. Arazi sent his emissaries to invite Lasky to come to La Spezia to see our predicament. Had he refused, the publicity drums were prepared to be activated at the congress, pointing out the insensitivity even of the British labor leaders. If he accepted the invitation, Arazi decided to coax the British Ambassador to come by inviting the American Ambassador.

Harold Lasky arrived at Zion Gate at La Spezia, if I remember correctly, on the fourth day of the hunger strike. He was told that a number of the DPs had offered to hang themselves on the gate to greet him in order to display the desperation of the DPs but were dissuaded with difficulty. I rather doubt whether anyone really contemplated such a deed. It was yet another display of Arazi's flair and a propensity to introduce a dramatic effect. Harold Lasky and the ambassadors were invited to Arazi's cabin. There some of the leaders of the groups were assembled, among them myself, waiting to answer questions posed by the distinguished visitors. We conveyed to the visitors our determination not to continue to live in camps.

We wanted to travel to Palestine, and if prevented, we would blow up the ship with the people in it.

I doubt whether this was indeed contemplated, as we had no explosives or any weapons on board. The statement was made for its impact. Lasky and the British Ambassador were visibly shaken, realizing the damage this could do to the image of the British Empire. Both promised to intervene on our behalf. Harold Lasky pleaded with us to stop the hunger strike and trust him that on his return to London he would do his best to find a solution and would communicate the results directly to us. We thanked him for his interest in our lot and for his assistance. We agreed to comply with his request. The hunger strike was over.

We were weak but happy that there was a chance to obtain a permit to sail. After the strike was over we were given only a biscuit and a little milk diluted with water. The second day smaller-than-usual quantities of simple food were served. Life on the *Fede* returned to its "normal" routine.

The inhabitants of La Spezia were shaken by the story and quite sympathetic. Every morning during the strike people gathered at the gate, where packages with food and fruit were left. Some stood at the gate and watched the DPs milling around; others cried, moved by yet another plight of the survivors of the Holocaust.

After the hunger strike was over, a petition was delivered to the British Ambassador in Rome asking for his intervention on behalf of the jailed captain of the ship and the mayor of La Spezia. Shortly afterwards both arrived at the pier to be greeted by Arazi, the Palyam members of the crew, and representatives of the DPs.

Arazi was prepared for the occasion. Beautiful silver medals attached to blue-and-white ribbons were specially designed and minted for this occasion. This was a decoration awarded on behalf of the Jewish Agency to the heroes of the illegal immigration. On one side was a sailing ship and the words of a Prophet, *"Ve Jashuvu Banim Lygvulam"* ("And the Sons will return to their Land"). On the other was the Zion Gate with the words *"Judea rebuilt."* The mayor, the captain, and a few of the DPs were decorated by Arazi, with everyone assembled at the flagpole.

A reception followed the simple ceremony for the city dignitaries, the harbor master, and all who were helpful to us in the struggle. A few days later the British Ambassador arrived from Rome with a personal message from Harold Lasky asking for more time and patience.

We waited for the outcome of Harold Lasky's intervention. The day on the pier and ship started usually around 7 A.M. when men and women were lined up in front of the separate bathrooms with toothbrushes, soap, and towels. Most slept outdoors and now collected their blankets, tidying the place and carrying everything back to their hammocks in the hold of the ship. Not far from the gate was the makeshift kitchen, and there breakfast was served, usually a piece of dry cake and tea. Then the DPs strolled back and forth on the pier enjoying the cool morning and the splendid view. On a clear day we could see Portovenere and observe the fishermen returning with the catch of the night. Later in the morning a search went on for shade; although it was April the midday sun was very strong. Lunch consisted of bread, a piece of mortadella, cheese, and fruit. In the afternoon it was quiet as a siesta was enjoyed by most, some outdoors on the pier and others retired into the hold of the ship to escape the sun. The pier again came to life in the afternoon with the DPs doing their laundry, playing chess, reading the papers left at the gate courtesy of the Italians, arguing. The pier was indeed a lively place. Then dinner similar to lunch was served and slowly the DPs settled down for the night.

This strange community assembled at random by a series of events was a reasonably cheerful and constructive lot. Their objectives were clear and uncomplicated. They yearned to find a place to settle, to be able to earn a living, to marry and to raise a family. They were able to function reasonably well as a group and as individuals, interrelating within reason despite different backgrounds and outlooks. All this was achieved without the benefit or the assistance of psychiatrists, therapists, psychologists, or mental health clinics.

While waiting for a decision to be made in London, the *Fede* community was not without its problems. The agitation started after the hunger strike with the arrival of an assortment of "messengers." They were not allowed to enter the pier but were able to agitate from the outside by sending in messages to their followers, or meeting them at the gate. The discussions became more heated, and the growing controversy already present in Lido di Roma was visibly amplified. The religious group, approximately 15 percent of the community, forced me to request kosher food in observance of the dietary laws. The request was complied with to avoid potential controversy. This added to the headaches of the Haganah personnel, who had to provide for over a thousand people squeezed into a limited space. In effect we were still imprisoned and restricted to existence on the ship and on the pier. Only once were we allowed to leave the harbor—one Sunday afternoon when our soccer team was challenged by the city's team. It was a pleasant occasion and a diversion. Only a few of us spoke Italian, and we were eager to express to the local inhabitants our gratitude for the support and the compassion shown to us. It was a lovely afternoon and an opportunity to mingle with the inhabitants of La Spezia.

Shaar Yashuv in Lido di Roma sent a messenger who brought news about the new arrivals from Austria and Germany. He was pleased to find us after the ordeal in good spirits and in good health. He inquired of the members of Shaar Yashuv on the *Fede* what to do with our share of the money the Shaar Yashuv had earned during the winter months. I instructed him to buy Palestinian pounds to be distributed to the members on the ship. Indeed a few days later the same messenger, a Hungarian and an enterprising young man formerly from Budapest, returned. I was pleased that everyone would have at least a little bit of pocket money on arrival in Eretz Israel.

Finally long-awaited news arrived. We would be issued certificates (entry visas) at the pier by a British consular official. The joint efforts of Harold Lasky and the British Ambassador apparently succeeded in persuading the Labor government and its Foreign Secretary to be somewhat more flexible. After a few days additional news was delivered. We would not be permitted to sail on the *Fede* because she was not suited to carry a thousand passengers safely. Arazi conveyed the news and informed us that another ship would join the *Fede*. Indeed the next morning alongside the *Fede* another ship was docked, the *Fenice*. Arazi commented that our struggle took place on the *Fede*. Therefore, we would sail on her and on her sister ship. Both were renamed to honor two founders of the

Haganah. The *Fede* was renamed *Dov Hoz* and the *Fenice* was renamed the *Elijahu Golomb.*

A few days later a British consular official arrived, accompanied by the representative of the Jewish Agency. A photographer took passport pictures that were attached to an identity card issued and signed by the representative of the Jewish Agency. At a separate table was the British consular officer, who stamped the entry visas on the identity cards. It was an extraordinary event as the British for practical purposes were recognizing a document issued by the Jewish Agency.

It was Passover and a Seder was organized on the pier. A cantor from Budapest, who had composed a song that served as an anthem of the *Fede,* presided over it with the community sitting on the ground. The Seder was conducted combining the story of the Exodus with recent events, including our struggle with the British, following a custom popular in Eretz Israel. The orthodox group did not appreciate it and we separated to conduct our own traditional Seder. It was a telling foretaste of what was to develop years later after the creation of the State of Israel.

This was an extraordinary, an emotional, and a memorable evening. The sky was cloudless and the stars were shining brightly. While telling the ancient story of the Exodus, we were living our own from Europe. The next Passover would be celebrated in the Holy Land. It was also a sad moment because we were leaving Europe, only a remnant of a destroyed people. We had survived the tragedy and the hardship. We apparently had won and we wished one another the traditional "Next year in Jerusalem."

I sat in my favorite corner on the pier in La Spezia watching the lights on the other side of the bay and reflecting on what tomorrow might bring. Somehow it must have been the feeling of our ancestors millennia ago when leaving Egypt. An extraordinary closeness with the past was felt by all of us, an experience that would be repeated not long after this Passover night in La Spezia while fighting in the places described in the Bible and defending Jerusalem.

The long awaited day arrived. It was a sunny beautiful morning. The ships were spruced up and displayed Israeli and Italian flags. We were all on the decks. On the pier were assembled Italian dignitaries, representatives of all political parties, bands, and people who came from La Spezia to see our departure. A few brief speeches were made. Arazi thanked the city, its people, and the Italian authorities for the kindness and support so generously extended. The bands played the anthems and the crews hauled in the ropes. The engines dead for so long were cheerfully humming, and the ships, slowly at first then gaining speed, left the pier. The first to depart was the *Fede–Dov Hoz* followed by the *Fenice–Elijahu Golomb*. The pier with the people, and the flags, and the music started to recede and eventually became a small speck on the horizon. The sailors on the Italian corvette who had guarded us all these months were waving, and its siren sounded a farewell greeting. After reaching international waters, a launch approached the *Fede–Dov Hoz*. Yehuda Arazi descended on the lowered gangway to the launch bouncing in the somewhat choppy water, and sped away to another project and another struggle.

London later informed the Jewish Agency that the certificates issued to us would be taken off the annual assigned quota of 2,000 permits. It was a malicious act, because it forced the individuals entitled by law to a certificate (members of the family) to wait another year. In order to accommodate Harold Lasky, the certificates were issued to the DPs imprisoned in La Spezia. However, the existing quota was reduced by the corresponding number of certificates. The La Spezia saga attracted attention to the plight of the survivors of the Holocaust, but little else was accomplished and the struggle was in vain.

ల

The brutality with which other ships were boarded while approaching the shores of Eretz Israel, and especially the ugly incident of the *Exodus* with many DPs hurt and taken back to Germany, demonstrated the hostility if not outright anti-Semitism of the Labor government. The declaration of Lord Balfour and the mandate of the League of Nations calling for even-handed treatment of the Jews and Arabs were ignored. The bitter struggle during World War II and the brotherhood of arms were quickly forgotten.

The Arab world was hostile to the British and had looked forward to a German victory. Some of its leaders, like the notorious Mufti of Jerusalem Amin al Husseini, during the war remained in Berlin as guests of Adolf Hitler. An SS unit was formed from Moslems recruited in Bosnia with the blessing and the support of the Mufti. The Iraqis rose against the British, which required an intervention in 1941 to protect the oil fields of the Iraqi Petroleum Company. All this meant little to the architects of the destruction of the British Empire. The Labor government was determined to woo Arabs and pursued a consistently pro-Arab policy. The wooing of the Arabs at the expense of the Jews did not prevent the ultimate loss of the Middle East by the British.

The Haganah, which had refrained so far from challenging the British, was ordered by the Jewish Agency to respond. Selected bridges leading from Eretz Israel were simultaneously blown up by the Palmach (companies of attack, a permanently mobilized force of the Yishuv, highly trained, armed, and stationed throughout the country in kibbutzim.) This demonstrated that Palestine and the British forces stationed there could be cut off at will. A few weeks later all the radar stations, which were instrumental in locating the ships carrying illegal immigrants, were attacked and some were destroyed.

The British mandate authorities retaliated by interning the leaders of the Jewish Agency in a detention camp near Latrun, imposing curfews, and by initiating searches in settlements to locate and confiscate hidden weapons. As a consequence the British found themselves imprisoned in what was referred to then as Bevingrads (fortified zones) in the cities and in military camps. Begin's terrorists succeeded on several occasions to penetrate these zones, inflicting casualties. The Haganah as matter of policy refrained from activities that could involve killing British personnel.

Eventually, the British government, tired of the perpetual self-inflicted crisis, referred the matter of Palestine mandate to the United Nations. An era that had started with great hopes and expectations, that had produced many years of cooperation and respect for the correctness of the way with which the mandate authorities at first discharged their responsibilities, was over. The La Spezia affair,

a minor episode after all in the chain of events, convinced the
Yishuv that negotiations and restraint would lead nowhere.

಄

I was sitting in what used to be my favorite corner on the pier
during the La Spezia affair looking at the shore across the bay. The
abandoned pier was overgrown with weeds, and the mushroom-like
iron posts to tie the docking ships were unused and rusty. Only the
mongrel woke up and approached to have another look at me, possibly in anticipation of a tasty morsel. The guardhouse, once bustling
with activity during the La Spezia affair, was empty. The din, the
milling people, the *Fede* docked at the pier were only memories. It
was time to return to Monteroso del Mare in Cinque Terre. I approached the wrought iron gate called once "The Gate of Zion" and
looked back on the pier, a site of a struggle almost half a century
ago, thinking that possibly the La Spezia affair was after all only an
illusion within another larger illusion.

PERMIT TO ENTER EREZ-ISRAEL (PALESTINE)

N.° *C 715*

SURNAME *Levin*   Name *Jechar Jenry*
Father's Name *Jcheszkel*   Mother's Name *Eva*
Place of Birth *Poland*   Date of Birth *1925*
Nationality by Birth *Persian*

HAS BEEN FOUND QUALIFIED BY THE REPRESENTARIVES OF THE YISHUV
FOR RE-PATRIATION TO PALESTINE.

Authority: a) " And they shall abide in the land that I have given unto Jacob my
servant, wherein your fathers abode, and they shall abide therein,
even they, and their children, and their children's children, for
ever ". (Ezekiel, XXXVII).
b) " With great mercies will I gather thee ". (Isaiah, LIV).
c) Lord Balfour's Declaration of 2nd November, 1917.
d) The Mandate for Palestine.

FOR OFFICIAL USE ONLY

Immigration Office

Quarantine Office

. 9 5 MAR 1946

HEALTH DEPARTMENT

*A document issued by the Haganah to the DPs at the pier in
La Spezia to be shown to the British authorities.*

*The medal of the Alija B (illegal immigration) awarded by Jehuda Arazi to the
mayor of La Spezia, the Italian captain of the ship, and a few selected DPs.*

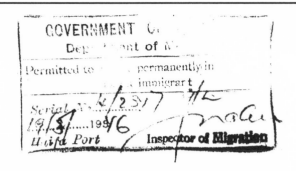

The Jewish Agency for Palestine
Palestine Central Office - Rome

IDENTITY CARD

Surname   L E W I N

Name   JCCHAK KURT

Fathers Name   JECHESKEL

Mothers Name   EWA

Place of birth   LUBACZOW (Poland)

Date of birth   28/2/I925

Nationality by birth   JEWISH

Date of issue   6/5/I946   N.°

Signature of Holder

... OF FRONTIER CONTROL
... HAIFA PORT ...

A travel document issued by the Jewish Agency in Jerusalem and recognized by the British authorities with an official certificate and a landing permit stamped on it.

CHAPTER 5

The Clandestine Commanders School
of the Haganah

OPERATION OR DROR (a code name of the exercise) was in its initial stages. We were brought by trucks into the vicinity of the staging area, which was a few miles away. We reached it in the late afternoon after marching in parallel single lines separated by a mile or so in order to arrive from different directions. Our movements were observed by the British. Therefore the plan called for an assembly in stages, so as not to arouse unnecessary attention. At the staging area in an olive grove we found equipment waiting for us: small scout tents, blankets, inflatable boats, and other supplies required for the fourth graduating class of the clandestine commanders school of the Haganah.

The camp was set up in a half hour, dinner was served, and we tried to catch some sleep, because we had a hard night ahead of us. We were camping in the vicinity of Menahamiya at the edge of a plateau before a sharp drop to the Jordan valley. The rather wide valley, a tear in the earth's crust due to some tectonic explosions millenniums ago, is enclosed at both ends by sharply rising cliffs. The Jordan River makes its way from the Sea of Galilee to the Dead Sea through this valley, twisting and changing its course unexpectedly. It is a rather insignificant river, flowing swiftly through a narrow but rather deep bed, its banks hardly visible and overgrown with high reeds.

The objective of Operation Or Dror, planned and commanded

by one of the instructors, Shmulik M., was to simulate an attack on the settlements in the Jordan valley. The exercise was a maneuver designed to test the performance of the graduating class and the degree of preparedness of the regional units of the Haganah. Our assignment was to descend at night from the plateau, cross the Jordan on inflatable rubber boats, and, assisted by a unit of the Pal-yam (the naval arm of the Palmach that consisted of permanently mobilized elite units of the Haganah), attack the kibbutzim Degania A, Degania B, and Beit Zera. Our weapons consisted of whistles rep-resenting rifles, noisemakers acting as light machine guns (the Bren variety), and flashlights signifying mortars.

It was the first exercise of the Haganah on such a scale. The set-tlements in the Jordan valley, the district[1] organized for defense in case of hostilities, were mobilized and were on alert. We were to dis-play our newly acquired skills and penetrate the region, simulate blowing up the bridges, and inflict as many theoretical casualties as possible, employing whistles, noise makers, and flashlights. Crossing the Jordan at midnight, three combat teams were to attack the kib-butzim. Another team was to block all the roads, preventing rein-forcements from reaching the region. The Palyam unit, protected by a small detachment, was supposed to guard the river crossing, wait-ing for our return after the attack.

The descent from the plateau to the valley was somewhat tricky. We clung to the cliffs, descending on paths suitable only for moun-tain goats. We carried with us inflatable rubber boats, oars, and stretchers to evacuate "casualties." I kept thinking about the climb back to the staging camp on the plateau from the valley.

On arrival in the valley after a difficult and tiring descent, which took some time, the rubber boats were inflated and six of us were ordered to carry one boat. I led the group with the rubber boat rest-ing on my head; four men, two on each side, supported it, and the last man held the other end on his head, supporting it as did the oth-ers with his arms. We were supposed to march in unison. That was easier said than done as the terrain was uneven and full of rocks. The last one was Itzko, a Bulgarian, a member of one of the kibbutzim in the Jordan valley, a tall and husky young man. Each time he stum-bled or fell out of step the rubber boat slapped my head. The crossing was not too far, and I was much relieved to get rid of the boat, which was taken over by the Palyam. They were rather large and capable of accommodating twenty to twenty-five men in a pinch.

Two men from the Palyam unit secured a rope to a trunk of a tree and then swam with its other end to the opposite shore of the river, attaching it there to another tree. The commander of the Palyam divided us into three groups: strong swimmers, swimmers, and non-swimmers. Twenty men at a time were ordered into a rubber boat and, pulling the rope stretched over the river, crossed to the other shore. As there were only four boats, it took some time to get all of us across.

First the strong swimmers were brought over to the other shore. I was in the second category. On entering the boat I noticed a little bit of water at its bottom. Apparently someone had made a hole in it with heavy nailed boots. When the non-swimmers started to cross, one of the boats sank in the middle of the river. Most of them reached the other shore one way or another, assisted by the Palyam and the swimmers. One, however, was carried away by the swift current and started to drown. He was quickly rescued by the Palyam. However, he had to be transported to the nearby kibbutz, Degania B, and an ambulance was called.

An alarm was sounded in all the settlements, and dogs started a concert that was answered by the dogs from Arab villages on the other side of the river. Whistles were blowing, noise makers were making a racket, flashlights were blinking, and the wailing of sirens in the settlements complemented the commotion.

Mundek, the commander of the school, and the instructors were driving around in pickup trucks in the Jordan valley, observing the exercise and acting as umpires. The British police and some military units, alarmed by the commotion in the valley, set up road blocks and arrested the instructors, pondering what grown men were doing in the middle of the night riding through the valley armed with whistles, noise makers, and flashlights. The instructors were sent to Haifa[2] for interrogation and a routine check.

I with two other classmates sat under a bridge we were supposed to "blow up." On a signal we all reassembled, this time at a ford, and crossed the Jordan on foot. Exhausted and amused, we returned to the staging area and our base, happy to be left alone to rest and sleep for two days or so until the instructors were released from jail.

Operation Or Dror, a fumbling and possibly slightly silly exercise, might give a wrong impression of the graduating class, the instructors, and the defense arrangements in the Jordan valley. The class consisted of approximately 130 men and one woman, Ziva the Turk. (For security reason most of us used nicknames. Ziva had come as a child from Turkey with other children in a rescue operation organized by an American, Henrietta Szold; hence the nickname.) These were hand-picked veterans of either the Palmach or Chish (Chayil Sade—reserve units of the Haganah that could be mobilized on short notice when needed). They were tough, experienced, and resourceful, and some had an impressive combat record. The class was completing an extensive program that, after thorough physical training, covered every subject involved in preparing a participant to command a platoon and eventually an infantry company. In addition, we were taught all the skills of a commando, including handling of explosives. It also included some theory but mostly comprised practical training and exercises in the field. We were taught to fight in the mountains, in valleys, in the desert, and in a city. We were future Haganah field commanders approaching the end of an accelerated three-month training program.

The highly professional elite that graduated in October 1947 was mobilized shortly after the partition of Palestine by the United Nations in November 1947 to confront escalating Arab terrorism. After a few weeks of hit-and-run attacks, the Arab leadership switched to forming large well-equipped units that infiltrated from Syria. Attacks on Jewish settlements were carried out sometimes even with the use of artillery. The British authorities either ignored this activity, or at times openly abetted the Arab irregulars.

The British Police were especially hostile to the Jewish population, and some of its members joined the Arabs in attacks on transportation and settlements. A bitter and bloody struggle resulted, which lasted almost until the the end of the Mandate (May 15, 1948). At the end of April 1948, on the eve of the departure of the British High Commissioner, the Arab bands were neutralized by the Haganah and the Palmach.

The fourth class of the clandestine commanders school of the Haganah, which graduated in October 1947, took the full impact of the struggle of the Yishuv for survival. This class provided platoon commanders for the Haganah and Palmach units engaged in combat with the attacking Arab irregulars from the Galilee to the Negev. Of the twelve classmates who arrived with me from the Jerusalem District, six were killed during the siege of the city. The list of the fallen is a long one, and to my knowledge half of the graduates perished in the war of 1947-48. The survivors led the Israeli Army in the three wars of 1956, 1967, and 1973.

Hardly a year after my arrival in Eretz Israel/Palestine from La Spezia in May 1946 I joined this extraordinary group and graduated as a platoon commander (MM). After the Holocaust in Poland and the La Spezia affair this was another new adventure for me.

Following a short stay at Kibbutz Tel Yitzhak in the summer of 1946, I was able to enroll as a regular student at the Hebrew University, thanks to the considerate school mistress in Boernerowo, near Warsaw, who had arranged for me to graduate before I left Poland with a matura-abiturium, the equivalent of a bachelor of arts degree. These were happy days, and I relished the return to a life of a student. I studied classics under Professor Moshe Schwabe, history under Professor Joseph Klausner, the author of the book "Jesus of Nazareth," and Talmud under Professor Gedalia Alon.

I was grateful that I could start the rebuilding of my life. This was made possible by Dr. Poznanski and Dr. Emil Schmorak. Dr. Poznanski, the registrar of the Hebrew University, freed me from paying tuition; Dr. Emil Schmorak from Lwów, an associate of my father in the Zionist Executive Council of Southern Poland before his departure for Eretz Israel, was a member of the Jewish Agency[3] and arranged a small scholarship for me. My father's contribution was still remembered in some quarters in Jerusalem, and this paved my way.

In those days studying at the Hebrew University on Mount Scopus was an extraordinary experience. From the University built on a ridge that is a continuation of the Mount of Olives, looking downward on the other side of the valley covered with olive trees, Jerusalem could be seen in all its glory. The plateau, on which once stood Solomon's Temple and subsequently the Second Temple, is occupied by the Dome of the Rock (referred to also as the Mosque of Omar) with its gleaming golden dome. The many churches range from the strange spectacle of a Russian Orthodox church with onion domes in the Gethsemane (Gat Shemen—in Hebrew, oil pressing place) to the fortress-like Church of the Dormition and its tower. In the distance beyond the old city is the campanile of the Italian Hospice.

One was never tired looking at the extraordinary panorama, always discovering something new in the changing light. There is some mysticism in the air that modern life cannot invade. The Judean mountains provide a backdrop for the plateau of the Temple and together with the quality of light create an atmosphere that has captured the imagination of many over recorded history. It is also the cradle of monotheism and Judeo-Christian ethics. Its holy places, usurped by Islam after the Arab conquest in the seventh century, have the same fascination for Moslems as they have for Christians and Jews. Jerusalem represented as it represents today an extraordinary mosaic of religions, cultures, and customs. To study at the Hebrew University was a unique privilege, and it was a short but happy interlude dedicated to academic pursuit and dreams.

Shortly after my arrival at the Hebrew University I was approached by a friend who casually inquired whether I would like to join the Haganah. My answer was positive, so I was asked to come late one evening to the clinic of the Kupat Cholim, a medical insurance system run by the powerful labor union, the Histadrut. On arrival there I was ushered into a dark waiting room. There were twenty or thirty others already assembled. After a short while I was escorted to an office.

In the center of the room was a plain wooden table with two candlesticks, a Bible, and a pistol. At the table were Nathan Perlman, one of the leaders of the Association of Students of the Hebrew University (killed in Atarot in 1947), Ephraim L., and another individual. I was given the text of the oath[4] and was instructed to put my right hand on the Bible and to read it. Thus I became a member of the Haganah, the military arm of the Yishuv and its elected government, the Jewish Agency. It was a simple and meaningful ceremony. From then on, every Saturday I had to participate in a clandestine training program primarily designed to familiarize the members with small arms. Once a month we went out of town for field exercises.

This activity interfered with my studies, which were quite rigorous. Therefore I proposed to the Haganah commander of the Hebrew University that I use my summer vacations for training or any other service required, in exchange for leave until the completion of studies. This offer was accepted, which launched me into this new adventure. I am fortunate to be alive to tell it.

At first I was sent to an NCO school in Revadim in Gush Etzion in the mountains of Judea not far from Hebron. There after a day in the field I was asked by its commander whether I had had any previous military experience. After learning that I had served in the Polish army, I was told to return to Jerusalem and speak to Shalom B., a senior commander of the Haganah in the Jerusalem District. He arranged for me to join a team prepared for the clandestine commanders school.

This team was a carefully selected group of young men chosen by the command of the Jerusalem District. A brief but intensive physical education program at the kibbutz "Maale haHachamisha" (named to commemorate the five members who were slain by Arabs during the 1936-39 riots) was followed by a review of the usual training of an infantryman. At the end of the preparation, we were driven to kibbutz Beit Haarava near the Dead Sea, where we spent the night. We were driven early the next day to the secret shooting range of the Haganah. It was an interesting experience to fall asleep outdoors on the lawn of the kibbutz while listening to classical music played on an old record player for the members sitting in a circle near us. At dawn we were driven to a wadi (canyon) not far from Khirbet Qumran where the Dead Sea Scrolls were found. An impressive set of weapons with live ammunition had been prepared for us. We spent the day on the shooting range, ignoring the heat. Such an exercise could be carried out, without alerting the British Police, only on the desolate shores of the Dead Sea.

After the return from the Dead Sea we were given a day off to pack and to put our personal affairs in order. The following morning

Shalom B. drove us to kibbutz Yagur in a pickup. There were twelve of us sent to the commanders school by the Jerusalem District. Moshe Rusnak, a Jerusalemite, was soft-spoken and kept to himself. Kiki, a Palmachnik (Hebrew slang describing a member of the Palmach), jovial and pleasant, was on vacation from the Palmach and joined us in the preparatory program. Amnon Vigolik, a cheerful youngster, was a friendly and outgoing Jerusalemite. He and Kiki kept us from becoming too serious. Motke, a son of one of the prominent Zionist religious leaders and a husky young man, told anecdotes relating to known public figures. Abrasha, a former soldier in the Jewish Brigade, kept entertaining us with stories of whorehouses he had visited in Rome and Paris. Johnny, from kibbutz Kiryat Anavim near Jerusalem, had been released from Kishle, the jail in Jerusalem where he was serving time with other Palmachniks and Moshe Dayan. They all had been sentenced after being caught exercising with weapons in the Dead Sea area. His head was still shaved as he had left Kishle (British prison in Jerusalem) only a few days before joining us. (He died in the first battle for the Kastel in the winter of 1948.)

Noam Grossman and Rabi (a nickname), students of the Hebrew University, Yaakov S., two other students whose names I no longer remember, and I completed the Jerusalem contingent. It was a motley and cheerful crowd that travelled to kibbutz Yagur, which we reached in the late afternoon. There more than a hundred other arrivals were already assembled on its large and meticulously manicured lawn. Some knew each other and exchanged greetings; others were just milling around. Looking at these young veterans of the Palmach and the Haganah, I pondered whether I would be able to manage. After all, I was a newcomer and unfamiliar with the ways and customs of this crowd, most of whom were Sabras.

We were divided into two groups and instructed to climb into large trucks waiting for us. These were the usual nondescript commercial trucks seen on the roads. The participants in the program were all dressed alike in khaki shirts, khaki pants, a sturdy belt, a long-sleeved woolen sweater rolled and tied around the waist, and obviously a *kova tembel* (literally an idiot's hat, a headgear sometimes seen in the U.S. in amusement parks and in European mountain resorts). As practically everyone with a few exceptions walked around dressed in this fashion, there was nothing unusual in this uniformity. The trucks took off, and after an hour or so of driving through the Emek Jizrael (Valley of Jezreel) we reached our destination, kibbutz Sarid. There in an apple orchard outside the kibbutz tents were waiting for us. We left the trucks, picked up our knapsacks and kits that had travelled separately, and were assigned six to a tent.

After half an hour or so we were requested to assemble in a large tent serving as a classroom and dining room. There waiting for us were the commander of the Sarid camp, Danny Mass (who fell in December 1947 leading a platoon sent to reinforce the kibbutzim in the Gush Etzion region), Oded Messer, and "Chytrun," whose real name I never learned. The instructors explained the procedures. Everyone was assigned a folder with a number. There we kept all the papers, a compass, and other paraphernalia connected with our studies. These folders were distributed before the start of the meetings and collected at the end of each meeting. Therefore, there was no trace of names or evidence that could be used against us if found by the British. The simple meals, at 6 A.M., at noon, and at 6 P.M., were served in a large tent.

Instructions would be given orally every evening, explaining the activities of the next day. Officially we were an intercollegiate summer school for instructors of physical education. Whenever notified of the approach of the British, we had to gather next to the specialized equipment assembled near the camp and exercise. Finally, the kibbutz was out of bounds. Past experience demonstrated that the Palmachniks, or participants in the Haganah training programs, had an inclination to be too attentive to the women in the kibbutz. This caused friction and trouble, which had to be avoided. The instructors wished us success in our endeavor. They were a competent, pleasant, and fair team. They kept to themselves and did not socialize with the students.

We dispersed and returned to our tents. There were six of us. I shared a tent with Dodik, Amnon Vigolik, Motke P., Noam Grossman, and Mati. Before we could get acquainted it was time for dinner. Following it was a lecture on map reading and correcting, essential skills for this type of training. The next morning at 5 A.M.

we started the physical conditioning program. After two days of this treatment I ached in every muscle and sinew. However, I was astonished to learn what a young, properly conditioned, and healthy human body could do. Eventually the pain and the discomfort receded and I started to appreciate the suppleness and control this rigorous training gave me. A daily routine of exercises and lectures carried us uneventfully through the first part of the program. It was designed to condition the students for a series of strenuous exercises all over Galilee in situations that might be encountered in a possible future military confrontation.

The school was divided in two separate camps. Our base was in kibbutz Sarid, while the second unit was stationed in kibbutz Ganigar a few kilometers away. Occasionally both camps met, usually in Ganigar for lectures or when a prominent visitor arrived. (A lecturer on military history was one of them, Dr. Israel Beer, Ben Gurion's military advisor, unmasked twenty years later as a Soviet spy.) At the end of the first part of the program, we also reviewed the use of medium mortars and machine guns in support of infantry. This equipment was stored somewhere in a secret hiding place in Ganigar by the Haganah armorers.[5]

We shuttled there from the nearby Sarid to be introduced to a strange assortment of weapons of British, French, Polish, and Italian origin. The exercise consisted of familiarization with these weapons, their characteristics, disassembly, assembly, and servicing. Some of them were quite exotic, like a water-cooled heavy machine gun used in the Austro-Hungarian army in World War I, called Schwarzlose (the name of the manufacturer), an interesting museum piece. Obviously no ammunition was involved. After the exercise, a number of my classmates were assigned to clean and oil the weapons before returning them to the armorers of the Haganah to be stored in the secret storage referred to in our slang as "slicks."

One day we were caught red-handed by a British squad in the nearby kibbutz Ganigar. While the students were sitting on the ground cleaning and oiling the assortment of weapons neatly arranged on canvases, a platoon of the British Sixth Airborne Division suddenly emerged from an orchard. Its surprised commanding officer, a youngish man with a baby face, ordered the petrified men to pack the weapons, probably the total heavy equipment of the lower Galilee district of the Haganah, and to follow the soldiers.

The camp was alerted, weapons distributed, and orders given. Zvi Hurwitz, the deputy commander of the school, after quietly surrounding the British platoon with his men, walked smilingly to the lieutenant in command and inquired what was going on. The lieutenant explained that his commanding officer, suspecting illegal activity, had dispatched him to inspect the kibbutzim in the area. Here by chance he had stumbled on men cleaning machine guns, and he was going to take them and the evidence to Haifa to his command post. Zvi suggested that this would not be prudent because the platoon was surrounded.

The young lieutenant looked around and only then noticed Sten guns (British-designed light infantry machine guns commonly in use) pointing at him and his men from every direction but one. Zvi prudently had left open a way out and told the lieutenant that either he collect his men and leave quietly, or no alternative would be left but to open fire. The lieutenant looked around, evaluated his chances and followed the suggestion. He ordered his platoon back to the command cars waiting outside the kibbutz gate and left.

The camps in Sarid and in Ganigar sprang into frenetic activity. Everything was dismantled. Knapsacks and kits and other paraphernalia were loaded on the nondescript commercial trucks, which left at once in a variety of directions. Weapons were returned to the armorers to be stored. The students left as they were (without changing) on a forced march, heading for the mountains. In half an hour or so the school no longer existed. Shortly afterwards a British column of armored and command cars filled with troops arrived at the kibbutzim, took positions, and started a thorough search. All that was found was an old pistol, a German Mauser, left in the nearby forest by the retreating Turks in 1918.

Avoiding roads we marched through the countryside and late at night we arrived at our new camp in Juara, a hill in the mountains of Ephraim opposite the kibbutz Ein Hashofet. The tents were already set up for us, a warm meal was ready, and the school was back in business, no longer divided into two camps.

Having discovered our activities, the British kept us under surveillance. Every few days British units including Humber armored cars maneuvered on the ridges facing the area where we were exercising. It was a somewhat strange spectacle. The British realized that this was the clandestine commanders school of the Haganah. We no longer pretended that we are training to become instructors of physical education. Moreover our activities on the ridges of the hills clearly pointed to their military character. All that was missing were weapons. We were not bothered by it as it was clear that no shred of incriminating evidence could be found either on us, or in the camp in Juara. We carried on our activities and the British theirs, ignoring one another.

Life in Juara was more interesting. There the whole design of the program and its scope became visible. There were more opportunities to meet other students and get better acquainted. The new dining hall was an ideal place for it. It was airy and spacious, and we sat comfortably on benches at long tables. After the customary reading of a short passage from the Bible by a student, usually a lively conversation developed at the tables. The long lines of students waiting to enter the shower room provided another brief opportunity to socialize. While in the field there was no chitchat and a high level of discipline was maintained at all times.

Mundek Pasternak, the commander of the entire school, became more visible. He lived in a nondescript concrete building, probably purchased from the Arab owner together with the hill. There was the storage room, Mundek's office, and an infirmary. On a sort of parade ground in front of the building was a leveled plateau where the neat rows of our tents were erected. There we assembled every morning after breakfast where Mundek reviewed the assembled class and made a brief comment on the program for the day.

He was a tall, slim man in his early forties then, a chain smoker, always neatly turned out in khaki shorts and a starched and pressed shirt, with a white handkerchief folded in a sort of improvised collar. His features and the way he carried himself made him appear as a Polish cavalry officer would. Mundek's colorful language was remarkable. The Hebrew language generally does not lend itself to cursing. However, Mundek's command of it was unique. If he did not like something, or called someone to order, he expressed it in a fashion that made even the tough Palmachniks cringe.

Mundek had emigrated from Lwów to Eretz Israel in the early 1930s. He was a highly erudite man with a doctorate in fine arts taken at the University of Rome. He was a sensitive, kind, fair, and decent man. Outwardly he projected an image of a tough soldier with a touch of cynicism. His erudition was a well-kept secret, which I later discovered while serving as his aide for a short while on the general staff of the Israeli Army. (Mundek was a deputy to the chief of operations responsible for the Central and Southern fronts; I was heading the Egyptian desk at the Military Intelligence Department in preparation for Operation Ten Plagues in 1948.[6])

Poles, always anti-Semitic, became more so after the death of Marshal Pilsudski. The official slogan popular then was "Jews to Palestine" ("Zydzi do Palestyny"). Somehow the conclusion was reached in official quarters that, if military assistance were offered to the Haganah, the process of getting rid of the Jews would be speeded up. I would not be surprised to find out that Mundek had engineered this whole affair. He went to Poland and graduated from a Polish officers school and organized clandestine shipments of weapons from Poland to Eretz Israel.

His deputy, Zvi Hurvitz, was responsible for administration. His reputation among us was well established after the Ganigar episode, when the British platoon stumbled on the students cleaning machine guns. The instructors were generally an impressive, highly professional lot. Some were more popular than others, but they all were respected and followed.

The students consisted of two distinct groups, the Palmach[7] and the Chish (Haganah members serving as volunteers in field units; "Chish" was an abbreviation of Chayil Sade-field or infantry units). There were also among us a few former soldiers of the Jewish Brigade. The Palmach contingent generally stuck together. Most of them had combat experience because they had served in the Palmach units since the age of seventeen. Therefore, while only in their early twenties, they were already seasoned veterans. They were a dedicated and highly motivated lot with somewhat narrow horizons, understandable in view of the life they led after leaving high school.

Most of the students preferred the use of pseudonyms because of security reasons. They had a strange inclination to be called by popular English names or nicknames. Each carried a Bible, which he read and knew well. Strangely enough they also carried a Hebrew translation of a Russian book, *The Men of Panfilov*. This was a nonfiction description of the battle in 1941 on the Volokolamskoe Shose (highway) near Moscow, and the role the Panfilov Division (named after the general commanding the division) played in saving Moscow. The book fascinated them and represented the ideal of a few men stemming the tide, facing up to a better equipped and more numerous enemy. The soldiers of the decimated Panfilov Division prevailed because of their dedication and superb leadership. Somehow they identified themselves with the men of the Panfilov Division, who, while suffering horrendous losses, stopped the German assault.

They carried out whatever order was given without questioning it. Otherwise, it was a tough, abrasive, slightly arrogant group, somewhat resembling in their behavior the military orders in the days of the crusades. They had a touch of military asceticism and mannerisms popular within this elite and dedicated group. Once they learned that I had served in a Soviet controlled army I was questioned with great interest about life in it. My answers were not to their liking, because they did not correspond to the image formed in their minds. They were by and large disinterested in the Holocaust, taking the rather naïve position that if they had been there they would have taught the Germans a lesson.

I belonged nowhere because there were no other new immigrants or survivors of the Holocaust among the students. The subject was of no interest, and after initial curiosity I was left alone. As I participated in the program like everyone else and performed as expected, I was accepted. However, it was prudent to keep my ideas to myself. There were a few exceptions. I befriended individuals like Amnon Vigolik, a highly sensitive Jerusalemite, who like me was somewhat like a fish taken out of water; Filon Friedman (who fell in Nebi Jusha 1948), a Palmachnik, the only son of a superintendent at the Hebrew University who originally was from Lwów and who befriended me while I was studying in Jerusalem; and Noam Grossman (who fell near Atarot 1947), with whom I studied history.

Another one was Bren, a Palmachnik who looked like a teenager. When I saw him first I asked, "What is this kid doing among us?" I was told, "Don't be silly, this is Bren." A few weeks before joining the commanders school he was escorting a team of surveyors in the Negev desert. Two Bedouins armed with knives and rifles stopped them. Most probably they planned to kill the party and disappear into the desert with their belongings after setting their pickup truck on fire. Bren, taking advantage of the fact that the Bedouins ignored the "kid" and were busy stripping the surveyors of their possessions, grabbed the rifle of one of the Bedouins and shot him with his own weapon. The other Bedouin ran away with Bren in pursuit. After a while Bren returned carrying two rifles and two leather ammunition belts.

Bren and I were dropped at night on the Carmel range with a small cutout of a map and no compass. The exercise called for us to find our way back to the camp and to report at the base the next day not later than one o'clock in the afternoon. The cutout of the map was of limited use after dawn. The night hours were critical and, unless we were able to navigate through the ridge and the wilderness with the assistance of stars, precious time would be lost and we could not reach the base as ordered. We collaborated very well and without much difficulty identified where we were and selected the shortest route to the camp while avoiding Arab villages. We arrived tired, hungry, and pleased that we had met the deadline.

On another occasion he and I were sent to scout out an Arab Legion camp on a *tel* (elevation, usually ruins of a destroyed ancient village or town covered with earth over the centuries) at a crossroads. Our assignment was to return with a plan and a description of the location and the activities in the Legion's camp. I was impressed with the coolness and the ingenuity with which he approached the task.

I learned to appreciate Bren's dry sense of humor and laconic comments. He on the other hand realized the reservoir of experience at my disposal. In short, we hit it off well. Our paths crossed several times later during the battles in the Negev, and in 1950 we graduated again in the same class from battalion commanders school.

Bren was the first Sabra with whom I was able to strike up a friendship. Later over the years the task became much easier.

We were constantly on the go. There was little time, and therefore not much socializing took place. Every free moment was used to
catch up on sleep as most of our training shifted to exercises carried
out at night, our preferred environment for military operations. The
landscape, stripped of vegetation by grazing goats since the Arab
conquest, provided little cover and during the day one was visible
and vulnerable. Only the terraces outlined by stone walls, traces of
extensive cultivation millenniums ago, following the contours of the
rocky hills, provided nooks where shade could be found and the day
could be idled away until sunset. Then we could move again. Night
offers protection from hostile observers; it provides cover and a shelter. One could move freely, limited only by obstacles that could be
circumvented. After leaving the camp, our eyes after a while adapted
to darkness, and it was possible to see within reason and move
without much difficulty. A full moon was an enemy because it compelled much more cautious behavior and avoidance of moving along
ridges.

The terrain could be studied during the day on corrected topo-
graphical maps. However, at night it was essential to navigate following stars to reach one's destination. The rainy season in Israel is
short and most of the time the sky is clear. At night constellations of
stars are easily identified and serve as guides. The North Star,
Cassiopea, Orion, the Great and Small Bears, and others became
trusted friends. Identifying the stars and keeping one's course in relationship to them after leaving the base was comforting and provided
a feeling of security.

At this stage of our training we were assigned an objective. The
planning of the exercise and its execution were left to us. The
instructors appointed students to take charge, accompanied the
units in the field as observers, and offered comments and critique
the next day. We executed deep penetration raids, launched surprise
attacks on remote targets, and entered settlements to "blow up"
strategic objectives. We departed Juara with twilight and had to be
back in the camp not much after dawn. A lost way on approach to
the target meant that it was impossible to get out from the territory

controlled by the "enemy" before dawn. This required camouflaging oneself and staying motionless until darkness offered the possibility of moving undetected again.

The sunrises in the hills of Ephraim and in the lower Galilee were breathtaking. The sky was a deep blue, practically black, with stars shining brightly and changing position in the firmament as the night progressed. Shortly before dawn, a red stripe started to emerge on the horizon in the east. It progressively widened, changing colors from deep purple and red, shifting hues until its lower part turned bright yellow with the red disk of the sun slowly emerging from behind the still-dark horizon.

It was an unforgettable sight that the ancient Greeks saw as the chariot of Apollo emerging from the darkness to start its trip westward high in the sky. I always enjoyed exercises that called for a surprise "attack" with the first daylight. Arriving at the staging area at night before the zero hour permitted observing a spectacle of nature still etched in my mind.

It was autumn and nights were getting cold. The Jewish New Year was approaching and I inquired about the possibility of attending services. I found out to my surprise that there were no synagogues in the nearby kibbutzim. The nearest was about twelve kilometers away, which was not a problem because we were conditioned to march briskly and cover rather impressive distances.

However, I was amazed to learn that there were only five of us who were interested in attending services. Moshe Rusnak, Amnon Vigolik, and Motke were Jerusalemites. Technically, so was I as a student of the Hebrew University. We were joined by another classmate from Haifa. We got a day off and left early in the morning to attend the Atonement services. We inquired on arrival at the kibbutz where the synagogue was. A member directed us to the parents' quarters (an old-age home for the parents of the members of the kibbutz). There we found a modest synagogue and a small congregation.

Marching back to Juara we discussed the matter. The explanation given was that, as we now lived in Israel, it was no longer necessary to follow the rules important in keeping us together in the Diaspora. In the Diaspora the network of restrictions was our fortress and protection, while in Israel we were building our own country. The ratio-

nale was interesting but not altogether convincing, because it contributed to creating a chasm between the Israelis and the Jews in the
Diaspora.

The reading of the Bible before every meal contradicted this
argument in a way. It represented a search for one's roots. However,
paying attention to the passages chosen each day it became apparent
that they were selected because of their nationalistic character or
because they dealt with the region in which we were exercising. The
intensive training left little time for reflection. However, the occasional comments made provided insights into the society in which I
found myself. The Holocaust was beyond comprehension for this
proud and tough group of mostly Sabras. It was difficult for them to
comprehend how one could exist in an atmosphere of hatred and
contempt. They preferred to be satisfied with little and defend it if
need be with their lives, rather than exist in constant humiliation.
The fact that the conditions prevailing in the Diaspora were tolerated by Jews was simply beyond their comprehension.

Their espoused values and way of life narrowed their horizons,
especially those of the members of the Palmach. Abrasha T. once was
telling us about the excellent restaurants in Paris during one of his
descriptions of experiences during his service in the Jewish Brigade.
My neighbor in the tent hailing from Be'er Tuvya (an agricultural
community consisting of a few hundred families), responded with a
question, "Abrasha, have you ever been to the Tnuva (a dairy restaurant chain) in Be'er Tuvya? If you had you would not boast about
restaurants in Paris." There is no argument with such a point of
view.

The political fragmentation in the commanders school was as
pronounced as it had been in Lido di Roma, or on the pier in La
Spezia. My classmates belonged to or identified themselves with the
then-political mainstream in Israel. The members of the Palmach
identified with the left wing of the political structure, some of which
was in opposition to Ben Gurion. The Chish contingent leaned
more toward the center, with what later became Mapai, the dominant political party in Israel for a long time. There were also a few
individuals from other political quarters. I was bored by all that, and
in addition we were too tired after an exhausting day to engage in

political discussions. However, one afternoon the issues came into sharp focus. An instructor alerted two platoons to assemble. They were issued *nabbuts* (a short stick used by Arab shepherds as a weapon), and we were ordered to climb into two trucks that left Juara in the direction of Beniamina, a large and wealthy settlement controlling citrus groves in the region. I inquired about the significance of it. It was explained that Shuni, near Beniamina, served as a base for IZL (National Military Organization, a clandestine military arm of the movement headed by Menachem Begin). Members of IZL beat up members of the Haganah living in this settlement. Our task was to teach IZL a lesson. It was astonishing to see units of my class going into action vandalizing the premises and beating up other Jews for admittedly political reasons, without sending them to a hospital.

To understand the proper perspective of this episode, one has to remember that the Haganah was a military arm of an elected body, the Jewish Agency, which had approximately sixty thousand members. IZL, which rejected the authority of the Jewish Agency, had about two thousand members and led by Begin engaged in some highly controversial terrorist activities condemned by the majority of the Yishuv.

There was no time to read newspapers because we either were in the field, or were preparing an exercise, or were catching up on our sleep. Noam Grossman, who had joined the commanders school after his return from the United States, brought with him a small portable radio that worked on batteries. It operated employing vacuum tubes and was an amazing novelty from America. It kept us in touch with the world. Every now and then Noam listened to broadcasts from Jerusalem and the BBC and informed us about developments in the international arena.

The cold war was on. The Chinese communists were making progress in taking over the mainland of China. Atomic tests were conducted in the Pacific. Marilyn Monroe had been introduced to the American public and was gaining popularity. All this meant little to us. We were focused on the debate going on in the United Nations at Lake Success about the future of the British Mandate for Palestine and the solutions proposed by its special commission.

A JOURNEY THROUGH ILLUSIONS

Noam was the source of latest news and visitors always gathered at his tent.

Unexpectedly one day Ben Gurion visited the commanders school. We assembled in the dining room and he addressed us, explaining the situation. Ben Gurion was a short man with an extraordinary presence, radiating magnetism. He made his points forcefully and convincingly. He certainly was an impressive leader of men and in some respect a visionary. It was not generally known that he was quite erudite and was studying, while I was there in 1946, in the Department of Classics headed by Professor Schwabe, my teacher. After his formal comments, a discussion followed with sharply focused questions posed to him, as my classmates were not easily intimidated, especially not by politicians. He responded to these questions with frankness and clarity, ignoring the fact that the ones coming from the left wingers among us were quite aggressive and almost offensive.

He then posed a series of questions inquiring about the program, our ideas about the future, and our vision of the state when it would be established. He was interested in the composition of the graduating class and in particular how many members of the Oriental (Sephardi) community were among the students. Jerucham Cohen, a Yemenite, was the only one. Ben Gurion was pleased that there was at least one, stressing that this must be swiftly corrected. He mentioned the Holocaust briefly, and I was struck by the coldness of his comment. Ben Gurion saw the Holocaust only as a stepping stone to the redemption of Israel and a rationale for gathering exiles into their own land.

He impressed me as a powerful leader, if somewhat cold and detached. He was a visionary but not a fanatic, and it was apparent that he was a dominant personality in the Jewish Agency. He had been bitten by socialism of the 1905 vintage from which he never succeeded in detaching himself. He did not tolerate opposition and was visibly irritated if his persuasive comments did not convince one of my classmates. The record of his contribution to Zionism and to the creation of the State of Israel is well established. I had met before him men greater than he, and I also knew other political leaders of the Yishuv. Therefore, while impressed, I was not overwhelmed.

Subsequent encounters with Ben Gurion confirmed the impression he made on me in Juara. I met him again while attached briefly to the Prime Minister's office before my discharge from the Israeli army. I respected the man and his accomplishments. The original impression, however, remained.

Our field exercises were coming to an end. After completion of work with explosives and their use, we were ready for the final part of the program, the techniques of combat in a built-up area. The school moved to an encampment in the vicinity of Haifa that consisted of small two-man tents. We spent some time in an abandoned failed real estate development practicing techniques of moving without exposing oneself to enemy fire, breaking into a house, and preparing a house for demolition. All this became very useful in a few weeks in the battles defending Jerusalem and in Haifa.

We moved on to Haifa, a lovely city on the Carmel, with splendid views on the bay. We meant no harm and did not intend to cause any mischief. However, the appearance of over 130 men walking in twos or threes through the city's streets did not go unnoticed. The British police were put on alert, which we found rather amusing. We were studying imaginary lines of defense, exploring desirable locations for machine gun emplacements, studying lines of attack. While strolling through the city we were followed by fully armed British policemen, who observed what we were doing. We were chatting, taking notes, and occasionally making a diagram. Then we stopped at a falafel (deep fried balls of chick peas in a pita bread) vendor on the street to buy our lunch. All this puzzled the British police.

Our assignment called for planning the demolition of all government offices, banks, British firms, the railroad station, and the harbor installations. Two colleagues and I were given the task of planning demolition of the Barclays Bank DCO building. Obviously no one meant any harm, but it was essential for making plans to have a peek inside the bank to identify critical areas suitable to place explosives for maximum effect.

As we lingered on the banking platform, the manager, a redhead in slacks and a shirt with a tie, got suspicious and inquired what we wanted. One of us spoke English and responded that, as we planned to go to Australia, we were interested in acquiring Australian currency. The response angered the Englishman, and he told us to get out or he would call the police.[8] Others had similar experiences trying to enter Thomas Cook and Sons and other British institutions.

We returned to Juara to finish some odds and ends and to prepare for Operation Or Dror. One morning we were taught how to lay a minefield, mark it properly, and record it on a map. Marching back to Juara, we saw fire and smoke on the ridge ahead of us where the camp was located. Someone carelessly had thrown a cigarette near a tent. The dried grass caught fire and the tent went up in smoke.

(It is strange that later its inhabitants were killed in different parts of the country in unrelated battles but in the order in which they slept in the tent. In May 1948 during the first armistice, Rabi, the student of Hebrew University who came with me to the school from the Jerusalem District, stopped in Abu Gosh where I was stationed to say goodbye. He was on his way to the Negev where he had been transferred from the Sixth Jerusalem Brigade—Etzioni. I offered him some spam, bread, and an excellent wine. Rabbi sipped the wine, and we remembered our days in Juara. Before leaving he commented, "Well, it's my turn. Do you remember the burnt tent? I am its last inhabitant." Two weeks later the news reached me that Rabi had died in the south in an attack on the Taggart Police Station.)

The concluding exercise of Operation Or Dror accomplished its objectives despite the mishap with the boat while crossing the Jordan. The Haganah operated in squads and rarely in platoons. A battalion and a company were administrative units. The concluding exercise was designed to test the moving of a reinforced company with heavy weapons and auxiliary equipment provided by the Haganah's naval arm into a staging area, and carry out a coordinated attack simultaneously on a series of objectives. Equally, its objective was to provide the commander of the district with an opportunity to test the defense network.

Although the mishap at the Jordan messed up the exercise, the set objectives were achieved. The logistics, the chain of command, and the communication setup were tested. Our presence was

detected in the early stage of the enterprise and the element of surprise was lost. Nevertheless, we were in a position to blow up
the roads and bridges. If the commander of the operation chose, he
could shift to other targets in the middle of the battle and still withdraw before daylight. The defenses of the region were tested in conditions as close to a real battle as one can create in such circumstances. Seven months later the defenses of the Jordan valley were
tested by Syrian infantry and tanks.

We were delighted to be back in Juara with nothing to do, waiting for the instructors to be released from jail in Haifa. The program
ended and we were preparing for final examinations. Two senior
Haganah commanders arrived in Juara. A large sandbox was set up
and a three-dimensional model of an imaginary region was prepared
representing nicely contoured mountains, valleys, roads, and bridges
all scaled down. A great deal of ingenuity was displayed in improvis-
ing forests, houses, bridges, railroad crossings, and military installations out of a variety of materials like cardboard, matches, cotton,
and string. The total effect was interesting as with limited means, a
little paint, and great deal of improvisation a varied landscape was
recreated in miniature. The students were called individually before
the examiners, who presented each with a tactical problem and outlined the resources and manpower allotted to the operation. A few
minutes were allowed for the development of a plan of how to
accomplish the objective. The student then made a brief presentation describing how he proposed to deal with the task.

The examination was a formality. The instructors knew everyone's limitations and strengths. They had seen us performing during
the hot summer months in a state of almost total exhaustion. We
had been observed moving through the countryside at night, going
unerringly to a variety of targets. They had seen us functioning as
soldiers and as commanders.

We equally had observed them and had learned a great deal about
each—his stamina, leadership, strength, and weaknesses. The evaluation and the tests had taken place while performing in the hot and
unrelentless subtropical sun, or in the cool nights in the lower Galilee
and the hills of Ephraim. In a way they too were trained for future
positions of leadership. Some were popular, others less so. However,

their dedication, professionalism, and correctness were respected. There was no authority vested in a commander or an instructor in the Haganah. One had to earn it by commanding respect, providing an example, and performing according to expectations.

It was a rewarding experience to stand in front of the commission and the instructors with a pointer, showing on the sandbox the routes of approach, the lines of attack, and the method of disengagement. It was an opportunity to display the skills acquired over the hard months of intensive training. We had changed, gained self-confidence and inner strength, and acquired the assurance that we were ready for whatever the future might bring. We were all cognizant that we were headed toward a showdown after the United Nations decided the future of the Yishuv. We were fully aware of the risks involved and the burden of responsibility.

The fourth class of the commanders school of the Haganah was ready for the graduation ceremony. We assembled next to our tents in freshly laundered khakis and had even polished our well-worn heavy shoes for the occasion. Platoon after platoon marched to the assembly square in front of the old house. The instructors assembled in front of the school. We were all volunteers. No social advantage was involved as one did not boast about being an officer of the Haganah. We came from many different walks of life. Our motivation was to fulfill our duty, and it was a privilege to be entrusted with the defense of the Yishuv. The sun set and it was dark. In front of each platoon, cans filled with sand and kerosene were lit, illuminating the faces of the men.

On top of the building out of burning rags soaked in kerosene letters were fashioned to spell *"Ly Pkuda Tamid Anachnu!"* ("If called we are always ready!")—the theme of the song of the Palmach. The Israeli flag was hoisted on the pole; we sang "Hatikvah," the national anthem; and Mundek wished us all good luck and commented that we had done our best and that he and the instructors were privileged to command the fourth class of the commanders school.

This ended the simple graduation ceremony, and we proceeded to the dining hall. The passage from the Bible was read, dinner was served, and then came a surprise. A makeshift stage was set up, songs were sung, the instructors were roasted, and little skits were performed. I had never suspected that there were so many hidden talents in our group. There were comedians, actors, playwrights among us and the entertaining performance was staged with ingenuity, humor, and tact.

Three months later the graduates of the fourth class 1947 were decimated. Johnny fell on the Kastel, an operation in which I participated. Arab bands assembled in this village, built on the ruins of a Roman fortification. It dominated the approaches to Jerusalem and was a base for daily attacks on the civilian transportation and the trucks carrying supplies to the city. My platoon laid ambushes to block reinforcements from reaching the attacked Arab bands, while Johnny's platoon attacked the village. The operation was successful, but Johnny was killed by a stray bullet.

Noam Grossman fell on a ridge near Atarot; Amnon Vigolik lost his hands and eyes clearing mines near Nve Yaakov. Filon Friedman fell in an attack on the strategically located police station of Nebi Jusha in the upper Galilee that had been surrendered to Arab bands by the British. A scout guiding the platoon led by Danny Mass, the commander of the Sarid camp of the school, to Kfar Etzion erred and entered the wrong wadi (canyon). At dawn they found themselves surrounded by Arabs on a small hill only four kilometers from their destination. Ammunition ran out. . . . Their horribly mutilated bodies were brought to Jerusalem in sacks by British soldiers.

Years later visiting Israel I located the modest museum of the Haganah on Allenby Street. There I inquired about records of the fourth class of the clandestine commanders school that had graduated in 1947 in Juara. A folder gathering dust was located on a shelf. It had a few papers in it, including a handwritten list of thirty-odd names, among them mine. This was all that remained except the memories of those graduates who had survived the 1947-49 war.

We dispersed the morning after the graduation ceremony. I returned to Jerusalem and went to the Association of Students of the Hebrew University to get my assigned place in a student shelter in Beit Hakerem, a suburb of Jerusalem. I was told that I had been assigned a room in a small elegant hotel on Abarbanel Street in Rechavia not far from the Jewish Agency. I objected, stating that I could not afford it. I was told not to worry because my rent was already paid. I checked in at the hotel and found there an envelope with a paycheck waiting for me from Tnuva, a cooperative belonging to the Histadrut (Trade Union) specializing in the processing and distribution of agricultural products. I went there to inquire what my duties were. I was told not to worry because there was nothing for me to do. A few days later I received a letter stating that my life was insured for 1,000 English pounds by Lloyds of London and would I please appoint a beneficiary. Puzzled, I checked with Shalom B. (the senior Haganah commander in the Jerusalem District who arranged to send me to the commanders school) about the meaning of all this. He replied that I was now a member of the regular staff of the Haganah on a leave of absence until I completed my studies.

My book written in Lido di Roma in the winter of 1945-46 was published by Am Oved (a prestigious publishing house belonging to the Histadrut) and I received royalties. Finally I was well established and could address myself to my studies. I returned to the Department of Classics and concentrated on Greek and on the reading of *Anabasis* by Xenophon.

Rather late one evening there was a commotion in the streets. People were yelling, dancing, running. I went out to inquire what this was all about. I was told that the vote in the United Nations taken on November 29, 1947, was in favor of the partition of Palestine into an Arab and a Jewish state. The euphoria lasted the whole night. In the morning I was asked to report at the Jewish Agency, where an armorer gave me a pistol and told me to join Golda Meir as her bodyguard. I followed her to the balcony, where she made the historic speech calling on the Arabs to accept the partition and join the Jews in building a better future for the inhabitants of the land. She was the only member of the Jewish Agency present in Jerusalem on that day. In old photographs taken of Golda Meir speaking from the balcony, a young man can be seen standing next to her. My features could possibly be recognized among the group of individuals standing on the balcony of the Jewish Agency although almost half a century has passed since the event. When the ceremony was over I got rid of the pistol and went back to my studies, happy that I would be left alone for two years to finish my studies in peace. This too was only an illusion.

On December 1, 1947, I was in the library of the Hebrew University working on some papyri for Professor Joseph Klausner. A member of the Haganah whom I knew from the winter training sessions came to me and whispered orders from the commander of the Haganah District. Would I please at once collect a platoon of Haganah members in the classes and proceed to the city, because Arabs were killing Jews at the commercial center near the Tanus Building. He informed me that I would find a bus outside the Humanities Department in the Rosenblum Building and in it was waiting an armorer with small arms.

I left my books on the table to return to my studies later in the afternoon and walked to the other building where classes were held. I entered the classrooms and ordered Haganah members to assemble at the bus. The lecturers were annoyed by the intrusion and the students were puzzled, realizing that something was going on. The platoon assembled swiftly at the bus, arms were distributed, and we took off for the commercial center. I did not realize it then, but in effect I had been mobilized, given a command, and sent to defend Jews attacked by their Arab neighbors.

One completed assignment was followed by another. For a while I commanded the center of the city around the Moslem Mamillah cemetery. Then I was sent with the first field unit, consisting of a platoon of former soldiers of the Jewish Brigade and a platoon of Jewish Auxiliary Police (Notrim), to secure the road to Jerusalem. I did not return to the Hebrew University and my books that were left on the table in the library. I fought in Jerusalem, and after the armistice I was transferred to the General Staff for a short while, and then back to the Southern Command (the Negev and the Sinai). I was not discharged from the Israeli Army until the autumn of 1954.

I still remember with pride that I was privileged to join the fourth class of the clandestine commanders school of the Haganah. The graduates were part of the silver platter on which the State of Israel was brought to the Jewish people everywhere. This term was coined by the poet Nathan Alterman in his moving poem "The Silver Platter"[9] dedicated to the selfless generation that defended the Yishuv in the years 1947-49.

This silver platter consisted of the companies of the night (Special Night Squads) organized by Capt. Charles Orde Wingate to neutralize the bands that had terrorized the Arab and Jewish population of the Palestine Mandate in the 1930s. They were joined by the legendary commanders of the Palmach, the officers and the NCOs of the former Jewish Brigade of the British Eighth Army, and the graduates of the Haganah commanders school. They led the men and women of the Yishuv in the defense of their homes and settlements. On May 15, 1948, with the establishment of the State of Israel, they became the Israeli Defense Forces. They paid a terrible price in dead and maimed in this battle for survival. I was privileged indeed to be a part of this saga.

Three decorations:
(a) A decoration awarded to members of the Haganah for the defense of Jerusalem in 1947-48. (b) An original Haganah commander's (MM) pin issued to graduates of the clandestine officer's school. (c) The badge of the Sixty-second Battalian Beit Choron of the Sixth Brigade Etzioni worn on the beret.

משרד הביטחון

№ 1839

שם משפחה ___ לוין ___

שם פרטי ___ יצחק קורט ___

שם האב ___ יחזקאל ___

מס. זהות ___

בזה ניתנת לך
הזכות לעונדת

אות ההגנה

מרדכי צפורי
סגן שר הביטחון

תאריך

An award by the State of Israel to former members of the Haganah.

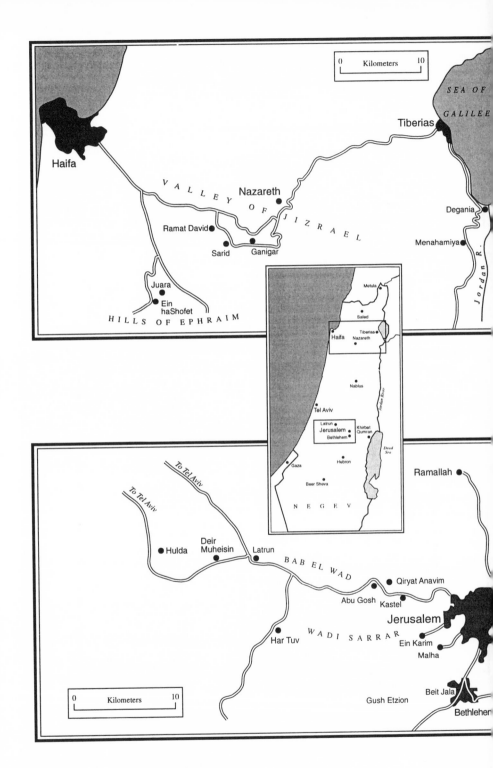

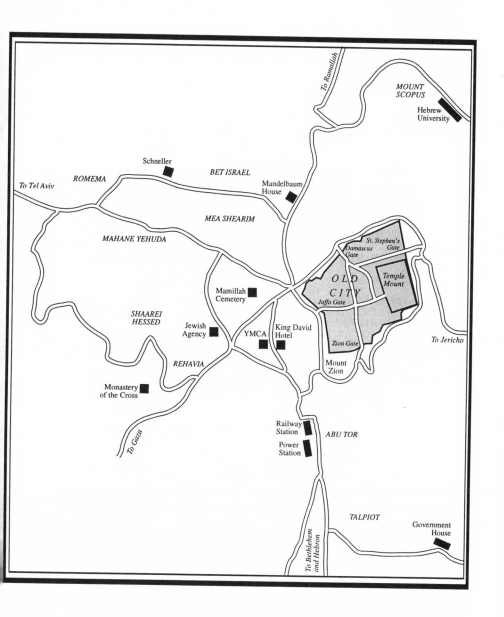

To Ramallah

MOUNT
SCOPUS

Hebrew
University

Schneller

BET ISRAEL

ROMEMA

To Tel Aviv

Mandelbaum
House

MEA SHEARIM

MAHANE YEHUDA

St. Stephen's
Gate

Damascus
Gate

Mamillah
Cemetery

OLD
CITY

Temple
Mount

SHAAREI
HESSED

Jewish
Agency

YMCA

King David
Hotel

Jaffa Gate

To Jericho

Zion Gate

REHAVIA

Mount
Zion

Monastery
of the Cross

To Gaza

Railway
Station

ABU TOR

Power
Station

TALPIOT

Government
House

To Bethlehem
and Hebron

JERUSALEM, 1948

CHAPTER 6

The Story of Moshe Dayan

A S IT HAS from time immemorial, the road from the Mediterranean coast to Jerusalem, after passing Latrun with its vineyards and the Trappist monastery, enters Bab el Wad, a twisting canyon, which ends near Saris. From there it continues to Abu Gosh, an Arab village. The final approach to Jerusalem is dominated by the forbidding Kastel. This was the route followed by Egyptians, Israelites led by David; Assyrians, Babylonians led by Nebuchadnezzar; Persians, Greeks, Romans led by Titus; Byzantines, Arabs, Crusaders led by Gotfryd de Buillon; Saracens led by Salah ad Din; Turks led by Suleiman the Magnificent; and the British led by Allenby. Now it was our turn to fight for this lifeline to a city with over 100,000 Jews living in it.

The village of Abu Gosh is located near a water well around which was once the winter camp of the X Legion of Titus. An old French priest living in a monastery next to a church built by the Crusaders showed me a stone over a well near the altar with the inscription LEGIO X carved on it. It was a strange feeling to be stationed where the Romans had had their winter camp centuries ago. This Roman Legion, according to the historian Josephus Flavius (Joseph Ben Matatyahu), was responsible for the destruction of the Second Temple.

The base of the Sixty-second Battalion of the Sixth Brigade, commanded by Meir Zorea (Zaro),[1] was a Taggart police station built by the British during the Arab riots in 1936. Taggart apparently headed the Public Works Department, which constructed a network of these stations throughout the land. Whoever planned the location of these fortress-like structures had a keen sense of history and was a military expert. All of them were constructed in key strategic points dominating the surrounding countryside. They were solidly built, painted in a color matching the yellow brownish hue of the soil, and they blended well into the landscape. It took a battery of six-pounder anti-tank guns to get the Egyptians out of one of them in Iraq Suidan that was blocking the approaches to the Negev.

The Taggart station at the pass near Abu Gosh had been abandoned by the British police some time in April 1948, and we took it over. There, hardly a kilometer and a half from the front line, we could rest and catch our breath.

The battle for the approaches to Jerusalem started shortly after the partition, with Arab irregulars attacking buses and trucks carrying supplies to the beleaguered city. The road through Bab el Wad was like a shooting gallery through which one had to pass to reach Jerusalem.

In the beginning of April, the Sixty-second Battalion Beit Choron[2] was detached from the Sixth Brigade Etzioni defending Jerusalem and transferred to reinforce the Tenth Palmach Brigade Harel, referred to as *"haPortzim"* (the ones who broke through), which was newly arrived in the Jerusalem sector. This brigade, commanded then by Itzhak Rabin, a future Prime Minister, had infiltrated the blockade of Arab irregulars and joined the defenders of Jerusalem. In a way it saved the city while paying a high price in heavy casualties.

On arrival in Abu Gosh, Zaro and I went to meet the brigade commander in Beit Pfefferman, a convalescent home in a pine forest on a ridge above the kibbutz Kiryat Anavim, where the headquarters of the brigade was based. There in one of the rooms pointed out to us we found him. On a bed covered with a sheet was a blond youngster, just waking up and unceremoniously scratching his behind. Zaro and I had been officers in a regular army. We looked at each other, somewhat puzzled seeing the youngster. Zaro reported the arrival of the battalion, its strength, and its equipment. We left Itzhak Rabin, somewhat perplexed. He proved to be a thoughtful, highly competent commander with considerable analytic ability, rather laconic, and surprisingly shy. We were sorry to see him go a few weeks later to become chief of staff of the Southern command.

Shortly after we settled in Abu Gosh and took over the strong points (mountain peaks) along Bab al Wad, Mickey Stone arrived. The mysterious American was to take over command of the newly formed central front. This included the brigades Third Alexandroni and Fourth Kiryati defending Tel Aviv and responsible for opening the road to Jerusalem, the Tenth Palmach Brigade in Bab el Wad, and the Sixth Brigade Etzioni defending the city. A brigade was still an administrative concept only, as the Haganah[3] operated in platoon, company, and occasionally in battalion strength. Mickey Stone,[4] a pseudonym of the American, was given by Ben Gurion the task of forging its forces into a regular army.

I was asked to provide wine for the *kumsitz* (party in Hebrew slang) planned for the evening. My access to wine resulted from an accidental discovery of a winery in Motza. In December after a brief stint of commanding the center of Jerusalem, I was relieved and assigned to take over the first field unit dispatched to protect the road from Kastel to the outskirts of the city. My base was a convalescent home of the Kupat Cholim (a medical insurance system organized by the Histadrut, the Labor Union) located in Arza on the top of the ridge. One squad of my platoon, disguised as convalescing patients, was with me at the sanatorium. A second squad was located in private homes in Motza Elit (upper) a few hundred meters below it, and one in Motza Tachtit (lower), down the road at some distance.

I noticed that the squad in Motza Tachtit was always tipsy. I found out that an old winery was located there and in its underground cellars were large wooden barrels of excellent wines stored to age. With the outbreak of Arab terrorism following the partition, the owners locked the place, camouflaged the entrance, and left for Jerusalem. Somehow one of my men discovered the cellar and found a way to get in. We kept the information to ourselves and enjoyed a regular supply of superb wine brought in milk cans to wherever we were at the time. My scouts made it available to the quartermaster, who bartered it with other units for ammunition, food, and other supplies.

The *kumsitz* was set for the evening in the monastery of Abu

Gosh where a monk, Pere Joseph, a Frenchman and former Foreign Legionnaire, resided. There Mickey Stone, his deputy Harris (also an American), and his driver Rivka settled for the night. I arranged for the wine and did not join Zaro and others at the *kumsitz*. I was a field commander, and strategic and political questions were of little interest to me. Three months of facing constant danger, protecting convoys, scouting the southern region of Jerusalem, and helping Zaro to form the battalion had tired me out. Besides, my girlfriend, also a student at the Hebrew University, served in a unit in the nearby kibbutz Kiryat Anavim.

I learned in the morning the shocking news that Mickey Stone had been killed during the night. Colonel David Marcus, a graduate of West Point, known as Mickey Stone, did not die, as the official version stated, in Abu Gosh. He was taken by ambulance, I was told by eyewitnesses, badly wounded but still alive, to a hospital in Jerusalem where he died. The official version is probably correct that he left the monastery in the middle of the night wrapped in a white sheet to urinate, was challenged by a sentry, responded in English and was shot.

It was rumored then that British policemen had joined the Arab irregulars. Besides, we were facing the Arab Legion,[5] which was commanded by British officers and NCOs, and whose outposts were not more than a few hundred yards away. The sentry did not speak English. Still there remained a lingering doubt about what had happened. The official version probably contributed to this doubt by not adhering to the facts. It was rumored that there were those who resented the appointment of an American as the first general of the newly created Israeli Army. I don't believe this version, and there is not a shred of evidence to support it. There was a considerable dose of carelessness, amateurishness, and bravado in those days, which was conducive to that sort of incident. The body of Colonel Marcus, accompanied by Moshe Dayan, was returned to the United States to be buried in the Arlington cemetery.

Moshe Dayan was born in Nahalal, the first *moshav* (an agricultural settlement) in the Valley of Jezreel, referred to also as Emek. He was among the young men of the Haganah trained during the riots of 1936-39 by Captain Charles Orde Wingate. He lost an eye in Syria while acting as a scout for the British troops fighting the

Vichy French. A few months before the end of the Mandate he was caught with Johnny, my classmate at the clandestine commanders school, and others carrying arms and was sentenced to jail by the British. They were all released shortly after the partition. Johnny knew him well and so did others. This was the first that I heard of Moshe Dayan. He played a key if controversial role in Jerusalem following his return from the United States in the summer of 1948 after the first armistice.

Moshe Dayan was the third commander of the Jerusalem District, which included the Sixth Brigade Etzioni. At the time of the United Nations vote on partition in November 1947, the Jerusalem District was commanded by a political appointee, a bureaucrat and an administrator. This would still be a somewhat charitable description of this official, who was also an amateur in military matters. He was replaced by the colorful David Shaltiel, a former French Foreign Legionnaire, who was an interesting if controversial man. Shaltiel organized the defenses of the city in a somewhat more rational fashion. The field commanders, a rather competent and resourceful lot, did their jobs and the brigade did not interfere.

The regular Arab armies crossed the borders of the Mandate and attacked the newly proclaimed State of Israel on May 15, 1948. The Jerusalem sector was invaded by the Arab Legion, well-trained, well-equipped, and led by seasoned British officers.[5] It was a frightening moment, because we did not have the necessary equipment and adequate ammunition to defend ourselves. The Jerusalem District was in disarray; its Sixth Brigade was decimated. At a meeting of Palmach commanders with the staff of the Sixth Brigade, Itzhak Sade,[6] the legendary commander of the Palmach who had arrived with the Tenth Brigade Harel that was sent to reinforce the Jerusalem front, slapped the face of one of the senior staff officers. The individual, a former British officer, had suggested not without reason that Jerusalem, cut off from the rest of the country, could not be held by irregulars against the Arab Legion and suggested surrender. The atmosphere prevailing in the headquarters of the Jerusalem District reached a point that the commander of the Tenth Brigade Harel, Tabenkin, who replaced Rabin, wired the General Staff in Tel

Aviv that under the prevailing circumstances he was compelled to take over temporarily the command of the District.

We were glad to be attached to the Tenth Brigade Harel, because we had reservations about the competence of the leadership of the Jerusalem District and did not care much for the mannerisms they had introduced. The Haganah took pride in simplicity and a low profile, which was no longer observed at the headquarters of the Jerusalem District. One morning Zaro and I returned to the city from the front lines in Bab el Wad and called on the headquarters of the District, which was located in the building of the Jewish Agency. We came from the front sweaty, covered with dust, and armed with rifles. At the headquarters everybody wore neatly pressed khakis and curiously walked around in helmets. We were led to a well-stocked bar where a barman in a white jacket and a black tie first inquired whether we were officers and then offered us a drink. We asked for a lemonade and left.

The battle for the approaches to Jerusalem was fought from Bab el Wad by the Tenth Brigade Harel and the Jerusalem garrison. The assembled forces in Hulda, on the plain facing Latrun, were given the task of taking the Taggart police station and establishing control over the highway crossing. There the two forces were supposed to meet, ending the siege. Our primary target then was Latrun, on a hill with a Trappist monastery on it dominating the entrance to Bab el Wad. On it was entrenched a unit of the Arab Legion blocking the road to Jerusalem.

The engineers of the Haganah found an alternate route that circumvented the lines of the Arab Legion, allowing trucks to deliver supplies to a point near the entrance to Bab el Wad where only jeeps could pass. From there the supplies had to be carried by porters for a few miles to the entrance of the canyon. This secretly opened route to resupply the starving population of Jerusalem was referred to as the "Burma Road." At night at its end one could see long lines of men from all the communities in Jerusalem: Hasidic, Bukharan, Yemenite, and European Jews. They carried on their backs sacks of flour to be reloaded onto trucks waiting in the relative safety of the entrance to Bab el Wad and sent up to Jerusalem.

A coordinated attack was planned for the units of the Jerusalem

District stationed in Bab el Wad and units from Tel Aviv District assembled in Hulda, opposite Latrun, to take Latrun and break the siege of Jerusalem. I was sent by Zaro to Strong Point 21, a mountaintop permitting observation of the highway leading from Ramallah to Latrun. I joined a platoon holding it and with powerful artillery binoculars observed the traffic on this highway. A few days before the attack, I observed a convoy of at least two hundred trucks moving from Ramallah, the base of the Arab Legion, reinforcing the unit entrenched in Latrun.

On the eve of the attack I was sent by Zaro to Deir Muheisin, on the other side of Latrun, to warn Chaim Laskoff, commander of one of the battalions, a former British army officer and a close friend of Zaro, that Latrun was significantly reinforced. I had to cross enemy-held territory at night to reach him in his headquarters in Hulda, the staging area of the operation. I spent the day with Chaim Laskoff outlining the positions of the Arab Legion and the strength of its units defending Latrun. Our paths crossed many a time in later years and Chaim always remembered my visit to Hulda. He was a soldier's soldier, perhaps too influenced by his experience in the British Army.

The following night I returned to Bab el Wad, convinced that the attack would be either postponed or canceled. To my surprise and horror that was not the case. Units moved into positions at twilight from Hulda and Bab el Wad, and shortly after nightfall the attack started. It was beaten off by the units of the Arab Legion. The experienced Palmachniks of the Tenth Brigade Harel retreated back to Bab el Wad before daylight, suffering only light casualties. The units attacking from the Tel Aviv side were ordered to continue. It was a veritable slaughter, as in daylight without artillery and mortars the attackers became targets for concentrated crossfire of the Arab Legion directed from the hills dominating the juncture, the Taggart station over it, and the monastery of Latrun.

A great number of the fallen were survivors of the Holocaust. Some were graduates of the concentration camps; others survived having joined partisan units in the forests of Byelorussia. There were those who had hidden in cellars or bunkers. All had been caught while attempting to break the British blockade at the shores of Eretz

Israel in the crowded rickety ships of the illegal immigration. They were then deported and interned in Cyprus. After the end of the British Mandate they were released and brought to Haifa. Some of them arrived at the harbor in the afternoon, were sent in buses directly to Hulda, and on the way there were issued rifles and shown how to use them. In the early morning they faced the experienced and well-equipped Arab Legion. Hundreds of them died in the withering fire in the fields before Latrun without anyone's knowing, or for that matter caring, who they were. The thoughtlessness and callousness of this made a strong impression on me. In the evening I collected a few stragglers who were wandering around bewildered and had stumbled into our patrols at the exit from Bab el Wad.

Shortly after this failed attack, the seventh unsuccessful attempt to dislodge the Arab Legion from Latrun, we were ordered back to the city to rejoin our brigade (Sixth Brigade Etzioni). We were worn out, having suffered losses starting with a platoon wiped out by the Arab Legion shortly after our arrival in April 1948 from the city in Abu Gosh. This platoon, commanded by Ami Rozanski, a young and promising officer, was entrenched on the Radar Hill, a former British army camp, to protect the approaches to Beit Pfeferman and the kibbutz Maale haChamisha. It was attacked by infantry of the Arab Legion supported by artillery, and within five minutes the platoon was wiped out. From then on we were in constant skirmishes with the Arab Legion. Our task was to hold the strong points controlling the approaches to the road leading to Jerusalem, from the entrance to Bab al Wad up to the western outskirts of Jerusalem. After almost three months on the front line under shelling, sniping, constantly patrolling the no man's land, and occasional counterattacks, we were battle worn. We had suffered casualties and the battalion's strength was reduced. The battle for the road to Jerusalem was a hard and bloody one. The battalions of the Tenth Brigade Harel were in not much better shape.

We were sorry to be detached from the Tenth Brigade Harel with whom we had shared many difficult days. However, we were looking forward to rest and to replacements to bring the battalion to full strength again. The Sixty-second Battalion, or what was left of it, returned to Jerusalem and settled at Schneller, a former Syrian orphanage used in World War I by the German troops assisting the Ottoman Turks fighting General Allenby. It subsequently had become a British army camp, and presently served the Israeli army.

One quiet morning we were alerted that the Arab Legion was breaking into the city. Its armored spearhead had already reached the Mandelbaum House, a key strong point controlling the entrance to Mea Shearim, the quarter of the ultra-orthodox Jews. The battalion was assembled, and its first task was to stop the approaching armored column. This was accomplished with Molotov bottles and PIATs (a British infantry anti-tank weapon). At night we launched a counterattack, retaking both Beit Shchori and Beit Mandelbaum, referred to for years as the Mandelbaum Gate (a crossing point between Israel and Jordan until 1967). The Arab Legion was stopped and resorted to regularly pounding the city with artillery, twenty-five pounders and even six-pounder anti-tank guns.

The Sixth Brigade Etzioni made one final effort to retake the Jewish quarter of the old city. (Cut off from the new city, it had fallen in May 1948.) The attack was carefully planned and prepared. The task assigned to the Sixty-second Battalion was to blow a hole using an explosive device in the wall and break into the old city through the Zion Gate. We marched into positions at twilight. It was the first time I had seen the whole battalion assembled and going into a battle as a unit with all its equipment, including the newly arrived wireless sets, the American-made SCR 300. We were proud to have forged, while in combat, a regular unit out of conscripts. There were no longer Haganah volunteers available to replace the losses. They had all been mobilized in December 1947 and had been serving for a long time already in a variety of units on the Jerusalem front.

The operation failed because the wall built by Herod the Great and then reinforced and raised by Suleiman the Magnificent could not be breached. A conic explosive device, carefully calculated and designed by scientists, had to be dragged up Mount Zion with considerable difficulty and attached to the ancient wall under fire. It exploded, shattering every window still intact in the city and leaving only a black spot on the old wall. In the morning, having made a lot of noise without gaining anything, we returned to our positions.

The wags in the battalion painted a black spot on the insignia worn on our berets to commemorate the occasion.

This was the last operation of the brigade under the command of David Shaltiel. He had taken over a demoralized city under attack, defended by dedicated Haganah members, a large percentage of them students of the Hebrew University. He succeeded in forging them into fighting units and had the good sense to leave tactical decisions to professionals. He gave enough leeway to the battalion commanders, permitting them to develop their own initiatives within assigned responsibilities. The Jewish quarter in the old city, the kibbutzim of Gush Etzion, and the settlements of Atarot and Nve Yaakov, which either fell or had to be abandoned, could not be defended. In the final analysis, the city survived the siege thanks to David Shaltiel. His flamboyance and preoccupation with military symbols were perhaps irritating to the combat units, which saddled him with a reputation as something of a buffoon. Nevertheless, he developed a coherent plan of defense after taking over from his predecessor, successfully defended the city, and led the population through the horrible siege. The battle for Jerusalem had started with the decision of the United Nations in Lake Success on November 29, 1947, to divide the country into a Jewish and an Arab sector, and was nearly over in July 1948.

Harel's intervention was essential because the Sixth Brigade Etzioni was worn out from escorting convoys and from battles with the Arab irregulars fought in the daily effort to protect the various Jewish quarters. Moshe Dayan was away in the United States and had nothing to do with the defense of Jerusalem, the battle for the strategically critical Kastel, or the road leading to the city.

It was amazing and disturbing to learn from the press that Moshe Dayan was lionized in the United States as the defender and hero of Jerusalem. He arrived in the city after all the battles were practically over. The ones he directed, the attack on the Government House and on Beit Jalla, were unmitigated disasters. A very important lesson was brought forcefully to my attention then that one should not confuse issues with facts, and that the ability to manipulate the media is of critical importance. Moshe Dayan was the darling of David Ben Gurion and the epitome of the fearless and heroic new

Israeli generation. Therefore, he felt he was above conventions and accepted patterns of behavior.

Originally we assumed that it was the American press that had distorted the truth. With time we learned that it was Moshe Dayan who deliberately was spreading the story about Jerusalem and without any compunction took credit for accomplishments of others. This was a pattern he followed with great skill and flair for publicity to the end of his days. He unquestionably was a brilliant and personally courageous man. He was endowed with a quality of leadership that at times was exercised with a flash of greatness. He inspired confidence as was the case in the frightening days on the eve of the Six-Day War in 1967. He was also a totally amoral individual with a streak of cruelty, cunning, and scheming, using others to accomplish his objectives. He did not hesitate to force individuals to act on his behalf and then abandon them to the consequences.

The staff of the Sixth Brigade Etzioni was changed with the arrival of Moshe Dayan. We were not particularly sorry to see some of them go. For practical purposes the brigade was only a conduit of orders and an administrative framework at this stage of the war. The broad outline of the assignments was worked out in the general staff and was transmitted to the brigade for execution. The brigade in turn allocated parts of the assignment to the units involved. The choice of tactical solutions was left to the commanders in the field. "Konrad" (Mundek Pasternak, former commander of the Haganah commanders school) in the general staff was responsible for the broad outline of operational plans for the Central and Southern fronts. Israel Beer was responsible for the coast (the Tel Aviv–Haifa line) and the North. Both reported to the chief of operations, the young and highly regarded brilliant archeologist Yigal Yadin.

There were other changes made. Mart was the commander of Moria, the Sixty-first Battalion of the brigade, the counterpart of the Sixty-second Battalion. Before 1947 he was responsible for training cadres of the Haganah in the Jerusalem District. A Russian Jew, not very imaginative or sparkling, he was competent, brave, and inspired confidence. He, like Zaro, was careful in committing his unit to a battle. Nevertheless, the losses suffered in the siege of Jerusalem were horrendous. The Sixty-first Battalion Moria and the Sixty-second Battalion Beit Choron were not spared their share. However, it was recognized in both battalions that every effort humanly possible was made to limit losses to a minimum. Mart understood Jerusalem and its complex problems. One of them was the ethnic composition of the population, which included a large orthodox community, some of it openly hostile to Zionism and the State of Israel. A Hasidic sect originating in Hungary gathered in Mea Shearim carrying white flags to greet the Arab Legion, while we fought to prevent it from breaking into the city.

Mart had been with Dayan in Syria and had carried him out at considerable risk when Dayan was wounded by a sniper's bullet, which cost him an eye. It was assumed that Mart, Dayan's friend, would become his deputy, because no one knew better than Mart the complexity of the tactical problems of defending Jerusalem. To our amazement Mart was removed from the command of the Sixty-first Battalion Moria and was sent to take over a recently formed battalion of conscripts, an equivalent of civil defense. It was a strange and humiliating appointment that puzzled everyone. This too proved to be a pattern frequently repeated.

Visitors started to arrive in the city calling on Moshe Dayan. This was his old command, a hastily formed unit armed with machine guns mounted on jeeps, rather unruly and arrogant, arriving from the coastal plain. To impress everyone they removed mufflers from their vehicles, making them roar when accelerated. They wore Australian hats, scarves of many colors, and walked in sandals. It was a somewhat bohemian-looking crowd, living according to its own rules on the fringes of the Israeli fighting machine. We were preoccupied with other things and did not pay too much attention to these disturbing signs.

The battalion was slowly recovering from the long months in Bab el Wad. We were at last properly armed, and the early days of the war when there was only one rifle for three men were forgotten. Later after the siege of Jerusalem ended we received machine guns and mortars to support the infantry units as they arrived from abroad after the State of Israel was proclaimed.

Zaro, a bear of a man, was highly regarded and respected. He was curt but considerate and took excellent care of his men. Uzi, his deputy, a no-nonsense officer with an excellent sense of humor, had formerly been a sergeant in the Jewish Brigade. He was in charge of the logistical support essential for the combat readiness of the units.

David Shaltiel, the commander of the city, once came to the wireless station of the command post of the Sixty-second Battalion during the first battle for the control of the Kastel to address the beleaguered garrison. He started with a statement, "You eagles of the Kastel, the nation's eyes are on you. . . ." Uzi, then in command of the units engaging the bands led by Abdel Kadr el Husseini, the nephew of the notorious Mufti of Jerusalem, Amin al Husseini, interrupted him, "See to it that we get food and ammunition and don't bother us with nonsense." An expletive ended Uzi's response.

Meir Hafetz and Zvi Zellner, both company commanders, were completely different. Meir was a Sabra, cheerful, informal, competent, and liked by his men. Zvi Zellner, born in Germany, spoke Hebrew with a heavy accent and was always neatly turned out in freshly laundered and pressed khakis. He even polished his boots. A yellow-green commando scarf was always around his neck, a souvenir of the days when he had been a sergeant in the commando units of the British army led by Lord Mountbatten and a veteran of quite a number of combined operations. Zvi often looked at us, shaking his head and commenting that we were only partisans and it would take a long time, if ever, before we became real soldiers. He was fearless in battle, cool, and decisive.

David Shoham, a university student who commanded the support company, Shmuel Matot (the instructor in the officer's school of the Haganah responsible for Operation Or Dror), Miki Haft, and I completed the team. I had joined Zaro as his Intelligence and Reconnaissance officer in the winter of 1948 shortly after his arrival in Jerusalem. Zaro's newly started battalion was my third, because the other two had been decimated in the first two months of fighting. I refused a permanent command appointment because I had reached the conclusion in the early days of the battle for Jerusalem that it was safer to operate behind enemy lines with my scouts than to direct troops in battles planned by the staff of the brigade. Therefore, while the Sixty-second Battalion was led by a competent commander, it suited me nevertheless to serve as its intelligence and reconnaissance officer and to be given temporary assignments. Occasionally, I was ordered to lead a reinforced combat team, or to replace a killed company commander.

Orders arrived from the brigade to secure the Government House, formerly the seat of the British High Commissioner, which had been declared a "neutral zone" and handed over to the International Red Cross. We suspected that the Arab Legion occupied the beautiful gardens of the Government House and from there controlled access to the southern quarters of the city. I set up shop in Talpiot, a suburb of Jerusalem, adjacent to the Government House. My second in command, also a former student at the Hebrew University, was busy checking and correcting maps. At night accompanied by two scouts I sneaked into the grounds of the Government House and, as I expected, found emplaced machine guns and Legionnaires moving freely in the well-manicured gardens left by the British only a few weeks ago.

I checked the orders issued by the brigade to the battalion and signed by Dayan. They called for two companies to move on two axes along the ridge without entering the grounds of the Government House and then link behind it. This posed two problems. One was to check the maps and the distances to determine the feasibility of the two companies linking around the grounds of the Government House. The second was to determine whether the Arab Legion was stationed inside the "neutral zone." I invited Meir Heifetz to join me on another reconnaissance inside the "neutral zone," as his company was to move along the southern axis and would be exposed to cross fire if the enemy was inside the grounds.

At night we sneaked into the grounds of the Government House and confirmed the presence of the Legion there. Study of aerial photographs stolen from the RAF (Royal Air Force) showed that the ridge was much wider than it appeared. The ridge was carved by numerous little wadis. In Jerusalem the watershed passes through the city from South to North, making this plateau strategically critical, a fact recognized long before the three main monotheistic religions became obsessed with it.

I drew to Zaro's attention that the order as issued could not be executed because of the topography and the presence of the Arab

Legion in the premises of the Government House. The only practical way to accomplish what the brigade wanted was to occupy the Government House at the start of the operation and after removing the Legionnaires from its grounds to occupy positions on selected high points on the ridge. Zaro had discussed it earlier with Moshe Dayan, who had refused to modify the order.

I told Zaro at a staff meeting that it was preferable to refuse to carry out the order unless it was modified. He answered that a commanding officer has to give an example. Otherwise, it would be disastrous if every commander demanded to modify orders given to him. I admitted that he had a point, but expressed my opinion that the orders were issued by the brigade ignoring available intelligence. I reiterated that I had reconfirmed that the grounds of the Government House were occupied by the Arab Legion and that our units would find themselves in a crossfire from within the Government House and from without. We all failed to note that the order also included a paragraph stating that, should a retreat be dictated by circumstances, it had to be approved personally by the brigade commander.

The units left Talpiot as planned, and the battle unfolded as I foresaw. Meir Heifetz was killed by fire from the Government House and his company continued the futile effort to link up with the company of Zvi Zellner. Zvi tried to advance around the grounds of the Government House and he too got stuck. Normally, a unit would retreat at once in such circumstances to avoid additional casualties. On this occasion the retreat had to be personally approved by the brigade commander.

Moshe Dayan was nowhere to be found. We erroneously assumed that in view of the importance of the operation he either would establish a forward command post not too far from where the action was, or at least stay at the headquarters of the brigade. That was not the case. Moshe Dayan was finally found in the house of his mistress at three o'clock in the morning. A retreat was approved, but it was already too late. Zvi Zellner, forced to retreat in daylight under fire, succeeded in extricating most of his company. The battalion suffered sixteen killed, and over thirty wounded.

An efficient fighting unit, seasoned in many battles, forged by dedication and the effort of many, was badly mauled owing to carelessness. We were used to suffering casualties, as we had been in combat since March. However, the fiasco at the Government House was an unnecessary and an avoidable waste of human lives. In normal circumstances an inquiry would be arranged and most probably the brigade commander would be relieved. This was not the case, and Moshe Dayan decided to shift the blame to Zaro.

A few days later Dayan arrived at the battalion to discuss and summarize the operation. He drew a finger-like ridge on a blackboard and stated that, if the two companies had performed as ordered and met at the appointed place, the operation would have been a success.

Zaro took over and briefly summarized his views, stressing the location of the strong points of the Arab Legions forces. He was interrupted by Moshe Dayan, who denied that Legionnaires were inside the Government House. Zaro turned to me and requested that I report what I had learned during and after the attack. I took out a mosaic prepared from aerial photographs and described the topography of the ridge. I also stated that I had been inside the Government House grounds twice before the battle and found Legionnaires entrenched there. Moreover, after the operation failed I had removed bodies of our soldiers from the "neutral zone" under a temporary armistice arranged by Dayan through the Red Cross and with some difficulty avoided being taken prisoner by the Legionnaires. I had gotten out of there thanks only to a young Swiss officer, a Genevoise, who drove me and my two scouts out of the "neutral zone." Moshe Dayan without saying a word got up and left the room with his two aides.

A new company commander arrived to take over Meir Heifetz's company. Shimon Smaragd was a graduate of Sandhurst (the British equivalent of West Point) and on arrival in Israel had been sent to the Sixty-second Battalion. We were then responsible for the defense of the southern part of the city. Opposite our position on the other side of the deep Wadi Sarrar (mentioned in the Bible in connection with Samson) were units of the Moslem Brotherhood, volunteers from Egypt, equipped with old howitzers that were shelling the city. The next project of the brigade was to dislodge them and take Beit Jalla.

Shimon was stationed in Malcha in an abandoned Arab village facing the positions of the Moslem Brotherhood volunteers on the other side of the Wadi Sarrar. Zaro decided to inspect this sector, and after dinner we took off for Malcha. There we found Shimon ready to leave on a patrol to survey the area. He expected to be back in two hours. We decided to rest and to wait for his return. The scouts who were with him returned late at night reporting that Shimon had disappeared. To this day no one knows what happened to him.

I was ordered to take over Shimon's company, or what was left of it, after the Government House fiasco. There were in Malcha thirty-odd soldiers and two NCOs. We concluded that the line could not be held as there was no adequate manpower. Therefore, I moved two sections forward and ordered them to dig in and kept the third one with me as a reserve. A three-inch mortar with its crew was also attached to our unit by David Shoham. This setup provided me with the flexibility to counterattack if need be and secure time for Zaro to reinforce the sector.

A day or so later Moshe Dayan showed up unexpectedly in my command post. After listening to my description of the defense setup, he said that the arrangements were all wrong and demanded that changes be made forthwith. I politely replied that the arrangements had been worked out jointly with the battalion commander and were coordinated with neighboring units. Should he wish to change the defense setup, I would be pleased to comply. However, the order to do so had to come from the battalion. He left the command post, not saying a word. A few days later orders arrived from the brigade, transferring me to a civil defense battalion.[7]

I told Zaro that I would follow the example of Kantarshi, an NCO from Hadera, who had come with reinforcements sent to Jerusalem. After our arrival in Bab el Wad, Kantarshi had declared that war was dangerous and that he did not wish to fight. As no amount of persuasion worked, he was jailed. His reaction was that we all were foolishly risking our lives while he, Kantarshi, was in a safe place. He was sitting in the Abu Gosh Taggart station in a holding cell opposite my quarters. When bored he used to hammer his tin plate and utensils on the steel bars. I had to bribe him with cigarettes to be quiet so that I and my scouts could catch some sleep after a night behind the enemy lines. (Many years later I read some-where that Kantarshi had published a book describing the heroic battles he participated in Bab el Wad.) A jail seemed to be a rela-tively tranquil place in those days, as Kantarshi found out. I decided to follow his example.

Zaro came up with a different suggestion. He proposed that I take a two-week medical leave to "remove my tonsils." He proposed that I go to Tel-Aviv and call on Arie Simon, his friend from the Jewish Brigade, who was deputy director of Military Intelligence on the General Staff. He would provide me with a letter of introduc-tion, and, as there was a shortage of qualified personnel, there would be no difficulty in my finding a suitable appointment. He would keep the brigade off my back as long as he could, and afterwards I would be on my own. I agreed, and the next day I was on my way to Tel Aviv.

On the road from Jerusalem to Tel Aviv, passing the places where we had fought during the siege, I reflected on the events of the last two years since the *Fede–Dov Hoz* docked in Haifa in May 1946. I was then twenty-three years old and was caught once again in a whirlwind of history. I was embarking on a new adventure and did not have the foggiest idea where it would lead.

The bus travelled through Romema, past Motzas where I had been stationed in the early days of the war, the Kastel that had been so bitterly contested, and started the long climb toward Abu Gosh and its Taggart police station. The ride on the bus to Tel Aviv pro-vided the first opportunity to reflect on the events of the past few months and the direction my life suddenly had taken. My studies, resumed with considerable difficulty in the hope of building a future, had been interrupted. After participating in practically every battle fought in Jerusalem since the partition, all I had to show was desertion from the Sixth Brigade Etzioni.

The events before and after the battle for the Government House left me bitter and disillusioned. Meir Heifetz and I had been through a great deal together during the siege. He died because of a whim and incompetence, as did a combat engineer Itzhak Levy with whom I had been in several hot spots since the war started. Itzhak Levy, a Jerusalemite, a cheerful fellow assigned to accompany me on a number of operations, had always worn blue shorts, which he claimed brought him good luck. I saw his body spreadeagled on the fence of the Government House in front of the position of a Bren gun of the Legion. I identified him because of the blue shorts no one else was allowed to wear.

I had been shaken by the spectacle of the nameless survivors of the Holocaust marched callously into the fire of the Arab Legion in Latrun. At night in Malcha inspecting a foxhole on the outskirts of the village, I had heard someone crying. It was a Polish boy who hardly spoke Yiddish and no Hebrew. He was astounded when I addressed him in Polish. He was sobbing and with difficulty told me that he did not know what had happened to him. He was brought by ship to Haifa from a camp in Cyprus where he had been interned by the British, given a rifle, and the next day found himself in a battle. After wandering around, he was picked up by soldiers and brought here. He was lucky to be one of the few who had survived the attack on Latrun. I promised to help him. Regretfully shortly afterwards I was relieved from my post and could not keep my promise.

The bus descended through Bab el Wad, passing on the way the wrecks of the burned-out trucks and armored cars of the convoys that did not get through. I was greatly relieved to get out of Jerusalem. Years later I was reminded of this feeling seeing the movie *Mr. Roberts* with Henry Fonda. In one of the scenes, while sitting on the deck of the rickety supply ship on which he served and watching a task force consisting of an aircraft carrier and its escorting ships passing by, he remarked to the ship's doctor that it would be nice one day to join forces fighting a real war. He was dreaming of leaving the depressing environment of the supply ship. I was pleased to leave Jerusalem, the Sixth Brigade, and rejoin a real army fighting a different war. Or so I thought. It was yet again another illusion.

Serving with Zaro was a rewarding experience. We had met early in March 1948 shortly after his arrival in Jerusalem. Shalom B. was liquidating what was left of his battalion and thought that joining Zaro was a good idea. Although Zaro was only four years older than I, he was much more mature. He was respected and trusted by all who met him.

As an observer, he had accompanied a reinforced company of the Tenth Brigade Harel of the Palmach that attacked Nebi Samuel, a key strong point of the Arabs in a village high on a mountain controlling the approaches to Jerusalem. Posa, the commander of the attacking unit, was killed by a sniper in the middle of the battle. Zaro took over and skillfully led the unit out of the predicament. We were together in a variety of tight spots during the battle for Jerusalem. I never saw him tense or not in control of his emotions.

Travelling by jeep, after our return from Bab el Wad in July 1948 to Jerusalem, we went to inspect our position at Miss Kerry, a building on the top of a ridge over Ein Karim. It was probably named after a British missionary bent on repairing the world. We were compelled to cross an open stretch of a road exposed to the fire of an Egyptian machine gun in a fixed position on the other side of the Wadi Sarrar. As the gun was locked on the target, it could not miss. Therefore, one's luck depended on the degree of alertness of the gunner. In a way passing this stretch of the road was a version of Russian roulette. We stopped the jeep, took a deep breath, gunned the engine, and took off. When we arrived almost at the end of the stretch, the gunner started to fire but we were already out of danger. Zaro cringed and flattened himself on the steering wheel; he too had had enough.

The fiasco at the Government House was due to Zaro's battle discipline. He assumed that there were political considerations that forced Dayan to impose the limitation of not entering the "neutral zone." Little did he know Dayan. It did not enter Zaro's mind that during a battle a brigade commander would not be at his command post. He made this error of judgment only once. Subsequently, he challenged Dayan on several occasions in the course of the years. After my departure from Jerusalem, Zaro was transferred to join his friend Chaim Laskoff, who was in charge of the training of the Israeli Army. Zaro was appointed to the critical position of commanding the Israeli Army's first officers training school, the first of the newly formed Israeli Defense Forces. We remained in close contact. However, to my regret we never served together again. Years later while visiting Zaro in his kibbutz Maagan Michael, I told him that if he embarked on a political career I would join him. He became for a while a member of the Knesset (Parliament). He gave it up because the man was too honest to become a successful politician.

After reading the letter of introduction of Zaro, Arie Simon at the General Staff in Ramat Gan near Tel Aviv received me with open arms. There were many competent individuals and a number of scholars in his department. However, none of them had any combat experience. Most of them were graduates of the SHAI (Sherut Yediot), the intelligence arm of the Haganah, which concentrated on surveillance of the Mandate authorities, the programs developed by the British to stem illegal immigration, and following Arab affairs. The SHAI also tried to keep open channels of communication with Arab leaders and learn what they were up to.

Israel in 1948 was defending itself from a coordinated attack of the regular armies of neighboring Arab states. The intelligence requirements were of a different nature, for which the graduates of SHAI were not prepared. Therefore, I had no difficulty in obtaining a position and settled quickly in the General Staff.

A few days after my arrival at the General Staff, Mundek Pasternak, the former commander of the Haganah's commanders school, invited me to his office, opened a safe, and took out maps marked "top secret." These were plans for a major offensive prepared to break the Egyptian hold on the Negev. The Egyptian army had stopped at the kibbutz Negba, south of Tel Aviv, and was blocking access to the Negev from the Taggart police station in Iraq el Suidan. From Ishdud, or the ancient city of the Philistines Ashdod, Egyptian forces presented a potential threat to Tel Aviv, thirty miles away.

Mundek put all sources of available information at my disposal. My function was to activate these sources and collect specific information in such a way that the thrust of the plan and its details would not be disclosed. Consequently, I developed a program for each intelligence-gathering agency delineating a specific assignment. Only Yigal Yadin, Mundek, and a few other officers in key positions knew the details of the plan. In preparation for the offensive, I was given the responsibility for the Egyptian desk in the military intelligence unit of the General Staff.

The General Staff of the fledgling Israeli army in August 1948, located in a cluster of homes and villas on a hill in Ramat Gan, was an interesting if somewhat strange place. There a war was fought between 8 A.M. and 5 P.M. It was quite a change from the daily routine in a fighting unit. Operations, the heart of the General Staff, was located in a villa. On the upper floor was a large war room with walls covered with detailed maps of the front, as well as the offices of the chief of operations, Yigal Yadin, and his deputies, Mundek Pasternak and Israel Beer. Two secretaries and an officer on twenty-four-hour duty made up this compact but efficient team. The officer's responsibility was to sort and distribute incoming cables and messages according to their significance to the Prime Minister or the chief of staff, or pass them on for routine processing. This task was given to officers in rotation. Occasionally it was my turn to spend twenty-four hours in the map room. It was a disturbing and frightening picture at times. The Arab Legion was threatening Jerusalem and the access to it could be cut at any moment. The Iraqi army was in a position to cut Israel in two, because the narrow strip of land between Tel Aviv and Haifa was only about fifteen kilometers wide and the Iraqi positions were in what is referred to today as the West Bank. The Egyptian expeditionary army was stationed at the crossroads south of Tel Aviv, blocking the way to the South and the Negev.

Life on the hill in Ramat Gan was an illuminating experience. A large number of officers were strutting around in meticulously pressed khakis, all with pistols. This angered me, because there were no side arms for our combat engineers. As the combat engineers carried either satchels with explosives or mines, they had to have their hands free. Consequently, except for a knife they had no other weapons for self defense. A pistol, although useless in combat, could provide protection at night for combat engineers in the field. Armorers told us that there were no side arms available, but they seemed to be in ample supply for the military clerks fighting an 8 A.M. to 5 P.M. war at their desks.

There were three separate dining halls: one for officers, one for NCOs, one for other ranks. This too was an innovation, as in the tradition of the Haganah there were no ranks and everyone was called by his first name. My neighbor at an adjacent desk was from a prominent Tel Aviv family influential since the days of the Ottoman Empire. He arrived every day smartly dressed in slacks, a silk shirt with a tie, and on occasions in a well-tailored linen jacket. His excellent manners prevented his commenting on my attire. Nevertheless, he was disdainful of my faded khakis and scuffed boots, which had no top leather left to be polished after negotiating the stony hills of Jerusalem. He did not serve long on the General Staff. In the middle of the crucial battles for the survival of the State of Israel, this young and able-bodied man was sent to serve in one of the embassies abroad. I expected to return to the front as soon as possible and did not bother to outfit myself to emulate the elegantly turned out officers, strutting around on the hill with side arms to create a martial look.

I expected that in a week or two Dayan would look for me. Life in the Soviet Union and the service in the Polish Special Battalion had taught me lessons that remained etched in my memory. Before leaving the Sixty-second Battalion for Tel Aviv, I had prepared a folder with the brigade's order to secure the hill of the Government House, the reports of the company commanders to Zaro, and Zaro's report to the brigade, aerial pictures, and anything else I thought could be helpful.

My draftsman prepared copies of all these in a neatly organized folder. Shortly after arriving at the General Staff, with access to all files, I retrieved the original order issued to the central front for transmission to the brigade and also Dayan's report. I added these to my folder and waited for developments to unfold.

The space in the villa where Operations were located was rather limited. We sat squeezed at the few available desks. Due to the nature of my assignment, I shared the room with Arie Simon. One morning Yigal Yadin's voice came in on the intercom, "Arie, is there in your unit a young officer wearing glasses from the Jerusalem brigade?" "Yes," answered Arie. "The fellow deserted from his unit. Send him immediately to my office." Arie was perturbed and puzzled—after all I had come with a letter of introduction from my battalion commander. I picked up my folder and went upstairs. There in Yigal Yadin's office was Alex B., a combination of Dayan's assistant, personal secretary, and point man, who had come to escort me back to Jerusalem. Yigal came straight to the point and asked what I had to say. I replied that everything he might find of interest was in the folder.

In it Yigal found the original order issued by Mundek Pasternak that called for occupying the Government House. An identical text was transmitted to the brigade by Zvi Ayalon, the commander of the Central sector. The order issued by the brigade to the battalion modified the order, calling for completion of the task without entering the "neutral zone." The report of Dayan to Zvi Ayalon after the battle stated that Zaro modified the original order on his own initiative. There was no need to provide any further explanations, or show the aerial pictures. Yigal Yadin asked for references. I responded that Mundek Pasternak and Zaro would be pleased to provide additional details. I was told to return to my office and wait for instructions.

There was a great deal of curiosity and excitement downstairs, but no one asked what had happened. After some minutes Yigal again came in on the intercom, "Arie, let the fellow carry on."

The story was not over yet. Mundek called me and asked for a detailed description of what happened. He listened attentively and did not comment. I left the prepared folder with him and as far I was concerned the matter was closed.

There were some administrative matters to straighten out. As I had not been formally transferred from the Sixth Brigade to the General Staff, it was simpler to enlist me again. The quartermaster of military intelligence made the necessary arrangements. As a result, I had two personal numbers. One was 30577, the code three zero indicating that I had been originally a Haganah commander on its regular list transferred to the Israeli army. The new personal number issued in Tel Aviv was 33143, with thirty-three the code for the Military Intelligence Corps. This caused some confusion and had to be sorted out after the war.

Alex B. returned to the brigade without me. I resumed my activities at the General Staff and started to explore the possibilities of being reassigned back to a combat unit. Zaro would visit me from time to time as the office of Chaim Laskoff, to whom he reported, was in a villa next door. On one occasion he told me that a farewell was planned for him in Jerusalem. The Sixty-second Battalion arranged a "goodbye" parade, followed by dinner afterwards for the old-timers. Zaro invited me to join him and we travelled together to Jerusalem. It was a strange feeling to see my old friends and remember battles fought. Zvi Zellner and other officers on Zaro's request were transferred as instructors to the officers school and shortly afterwards the Sixty-second Battalion was only a name that remained from the proud unit commanded by Zaro during the siege of Jerusalem.

I stayed on at General Staff until the preparations for the next major offensive were completed. Then I was transferred as a liaison officer between the chief of operations, Yigal Yadin, and the commander of the Southern sector (Chazit HadArom), Yigal Alon.

During the day I and three officers who reported to me joined the brigades that were engaging Egyptian forces. We accompanied the fighting units all day long, observing the battle. In the late afternoon we either met to summarize observations, or kept in touch by radio. At twilight I was picked up by a Piper Cub and was flown to Tel Aviv to provide the chief of staff with a first-hand report. It was critical to keep the General Staff and the government up to date on the developments on the Southern front. Vastly improved means of communication facilitated the flow of information. Nevertheless, personal interpretation of the rapidly changing situation was essential to complement the cables received from the command post of the operation. This offensive was fought by mobile units utilizing long forgotten Roman routes and emerging from directions unexpected by the Egyptians. Israeli forces, after breaking through the Egyptian positions, penetrated deeply into the Sinai Peninsula. This created a delicate political situation, because British troops were stationed in the proximity of the Suez canal and could intervene on behalf of the Egyptians.

Yigal Alon, a personable and very able man, the commander of the Palmach, was directing this operation, Itzhak Rabin was his chief of staff, and an old pal of mine, Zerubavel Wermel, was the Intelligence officer of the front. I was delighted to be back in combat even if only as an observer.

The Southern front included the Palmach Brigades, the Tenth Harel, Eleventh Jiftach, and the Twelfth Negev. The Brigades Fifth Givati, Eighth and Third Alexandroni completed the battle order.

There were classmates of mine from the commanders school in all these units. I ran into Bren leading the brilliantly executed attack on an Egyptian brigade occupying Temila, Jerucham Cohen was an aid of Yigal Alon commanding the Southern front, Ghandi (Rechaveam Zeevi, minister in one of the Israeli governments) and Raanana were there, as was Moshe Kelman, who had executed the legendary long-range raid on Sasa in the Galilee to destroy the bands assembling there in the early stage of the war. I was especially pleased to encounter the Tenth Brigade Harel to which I had been attached during the critical stages of the siege of Jerusalem.

One day Moshe Dayan, accompanied by his aid Alex B., visited the Southern front. The battle for Jerusalem was over, and Dayan had little to do except to meet regularly with Colonel Abdalla Tal of the Arab Legion. Thus he took the initiative of negotiating directly with the Jordanians, allegedly to streamline the battle lines. However, in effect he usurped the function of the Foreign Office. Although this offered a certain element of publicity, the main show was elsewhere. No one paid much attention to him, as we all were too busy. We greeted each other politely, but no other word was exchanged.

After the Operation Ayin (Auga, Abu Ageila, El Arish, in December 1948-January 1949) in the Negev was over, I succeeded in convincing Benjamin G., the head of the Military Intelligence, and Arie Simon, his deputy, to let me go. I was transferred to join a command team consisting of Lt. Col. Benz Frieden, his chief of staff Iti Amichai, and Danny Dagan in charge of operations. This team was sent to take over and reorganize Third Brigade Alexandroni, badly mauled in Iraq Suidan by the Egyptian forces. I was delighted to be out of the General Staff and back in the field.

The Third Brigade was guarding remnants of an Egyptian division locked up in the Faluja pocket commanded by Brigadier Mohammed Said Taha Bey, a black Sudanese and a brilliant and a courageous man. His intelligence officer and my counterpart was Major Gamal Abdel Nasser, and one of the Egyptian companies in Faluja was commanded by Captain Anwar al Sadat. The revolution that subsequently overthrew Farouk, the king of Egypt, was hatched in the Faluja pocket, where all the key protagonists were trapped by the Israeli Army for several months.

I stayed with the Alexandroni Brigade as its G2 (Intelligence officer of the brigade) until the end of the hostilities in the late spring of 1949. Demobilization commenced, and I decided to continue in the regular army. I was appointed the first commanding officer of the combat intelligence training center.

General Chaim Laskoff assembled a small team responsible for the development of plans for the future Israeli defense system (Tzevet Hahafala), and a number of experts were asked to join it. I was fortunate to be among them. Those were busy and rewarding days, as they presented the opportunity to be part of a team planning the future Israeli army and developing its combat doctrine.

A special accelerated program for senior commanding officers was organized to assist them in the transition from leading an irregular force to directing a fledgling army with quickly growing artillery, air force, and eventually armored units. I was privileged to be invited as one of the lecturers in the newly organized General Staff School. One of my responsibilities was to introduce techniques of employing combat intelligence before, during, and after a battle. Among the participants in the program were senior commanders, including Moshe Dayan, Tzvi Ayalon, the commanding officer of the Central front, and other key commanders of the Israeli army in 1949-50. In the time allotted to me I was to review the function of combat intelligence on a battalion and brigade level. I chose the attack on the Government House in Jerusalem in 1948 as the backdrop for my presentation.

The technical staff of the school prepared a sandbox with the details skillfully presented, using cardboard, wires, cotton, and paint to recreate a miniature reproduction of the battlefield. My presentation concentrated on the techniques employed to gather information.

The story of the attack on the Government House and Dayan's treatment of Zaro was well known to the audience. Among them were commanders directly involved with the Jerusalem front. I avoided any mentioning of the order given or a discussion of tactical solutions employed. My comments concentrated exclusively on the utilization of passive and active sources of information available on the brigade and the battalion level, the reconnaissances executed, observations reconfirmed, and a summary of procedures with suggestions for improvements. This indirect message conveyed in an impersonal and technical presentation was understood by the audience. Moshe Dayan did not react to my completion of the presentation, similar to that which had been rudely interrupted by him during his visit to the battalion after the battle in Jerusalem in August 1948.

My last assignment before leaving for the United States in 1952 to complete my studies was to participate in a major maneuver of the Israeli Army as an umpire. Its objective was to test mobilization procedures, logistic support, communications, and transportation facilities of the army. The plan called for an attack to be launched by the armor of the Southern Command led by Moshe Dayan on the forces of the Central Command defending the approaches to Tel Aviv led by Zvi Ayalon. The carefully calibrated program set a timetable for a series of predetermined lines to be crossed by the armored units of the Southern Command. This limitation was deliberately introduced to prevent concentration on tactical solutions, as the objective was to test the systems.

I was appointed by General Chaim Laskoff to the small and select umpire corps whose task was to analyze the results of these maneuvers. We knew the details of the plan and were able to cross the "front" lines freely. At the zero hour the Central Command was put on alert, mobilized its units, and started to unfold its procedures. Moshe Dayan crossed the first line on the appointed date and suddenly, ignoring the imposed timetable, accelerated his attack northward, throwing into chaos the forces of the Central Command trying to respond to rapidly progressing armored columns of the Southern Command. Moshe Dayan and his forward battle command post disappeared, and neither the General Staff nor the umpires were able to get in touch with him. The chief of staff, Yigal Yadin, was livid and complained that millions of Israeli pounds and the effort of many were wasted because of the irresponsible behavior of Moshe Dayan. The usually calm and collected archaeologist was so infuriated at a staff meeting that he broke a pencil stabbing the spread-out map while making his point to the officers directing the exercise.

I commented to umpires in the presence of other officers that I could not comprehend the behavior and the objectives of Moshe Dayan. The next morning on the wireless on my jeep came a message inviting me to lunch with Moshe Dayan at his forward command post and providing coordinates of where to find him. I located his forward command post far more advanced than the position assigned to him by the plan of the maneuvers. His armored units were incessantly raiding the forces of the Central Command, which were thrown into confusion. Piper Cubs attached to him were releasing leaflets over the troops with the message, "Remember that it is preferable to be a live dog than a dead lion! Come to us and surrender! A hot bath and excellent food are waiting for you in our camp." Needless to say, all this infuriated the Central Command and frustrated the General Staff, which was thwarted in its objective of testing the logistic system.

Moshe Dayan and his forward staff were sitting on the ground in front of a canvas serving as a table in a corner of a cactus hedge. The usual rations were served, and while we were eating Dayan summarized the battle order of the Southern Command and issued orders for the next day. Then he turned to me and commented that the purpose of maneuvers was to test the systems in conditions as close to real combat as possible. Once a battle has started unexpected developments occur. The ability of forces to respond effectively to surprises is the real test of their readiness, and only surprises will draw attention to the weaknesses of procedures and systems.

I listened attentively without committing myself. His objective was to have me relate the comment to Yigal Yadin and Chaim Laskoff. It was also an olive branch extended to me. His arguments made sense, as indeed the confusion introduced by Dayan's departure from the original plan brought into focus a few fundamental issues requiring correction. I could see a certain logic in his argument. I repeated Dayan's comment to Yigal Yadin and Chaim Laskoff. However, I was not entirely convinced that the way chosen by Moshe Dayan to make his point suited the occasion.

Shortly afterwards in January 1952 I left for the United States, sent by the Israeli Army to study economics and political science. Although I was rather young I had been charged with critical responsibilities. I felt that I must complete my formal education if I wished to stay in the Israeli Army as a professional. I was admitted to Columbia University without any difficulty, after presenting the graduation certificate obtained in Poland and the transcript from the Hebrew University in Jerusalem. The only problem was to demonstrate that Roman Matkowski and I were the same person. In 1953, after completing the requirements for an M.A. degree in the School of Political Science of Columbia University, I returned to Israel to resume my duties. While in the United States I met my future wife Olga and we were married in May 1953.

Shortly after my return in September 1953 from the United States, I invited Zaro to meet Olga. We were newly married and arrived in Tel Aviv from a honeymoon in Europe. Zaro greeted me with a bombshell. While we were on our honeymoon Moshe Dayan was appointed the new Chief of Staff of the Israeli Army. Zaro let me know that he had resigned from the army and was returning to kibbutz Maagan Michael. The news disturbed me, because I did not expect Dayan to be appointed to this critical post.

The controversy surrounding him was spreading. Dayan's style and behavior hardly inspired confidence among seasoned professionals. Mundek left for the École de Guerre in Paris. I had no choice as I served in the army bound by a contract. Technically I was an officer on active duty assigned to the Military Intelligence Corps. In effect, I was attached to a special school for high government officials with the responsibility for the part of the program dealing with military science. Its director was Dov Harari, and David Kimche (future director general of the Ministry of Foreign Affairs) was responsible for the program on political science and economics. The objective was to present in a capsulized form an introduction to the disciplines and the bibliography essential in carrying out duties in the high positions in which the participants already served. I had no contact whatsoever with Moshe Dayan and I was pleased to be left alone to complete my assignment. After its completion I resigned from the army.

Moshe Dayan was a complex individual and his record and impact are well known if not always accurately interpreted. He was unquestionably able, gifted, and personally courageous. His competence as a strategist and military commander can be seriously questioned. The raid on Lydda in 1948 (an Arab town near the Ben

Gurion airport), described by him in a professional monthly *Bama-chane*, reflected reckless and impetuous activity. Its success can be ascribed to a variety of reasons but not sensible or responsible employment of his forces. He undoubtedly had charisma and a certain magnetism. All this was overshadowed by erratic behavior at times, intrigues, and the use of individuals put under duress to engage in activities to forward his objectives. The forgery of documents in the Lavon case[8] carried out by others on his instigation is a typical example. The carefully cultivated myth that he was a hero of the defense of Jerusalem is fiction. He was not involved in any way in the battles for the access to the city and the defense of the city during the siege. In 1956 during the war resulting from the seizure of the Suez Canal by Gamal Abdel Nasser, the Israeli task force responsible for the brilliant victory was commanded by a number of seasoned generals, among them Zaro. Dayan again managed to take credit for the achievements of others.

The spectacular victory in 1967, the Six-Day War, was a result of years of planning, systematic gathering of intelligence, and superb leadership of field commanders in charge of the task forces. Dayan's appointment as Minister of Defense on the eve of the battle was of critical importance as it restored the sagging morale and strengthened the confidence of the population. However, it had little effect on the operations.

Toward the end of his life he became less and less important and his style of life and challenging of accepted patterns of behavior made him increasingly controversial and eventually irrelevant. This story is restricted to a description of one episode by a participant and an eye witness. It was a minor and long-forgotten link in a chain of events. However, the sight of the spread-eagled dead soldiers of the Sixty-second Battalion on the fence of the Government House is etched in my memory.

I met Moshe Dayan for the last time in 1962 in Jerusalem. I travelled with Father Michel de Lattre, the Vice Postulator of the cause of beatification of Metropolitan Andrew Graf Szeptycki. We were interested in locating documents and witnesses related to the assistance extended by the Metropolitan during World War II to the Jewish community in Lwów. We stayed at the Hotel President in

Jerusalem. In the elevator of the hotel on my way to my room I unexpectedly met Moshe Dayan escorting a woman. We pretended that we had never met before.

He was a complex and twisted individual. Today he is almost forgotten. His impact at the time was felt in Israel, and it contributed among many other causes to the erosion of idealism. Idealism could not be maintained for prolonged periods of time at a pitch seen in the 1940s in Israel. Nonetheless, a small country in a precarious geographical, demographic, and strategic position cannot afford intrigues, corruption, infighting, and controversy. These are destructive anywhere, anytime. Israel, threatened from the first day of its existence with annihilation, could ill afford the intrigues and Byzantine schemes of this man.

CHAPTER 7

The Story of a Saint

LADISPOLI IS a popular resort by the sea in the vicinity of Rome. In June 1959 it was quiet with the beaches empty. The standard of living in Italy after World War II still had not permitted a large portion of the population to leave the city for summer resorts. My wife, Olga, Father Michel de Lattre, and I sat in front of a trattoria under a huge eucalyptus tree discussing my forthcoming testimony in the cause of beatification of the Metropolitan Andrew Graf Szeptycki.

We had arrived there in the morning from Rome and were going through the official acts of the postulation prepared by Father Michel to determine which points in it I should address in my testimony. Olga, a lawyer and a member of the State of New York Bar, grasped at once the nature of the procedure, which after all was a legal process. Father Michel, the vice postulator of the cause and a canon lawyer, found it easier to convey to Olga the importance of certain points. I was too emotionally involved in the issues and, having had no previous legal experience, required explanations to prevent me from taking off into subjects dear to me but irrelevant to the procedure. After a long and exhausting session, Father Michel and Olga were satisfied that I was on the right track. The table was set and lunch was served outdoors in the shade of the large tree, taking advantage of the beautiful day.

The encounter with Father Michel, the vice postulator of the cause of beatification of Metropolitan Andrew in Rome, had culminated in this long working session in Ladispoli. It was a turning point in the years of my generally futile efforts to generate interest in this extraordinary man to whom I owed my life.

An odyssey that commenced at age fourteen on September 1, 1939, with German bombs falling on Lwów had carried me through an extraordinary series of adventures, mostly sad and tragic, ending in May 1945. The search for a direction and ways to rebuild my shattered life was influenced by the Metropolitan Andrew and his brother Clement. Andrew showed compassion and made arrangements that saved my life and the life of my brother. Clement was in effect my guardian and in frequent meetings he always subtly outlined possible avenues I could take after the war was over, if I survived it.

He stressed that no effort should be spared to complete my education, which he pointed out would be the best way to start a new life after the war. He stressed the critical importance of adhering to fundamental values. He pointed out to me, as he did to the Studite monks, that it is easier to adhere to values in one's home, or in the environment of a monastic community. The real test, he always reminded us, would come once an individual was alone and had to depend on his own spiritual resources. He never proselytized, satisfied that I was a believing individual and adhered to a set of values. These comments were made to me during my frequent visits to the palace-residence at Jur during my stay at the monastery of St. Josaphat at Petra Skarhy Street, where I worked in the library.

The daily life in the Studite community for over two years and the contact with individuals who followed the lead of Ihumen Clement were equally important factors in my formation during these critical phases of my life. The atmosphere of the Studite community and the values permeating it were a backdrop for the guidance I was privileged to receive from Clement. I left them in 1944 for a series of adventures that eventually landed me in Israel. After ten turbulent years I was still guided by a rudder, yardsticks of comparison, and a sense of direction given to me by Clement.

Before leaving Lwów for Lublin after the arrival of the Red Army in 1944, I was asked by Ihumen Clement to contact church authorities if I ever reached the West and to report on the situation of the Uniate church and the events in Lwów. After the outbreak of hostilities in 1939, Jur maintained more or less regular contact with Rome.

Father Peters, a German member of the Studite Order, acted as a courier between the Metropolitan and the papal nuncio in Berlin, Ceasar Orsenigo. As a German citizen (Reichsdeutsche), Father Peters was free to travel without restrictions. However, after his arrest by the Gestapo in 1942, all contacts between the Metropolitan and Rome were cut. From then on only an occasional Italian officer returning from the eastern front on his way to Italy, who stopped at Jur to pay his respects to the Metropolitan, carried oral messages to the Curia Romana.

On my arrival in Lublin in the summer of 1944, I called on a monastery of the Bernardine Fathers and asked to see the superior. I assumed that there I would be able to get assistance to pass news from Jur on to Rome. I was instructed by a monk at the gate to go to the church and wait there. After a while two monks arrived and joined me in a pew.

I introduced myself and explained the purpose of my visit, assuming that I would be asked to the reception room outside the clausura, as was the custom, where we would have more privacy. When I mentioned the name of the Metropolitan Andrew Szeptycki, their attitude visibly changed. They explained to me that they had no interest in the subject and were not in a position to extend any assistance. I stressed that it was important that the messages I was entrusted with be conveyed to the church authorities, as persecution of the Uniate church has started. I was coldly told that they were not familiar with the matter and that the subject was beyond the scope of their activities. Later attempts made after the end of the war to contact Polish church authorities in Warsaw and Krakow produced the same results.

After weeks of wandering through postwar Europe as a DP (Displaced Person), I reached Rome in October 1945. I located the Collegium of St. Josaphat, or Collegium Ruthenum (papal seminary for Ukrainians of the Byzantine Rite) on the Gianicolo and rang the bell of a massive wooden door. After a while a doorman inquired who I was. As I speak Ukrainian fluently, I was invited into a large barn-like guest room with practically no furniture in it except a few chairs and some benches. On one of the walls hung an enlarged photograph of the Metropolitan Andrew. This was an encouraging sign. Two priests walked in, and we sat down in a corner of this cold and forbidding room. I introduced myself and explained the purpose of my visit. The priests asked some perfunctory questions. It became obvious that they had no interest in the subject, and after a while I gave up.

The priests told me that before I left I must see the wonderful doors carved by the former members of the SS Division Galizien staying in Rimini. (The SS Division Galizien had been formed in 1943. Remnants of it were interned after the war in Rimini.[1]) These heavy wooden doors leading to the chapel were carved in a typical Ukrainian design frequently found in the Carpathian mountains. The priests were enthusiastic about these wonderful young men and their deeds. Now it was my turn to be uninterested.

I left the Collegium Ruthenum, somewhat surprised to have encountered a reception quite similar to the one accorded to me at the monastery of the Bernardine Fathers in Lublin. The enthusiasm at the Collegium Ruthenum for members of the notorious SS units, many of them former Ukrainian policemen involved in the massacres of Jews, was disturbing indeed.

Before I left Lwów, Ihumen Clement had suggested that if I ever reached Rome I should contact Eugene Cardinal Tisserant. I located him at the Congregation of Eastern Churches. After waiting in the *ante camera* (formal waiting room) of the impressive Palazzo dei Convertendi on Via Concilliazione, I was ushered into the Cardinal's office.

Eugene Cardinal Tisserant was a small man, dressed in a black cassock with red piping, with a red cap on his head quite similar to the one worn by orthodox Jews. He received me graciously and on hearing the name of the Metropolitan Andrew Szeptycki his face lit up. Tisserant was then the Prefect of the Congregation of Eastern Churches and was familiar with the problems faced by the Greek Catholic church. He listened attentively to my report. As lunchtime approached I was asked to return the next day to continue. He inquired whether he could be of assistance to me. I thanked him politely for the offer and declined. I was pleased to have had an opportunity to carry out my mission, and I did not think that at that moment it was necessary to accept his kind offer. I assumed that declining an offer of assistance would give greater credibility to my mission. Besides the experience with the Catholic Church in Poland and at the Collegium Ruthenum made me suspicious and cautious.

After arrival in Israel my major preoccupation was to make ends meet, to learn Hebrew, and to keep up with my studies. The book I had written in Lido di Roma was published in Israel by Am Oved (publishing house of the Histadrut). It was called *Aliti Mi Spezia* ("I Arrived from La Spezia"—the title was chosen by the publisher) and included a chapter on the Metropolitan Andrew, and a separate one on the Studites. Shortly after my arrival in Israel events started to unfold with dizzying speed, culminating in partition and war. There was little time or opportunity to generate interest in Metropolitan Andrew and his assistance to the dying Jewish community in Lwów.

It was only after arrival in the United States in 1951 that I could again explore the possibilities of interesting Jewish organizations in this extraordinary saga of assistance. I contacted the American Jewish Congress, the Anti-Defamation League of the B'nai B'rith, and others. I found no response whatsoever. Furthermore I discovered that the story of the Holocaust was equally of limited interest. On several social occasions I was asked where I had been during the war. The attempt to respond to this question evoked an occasional comment that equally hard times had been experienced in the United States. There had been difficulties in obtaining gasoline, nylon stockings, and occasionally even butter. I gave up any efforts to communicate on the subject of the Holocaust.

In 1952, while in the United States studying at Columbia University on a grant from the Israeli army, I discovered that Studite monks from Luzky were in Woodstock, Ontario, and among them was Father Marko. During Easter vacation, I travelled from New York to Canada and was delighted to meet Father Marko, Brothers Joseph, Filotej, and Laurentij, and Deacon Teofan Shewaha. It was an emotional reunion, and it was great to see my friends again.

We picked up the threads where we had left them. From Father Marko I learned of his and Fathers Peters' efforts to start a popular movement in the refugee camps in Germany in support of the beatification of Metropolitan Andrew Szeptycki. He published articles and in the DP camps distributed pictures of the Metropolitan with a little prayer. This movement took off like a brush fire among the Ukrainian refugees in Germany, Belgium, and France. I assumed that the Ukrainian community in Canada and the United States led by the Greek Catholic bishops would pick up the thread. I returned to New York and to my studies full of enthusiasm and hope.

Olga and I left New York for Israel in 1953, where I rejoined the army and concentrated on my assignment. We were newly married, and it took time before we settled into a semblance of normal life. Soldiering lost its luster for me once Moshe Dayan became the chief of staff. Most of my old friends had left the army, and I was not too eager to embark on a civilian career in Israel.

On completion of my assignment in Jerusalem I submitted my resignation to General Benjamin G., then my superior. A variety of offers were made to find an assignment that would provide a challenge and would be of interest to me. This attempt eventually extended to a career in the Ministry of Foreign Affairs or the Ministry of Finance. I greatly appreciated the kind efforts of my friends and superiors. However, I was tired, I was not prepared to lead, and I realized that the development of the country was in the hands of individuals whose values I did not share. It was not a question of a disagreement, or criticism, or disappointment. It was a divergence of views, expectations, and interpretations.

I was proud to have been part of the effort to build and to defend the State of Israel. It had started in La Spezia, which led to service in the Haganah, and eventually a career in the Israeli Army. However, now the time had arrived to change direction and address myself to finding my way in life free from the terrible responsibility of leading others. The decision to leave Israel was a difficult and a painful one. I realized that if I stayed there I would eventually be either corroded or corrupted. The inner struggle was difficult; an assured and exciting career was open to me because of the contribution I had made in the war of 1947-49 and in a variety of key positions afterward. The start of a new life and in a new country at the age of twenty-nine was a formidable task, and I was not sure I would be able to manage it.

I was fortunate to be encouraged, supported, and guided in this difficult time of decisions and adjustments by my wife Olga.[2] She was born in Lwów and came to the United States in 1939 as a child.

She combined ideas and values similar to the ones observed in my home. She had the benefit of a broad education and the influence of an Anglo-Saxon civilization that formed her and gave wings to her abilities and extraordinary intelligence. She was familiar with my background, could comprehend the experience of the Holocaust and the life with the Studites, and could cope with the challenge of a new life for her as a wife of an Israeli army officer on active duty.

After our return to the United States from Israel in 1955, we visited Father Marko in British Columbia, where he was then serving as a parish priest in Vernon, B.C. Listening to our conversation reminiscing on the Metropolitan Andrew and Ihumen Clement, she commented that we both were lucky men because at one time in our lives we had been privileged to touch the stars.

After settling in New York, I resumed my efforts to interest the Jewish community in the assistance extended by the Metropolitan to Jews in Lwów during the Holocaust. Only Filip Friedman, a historian and the author of a book *Their Brother's Keepers,* followed the story with a great deal of interest. He put me in touch with Professor Michael Vetuchiw, then editor of the *Annals of the Ukrainian Academy of Science.* Professor Vetuchiw was a prominent Ukrainian scholar from the Great Ukraine (Velyka Ukraina, not Western Ukraine, a part of Poland before 1939) who had escaped from Kiev to the West after the occupation of Ukraine by the Germans in 1941. Eventually, he and his family emigrated to the United States.

We met at Columbia University where Professor Vetuchiw taught. I outlined to him the story and inquired whether he would be prepared to include it the *Annals of the Ukrainian Academy of Science.* His response was that Jewish-Ukrainian relations represent a delicate subject. Nevertheless, the truth had to be adhered to, and an historical record is of critical importance even if it should portray the attitude of the Ukrainians toward the Jews in an unfavorable light. I was impressed by this highly cultivated and far-sighted man. I had written the article with Olga's assistance, as my English was still not up to the requirements of this task. Professor Vetuchiw reviewed it, made minor corrections, and it appeared in the next issue of the annals.

Shortly afterwards I was invited to meet Professor Vetuchiw on a beautiful Sunday spring morning in New York's Riverside Park near his apartment. On the sidewalk of Riverside Park were assembled his friends, acquaintances, and his family. Professor Vetuchiw suffered from cancer, and this was the last opportunity to say farewell to this great man. Professor Vetuchiw greeted everyone and exchanged a few sentences. It was a beautiful Indian summer day. Those who were gathered there were survivors of the horrible purges in the Ukraine in the 1930s. A remnant of an almost destroyed intelligentsia, they were mostly scholars and scientists, colleagues of Professor Vetuchiw at Columbia University. I was included in the gathering because of my tribute to Metropolitan Andrew Szeptycki. Professor Vetuchiw and his friends were Orthodox Christians. Nevertheless, they fully appreciated the greatness of the Metropolitan Andrew and the contribution he had made to the Ukrainians.

The article in the *Annals of the Ukrainian Academy of Science* stirred interest in the life of Metropolitan Andrew Szeptycki in a variety of quarters and brought me in touch with the postulation of the cause of beatification. I received requests for permission to reprint the article in a number of publications in Europe and in Canada. I was pleased to see it widely distributed and allowed it to be printed provided that the text was reproduced verbatim. The Basilian Fathers in Canada reprinted it in their publication *Svitlo* without my permission, made some adjustments in the text, and added an offensive anti-Semitic introduction. A threatened legal action compelled the Basilian Order to reprint it verbatim again with an apology. A letter arrived in the spring of 1959 from the postulator of the cause of beatification of Metropolitan Andrew Szeptycki, Father Michael Hrynchyshyn, a Redemptorist priest, inquiring whether I would be prepared to testify in the process. My positive reply started an interesting chain of events and made it possible for me to make a contribution to the cause of beatification of this extraordinary man.

A great deal has been written and will be written about Metropolitan Andrew Szeptycki. He was a scion of an old family that had followed the Eastern or Byzantine Rite. However, it was quite customary in the Commonwealth of Poland for the leading Ruthenian families to switch to Roman Catholicism. Thus Andrew was born a Roman Catholic in a family deeply steeped in the Polish tradition. His grandfather, Alexander Fredro, was a well-known playwright; and other members of this prominent family made considerable contributions in a variety of fields.

The young Andrew dedicated his life to the service of others, joined a monastic order, became a priest, and subsequently a bishop. On the suggestion of Pope Leo XIII he returned to the rite of his forefathers and addressed himself to the spiritual renewal of the Uniate or Greek Catholic Church.

The Ruthenians, later known as Ukrainians, one of the three nations of the Polish Commonwealth, had drifted away from Poland after the extinction of the Jagiellon dynasty in the sixteenth century. The country was subsequently ruled by a variety of elected foreign kings who were less sensitive to regional and ethnic differences. The Chmielnitzky rebellion of 1648 represented a watershed in the relationship of these two nations.

The chasm deepened with time, and a tragic chain of events led to increasingly bitter fratricidal conflict following World War I. The oppression of the Ukrainian minority by the Polish government in the 1930s, and the bloodbath encouraged by the Germans during their occupation of Poland and Western Ukraine in World War II, were the backdrop for the final tragic phase of the Metropolitan's life.

The diocese of the Metropolitan Halicz and Archbishop of Lwów was located in a region where two interpretations of Christianity met. The Western Slavs, the Czechs, and the Poles were evangelized by Rome and followed the Latin tradition. Most of the Western Slavs had been systematically destroyed by the German invasions to the east at the turn of the first millennium. The threatened Poles stopped the onslaught by accepting Latin Christianity with the assistance of the Czechs. Their king, Boleslaw Chrobry, received a crown blessed by the Pope, which was brought to him by a delegation of bishops from Rome in the year A.D. 1025, legitimizing his reign.

Eastern Rite Christianity, known as Orthodox, was introduced into Rus, later known as Ukraine, from Byzantium by the ruler in Kiev, Valdemar or Volodymyr, probably a Viking. The then-powerful Byzantine Empire was expanding its influence throughout Asia Minor and north to the Rus. Religion was a powerful political tool and provided legitimacy to the rulers. The two rites, Latin and Greek, of a split Christianity met on the borderline of Poland and Ukraine, adding religious conflict to a smoldering ethnic one.

A splinter of the Eastern Rite (Greek or Orthodox) church active in the rather liberal Commonwealth of Poland signed articles of union with Rome in the sixteenth century. The historical background for the articles of the Union signed in Brest Litovsk in 1596 and reasons for it are analyzed and described in great detail in books dealing with the history of this period. The reasons were primarily political and economic, as this rather important part of the Orthodox Church had to function in the Commonwealth of Poland and was governed by its laws. The Eastern Rite Church, united with Rome, thrived for a while in the liberal Commonwealth of Poland, which consisted of three nations: Poles, Lithuanians, and Ruthenians (later referred to as Ukrainians). The Poles and the Lithuanians were Roman Catholic, while the Ruthenians were divided between the Eastern Rite Catholics, referred to at times as Greek Catholic, and Orthodox (not in communion with Rome). The disintegration of the Polish Commonwealth, the protector and the sponsor of the Greek Catholic Church, brought with it persecution and martyrdom to its followers.

The Tzars and Russia became a successor to Byzantium after the fall of Constantinople in 1453. The Russian Orthodox Church and Tzars made every effort to obliterate the Greek Catholic Church, which was perceived as a Latinized and wrong version of Eastern Christianity presenting a threat of spreading the influence of Rome. Interestingly, this did not prevent the chauvinistic Polish church from treating the Ruthenian followers of the Eastern Rite united with Rome for centuries with equal hostility if not contempt. This conflict between the Western and Eastern interpretations of Christianity, always present in the Slavic world, varied in intensity, depending on the leadership of both churches at the time. After the partition of Poland in the eighteenth century, most of the Uniates or Greek Catholics found themselves in Austro-Hungary, for those times a relatively liberal political entity. The Uniates in the part of Poland annexed to Russia were brutally persecuted and their church eventually obliterated.

Young Szeptycki stepped into this difficult environment and dedicated his life to building a bridge between Western and Eastern Christianity, to the spiritual renewal of his church, and to improving the lot of his impoverished and downtrodden flock. His contribution to the welfare, education, and cultural life in Western Ukraine equaled his pastoral activities. All this is amply reflected in the writings he left and in the archives of the postulation, which are a rich legacy of the man and his contribution to the people of Western Ukraine.

He commenced his pastoral activities at the end of the nineteenth century when the political climate was conducive to building bridges and defusing conflicts. The collapse of the Austro-Hungarian Empire in 1918 accentuated ethnic and religious conflicts, which were subsequently cultivated and encouraged by the Third Reich in preparation for the onslaught eastward unleashed on September 1, 1939, with the attack on Poland.

The Metropolitan Andrew was suspected by Ukrainian nationalists of supporting Polish interests. The Poles considered him a traitor, and the Polish church was openly hostile, seeing him as an obstacle to the Latinization and the assimilation of the Ruthenians. The Curia Romana was suspicious of his interest in bridging the chasm between Western and Eastern Christianity. The Soviets and the KGB accused him of collaborating with the Third Reich and harboring political ambitions to become a ruler of a fascist Ukraine. The French denounced him during World War I as an Austro-Hungarian spy and arrested some of his collaborators.

This controversy continues to this day in a variety of quarters including the Yad va'Shem (a research institute dedicated to the documentation of the Holocaust) in Jerusalem. This Israeli institution seems to have difficulty in recognizing the man's compassion and assistance extended to the Jewish community in his diocese at the time of its martyrdom and destruction.

The man was loved and revered by all who came in contact with him. His church, thanks to spiritual renewal and his guidance, survived forty-five years of persecution by the Soviet regime and emerged from the underground strong and vibrant. His ideas of bridging the two Christianities, a guiding motive of his pastoral activity, are reintroduced now in Eastern Europe to cope with the crisis of values and the collapse of Marxist-Leninist ideology. He was the only church leader who had the courage to protest the horror of the Holocaust in his pastoral letter "Thou shalt not kill," which was issued in 1942 and warned of the consequences of participation in the persecution of Jews. His contribution and impact can be seen in the United States and Canada, where he organized the religious life of the Ukrainian emigrees.

Metropolitan Andrew died on November 1, 1944, observing his life's work destroyed by the war and its consequences. His church was dissolved by the Soviets, driven underground, and its leaders, monks, priests, and nuns, deported to labor camps in Siberia. His legacy was treated with indifference by the Ukrainian bishops in the West. Nevertheless, the popular movement in support of the beatification of the Metropolitan Andrew was started after World War II in the DP camps in Germany by Fathers Marko Stek and Johannes Peters. The deep affection the deportees and refugees from Western Ukraine had for this unique man of a Mosaic stature sustained the postulation. A comprehensive archive has been assembled that preserves the legacy of the Metropolitan.

Arrangements were made for me to appear before the Ecclesiastic Tribunal in Rome in June 1959 as a witness for the postulation. This phase of the process is normally conducted in the diocese of the deceased, which was Lwów. As the diocese had been destroyed by the Soviets, the Pope permitted the first phase of the process to be conducted in Rome, the Pope's official diocese.

On arrival in Rome, I contacted the vice postulator, Father Michel de Lattre, and we met at the Hotel Quirinale to discuss my testimony. Father Michel, a Frenchman, pondered what motivated my interest in the postulation. Olga, educated in the United States, was influenced by a Protestant way of thinking and therefore was somewhat suspicious of the Curia Romana. I had difficulty in understanding why a Frenchman and a Latin priest should be interested in this somewhat obscure cause.

We sorted out all these questions and, having clarified our respective positions, addressed the subject of my testimony. Father de Lattre informed me with some embarrassment that the process had been suspended by the Pope because of the intervention of Stefan Cardinal Wyszynski. The argument advanced by that Polish churchman was that the Metropolitan was a controversial figure involved in politics, and the present situation in Poland made the process undesirable. Father de Lattre mentioned that, possibly with the assistance of Eugene Cardinal Tisserant, the difficulty could be overcome. He was surprised to learn that I had met the Cardinal in 1945 in Rome, and we agreed that I would visit the cardinal to reestablish contact.

Eugene Cardinal Tisserant had met Metropolitan Andrew and Ihumen Clement, and as the Prefect of the Congregation of Eastern Churches was familiar with their work and ideas. A French priest, Father François Charon, had been stationed in the Middle East at that time and, interested in Eastern Christianity, became fascinated with the ideas of the Metropolitan and decided to join him in his ambitious projects. A close friendship had developed, and all three kept in touch for many years. Cardinal Tisserant followed the activities of the Metropolitan in the Congregation of Eastern Churches, while Father Charon was invited by the Metropolitan Andrew to act as his official representative at the Curia Romana. During World War I, the French arrested Father Charon, accusing him of being an Austro-Hungarian spy because of his involvement with the Metropolitan Andrew, an Austro-Hungarian subject and a member ex officio of the Parliament in Vienna. This enraged Father Charon, who after his release changed his name to Korolevskij and spent the rest of his life in Rome, never returning to France, but representing in Rome the interests of the Metropolitan and the Uniate church.

The archives in Father Korolevskij's possession were the nucleus of the postulation. The two dedicated friends of the Metropolitan, Cardinal Tisserant and Father Korolevskij, were responsible for giving the postulation a formal framework.

The Uniate bishop residing at the Collegium Ruthenum, Ivan Bucko, who had assisted the Metropolitan in his diocese before World War II, was an opponent of the Metropolitan. Driven by jealousy, he created circumstances that resulted in his own removal from Lwów. After a short stay in New York, which he had to leave because of pro-German sympathies, he settled in Rome. There he represented the interests of the Uniate Church for many years. Although he provided some support for the cause of beatification, his primary interests were elsewhere. He was preoccupied with extending assistance to former members of the SS Division Galizien, and he sheltered the assassin of Chancellor of Austria Dolfuss, Dr. Otto Wachter, the governor of the District Galizia in the General-gouvernment of Hans Frank.[3] Dr. Otto Wachter was a war criminal responsible for the destruction of the Jewish communities in Southern Poland.

A postulator appointed by Bishop Bucko, Father Peter Kreusa-Rzewuski, had known the Metropolitan, and probably was a well-meaning individual. Regretfully, he was somewhat unstable and had settled in Llandulas in Wales. From there he attempted to conduct the affairs of the postulation. In these circumstances the postulation would have died, as many such causes of beatification do after the original enthusiasm and support wear out.

Father Michel de Lattre, a priest from the diocese of Paris, had been attached to the United Nations as an observer for the Curia Romana, with special interest in the internationalization of Jerusalem. Having completed his mission in New York, he returned to Rome to find a new assignment. Eugene Cardinal Tisserant, whom he knew personally, suggested he review the cause of beatification of Metropolitan Andrew Szeptycki while waiting for his new assignment. He was introduced to Father Korolevskij, who befriended the young priest and put at his disposal the archives that were kept at his residence.

Father Michel de Lattre, a French aristocrat, became interested in the cause of beatification because of the suggestion of Cardinal Tisserant. The friendship with Father Korolevskij provided an introduction to the full scope of activities of Metropolitan Andrew. The guidance of Father Korolevskij was critical in providing Father de Lattre with insights. Father Korolevskij died in 1959 shortly after the formal opening of the process, leaving the archives to Father de Lattre in his will, as he did not trust the Ukrainian clergy at the Collegium Ruthenum.

The scope of activity of the Metropolitan and his ideas as reflected in the documents fascinated the French priest, who started a systematic review of the archives of Father Korolevskij and the documents pertaining to the Metropolitan that could be found in the Congregation of Eastern Churches. Father de Lattre, trained in canon law, was ideally suited to take over the cause. He was appointed vice postulator of the cause, and he located a young promising Redemptorist, Father Michael Hrynchyshyn, a Ukrainian born in Canada whom he met while he was completing his studies in Rome. Father De Lattre suggested that Father Hrynchyshyn be appointed the postulator of the cause, because sensitivities of the situation made it imperative that the postulator be a Ukrainian.

This started a partnership that produced the most constructive phase in the evolution of the postulation. A French priest, well versed in the ways of Rome with excellent connections, and a young Ukrainian, born in Canada and free of the complexes these people brought with them from the old country, together launched this complicated cause. The acts of postulation were prepared by Father de Lattre and the formal opening of the cause took place on December 5, 1958, in Rome. Matters were progressing satisfactorily until the intervention of Cardinal Wyszynski stopped the process.

Father de Lattre decided to take advantage of my arrival in Rome to reopen the process. An audience with Pope John XXIII was arranged for Cardinal Tisserant accompanied by Father de Lattre, at which a petition was presented asking the process be reopened to make my testimony possible. It was stressed that I had arrived from New York at my own expense to testify, and it would be embarrassing to inform me that the process was closed. It was also stressed that the testimony of a Jew in this cause was of special significance. These were times when the silence of the Church and Pope Pius XII during the Holocaust was under scrutiny and criticism. A play by a German writer R. Hochhuth, *The Deputy*, was stirring a lively debate and causing criticism of the lack of any reaction by Rome and the silence of Pope Pius XII while this crime against humanity was perpetrated. My testimony offered to bring into focus a stand taken by Metropolitan Andrew on the Holocaust and his effort to save at least a number of individuals.

The Pope granted permission to reopen the process to make it possible for me to testify. This was great news for the three of us and, on that nice day in Ladispoli at the seashore, we completed the preparations for my deposition. We once again went over the acts of postulation, identifying the points I could address in my testimony.

On the appointed day the three of us drove in Father Michel's old Citroen to the Tribunal of Rome. We parked the car in the courtyard of the massive old building in the center of the city. We were escorted by ushers to a waiting room, and I was called in to the large chamber where the tribunal (court) was in session. A massoretic Bible (Hebrew text of the Bible) and a hat, (by custom a Jew covers his head while praying or taking an oath) were waiting for me at the witness stand, and I was sworn in.

Behind a massive table sat the President of the Tribunal and two judges, one of them a Pole, Msgr. Marian Strojny. The court's interpreter translated the questions and my answers. The first question posed by the president of the tribunal was whether I was a practicing Jew. I found the question somewhat unusual and not to the point. Msgr. Strojny, observing my reaction, alerted me that, unless I was a God-fearing individual and practiced the precepts of my religion, my testimony would be of little value to the cause. I was pleased that at least one of the judges was favorably disposed to the cause and had an understanding of the background. His questioning was indeed helpful and allowed me to elaborate on the pertinent points in my testimony.

The first phase of the testimony concentrated on the description of the assistance extended to the Jewish community by the Metropolitan during the Holocaust. From the questions posed by the President of the Tribunal and the other judge, I realized that they had no knowledge of the historical background, and the assistance extended to Jews was of secondary importance to them. I shifted the emphasis of my testimony and briefly outlined the political, economic, and social circumstances prevailing in Western Ukraine during the life of the Metropolitan.

I described the causes of the conflict between the Ukrainians and the Poles, which was exacerbated by developments after World War I. I concentrated on the role of the Metropolitan in making every effort to bridge the gap between the two nations, to reduce tension, and his persistent warnings that violence in any form is self-defeating. I stressed the dedication of the Metropolitan to union with

Rome and his untiring effort to bridge the differences between Western and Eastern Christianity. I concluded that my observations were that of a neutral observer, as I was neither a Pole nor a Ukrainian.

The President of the Tribunal asked why as a Jew I was interested in the beatification of Metropolitan Andrew. My answer was that the sanctity of the man was recognized by Christians and Jews during his lifetime. The Jews demonstrated their respect for the Metropolitan by greeting him carrying the Scrolls during his frequent visits to towns and villages where Jews were living next to Ukrainians. Any effort to preserve the legacy of the man and make his ideas and accomplishments known was a worthwhile undertaking, and I was pleased to make a contribution to it. I handed them a prepared summary of my comments, which covered some of the subjects discussed in my testimony. This concluded the formal session of the Tribunal.

The three of us, Olga, Father Michel, and I, breathed a sigh of relief after my testimony was over and continued over an excellent lunch in a typical Roman trattoria near Fontana Trevi. This was the start of a remarkable friendship that continued after Father de Lattre's resignation from the position of a vice postulator of the cause and until his premature death in 1976.

I was particularly pleased to learn that after the deposition Msgr. Strojny told Olga that my testimony was important for the cause. He was a broad-minded individual favorably disposed toward the cause of the Metropolitan Andrew. Msgr. Strojny had been a rector of the Papal Polish seminary in Rome, an equivalent of the Collegium Ruthenum. He was abruptly removed by Cardinal Wyszynski from his post and replaced by an individual more representative of the militant, chauvinistic, and somewhat narrow-minded Polish church. The Curia then arranged for him to become a judge of the Rota, the highest court of the Church. In later years he often joined Olga and me for dinner at the Hotel Quirinale during our frequent visits to Rome. He was a tall, elegant man always wearing a Roman cassock with red piping and wearing old fashioned leather shoes with silver buckles. Our standing in the hotel increased considerably because we were entertaining as distinguished a member of the Curia Romana as Msgr. Strojny.

The process that was reopened to take my testimony was not closed, probably because of a deliberate oversight. Other witnesses were called to testify and documents were presented as evidence to the Tribunal. However, Cardinal Wyszynski again intervened during one of his frequent visits to Rome, having learned that the process continued. He petitioned the Pope, asking that the process be closed. He advanced the argument that the Metropolitan had been involved in politics and his actions were controversial. A similar objection was formally presented by the KGB-controlled Russian Orthodox Church on the grounds that the Metropolitan had collaborated with the Nazi regime and was directly responsible for atrocities committed against Soviet citizens (a term used by the Soviet government to describe the Holocaust).

The hostility of the Soviet authorities to the Metropolitan did not surprise me. However, the attitude of the Polish church, and in particular Cardinal Wyszynski, who had known the Metropolitan personally, was difficult to explain and understand. Cardinal Wyszynski in 1962 obtained another suspension of the process through his intervention at the Holy Office.

Father de Lattre, well versed in the ways of the Curia Romana, knew how to overcome these obstacles, and the process proceeded without much difficulty for a number of years until the arrival in Rome of Archbishop Joseph Slipyj,[4] successor of Metropolitan Andrew, who had been released from prison by Khruschev as a gesture to the Pope. He later obtained the removal of this second suspension after he arrived in Rome and requested to testify in the cause. This changed the situation somewhat and introduced new elements into this complicated cause, which I will discuss later.

After my return from Europe to New York following my testimony, I was requested in 1959 to organize a foreign department of a brokerage firm on Wall Street. This was very timely because it called for frequent travelling to Canada and to Europe, which facilitated contacts helpful to the cause of beatification. It also provided the opportunity to befriend the new postulator, Father Michael Hrynchyshyn, then a superior of a Redemptorist monastery in Winnipeg. I was to play a different and constructive role for a number of years. The postulator was born in Canada and his knowledge of the historical, political, economic, and social evolution of Poland and the Ukraine was limited and derived from studying the documents in the archives. Father de Lattre, a Frenchman and a Roman Catholic priest, had difficulty at times understanding the mentality of the Slavs and the intricate and complicated relations between the Poles and the Ukrainians. I was born in that part of the world and spent twenty years of my life in Central Europe. I had lived as a Ukrainian and as a Pole. Therefore, I was in a position to provide insights and explanations that clarified a variety of issues encountered in studying the complex relationship between the Metropolitan and the Polish church, and the equally complex relationship between the Metropolitan and his flock. The surrealistic and perverted environment in which the Metropolitan had to function in the last years of his life was not easily comprehended by a Ukrainian brought up in an Anglo-Saxon civilization, or a Frenchman whose mind was formed by the best Western European culture had to offer.

These years were the most productive in the evolution of the postulation and contributed to building an almost complete archive of the Metropolitan's writings, correspondence, and other related documents.

Father de Lattre, in addition to a systematic search for documents in the archives of the church, extended his research to archives throughout Europe, trying to locate information and documents related to the wide range of activities of the Metropolitan outside of his diocese. Olga, Father de Lattre, and I went to Vienna in spring 1960 in the hope of finding documents in the archives of the Greek Catholic parish of St. Barbara.

Vienna in 1960 was still a sleepy Central European city dreaming of its past. Only a short while ago, it had been a divided city with the Soviets occupying a part of it. It tried to forget the short euphoria of the Anschluss in 1938 when huge red flags with swastikas decorated the ancient St. Stephen cathedral, and later the horror of the war, bombing, and the Soviet occupation of Austria. It had drifted back into the memories of the Austro-Hungarian Empire, Vienna of the turn of the century. Walking through the narrow streets of the old city, one could indeed have the illusion of being in Vienna of the good old Habsburg days.

We stayed in a hotel in the Theresianum district near the residence of the papal nuncio. Our first contact in Vienna was Dr. Dzerowycz, whose father had been a canonic at Jur. (Greek Catholic priests according to the articles of the Union, like Orthodox priests, could be married) Dr. Dzerowycz had lived in Vienna since the 1930s. After the arrival of the Red Army in Vienna, he was called to attend a sick Soviet colonel. He disappeared, to return ten years later from a labor camp in the Soviet Union after Austria regained its independence. Mrs. Dzerowycz, a brave and determined woman, was left with three small children. She somehow had managed all these years, and fortunately the family was eventually reunited. The Dzerowycz family lived in a suburb of Vienna not too far from the villa of Katherine Schratt, a famous opera singer and a mistress of the Emperor Franz Joseph. We were warmly received there. However, we were not encouraged by the comments made by Dr. Dzerowycz about St. Barbara.

The next day Father de Lattre and I called on the parish priest, Father Gavlicz, a Basilian monk. We were received by him practically in the corridor of the parish and were informed that there were no records at the parish house and therefore he could not be of much assistance. It was very hard for me to accept that in this parish that had escaped the ravages of war intact no publications or documents were available that could be of interest to the postulation. We invited Father Gavlich and his vicar for lunch the next day and left the parish rather discouraged.

The Austrians, like the Germans, are addicted to keeping accurate records. Lwów was an administrative center of the Province of Galizia and Lodomeria in the Austro-Hungarian Empire. The clergy of all denominations were part of the bureaucratic system. I suggested that it might be useful to check whether in the state archives there were documents that might be of interest. Father de Lattre visited the papal nuncio and through his introduction secured for us access to the "secret" archives of the Austro-Hungarian Empire. There in an old building, probably erected in the days of Maria Theresa or Joseph II, we found a veritable gold mine. To our amazement all the records of the Austro-Hungarian Empire were kept in perfect order, gathering dust on shelves. Officials in gray coats were delighted that someone showed interest in the archives. The records were intact until November 1918 when the Empire ceased to exist. In one of the rooms we found files of the Ministry of Religious Affairs and records relating to the Greek Catholic Church. There were literally hundreds of documents of interest to the postulation that we asked to photograph.

Among them Father de Lattre discovered a communication of the Apostolic Emperor of Austria to the Pope nominating Andrew Graf Szeptycki for appointment as cardinal. Apparently it was a privilege accorded to the Emperor of Austria to appoint cardinals. The communication was dated August 1, 1914, a few weeks before Metropolitan Andrew was arrested by the invading Russian troops and deported to Russia, where he spent the war years imprisoned in a monastery until the revolution.

We followed this lead to the Parliament, assuming that there we would also find documents of interest. Indeed at the Parliament we found all the speeches the Metropolitan Andrew had made addressing the Parliament on many occasions as a member ex officio. This proved to be another gold mine as the speeches clearly reflected the concern and the effort to reconcile the ethnic conflicts intensifying in his diocese. Our trip to Vienna was successful even if the visit to St. Barbara did not produce results. In the mornings we sat in the archives sifting through the dusty folders identifying documents to be copied, and in the afternoon and on weekends we enjoyed the sights of this lovely city.

It was a pleasure to wander through the streets of the old city, to visit the museums, the many churches, and stop at Demel's for coffee and cake. Vienna was not yet overrun by tourists and offered a great deal. The Sparrow Mass by Mozart sung by the Vienna Boys Choir in the Hofburg chapel, followed by watching the Lippizzaner horses performing in the Spanish riding academy, and a lunch at Gosser Bier Keller or the Kapuziner Keller on a Sunday were memorable experiences. The opera season was on in the rebuilt Staatsoper and so were the performances in the Volksoper.

The *Bartered Bride* by Smetana at the Staatsoper and the *Merry Widow* at the Volksoper completed our sightseeing program. Father de Lattre was hesitant to join us, as in those times in Rome priests were not allowed to attend public spectacles. After a discreet inquiry during a visit to the papal nuncio, he was encouraged to see an opera and an operetta. It was only suggested that he wear a tie and not a priestly collar.

Passover was approaching and Father de Lattre tactfully inquired whether this was the time of the year when Jews are required to repudiate Christ. I was taken aback by this statement and inquired where he had learned this nonsense. Father de Lattre mentioned that this had been discussed once when he was in the seminary.

As the first seder was the next day, I suggested that I could organize a service, and he would be able to see what it consisted of. Father Michel readily agreed. Olga and I went to the Jewish community and obtained a Hagadah with a French translation and a box of matzah. Then in town we gathered the other necessary ingredients.

As the evening approached Father de Lattre was more and more uneasy. He apparently was apprehensive that he might have accepted an invitation to participate in a cult that could offend his beliefs. Olga set up a traditional seder plate with some limitations as not all the required ingredients were readily available. I said the blessing and started the narrative of the Exodus, followed by a meal and a thanksgiving service. Father de Lattre relaxed and finally joined us in reciting the psalms. He realized that he was attending a service identical to the Last Supper described in the Gospels. There was nothing in it that could be offensive to anyone. The service was held in the apartment occupied by Father de Lattre at the hotel because it had a sitting room. The next morning the maid probably was puzzled to find Jewish prayer books and matzah in Father de Lattre's quarters.

Father Gavlicz mellowed somewhat and invited us to attend the Easter service at St. Barbara. The old baroque church, a veritable architectural jewel, was filled to capacity. The service was conducted in the Eastern Rite's Slavonic version with a superb choir accompanying the priest. Closing my eyes I could recall the services at the Studite monasteries that seemed so long ago. After the services we were shown the grave of St. Josaphat, a bishop of Polotzk, martyred for his support of the union with Rome. The coffin had been secretly taken away by U.S. troops on the request of the Ukrainians a few hours before the Soviets came to remove it. It was flown to

Washington, where it was stored for safekeeping at the Library of the Congress. Subsequently it was returned to be interred in Rome under an altar in St. Peter's Basilica. Nevertheless, the changed attitude of Father Gavlich did not result in providing access to the archives of St. Barbara.

The preoccupation of the Soviet government with the Greek Catholic church had prompted an attempt to remove and probably to destroy the relics of this martyr in the cause of the Union with Rome. It also prompted the production of a movie portraying the Metropolitan as a power-hungry manipulator and collaborator with the Nazi invaders. Several articles were written on the subject by "historians," and a book was published describing the life and activities of Metropolitan Andrew. In it he was portrayed as an intriguant driven by unbridled ambition. In it there is a brief comment describing my cooperation with the Metropolitan in his efforts to destroy the Jewish community in Lwów.

On my return to the United States I tried to interest Jewish organizations and Roman Catholic clergy in the process of beatification of Metropolitan Szeptycki, again without any results. Calling on the Ukrainian bishops I was surprised to encounter indifference and at times hostility to the cause. Only Metropolitan Maksym Hermaniuk, the Archbishop of Winnipeg, who extended much assistance to the postulation, showed a keen interest in its progress.

The postulation was successful in securing documents and records illustrating the activity of the Metropolitan until the year 1939. After the outbreak of the war, channels of communication were broken and the records had to be painstakingly reconstructed. The testimony of witnesses was of critical importance, as in those tragic days it was difficult and possibly dangerous to keep records. The postulation had difficulty securing the cooperation of the Ukrainian bishops in gathering witnesses and documents.

The testimony of Father Marko Stek was obtained in a somewhat superficial way at the chancery of the Greek Catholic bishop in Edmonton. The official taking the testimony, Father Laba, was not familiar with the procedure. He had served as a chaplain of the SS Division Galizien, had little interest in the cause of beatification, and belonged to those who resented this great man. The testimony of Father Johannes Peters was secured in a similar fashion at the chancery of the Greek Catholic bishop in Munich. These priests had been the closest collaborators of Ihumen Clement and had played key roles at Jur during the war years. Their critical testimony was secured by officials who had little interest and no experience in legal matters. Other potential witnesses were either never called or their testimony was secured in a fashion that made them of little value. Precious years were wasted and slowly witnesses died and memories faded of events that had occurred long ago.

Nevertheless, the postulation progressed, thanks to the dedicated effort of the postulator Father Michael Hrynchyshyn in Winnipeg and the vice postulator Father de Lattre in Rome. It was fortunate that the postulation was domiciled in the Eastern rite province of the Redemptorist Fathers. This Order was dedicated to the memory of the Metropolitan, and its then provincial supported the activities of the postulation and provided a domicile for the archives. Its monasteries in Canada and the United States assisted Father Hrynczyshyn in his work and in the popularization of the cause among Ukrainians living in North America. The General of the Order in Rome, Father William Gaudreau, an American, became interested in the cause and was favorably disposed to it. This support was of critical importance and in contrast with the indifference of the Ukrainian bishops. It also gave Father Hrynchyshyn the freedom to act as a postulator.

Father de Lattre organized and expanded the archives, catalogued the contents in a systematic fashion, and followed the procedures of the first phase of the process. He befriended a prominent canon lawyer in Rome specializing in causes of beatification. Mr. Giulio Dante, highly competent and experienced in the ways of the Curia Romana, provided advice and guidance in the preparation of briefs and supporting evidence for future reference, responding to the various accusations and criticisms that could emerge in the second phase, the apostolic process, of this intricate legal procedure.

Archbishop Bucko residing at the Collegium Ruthenum provided support and a small monthly stipend of fifty dollars paid to Father de Lattre. It was of critical importance that he not interfere in the activities of the postulation because of his connections in the

1

Curia Romana. He was always friendly and courteous to Father de Lattre and me. The postulator provided financial support, which paid for secretarial services and legal expenses connected with the conduct of the cause in the tribunal. Father de Lattre supported himself by preparing other causes of beatification. The years of his painstaking anonymous work were donated because of the dedication to the memory of the Metropolitan Andrew and belief in the ideas and values he represented.

My professional activities called for frequent travel to Europe and Canada. This facilitated the development of many contacts that assisted the postulation indirectly. Anti-Semitism after the Holocaust was dormant. The interest and the support of a Jew for the cause of beatification attracted attention. I regularly visited Archbishop Ivan Bucko at the Collegium Ruthenum, Cardinal Tisserant at the Vatican library, Archbishop and subsequently Cardinal Coussa and Msgr. Rizzi at the Congregation of Eastern Churches, the Jesuit Fathers Reas and Horacek at the Pontifical Institute of Oriental Studies and Russicum, and the General of the Redemptorist Order, Father Gaudreau. These visits made together with Father de Lattre contributed to obtaining broad support in influential circles in Rome at that time.

The interest in the cause generated subtly and skillfully by Father de Lattre helped greatly to offset the occasional interventions of the Polish church to have the process closed. As the contacts between the Curia Romana and the KGB-sponsored Russian Orthodox Church developed in the 1960s, so did the possibility of a negative impact of their intervention on the cause of beatification of the Metropolitan. Persistent efforts were made by Zagorsk, a KGB-sponsored center of the Russian Orthodox Church, to obstruct the process of beatification while the brutal persecution of the Greek Catholic church in Western Ukraine continued.

In 1963 a cable arrived from Olga while I was travelling as a member of an American delegation in the Far East. She alerted me that Archbishop of Lwów and Metropolitan of Halicz Joseph Slipyj, the successor of Metropolitan Andrew, had been released from a Soviet prison and accompanied by Cardinal Willebrand had arrived in Rome. This was electrifying news indeed, and I sent a cable from

Hong Kong welcoming the Archbishop. His appearance at the Second Vatican Council made a great impression and produced many expectations. These regretfully have not materialized.

After several meetings with Joseph Cardinal Slipyj I realized that it would be difficult for me to communicate with him. He remembered me from Lwów and brought regards from a parish priest in Rawa Ruska, Father Blavatzky, in whose home I had spent a few days before crossing the border to Poland. Regretfully, the many years of imprisonment, while failing to break the man's spirit, had left a mark on his personality. This was exacerbated by the advisors surrounding him, who injected controversy and discord, and greatly complicated the reasonably friendly relations of the Greek Catholic Church with the Curia Romana.

Father de Lattre after encountering Cardinal Slipyj recognized that he would not be able to continue as a vice postulator. We met on the French Riviera where he was a guest of his family. There we discussed the desirability of his resignation. Olga and I supported his decision to resign from the postulation. He was a frail man and the aggravation connected with the postulation had started to affect his health. Besides we had the example of Father Johannes Peters, a German Studite, who was almost defrocked because of intrigues and calumnies woven by German bishops assisted by the Collegium Ruthenum. The situation of Father Marko was equally precarious. The position of a foreigner among Ukrainians without a strong sponsor was always rather delicate. The unexpected removal of Cardinal Tisserant from the Congregation of Eastern Churches, the death of Father Korolevskij, and the untimely death of Cardinal Accacio Coussa left Father de Lattre rather isolated. His resignation was certainly a loss for the postulation. However, he remained in close contact with the postulator and assisted with guidance and advice wherever he could. The archives were assembled and catalogued, and testimony of witnesses was secured.

An impressive and reasonably complete record of the Metropolitan's activities since his early days as a bishop of Stanislaviw until his death in 1944 was assembled. Thousands of documents were authenticated at the house of the Redemptorist Order on Via Merulana in Rome, and properly bound were deposited at the

Congregation of Rites by the postulator. Shortly afterwards Msgr. Hrynchyshyn was abruptly dismissed without any explanation by Cardinal Slipyj.

The Cardinal's interest lay elsewhere. He appointed a former member of the SS Division Galizien who had subsequently become a priest as the new postulator. This ended any meaningful activity and accomplished what Cardinal Wyszynski and the Russian Orthodox Church had failed to do. Twenty years later the postulator, who had not done a thing to advance the cause, was finally removed. However, a new one has not yet been appointed.

The years of effort produced an almost complete archive documenting the ideas and the contribution of the Metropolitan Andrew Graf Szeptycki. The collapse of the Marxist-Leninist ideology brought an end to the persecution of the Greek Catholic church in Western Ukraine in 1989. Literally out of modern catacombs a vibrant church emerged with bishops, priests, monks, and nuns. It had preserved the legacy of the Metropolitan Andrew and survived half a century of persecution. Its encounter with the materialistic west is another matter. That has produced new and different trials in the still fragile political environment of Western Ukraine.

Political capital is made today in some quarters, taking advantage of the popularity of the Metropolitan Andrew. Those who either attacked him, or at best ignored his teachings, lately have become active using his name as a rallying point for a variety of causes, some of which the Metropolitan fought against all his life. These political causes are presently introduced by interested parties, sometimes under the guise of religion, to the inhabitants of Western Ukraine. Regretfully, this partisan activity contributes to tension and discord, as the ideas of the Ukrainian émigrés in the United States and Canada do not always coincide with the views prevailing in Western Ukraine freed from the yoke of Soviet domination.

Msgr. Michael Hrynchyshyn, the former postulator, presently the Apostolic Exarch to Ukrainians in France, during a visit to Lwów discovered a complete archive of the Greek Catholic Church carefully preserved and catalogued by the KGB. Every scrap of paper, including personal exchanges between the Metropolitan Andrew and his brother Clement, were located. It will take years of research to complete the work accomplished painstakingly at considerable personal sacrifice by Father de Lattre. It is ironic that the KGB showed greater interest and care in preserving the records of the Metropolitan than did the Ukrainians in the West.

The ideas of Andrew Graf Szeptycki, Metropolitan of Halicz and Archbishop of Lwów, are as valid today as they were in his lifetime. They are universal and point the direction for pursuing the spiritual renewal essential to the survival of the civilization of Western man. A bridge between the Christianities of the West and the East, which the Metropolitan foresaw as a mission of his church, but which remained only a dream during his lifetime, became a possibility with the collapse of the Marxist-Leninist ideology in the Soviet Union.

I am grateful for the opportunity I had for a while as a young man to live in the Metropolitan's shadow. I am equally grateful for the opportunity to make a contribution to the preservation of his ideas and join the many splendid individuals I was privileged to meet and befriend over the years of association with the postulation of the cause of beatification of Andrew Graf Szeptycki.

Roma, 4 via Giovanni Prati
June 26, 1961

Dear Mr. Lewin,

I thank you very much for your letter of June 18th and for the article on Archbishop Sheptytsky and the Jewish Community in Galicia.

The article is very interesting. In the circumstances of the second World War the Metropolitan was always a great man.

Many thanks for your congratulations. It was a splendid coincidence that my election occurred exactly on the 25th anniversary of my elevation to the College of Cardinals.

Please accept my best wishes and believe me

Very sincerely yours,

+ Eugene Card. Tisserant

A letter received from Eugene Cardinal Tisserant acknowledging congratulations on his election to the Académie Française.

CHAPTER 8

The Story of Three Lives

THE EVENTS described in these three stories occurred almost half a century ago. The world around us is rapidly changing and so are our perceptions. The Romans had a proverb, "Tempora mutantur et nos mutamur in illis." (Times are changing and we are changing with them.) The values and yardsticks permeating society today will make this story of the three intertwined lives strange and difficult to comprehend. These are the days of the antihero, materialism, and success as measured by yardsticks entirely different from those employed by the three protagonists of this chapter —a Ukrainian, a German, and a Frenchman. All three were motivated by the same objectives, followed the same ideas, and dedicated their lives to the pursuit of the truth. All three paid a high price for their endeavor. Did they achieve what they set out to attain at the start of their journey through life? The answer depends on one's point of view and the values one pursues.

The first story deals with the life of a Ukrainian, Marko Stek. We met in 1942 in Lwów at the monastery of St. John the Baptist in Lyczakiw, a suburb of the city. From then on our paths crossed over the years, and in strange ways we were reference points for each other going through respective trials with which life presented us.

I was demobilized from the Polish army in the summer of 1945 and was determined to get to the West, assuming erroneously that assistance, compassion, and understanding were waiting there for the survivors of the Holocaust. I was equally determined to take Marko with me. He was one of the few close associates of the

Metropolitan Andrew remaining in Poland. As Ukrainians were routinely deported to the Soviet Union, it was only a matter of time before he would be arrested. The persecution of the Uniates had already started in Western Ukraine, and all indications pointed to a Soviet determination to destroy this church with its strong historical ties with Rome.

My life had been saved by this church, which had offered me and many others shelter. Now it was my turn to reciprocate by assisting Marko. It never occurred to me that the ideas of the Metropolitan would be rejected or ignored by the Uniate church in the West. Neither could I foresee that Marko was exchanging one exile for another. I saw him emerging in the West as a leader of his church, spreading the teachings and the values of the Metropolitan Andrew. I did not anticipate that he would be thwarted by a multitude of spiritual and intellectual dwarfs.

As a young man, Marko (the Ukrainian version of the name Mark) Stek had been a trainee in a bank. Handsome, always cheerful and outgoing, well-educated, he had a bright future ahead of him. He came from Rohatyn, a small service town in Western Ukraine. His parents were well-off landed peasants with roots in a part of the country where the soil is rich, the peasants are comfortably off and follow centuries-old traditions. Everything was within reach of this young and gifted man. Somehow he was not satisfied, and this brought him to the Studite Lavra of Assumption in Uniw, near Peremyshlany.

The fortress church and monastery, built to protect monks and the villagers from the seasonal raids of Tartars and Cossacks, who emerged from the steppes every spring until the beginning of the eighteenth century, were impressive and at the same time forbidding. The invaders bypassed it, interested rather in quick loot and the highly prized captives—*yassyr*—to be sold in the slave market of the Bakhczysaraj.[1] Marko was repelled by the gloomy first impression the Lavra made on him. Years later I reacted to it in the same way Marko did when I arrived at the mother house of the Studites in Uniw.

The first night spent on a wooden pallet with a mattress and pillow filled with straw was hardly a success. Marko woke up in the morning with a bleeding nose as he was not used to sleeping on a straw-filled pillow. The morning services sung by the monks and the mass celebrated in the old church compensated for the first negative impressions of this prison-like fortress-monastery, however, and Marko decided to remain in Uniw as a guest for a few days. The simplicity of life and the dedication of the monks attracted him, and his departure was repeatedly postponed until Marko decided to become a novice. These were days of hard work and tests. Marko was determined to stick it out and leave monastic life after finishing the novitiate.

The young Ukrainian in time reached the conclusion that he had found what he was searching for. He detached himself from the hustle and bustle of city life and social activities and dedicated his life to the Lord and to prayer. The correct technical term is that he developed a vocation. Marko thought that he was leaving ambitions, struggle, and human frailties behind. He repeated this to me on many occasions. His illusion did not last long.

Ihumen Clement, observing the young man, recognized the greatness of soul, the ability to inspire and lead, and the generosity of spirit. Therefore, responsibilities were entrusted to him, first in the realm of his experience as a banker. Then he was sent to a seminary and was ordained as a monk priest. Ihumen Clement in the years before the war increasingly relied on Marko. With time it became clear to the Studite community that eventually Marko would take Clement's place and lead the order. No one ever said anything on the subject. However, this was the perception of the monks, based on the way Marko led the monasteries of which he was superior and the simplicity and kindness he showed to all.

The war years brought new challenges and tribulations. A helping hand was extended by the Metropolitan and Ihumen Clement to Jews asking for help. The burden of making arrangements for them fell on Marko, on the Superior of the Studite nuns Josepha, and the Superior of the Basilian nuns Monika Polianska, formerly of Philadelphia. Marko, in addition to his responsibilities as a superior of a large monastery, was transporting Jewish children and placing them in a variety of shelters. He organized hiding places for those like Rabbi Dr. David Kahane, whose semitic features precluded existence under an assumed name, or placed Jewish women in convents disguised as nuns.

Marko, on one occasion while transporting two little Jewish boys on a streetcar from one hiding place to another, was confronted by a German soldier who was intrigued by the older one and tried to befriend the child. Marko was petrified that the boy might respond in German, which would betray him at once as a Jew. On another occasion in the middle of the night he was contacted by a Basilian nun, who was sheltering a few Jewish children in an orphanage. She informed him that one of the lay workers had discovered a circumcised boy and had notified the Ukrainian police. Marko had to remove the children from the orphanage in the middle of the night and keep them in his cell until a new shelter could be found.

Marko and I were close friends and shared our ideas and thoughts. I doubt very much whether Marko was especially interested in Jews, or had any affinity for them. He did what was asked of him because he saw it as his responsibility as a Christian and for the love of the Lord. He did not expect any recognition or gratitude.

In 1945 after I located Marko in Florinka, a village near Krynica in the western Carpathian mountains, I was determined to save him from deportation and possibly prison. I felt indebted to the Studites and the Greek Catholic Church for my and my brother's lives. To rescue one of their leaders and get him to the West where he would be able to resume his activities in peace seemed to me the best way to reciprocate in a small measure for all that had been done for us.

Before leaving Poland I showed up at the Studite monastery in Florinka and told Marko that this was his last opportunity to get out. A *rada* (conference) of the monks was convoked at which I presented the issues and asked for a decision. The monks agreed with me that there was no point in Marko's staying in Florinka. Marko agreed to travel with me provided that I would also take with us Father Anton Ryzak, a diocesan priest staying in Florinka after escaping from Lwów.

I was not overly enthusiastic but I had no choice. The three of us left for Krakow. The priests traveled in business suits and I in the uniform of a Polish officer. The confusion was still great after the war. Before demobilization I had arranged for a duplicate set of military identity documents and the required passes to be able to travel freely. Although demobilized, I still enjoyed all the privileges of an officer in the Polish Army. In Krakow I placed the two priests in the home of Jewish friends of mine and explored open avenues to leave Poland. The first step before our attempt to cross the border was to secure identity documents for Marko and Ryzak. The only sensible way to accomplish it was to register them as Jews with the Jewish Committee in Krakow.

Ryzak was not a problem. A thin, frightened, somewhat nervous man, he had the appearance of a survivor of the Holocaust. Thick glasses and a big hat completed the right impression. Marko was another story. Tall, with sharply etched slavic features, slightly slanted deep blue eyes, and a blond beard, he had the appearance of a good looking Slav in his late thirties. His powerful build and an erect self-assured posture by no stretch of the imagination could be those of a Jew. We decided that glasses could possibly improve Marko's disguise. We found an optician and inquired about glasses for Marko. The man asked for a prescription, or offered to test Marko's vision. I volunteered that this would not be necessary as any pair of glasses would do. The optician understood at once. He found black thick frames and fitted them with lenses made out of plain glass. Marko tried them on and, with a stretch of the imagination, he could pass as Marko "Weiss," a teacher of Jewish religion in a primary school before the war. We picked up Ryzak and together went to the Jewish Committee to register.

Marko's Polish was heavily accented and his Yiddish nonexistent. Ryzak was shivering, was nervous, and fit the requirements. I did most of the talking, and we walked out with the required identity cards attesting that they were Jews, survivors of the Holocaust.

From Krakow we moved on to Katowice, where I located friends from my old military unit who were stationed there. After establishing a contact in the case of trouble, remembering the offer of Colonel Henryk Torunczyk,[2] I explored ways to cross into Czechoslovakia. We were informed that UNRRA supplies arrived in Poland by trains from Munich, because the harbor in Gdynia, on the Baltic sea, was mined and could not be used. In the border station Dziedzice these trains escorted by American soldiers were unloaded and then returned empty via Czechoslovakia to Germany. We were also advised that it would be prudent to register before departure with the Polish Red Cross as former inmates of a concentration camp on the way home. This was accomplished without a hitch as the Jewish identity papers supported our story.

Before leaving Katowice for the Czech border I was advised to purchase Reichsmarks, which were worthless in Poland. For a few hundred zloty, a relatively small sum, I purchased 15,000 Reichsmarks (currency of the Third Reich), which I stuck in my knapsack. Marko "Weiss" and I, with Ryzak in tow, joined a group of Jews travelling illegally to Germany, led by a pleasant young man from Krakow, formerly a lawyer in prewar Poland. He acted as a guide for the group and was part of a network organized by the Haganah to assist the survivors of the Holocaust to get out of Poland. I introduced myself and had no difficulty joining the group, which consisted of forty to fifty men and women and even some children.

At the railroad station in Dziedzice on the Czech border we indeed found a long UNRRA train escorted by American soldiers. The boxcars were already unloaded and the escort was occupying a boxcar near the center of the train. They were preparing an evening meal on a camp stove, sitting around it wearing shiny helmets, chewing gum, with their rifles carelessly lying on the ground. This was our first encounter with a new world. We were instructed to climb into the empty boxcars away from the escort and hide in its corners. I went to the bathroom and changed into a suit and coat I had in my kit, left there my uniform and pistol and emerged as a displaced person. We climbed into the boxcar and waited.

Late in the evening, steam engines were attached and the train rolled toward the nearby Polish-Czech border where it stopped. Soviet soldiers inspected the boxcars, opening the doors of some. As Russians are generally short they were satisfied just to roll open the doors and check with a flashlight whether the boxcar was empty, without actually climbing into it. We were huddled in the four corners, and the Soviet soldiers missed us. After a while the train started to roll and gaining speed travelled southward. We arrived in Morawska Ostrawa after midnight. The train stopped at the station, and we were instructed to get off. We had arrived in Czechoslovakia.

We continued to Prague in commuter trains. There at the station we were transferred to a boxcar attached to a freight train continuing to Pilsen in the American zone.

The distance covered was approximately 300 kilometers. The trip took almost a week, with the train stopping at a variety of stations. Everyone carried his own provisions. Before departure in Katowice, we had bought two large loafs of peasant bread and a ring of dry sausage. Marko "Weiss" twice daily cut a small piece of both, which sustained us during the journey. We carried bottles of water, which were refilled at the stations where we stopped.

This trip in the boxcar differed from similar ones taking Jews to the death camps to be gassed and cremated. Our boxcars were occupied by thirty people and not 150 or more, and the destination was a new life hopefully waiting for us at the end of the journey.

After a day or two Marko "Weiss" caught the attention of the group. His accented Polish and distinct Slavic features made them suspect that he was not a Jew. I could hear whispered suggestions that he should be thrown out of the boxcar when the train was moving at high speed. I approached the leader of the group and disclosed that Marko "Weiss" was a Catholic priest who had saved a number of Jews including me, and I was taking him to Germany. As my family was well known among Jews, and there were some in the group who were from Lwów and its vicinity, my story was confirmed. The survivors were aware of assistance extended by Metropolitan Szeptycki. They were pleased to have one of "Szeptycki's men" among them. No one paid attention to Ryzak sitting quietly in a corner of the boxcar. Nothing was said directly to Marko. At mealtimes he was offered a piece of cheese, an apple, or a lump of sugar. When we approached the Soviet-American demarcation line before Pilsen, Marko "Weiss" was told to sit in a dark corner covered with blankets and shawls with women surrounding him. They were apprehensive that he might be recognized by Soviet soldiers as a non-Jew.

We arrived in the American zone in Pilsen. There we waited for a week or so before we were again sent in a boxcar attached to a train deporting Sudeten Germans to Munich. We arrived there early in the morning, with the train stopping before the station in a bombed-out suburb. We were dirty, unshaven, in need of haircuts, and hungry. First we found a water faucet and washed, then we took off for the city. On the way I discovered an open barber shop. I decided to walk in and get a haircut and a shave. Marko was worried about payment. I told him that first we would get a haircut and a shave and then decide how to pay.

The servile and excessively polite barber and his apprentice went to work on us. It was September 1945, and the members of the "master race" were apprehensive about the possible retribution for the suffering and horror inflicted on the "inferior" races. The notorious Dachau concentration camp, the prototype for a whole network of these institutions spread over Europe, was only a few kilometers from where we were getting our haircuts. When the barber finished I inquired how much I owed him. The answer was seven marks and fifty pfennig. I fished out a ten-mark bill from my knapsack and handed it to him. The barber returned two marks and fifty pfennig, which I left as a tip. He bowed almost to the floor, was brushing our clothes, and did not cease to chatter about his opposition to the Nazis and their policies. It dawned on me that I had 15,000 of these marks in my knapsack.

We did not register at the Deutsches Museum, where the UNRRA was housing the thousands of DPs passing through Munich on their way home. We rented a room in one of the few buildings left intact in the center of the city and rested after the ordeal of the trip. We could even afford a beer and a sausage of dubious origin in the nearby Augustiner Keller. Marko contacted the Greek Catholic Church authorities, and after a few days moved out with Ryzak to join them.

The time came to part and Marko and Ryzak came to say goodbye. I found Marko subdued and somewhat discouraged. I was bubbling with optimism, outlining the many things which Marko would now be able to accomplish. Marko did not reply and only smiled. This sad smile puzzled me, but I was young and inexperienced. I erroneously assumed that the Greek Catholic Church everywhere was permeated by the spirit and ideas I had encountered during my stay at Jur. It took me years to understand that was not at all the case. We parted hoping that soon we would meet again. I divided the marks into two. I kept half and gave Marko the balance. Marko remained in

Germany, and, after a few days of rest, I continued my journey to
Italy and Rome. I became embroiled in a whole series of adventures
and contact with Marko was lost. Only after my arrival in the United
States in 1952 to complete my studies at Columbia University did I
locate Marko in Woodstock, Ontario, in Canada.

The representatives of the Greek Catholic Church who had been
stationed in Germany during the war had been politicized and close
to the Nazi Ministry of Information and Propaganda (in charge of
religious affairs), which had skillfully manipulated them. They had
little interest in the ideas of the Metropolitan or in those who represented them. Marko was received with indifference, and no assistance was extended to him whatsoever. This sensitive man kept all
this to himself and addressed the crying need for spiritual leadership
and guidance in the DP camps. Thousands of Ukrainian men and
women had been dragged by the Germans to work as slave labor in
the munitions factories and later wound up in DP camps.

The camps were also filled with refugees who, afraid of the
Soviets, had decided to escape to the West until the storm blew over.
Many of them had been involved in atrocities committed against
Poles and Jews and were afraid of retribution. It was a frightened,
misguided, generally uninformed, and bewildered human mass subsisting on the handouts of the UNRRA. Marko untiringly moved
from camp to camp providing solace and spiritual guidance. He also
started the popular prayer movement for the beatification of the
Metropolitan Andrew Szeptycki.

In the camps he met Father Johannes Peters, a German member
of the Studite order,[3] a survivor of three years of the Dachau concentration camp. Together they continued their work, which eventually
also encompassed DP camps in the British occupation zone.

The small Studite monastic community from Luzky, the
monastery in the Carpathian mountains where I stayed for a while,
with the approach of the Soviet army was evacuated via Hungary to
Vienna and from there to Germany. They were located after the war
by Marko and Peters in one of the DP camps. The enterprising
Peters settled them in the house of a German widow in Buke, who
offered them shelter. Marko contacted Ukrainian church authorities
in Rome asking for assistance and guidance. He encountered the

same indifference, if not outright hostility, with which he had been met by the visitator of the Greek Catholic church in Munich. The Collegium Ruthenum in those days was preoccupied with the former members of the SS Division Galizien and had little use for, or interest in, the Studites.

Marko subsequently contacted the Benedictine Fathers in Chevetogne in Belgium and arranged for the Studites to be placed there. This Benedectine abbey was dedicated to the Eastern rite in an attempt to bridge the gap between the Christianities of the West and the East. Similar experiments were conducted by the Dominican Order in Paris, where they published a quarterly journal called *Istyna* (*truth* in Russian), and by the Jesuits in Rome. Most of these experiments were originated by Metropolitan Andrew during his frequent visits to western European countries. The Studites led by the Deacon Teofan Shevaha (after staying for a while in Chevetogne) complained to Marko that the Benedictine Fathers turned them into servants, that they did not speak French, and were generally miserable. This prompted Marko to contact Greek Catholic Church authorities in Canada and ask for assistance in emigrating to North America. Affidavits of support were arranged and eventually Marko and the Studites sailed for Canada in 1951.

Their first stop was the Redemptorist seminary in Woodstock, Ontario, where they were able to settle for a while. The Redemptorists treated them well and offered them a chapel and separate living quarters, enabling this small community to resume their daily routine. About this time I arrived in the U.S. from Israel, sent by the Israeli army to complete my studies at Columbia University. During the Easter vacations I visited Marko and my old friends in Woodstock.

There I found Marko, who because of seniority was acting as the superior of the Studites outside the Iron Curtain. Deacon Teofan headed the community, which originated in Luzky and consisted of Brothers Laurentij the apiarist, Brother Joseph, Brother Filotej, and three other monks who had joined the community in Germany. Their chaplain, a skilled painter of icons, trained at the Metropolitan's expense in Vienna, had left the community there when their train stopped briefly on the way to Germany.

Deacon Teofan, a soft-spoken, middle-aged monk with an engaging smile on his pleasant face, framed by a carefully trimmed grayish beard, projected a thoroughly misleading impression. He had joined the original community in Sknilow as a young man and therefore felt superior to Marko, who was much younger. He had assisted the ailing Metropolitan Andrew for a while. However, he had had to be removed from the palace-residence at Jur because of a tendency to gossip and to intrigue. He could not be sent to a seminary as his education was restricted to primary school. He was ordained a deacon, a purely ceremonial function, and from time to time performed the function of an administrator *(namistnyk)* of monasteries. He was frequently moved because he always caused discord and problems. Therefore, in anticipation of the return of the Soviets, he had been sent away from Lwów to Luzky in the Carpathian mountains.

He was jealous of Marko and Peters and as was his custom regularly wrote letters complaining to bishops and other church authorities about the transgressions of these two men. He accused Peters of locking himself up in a room with the old widow in Buke, who offered the Studites shelter after the war, insinuating impropriety. Marko was systematically accused of not partaking in religious services and neglecting the community. This activity with time produced poisonous and devastating results.

During my visit in Woodstock, on the surface all was well. Marko had aged in the seven years since our parting in Munich. The monks outwardly treated Marko with respect, and plans were made to move the community to a farm on the outskirts of the town that had been acquired through the mediation of the Greek Catholic bishop in Toronto. The diocese made a small down payment and Marko assumed the mortgage as superior of the order. He radiated kindness and was gentle as always. However, there was an air of sadness. I was too wrapped up in my own struggles to pay attention and to understand the situation in which my friend found himself. After a few days in Woodstock I left for New York, pleased that my friends had settled in North America.

After completing my assignment in Israel and after my discharge from the Israeli Army, my wife and I returned to the United States in January 1955. The adjustment to a new environment was a difficult one. I had no qualifications and did not know the country. Thanks to Olga's assistance I made rapid progress and I was employed in one of the investment firms on Wall Street. Once settled somewhat, I went to Woodstock to see how my friends were.

I recognized quickly that the situation there was precarious. Marko was practically isolated and Deacon Teofan had taken over the control of the community. His argument was that Ihumen Clement had send him as a superior to Luzky and therefore the jurisdiction was his. This was a preposterous idea because of the man's lack of qualifications and his record. Some monks, incited by Deacon Teofan, supported this. Marko would not fight as it was not in his nature.

The straw that broke the camel's back was the arrival of the painter priest from Rome. Marko was looking forward to his coming, assuming that he would help to carry the burden and assist him in curbing the intrigues of Deacon Teofan. The priest arrived by ship in Halifax, Nova Scotia, and Marko drove all the way from Woodstock, Ontario, to welcome him. Shortly after meeting Marko he told him brusquely, "Msgr. Coussa, the assessor of the Congregation of Eastern Churches, charged me with the responsibility of cleaning up the mess in Woodstock."

As the file of the letters of Deacon Teofan smearing Marko was growing in the Congregation of Eastern Churches, so was the concern about the future of the Studites. Msgr. Coussa probably had suggested to the priest before his departure from Rome for Canada that he check the situation and informally let him know what was going on there. This man, full of self-importance, blurted out that his mission was to clean up the mess. This was stated to Marko, who had arranged the emigration of the community to Canada, settled them in Woodstock, and was paying the mortgage on the property.

Marko was travelling in the area substituting for priests who were on vacation or sick to earn money for the purchase of a tractor and some livestock for the Studite community. All this while the monks lived without a worry, pursuing their usual activities, satisfied to be taken care of. The Studites, without letting Marko know, decided in a secretly held *rada* to submit to the jurisdiction of the Benedictine Fathers of the Eastern Rite in Chicago. The Benedictine Fathers assumed that they would get hold of a valuable property. Deacon Teofan and the brothers thought that they would be better off administered by the Benedictines. Both parties were deeply disappointed, and eventually the Benedictines abandoned the project.

Learning about it from my old friend Brother Laurentij, I went to Woodstock. I urged Marko to leave the community before the arrival of the new Benedictine superior and accept the jurisdiction of the Greek Catholic Bishop Nil Savaryn in Edmonton, Alberta, which had been offered to him. I remained in Woodstock until Marko left the community for the parish assigned to him in Kamploops, British Columbia. There he served as a parish priest until his death twenty years later in 1976. Although Marko was badly hurt by the attitude of his confreres, he never complained to me, nor to anyone else. He continued to pay off the mortgage on the farm in Woodstock from his meager earnings.

The community in Kamloops loved him and appreciated him because Marko was dedicated to his parishioners. His love of fishing was his only relaxation and escape from the drudgery of serving a small community, which was increasingly influenced by consumerism, television-induced fads, and extreme Ukrainian nationalism. (This nationalism started to arrive from the East Coast of the United States and Canada, brought there by the postwar wave of Ukrainian immigration.)

A year after his move to British Columbia, Olga and I visited Marko. It was a lovely summer and the three of us spent happy days together on the Okanagan, or nearby Shuswap and Kalamalka Lakes. Olga, more perceptive than I, understood Marko better. Marko tried to convey to me the gradual deterioration of the environment around him, sinking more and more into the morass of materialism and moral callousness. I thought that Marko was too pessimistic about where the world was headed. I tried to argue with him and cheer him up. Our friendship, always firm, was the only ray of light in his terrible loneliness. We remained very close, but we no longer shared the same interpretation of what was happening to our environment. I was too busy with my daily struggles and not sufficiently attentive to the trends that were emerging.

After my testimony in the cause of beatification of Metropolitan

Andrew, I made every effort to involve Marko in the process. My professional activities permitted me to travel from coast to coast in Canada. I invited Marko to travel with me, and we systematically called on the Greek Catholic bishops. I deluded myself that I would be able to generate interest in Marko and open new avenues for him. All this was to no avail. We were received everywhere politely, but the conversation always shifted to a discussion of current affairs. I gradually realized that Marko represented a different world and ideas in which the bishops were not interested. Notwithstanding, his spiritual depth was recognized, and when there was a need for retreats and spiritual renewal of the clergy, the bishops invariably turned to Marko to conduct them.

On one of these trips we were joined by the young postulator of the cause, the Redemptorist Father Michael Hrynchyshyn, and the three of us travelled to Woodstock after the Benectines abandoned the Studite community. A rada of the community was called in which the Redemptorist participated ex officio as a postulator of the cause of beatification of Metropolitan Andrew. I was invited to be present because of my long-standing and close relationship with the Studites, but I refused to join. At the rada Marko firmly stated that the Woodstock community was violating the rule of the Order and deviating from everything that Ihumen Clement had taught. He turned to Deacon Teofan and asked him why he had smeared him by writing letters to the Congregation of Eastern Churches and to bishops, and by spreading false rumors in the Ukrainian community.

The cornered Deacon Teofan admitted all and fell to Marko's feet, begging his forgiveness in the name of Christ. The monks were confused and sorry, but it was too late to repair the damage done over the years. The young postulator was quite shaken by the event. Before leaving for British Columbia, Marko had left in the care of the Studite community an archive of photographs of the Metropolitan, and of the Studites, and documents pertaining to the postulation. After the rada was over, Marko left the room looking for the valise he had left behind with the archives. He found it discarded somewhere in the attic with all the painstakingly collected documents gone.

We left Woodstock for Toronto in silence, as there was little to say. Marko returned to British Columbia where he served as a parish priest to the end of his days. He visited me at least once a year and played with my sons Andrew and Clement. He showed up in New York without announcing his visit the night Olga died. He helped me to bury her and stayed with me through the hard days of mourning.

On one of his frequent visits to New York he met Father Michel de Lattre, the vice postulator. They took to each other, as both were gentle and kind individuals dedicated to the same ideas. During the visit of Father De Lattre and Marko, I invited a monsignor from the curia in New York in charge of relations with the Uniate church in the diocese to join Marko and Father Michel for dinner. This well-meaning but ignorant cleric explained to Marko and Father Michel that the church favored a variety of rites. Lately a Basuto mass was experimented with in Africa, and even a mass with guitars and rock and roll music was permitted in the New York diocese. He was comparing these to the ancient Byzantine rites. I can still see Marko smiling sadly and Father Michel looking at the cleric with the condescension of a French aristocrat for a well-meaning but primitive native. Only years later did I understand the terrible chasm separating Marko and for that matter Father Michel de Lattre from the world into which we were sliding.

On his way to New York in 1976 to visit me, Marko stopped for the first time in years in Woodstock. Teofan Shevaha was dead. The Studite community was dwindling. It was the Assumption, the feast of the Studite Order in the Uniw Lavra. Marko got up early in the morning and celebrated the liturgy alone. He returned to his cell and died of a heart attack. He was buried in Edmonton, Alberta, in the plot of a diocese that gave him shelter and protected him from human evil and intrigues. There he rests far from the fields of Ukraine where he came from. I arranged to have carved on the black granite headstone the words of our favorite psalm, which we used to sing travelling with Olga through British Columbia, "I shall lift my eyes unto the hills, from here my help will come. My help will arrive from the Lord, the creator of heaven and earth."

❦

The next story in the chain is the extraordinary saga of Johannes Peters, a young Westphalian Catholic, who like Marko embarked on a search for the truth. His odyssey led him to Lwów, to the Studite Lavra in Uniw, to Dachau, and to many other trials and tribulations. He was almost defrocked, he was pronounced by the church authorities legally and morally innocent (an interesting distinction), and he returned to the Latin rite and retired as a parish priest in Bavaria. Ironically, Father Johannes Peters was decorated by the German Federal Republic for services rendered to the Ukrainians.

When Germans refer to the East they have in mind Central Europe and Russia. The Slavic world and especially Russia fascinated young Germans, who explored this frontier and at times settled there. The contact with Russia that started with Peter the Great intensified in the nineteenth century and then was cut by World War I and the Soviet revolution. The echo of this fascination with the East could be found in the Germany of the 1920s.

The tradition of the journeyman in the Middle Ages who travelled through Europe to perfect his craft before settling down was revived between the wars in what the Germans refer to as "wanderlust." The urge to travel, to explore the unknown, and to meet people of different cultures was rather strong in the 1920s. This and other expressions of intellectual ferment and curiosity were in contrast with the xenophobic, racist, and in a way primitive ideology embraced enthusiastically by the majority of the same people in the 1930s.

The young Westphalier, after graduating from a seminary in Munich, followed this urge and understandably first went to Rome, the center of Catholicism. While exploring Rome and its institutions, the German cleric was introduced to the Pontifical Institute of Oriental Studies. This brought him in contact with the philosophy and the traditions of Eastern Christianity. It proved a veritable revelation that prompted him to explore the teachings of the Fathers of the Eastern Church and monasticism as practiced in Byzantium. This fascination remained with Peters all his life. His inquiry about where the teachings could be found in practice brought the suggestion to meet Metropolitan Andrew Szeptycki. The Metropolitan's interests and ideas were well known in Rome, and it was easier for the young traveller to go to Lwów than to explore Eastern Christianity in Greece, Turkey, or the Middle East. Peters was not particularly interested in a pure academic pursuit of the subject. He looked for contact with people who followed this tradition, and leaders who could explain to him the direction of Eastern Christianity and who were dedicated to its revival. Before returning to Germany he travelled to Lwów. There he was told that the Metropolitan was in Pidlute, in his summer residence in the Carpathian mountains, not far from Luzky.

Peters continued there and spent some time with the Metropolitan, who became interested in the young German. This encounter made an extraordinary impression on the young cleric, who then and there decided that this was a bishop whom he wished to follow. In Pidlute, Peters got acquainted with Ihumen Clement, the Metropolitan's brother, who introduced him to the Studites and their mission of revival of the Eastern Rite while serving the community in a practical way. At that point Peters made a commitment from which he never wavered. He joined the Studites in Uniw, and completed the novitiate with Marko, Nikanor, and other young inspired men who came to the Studite Lavra.[3]

These were the best years in Peters's stormy life. He was closely associated with young, motivated men pursuing a vocation. The leadership of Ihumen Clement, a man endowed with an extraordinary intellect and deep dedication to the monastic order he was shaping, made an indelible impression on the German, who adopted this Ukrainian community in essence as his own.

The Metropolitan invited Peters to Lwów and charged him with the responsibility of organizing a library of Byzantica, probably the best in the West after the collections of books and documents in Rome. He lived in the monastery of St. Josaphat on Petra Skarhy and supervised the construction of Studion, a special building in which the library and the archives were eventually housed. Peters displayed an impressive ability to direct a project, control its finances, and organize teams who under his direction were able to deal with a variety of tasks with which this complicated diocese was confronted. Peters in time gained the confidence of the Szeptycki brothers, who were pleased with the progress of the team consisting also of Marko and Nikanor. They combined spiritual depth, dedication, leadership, and administrative ability. The Szeptycki brothers inspired this unique team and delegated to it ever-increasing responsibilities.

Peters, Nikanor, Marko and others were ordained a few years before the war. The political situation deteriorated after the Anschluss of Austria and the dismembering of Czechoslovakia following the shameful "peace" conference in Munich in 1938.

Germany immediately after World War I had addressed itself to circumventing the limitations imposed by the Treaty of Versailles. Its armed forces were rebuilt in the 1920s, ironically with the assistance of the Soviet Union following the secret clauses in the Treaty of Rapallo. Its intelligence service, the Abwehr, headed by Admiral Canaris, wove intrigues in the neighboring countries, building what was subsequently referred to as the "fifth column." These were the followers of Quisling in Norway, Degrelle in Belgium, the extreme right in France, the Croats of Pavelic, and the Ukrainian nationalists (O.U.N., Organization of Ukrainian Nationalists) in Poland.

The old alliance of the Poles, Lithuanians, and Ruthenians in the Commonwealth of Poland was a thing of the past. The national aspirations of Ukrainians in Austro-Hungary were cultivated by the regime in Vienna to offset the aspirations of Poles, who revolted from time to time to throw off the yoke of the three powers— Prussia, Austro-Hungary, and Russia. World War I had brought a collapse of the existing political structure in Central Europe. The new Polish government that took over Western Ukraine after 1918 was composed of nearsighted and oppressed minorities. The Ukrainians, thwarted in their aspirations, exposed to colonization and chicanery of the increasingly intolerant Polish government, reacted with violence. The Poles responded with "pacification"— burning Uniate churches, beating up peasants, and destroying their crops. All this was of interest to the German intelligence service, which cultivated and supported Ukrainian terrorism.

The Metropolitan and Jur kept meticulously out of politics, concentrating on religious, cultural, and social problems of the Ukrainians. The question was occasionally raised as to what extent Peters was motivated by his vocation; or did he act on behalf of his masters in Berlin, insinuating himself into the surroundings of the powerful and influential Metropolitan? This question can be answered without difficulty. There is no shadow of doubt that, during his stay among the Studites until the outbreak of the war in 1939, he was interested exclusively in the tasks entrusted to him by Ihumen Clement and the Metropolitan. There is no question in my mind that he enjoyed the confidence of both. His well-documented activities after 1939 point to a dedicated service to the church and willingness to use his German citizenship and position to serve the church at the risk of his life. Nonetheless, he maintained good relations with the German consul in Lwów.

Of course, it is customary in intelligence-gathering networks for contacts with nationals to be cultivated to obtain background information. This practice is followed routinely by the British and other intelligence services. Probably the German consul who created a network of local informers also maintained a social contact with Peters.

The German consul in Lwów a few days before the attack on Poland contacted Peters and advised him to get out of town. Peters alerted the Metropolitan and Ihumen Clement and with their blessing returned to Germany. The farsighted Metropolitan gave Father Peters a *hramota,* in old Slavonic a charter empowering him to organize an Eastern Rite center in Germany, to form a branch of the Studite nuns, and gave him a general power of attorney to act on his behalf in Germany. Peters arrived in Krakow at the outbreak of World War II with the German army in September 1939. He got himself appointed as head of a section dealing with the affairs of the Greek Catholic Church in the Nazi administration of the General-gouvernement, headed by Hans Frank, who was subsequently tried and hung as a war criminal in Nuremberg.

Peters did not disclose that he was an ordained Catholic priest, an offense punishable by death as clergy were not allowed to leave the territory of the German Reich. As a government official, he enjoyed freedom of movement and acted as courier between the Archbishop Sapieha of Krakow and the Metropolitan Andrew with the papal nuncio in Berlin, Msgr. Cesare Orsenigo. He assisted the Uniate clergy in the territories occupied by the Germans, observed the activities of the Nazi henchman Hans Frank, and bided his time.

After the German attack on the Soviet Union in 1941, Peters resigned his post, using health problems as an excuse, and left for

Lwów. There he rejoined the Studite Order and resumed the life of a monk and a priest. The German authorities in Lwów assumed that he was one of the many entrepreneurs following German troops looking for business. Peters continued his dangerous trips to Berlin carrying reports to the papal nuncio, which his German passport (Reichsdeutsch) made possible. The reports by the Catholic hierarchy from the territories occupied by the Third Reich were later found in the archives of the church in Rome and had been personally delivered to the papal nuncio in Berlin by Father Peters.

There was hunger in the city after its occupation by the Germans in June 1941, which did not spare Jur. Peters took over a shoe factory named Solid, which had been nationalized by the Soviets in 1939. As its German director, he secured contracts for production of shoes for the Wehrmacht (armed forces). Priceless allocations of leather were regularly obtained, and a team of Studite monks assisted by Jewish cobblers brought from the ghetto were in charge of production.

Access to leather resolved many a problem, as carefully cut leather left pieces that could be bartered for food, fuel, and medicines. The shoe factory organized by Peters provided for Jur, the monasteries, orphanages, and convents. It is hard nowadays to understand it. However, access to leather in those days was a priceless privilege, enabling the Studites to assist the starving community. In the summer of 1942, deportations leading to the liquidation of the ghetto intensified. Father Peters allowed the Studite monks to hide the Jewish cobblers and their families in the cellar of the factory.

The second enterprise of Father Peters was the printing of the many forms so beloved by the Germans. He obtained printing presses, which he transported to Jur with the permission of the German military authorities. He set up there a printing workshop run by Studite monks from the monastery of St. Josaphat on Petra Skarhy. Officially they were printing various forms ordered by the army and the administration of the District Galizien. Clandestinely this workshop was responsible for printing pastoral letters, the publication of the Diocese news, prayer books, and other religious literature. Peters was living at St. Josaphat where I was, and occasionally we met at the refectory or at the chapel.

Ukrainian nationalists persuaded lay workers to give them access to the print shop at night to produce anti-German leaflets, which were distributed throughout the city. As this was the only printing workshop in civilian hands in the city, it was rather simple for the Gestapo to trace their origin. They swiftly arrested the German director of the enterprise, Father Peters, and the superior of the monastery where he lived, Father Nikanor.

The preliminary interrogation of Father Peters conducted at the prison on Lackiego Street in Lwów, from which one rarely emerged alive, produced a startling discovery. The arrested German business-man was a Catholic priest and a former high official in the Nazi administration of Hans Frank in Krakow. The news of the discovery was wired to the headquarters of the Reichssicherheitsamt in Berlin. The head of the Gestapo, Muller, flew to Lwów to interro-gate the mysterious German personally. As the story unraveled, all the activities of Peters since the start of the war were discovered. Muller informed Peters that as a traitor he would be unceremoni-ously shot. Peters invoked a law stating that as a German citizen he was entitled to be executed in Dusseldorf, his home town. Muller agreed, assuming that further interrogation of Peters in Dusseldorf would help to uncover other anti-Nazis.

Peters was sent from Lwów to Dusseldorf to be executed, but the papers got lost somewhere in transit. As it was not clear what to do with him, he was transported with other prisoners to the concentra-tion camp in Dachau. This camp in the systematic and orderly pat-tern of Himmler's organization was designated also for clergymen. Over two thousand priests and ministers from all over Europe per-ished there. According to witnesses, Father Peters helped a number of priests imprisoned with him to survive the horror of the camp.

Peters survived the war, resumed pastoral activity in the DP camps, assisted in settling the Studites from the skyt in Luzky, and jointly with Marko started the prayer movement for the beatification of the Metropolitan Andrew. This extraordinary man befriended the Roman Catholic bishop of Aachen and, presenting the charter given to him by the Metropolitan, asked for permission to organize near Krefeld in his diocese a center for the Eastern Rite. The bishop read-ily agreed to the project, because it included an old age home to which the center would be attached. He allocated from his welfare budget (welfare was administered by churches in Germany) funds to start the project.

Peters promptly bought a farm near Krefeld, took out a mortgage, and started construction. The center consisted of an old age home, a church built in a Byzantine style, and a publishing house. A nucleus of dedicated women joined a Studite novitiate and were responsible for running the old age home. Thus Peters created a self-supporting enterprise and started to realize the dream of Metropolitan Andrew to generate interest in Eastern Christianity in Germany.

All this activity was very promising and constructive. However, the otherwise shrewd Father Peters ignored the Greek Catholic hierarchy in Germany, considering them spineless collaborators. Equally, he antagonized the German church hierarchy by criticizing them publicly for their passive attitude and silent acquiescence to Nazi war crimes. He failed to take into consideration that the ideas of Metropolitan Andrew were not necessarily shared by everyone in the church. Equally he relied too much on the sponsorship of the friendly and understanding bishop of Aachen.

In the midst of the construction of the center, the bishop of Aachen suddenly passed away. His successor had little understanding for the project of Father Peters or interest in Metropolitan Szeptycki's ideas. He unceremoniously cut the funds already allocated for the project, leaving Father Peters with a mortgage and an unfinished project.

Peters did not let this interfere with his plans. He went to Bonn and contacted his friends in the government whom he had met in Dachau. They were pleased to assist him, and the new bishop of Aachen found his budget cut by the amount originally allocated to Peters. These funds were transferred by the government directly to Father Peters to use as he saw fit. To make matters worse, these influential friends were mostly socialists. The enraged bishop decided to get rid of this meddlesome priest and his project. This was not so simple, because Peters, ordained in the Greek Catholic Rite, was subject to a different ecclesiastic jurisdiction.

Before leaving for Rome with Olga to testify in the process of beatification, I spoke to Father Marko in British Columbia, who informed me that Peters was having difficulties. Marko did not know the details, but according to the news he had received, Peters had been removed from the Center of Eastern Rite in Krefeld, and apparently resided in a monastery in Grotta Ferrata near Rome. Marko implored me to help Peters, mentioning that Ihumen Clement had always told him to defend Peters if need be. I remembered the Jewish cobblers from the ghetto hidden in the shoe factory Solid with the knowledge of Peters.

After my testimony I called on Cardinal Tisserant at the Congregation of Eastern Churches and asked his assistance in locating Peters. I was told that the case of Father Peters was known to the Congregation and everything was being done to assist him. It was suggested that I contact Father Dumont, a Dominican priest at the Istyna, a center for Eastern Rite in Paris. The patient and understanding Olga agreed to accompany me and participate in the search for Peters.

We learned from Father Dumont at Istyna that he also was trying to assist Father Peters. However, the case was complicated because it involved a joint intervention of German bishops and the Greek Catholic Papal visitor for Ukrainians in Europe, Archbishop Ivan Bucko, who resided at the Collegium Ruthenum in Rome. Father Dumont advised us to proceed to the Center in Krefeld where we could learn more about the affair and the whereabouts of Peters. We drove leisurely from Paris to Krefeld as it was vacation time.

At the Center in Krefeld I found my old Studite friend Deacon Christophor, a gifted icon painter, who had been transferred to the community in Luzky while I was there. Christophor showed us the center, an impressive modern nursing home managed by the Studite nuns, a beautiful small church built in a Byzantine style (a copy of one in Perugia), a conference hall, and a small library.

Christophor, who had stayed on in Germany, explained that, while Peters was dedicated to the ideas of the Metropolitan Andrew, he did not pay sufficient attention to the sensitivities of the Ukrainian clergy. He gave us the address of Peters, who was staying with his family in the nearby Moers am Rhein. We met with Peters, whom I had not seen since his arrest by the Gestapo in Lwów in 1942.

Peters told us the story of the funds, the predicament created for the center by the new bishop of Aachen, and how he had resolved it.

He had created a German lay board, which supervised the center and its activities and was the legal entity owning the property. The center thrived, with many visitors coming on weekends to attend the services. Peters, a Studite, was requested by Archbishop Bucko to go to Woodstock for a routine visitation of the monastic community there. While he was in Canada a Ukrainian priest was sent to Krefeld to take over the Center. Simultaneously a registered letter was sent to Woodstock by Archbishop Bucko requesting Peters to stay there.

Someone warned him about the developments in Krefeld, and Peters took a plane back to Germany before the registered letter reached him. Attempts to clarify the matter either in Aachen or in Rome were to no avail. Peters was punished without being told what the accusations made against him were and without an ecclesiastic trial. He ignored the request to go to the monastery in Grotta Ferrata and consequently was advised that he would be defrocked. In the meantime his celebret (permit to say mass) was taken away. Peters sued the bishop in Aachen and Archbishop Bucko in Rome for defamation in a German civil court and requested a formal ecclesiastic trial to which he was entitled under canon law.

The complicated affair was strange, to say the least. The nature of the accusations was equally extraordinary. After the completion of the center, the diocese in Aachen sent two Augustine fathers as observers. They spent a year in Krefeld, allegedly to familiarize themselves with the activities of the center. They produced a report accusing Father Peters of a long list of irregularities, claimed that he had twelve illegitimate children and had engaged in sexual orgies with the Studite nuns running the old age home. The German lay board was annoyed by the heavy-handed interference of the Ukrainian bishop into the running of a center financed by welfare funds provided by the German government and fully supported Peters.

Father Peters provided me with documents describing the affair and mentioned that with all these responsibilities he could not have fathered the twelve illegitimate children because he was too busy. Under the circumstances he had not lost his sense of humor. The next day we met for lunch in Moers with a German Jesuit, Father Dietz, and a Polish Benedictine priest, Father von Krasinski, a friend of the Metropolitan Andrew, who offered advice on how to help Father Peters. Olga, a lawyer, and I left Moers rather bewildered by this extraordinary story and reflected how to devise the next course of action.

On my next visit to Rome a few months later, I learned to my surprise that Eugene Cardinal Tisserant had been replaced by Amleto Cardinal Cicognani. The brilliant Frenchman, intimately acquainted with the problems of the Eastern Rite churches, was removed because of some internal intrigue hatched among the bureaucrats of the Curia Romana by Cardinal Tardini. Tisserant became the librarian and archivist of the Vatican, a harmless assignment without much influence. The French government, showing its displeasure at his abrupt dismissal, appointed him to the Academie Francaise and made him a commander of the Legion of Honor. The postulation had lost a staunch supporter, and I no longer could rely on my old friend to assist in the matter of Father Peters.

After consulting with Father De Lattre, I paid a courtesy visit to the new prefect of the Congregation of Eastern churches, Cardinal Cicognani, an elderly gentleman and a long-time papal nuncio to the United States who was interested primarily in the latest news from Washington. I then went to see Msgr. Accacio Coussa, a Syrian Melkhite (an Eastern Rite Church in the Middle East, a part of which is in union with Rome), a secretary of the Congregation of Eastern churches for many years under Cardinal Tisserant. He knew me well and greeted me warmly. After learning that I wished to discuss the issue of Father Peters, he said that he was rather busy, adding that the Syrian ambassador was waiting in the ante camera, and asked if I would please return the next morning.

The following day I was kept waiting in the ante camera for a long time. Finally I was ushered into the office of Msgr. Coussa, a short, corpulent cleric in an Eastern riasa (habit) somewhat similar to the one worn by the Studites, with sharp black eyes, bushy eyebrows, and a graying beard that reminded one of a respectable trader found in the bazaar of Istanbul or Damascus. I suggested that an interpreter would be helpful as neither my English nor his would enable us to be precise in discussing this delicate matter. The quick Syrian got the message and inquired whether I wished to have a witness to our conversation. I answered that under the circumstances it would be desirable.

Msgr. Raymond Etteldorf, an American from Des Moines, Iowa, a consultor to the Congregation, then joined us. I told Msgr. Coussa that I had known Father Peters since 1942, that I was aware that he had been close to the Metropolitan Andrew and had had his full confidence, and that he had rendered important services to the church during the war. I stated that I knew what the nature of the accusations were, that all the related documents were in my possession and were deposited at a bank in a safe. I commented that I was well disposed toward the church, and I assured Msgr. Coussa that I would be discreet. I concluded that I had no idea whether Father Peters was guilty or innocent. I asked only that he be given the opportunity to answer his accusers in an ecclesiastic court, which was his right under canon law.

The bewildered American cleric was quiet, observing an American Jew and a Syrian haggling over a German priest accused by German bishops of a variety of transgressions. Msgr. Coussa twisted his beard for a while and then commented that this was a delicate matter. He was unable to act against the German bishops, although he realized that an ecclesiastic trial was called for under canon law. He explained to me the situation and the consequences of a possible intervention, pointing out that the involvement of the Ukrainian bishop in Rome, Msgr. Bucko, added another dimension of complications. He asked me to be patient and to leave matters to him. I readily agreed and promised to communicate this to Father Peters, requesting him not to take any hasty steps. As we walked to the door Msgr. Coussa turned to me and said, "Mr. Lewin, you are like the Jew described in the Gospels; you are not perfidious." I thought to myself that, while the Catholic Church is blatantly violating its canon law, the Jews with only few exceptions are perfidious.

After the dramatic encounter at the Congregation I called on the consultors of the Congregation—the Jesuits, Father Raes, the rector of the Pontifical Oriental Institute, and Father Horacek, the rector of Russicum. These were courtesy calls during which I mentioned that I had visited the Congregation of Eastern Churches to discuss the problems of Father Peters. I did not mention either what they were, or what I knew. I just signaled my interest in the case.

A few months later I received a letter from Father Horacek informing me that he and another Jesuit had travelled to Germany on a mission entrusted to them by Msgr. Coussa and that the difficulties of Father Peters would be resolved in a satisfactory fashion. On my next visit to Rome I called on Msgr. Coussa. Msgr. Etteldorf was again present and I was told that Father Peters had been found morally and legally innocent. I learned to appreciate the intelligent and correct Syrian who had dealt with this mess in a skillful and just fashion. A few months later I received from Msgr. Coussa a personal invitation to attend the ceremony in the Sistine chapel at which he was to receive a cardinal's hat. I also received a formal letter from Cardinal Coussa countersigned by Msgr. Etteldorf thanking me for the courtesy and interest extended, without mentioning in what. It was a kind gesture to create a record in the files of the Congregation of Eastern Churches if and when I ever needed a reference.

The celebret of Father Peters was restored, and he resumed pastoral activities. The Eastern Rite Center was taken away from the Ukrainians as the German lay board would have nothing to do with them again. Throughout this ordeal Father Peters never lost faith and remained optimistic that justice would prevail. He resumed the pursuit of the ideas of the Metropolitan Andrew with the same energy and enthusiasm as before until the arrival of Joseph Cardinal Slipyj from the USSR.

Father Peters was attached to the Greek Catholic diocese in Munich and basically was left alone, subsisting on a pension from the German government and restitution for imprisonment and the years in the concentration camp. He called on Cardinal Slipyj after his arrival in Rome. The Cardinal treated Father Peters rather discourteously, as he did anyone who had been in direct contact with Metropolitan Andrew.

Father Peters asked to be released from the Studite Order and returned to the Roman Catholic Rite, serving as a parish priest in Bavaria until his retirement. He was always pleased to assist the Ukrainians or in the spreading of the ideas of the Metropolitan Andrew. The story of Father Peters raised a number of interesting questions. The fury of the German bishop of Aachen, an authoritarian sort of fellow referred to by his own clergy as "Timoshenko" because of his resemblance to the dour and humorless Soviet marshall, was understandable. After all, it was his budget that was sharply cut because of the intervention of Father Peters. The German bishops were infuriated by a priest who stated openly that if they were decent men they would have been with him in Dachau, a precise observation but not very diplomatic under the circumstances. Once together we visited the beer cellar in which Hitler had made some of his somewhat hysterical speeches. An "umpa" band was playing marches as in the good old days. At the long wooden tables men were sitting in front of huge beer steins, with waiters in leather aprons hurrying by with fresh mugs filled to the brim. Looking at the red faces inflamed by alcohol, Peters remarked to me in German *"Hatte ich mitgetanzt and mitgejubelt ware ich heute ein Bishof."* In free translation he stated that if he were a Nazi today he would be a bishop. He probably was right. Nevertheless, it would have been prudent to keep these observations to himself. However, Peters was not necessarily a man of compromises. He followed what was right regardless of the consequences. This probably explains the man's extraordinary tranquility and peace of mind displayed even in the darkest moments.

However, I could not comprehend the determination displayed by Archbishop Bucko to remove Peters, even if in the process the impressive Center for Eastern Rites serving the Ukrainian community in West Germany and of broad interest to the public was sacrificed. The answer was provided years later. Archbishop Bucko was sheltering Dr. Otto Wachter, the former governor of the District Galizien in the occupied territories of Poland. Dr. Wachter, an Austrian, had been one of the murderers of Chancellor Dolfuss in 1934 during a failed attempt to take over Austria by the Nazis. He had reappeared in occupied Poland and as governor of a large district was, with another Austrian, General of SS and Police Katzmann, responsible for the deportation to death camps of almost a million Jews.

This information, accidentally disclosed in a book[4] on another subject, was revealing indeed. It reminded me of the enthusiasm and interest shown in the remnants of the SS Division Galizien collected in Rimini when I had first arrived at the Collegium Ruthenum. Peters knew too much and was too close to the Metropolitan. He was aware of the circumstances that compelled Archbishop Bucko to leave Lwów after engineering an investigation of the Metropolitan's activities by a special commission sent by the Curia Romana. Both Peters and Marko represented a threat; consequently Marko was isolated and blocked and Peters almost defrocked.

ℰℐ

The next story is about Michel de Lattre, a Frenchman, who never met Metropolitan Andrew or his brother Clement. An accident brought him in contact with Father Korolevskij, the personal representative of the Metropolitan in Rome and a consultor of the Congregation of Eastern Churches. A review of his archives intrigued the young French priest, and he too became fascinated by the ideas and life of the two men as Marko, Peters, I, and many others were. His background, interests, and experience were far removed from Eastern Christianity, the Greek Catholic church, and Ukrainian affairs. Nevertheless, he dedicated eight critical years of his life to the postulation. Its archives reflect his meticulous scholarship and his dedication to the cause. As a result of this involvement, he became a displaced person in his church and he too shared the tribulations of Marko and Peters.

Michel de Lattre, the son of a banker, was born in Roubais, France, in 1910. He was one of seven children and was brought up in a traditional French family. His two uncles were Jesuit priests. Michel graduated from a seminary in France and was ordained in 1938 in a thirteenth-century church in a village near the summer home of his parents. His first assignment was in the diocese of Paris where he was a vicar in one of the parishes until the outbreak of the war in 1939. Father Michel served as a chaplain in the French army until the collapse of France in 1940. He became a prisoner of war of the Italians and was interned in Loretto, in Italy. After the war Father Michel went to Rome and after a few assignments, probably on the recommendation of Cardinal Tisserant, was sent as an observer for the Curia Romana to the United Nations. The question of internationalization of Jerusalem preoccupied the Catholic Church then as it does today. His responsibility was to follow debates dealing with this and other questions related to the newly established State of Israel.

Father Michel completed his mission sometime in 1954 and returned to Rome. Most probably he either would have found a position in the Secretariat of State or would have returned to the diocese of Paris to which he belonged. However, the suggestion of Cardinal Tisserant that he meet Father Korolevskij and review the cause of beatification of Metropolitan Szeptycki had far-reaching consequences and changed his life.

This casual suggestion launched Father Michel on a mission that became the center of his life for a number of years. He dedicated all his energy and personal resources to it as he was not paid for his work. He was given a leave of absence by the diocese of Paris, which allowed him to pursue this activity.

He discovered the extraordinary scope of activities of Metropolitan Andrew through the review of Father Korolevskij's archives. These led to a search for documents in the archives of the Congregation of Eastern Churches and the Vatican. Father Michel became intrigued with the activities of Metropolitan Andrew, which encompassed Austro-Hungary, Holland, Germany, France, Italy, the U.S., Canada, and Brazil. The primary interests of the Metropolitan were the renewal of his church and the Eastern Rite Catholics who, driven by poverty, had emigrated to these countries at the turn of the century.

These activities were eventually broadened to efforts to create a bridge between the Christianity of the West with that of the East. Father Michel to his amazement discovered that Metropolitan Andrew, imprisoned in Russia following the occupation of Lwów by Russian troops in 1914, had established close contact with the Synod of the Russian Orthodox Church. Using his powers as an Apostolic Exarch for the East, he had successfully negotiated an agreement between Rome and the Synod. Preparations for signing it were interrupted by Lenin's revolution in October 1917.

Access to the correspondence in perfect French between Metropolitan Andrew and a relative of his, the General of the Society of Jesus Ledochowski, was equally fascinating, as it offered an additional perspective on the scope of interests of this extraordinary man. The theological treatises written by Metropolitan Andrew were another subject that intrigued Father Michel.

The controversy surrounding the Metropolitan called for a careful research of the historical, political, and social background of the region. Father Michel, in anticipation of the challenges he expected would emerge during the second phase of the process of beatification, addressed himself to the preparation of briefs to be used to counter eventual objections and accusations.

He lived modestly in Rome in the Madonna del Riposo district where he acted as a vicar in a nearby parish, dedicating himself to the service to the poor. A legacy left by his parents provided a small income that he supplemented with historical research for other causes of beatification. At Easter and during summer vacations he would stay in Crans sur Sierre, in Valais, in Switzerland. There he continued his research, occasionally played golf, and visited his family and friends vacationing there. This provoked criticism that he was a "society priest."

All year long Father Michel worked in Rome on the cause of beatification of the Metropolitan and lived on the edge of poverty. This was overlooked by the "friends" in Crans sur Sierre, who begrudged him the little relaxation and a change that he could enjoy among people of his own social background.

I came to Rome to testify as a witness for the postulation. I realized that the assistance extended to Jews by the Metropolitan and the Greek Catholic Church was of little interest. It became apparent preparing my testimony that the real contribution I could make would be to guide Father Michel through the maze of political and social relations in this complicated region. This provided a basis for a friendship that grew with time and remained firm until the death of Father Michel in 1976.

Father Michel introduced me to Italian and French cultures while I guided him in his efforts to understand the intricate relations between the Poles and the Ukrainians. Of equal importance was the understanding of the social and cultural background of the Metropolitan. In the search for documents and witnesses, we travelled through Europe, always leaving time to enjoy the sights and a good bottle of wine. The war years had prevented me from learning how to enjoy life. Father Michel's wisdom and unobtrusive guidance helped me to mature and become a more rounded individual.

I used to spend my vacations with my sons in Crans sur Sierre and every day Father Michel and I lunched together at the hotel where I stayed. A mutual acquaintance of ours once asked Father Michel what subjects we had discussed for so many years. He replied with a twinkle in his eye that he was trying to convert me to Catholicism, and I was trying to convert him to Judaism. So far after ten years of discussions we had not made much progress.

The arrival of Msgr. Joseph Slipyj, the archbishop of Lwów and Metropolitan of Halicz, the successor of Metropolitan Andrew, changed the situation dramatically. Kyr (from Greek Kyrios) Joseph, a rather aloof, ambitious, and cold man, had been arrested in 1945 by the Soviets. He was released only in 1963 as a personal gift of Khruschev to Pope John XXIII. His unexpected appearance at the Second Vatican Council made a great impression.

Kyr Joseph had withstood the pressures exerted by the KGB and did not give in. He had even refused to leave Moscow for Rome after his sudden release unless he was issued a Soviet passport, so that he could eventually return to his diocese. Regretfully, he emerged with psychological scars, and the coldness and aloofness were accentuated by the long years in prison. Shortly after his arrival in Rome he engaged in a variety of controversies that continued until his death. The sad part of this was that he was manipulated by extreme Ukrainian nationalists. In recognition of his suffering and his stand on issues of faith he was made a cardinal. However, as he persisted in challenging the Pope and demanded the creation of a separate Patriarchate for the Ukrainians, he lost all influence in Rome and became quite isolated.

Father De Lattre, like many others including myself, paid our respects to Kyr Joseph. It became apparent that it would be impossible to relate to the authoritarian, unreasonable, and somewhat abrasive individual. His disregard for Fathers Marko and Peters signaled an attitude that did not augur well. Father Michel, remembering the predicament of Father Peters, decided to resign from the postulation. I supported him in this difficult decision, as I realized that sooner or later he would find himself embroiled in intrigues woven around the cardinal. He completed his work on the archives, catalogued them, and turned them over to the postulator. For a while he retained the private archives of Father Korolevskij, which had been left to him personally in the dead man's will. Shortly before his death he turned them over to Msgr. Marusyn, who took over as Apostolic visitor to the Ukrainians in Europe after the death of Archbishop Bucko. He parted from the Ukrainians in a friendly and elegant fashion.

Father de Lattre started a search for an association that would provide a challenge and an income. After so many years away from the diocese of Paris, nothing was available for him there, and Cardinal Feltin of Paris, legally his superior, advised him to stay in Rome. Father Michel was well connected in the Curia and his friends tried to obtain a position for him, either an appointment as a judge, or work in the archives of the church or in one of the Congregations. Despite his superb qualifications and an impeccable record, all these efforts were to no avail. The involvement in the cause of beatification of Metropolitan Andrew closed doors otherwise open to him.

He lived quietly, supporting himself doing research for causes of beatification, which paid modestly for his efforts. His magnificent historical research resulted in assembling an almost complete archive of documents related to the activities of Metropolitan Andrew, his writings, and correspondence. All this meticulously catalogued work shows no trace of the years of effort of this scholar. He published two books commissioned for other causes of beatification that were printed in Rome and signed by a Monsignor Frutaz who had commissioned the research. The ways of the Vatican's bureaucracy are strange at times.

Father Michel died in Rome in 1976, requesting in his will to be buried among the poor people in a cemetery in the outskirts of the city. After his death while in Crans sur Sierre I arranged a memorial mass in the little church of which he was fond. His many friends assembled there on a Sunday morning, and a local priest celebrated the mass. In a brief eulogy he mentioned that Father de Lattre had been a good and pious man even if he had had a tendency to be a "society priest."

ഌ

The Ukrainian Father Marko, the German Father Peters, and the Frenchman Father Michel de Lattre were individuals with entirely different backgrounds and characters. All three were linked by their love for the Metropolitan and their dedication to his ideas and his mission, which they tried to continue.

Father Marko dedicated his life to spreading the spiritual message of the Metropolitan among the Ukrainians. Father Peters dedicated his life to the Metropolitan and Ihumen Clement because to him they were true representatives of Christ. The mission entrusted to him by the Metropolitan and Ihumen Clement to build a center for the study of Eastern Christianity in Germany was a mission of the Lord. Therefore, regardless of the difficulties, dangers, and obstacles, he did his best to fulfill it. He realized that he was being thwarted and defeated. Nevertheless, he tried his best, which gave him the satisfaction that he was true to the mission. Father Michel, a man of remarkable intellect, understood the whole design of the efforts of the Metropolitan from his youth until his death. He too realized that through his research he had touched stars—an observation made years before by Olga. He carried on as long as it was constructive and left his legacy to the postulator whom he developed, cultivated, and prepared to carry this burden.

Measured by the materialistic standards of modern times, all three failed. Father Marko was thwarted by the intrigues of Deacon Teofan Shevaha and the betrayal of his confreres. Father Peters, after dedicating his life to this cause, found himself almost defrocked, and was compelled to secularize himself (leave the Studite Order) and return to the Latin Rite. Father Michel after his resignation saw the postulator, Msgr. Hrynczyshyn, with whom he had worked for years, removed abruptly from the cause by Kyr Joseph Slipyj and replaced with a former SS man. This ended any meaningful efforts to advance the beatification of the Metropolitan.

This superficial assessment does not reflect the inner strength of these three men. Each in the final analysis left a legacy and carried his work forward as long as he had strength and energy left. When they were prevented from continuing their mission, the three men knew that they had given their best. I was privileged to encounter them and share many of their trials. My rich reward was their friendship.

From my vantage point my conclusion is that Father Marko was thwarted first by the Ukrainian hierarchy in Munich, a hierarchy manipulated by the authorities of the Third Reich in charge of religious affairs and extreme Ukrainian nationalists. They were indifferent, if not outright hostile, to the ideas of the Metropolitan, whom they had always resented. Marko represented to them Jur and its ideas. The indifference of the Ukrainian bishops in Canada combined with the intrigues woven around Father Marko completed the tragedy of his exile.

Father Peters was resented, as a foreigner always is by Ukrainians. He was tolerated as long as he had the sponsorship of the Metropolitan and Ihumen. He could not grasp that these splendid and true ideas could be rejected. He despised the German Catholic hierarchy for having failed in their mission because they did not counteract evil when it was still possible. Their attempt to gloss over the genocide and horrors perpetrated during the war was equally abhorrent to him. He compared them to Metropolitan Andrew and found them wanting. These views landed him in a no-man's land, attacked with equal venom by the German and the Ukrainian clergy.

Father Michel involved himself unknowingly in the ancient conflict between Rome and Byzantium and ended equally in a no-man's land. He realized the greatness of the spirit of the Metropolitan Andrew and his vision. Also did Cardinals Tisserant, Coussa, Pope John XXIII, and the General of the Redemptorist Order, Father William Gaudreau. With these great men gone, a new generation took over of a different caliber and different motivation. In the new environment there was no place for him, and eventually he found his mission among the poor of Rome. He was vilified even at a memorial mass in a eulogy by a small-minded and probably jealous Belgian priest who had known him well. The Ukrainians have forgotten him, and the archive meticulously organized and catalogued by him has been utilized only by a Protestant theologian formerly at Yale, a Czech who was commissioned to write a dissertation on the theology of the Metropolitan Andrew.

These three men did not fail, nor were their lives an exercise in futility. But their individual odysseys represent a sad comment on the spiritual poverty of the environment in which they lived and worked.

The ideas of the Metropolitan Andrew and Ihumen Clement have survived for forty-five years after their deaths. The persecuted church emerged from the modern catacombs in Western Ukraine strong, annealed, if somewhat confused by the encounter with the values and ideas of the West. The collapse of Marxism-Leninism in the Soviet Union has been accompanied by a search for a spiritual revival. The culture of the Russians and the Ukrainians is deeply rooted in the Christianity of the East. This brought the ideas and the teachings of the Metropolitan into a sharp focus again. They are as valid today as they were when, after his release from prison, he was negotiating resumption of contacts between Rome and the Russian Orthodox Church in 1917 in St. Petersburg.

The economic transformation of the former Soviet Union and Central European countries is of critical importance. However, the transformation of societies deformed by a failed ideology is equally if not more important. The success in rebuilding these countries depends on ideas and a set of values these nations must find within their own cultures and their own environment. They cannot be imported from abroad. The archives of the Metropolitan Andrew, meticulously preserved by the joint efforts of Father Michel de Lattre and the former postulator Msgr. Michael Hrynchyshyn, and ironically also by the KGB in Lwów, and probably also in Moscow and St. Petersburg, represent a beacon of light in this darkness. Hopefully, it will not be dimmed by revived nationalism, old meaningless theological conflicts that once divided Rome and Byzantium, and by intrigues woven by religious bureaucrats. Hopefully, all this will be sorted out in time for the sake of the West and the East, fulfilling a dream of Andrew Graf Szeptycki, Archbishop of Lwów and Metropolitan of Halicz. His dream was shared among many others by the three splendid men described in this story.

CHAPTER 9

The Discovery of America

THE BOEING STRATOCRUISER of BOAC (the old name of British Airways), an impressive if somewhat slow plane, landed at Idlewild in January 1952. It was a long trip that had started in London and, with stopovers in Prestwick, Scotland, Gander in Canada, and Boston, finally brought me to New York. Here I was at the airport starting another adventure I hoped would lead me to a more peaceful existence. My dream to return to an academic environment was finally realized.

The trip by taxi to Manhattan was an introduction to this enormous city, its dynamism, and its lack of attention to esthetics. The skyline of Manhattan in the bright light of a winter sunset made an indelible impression. Thoughts were racing through my mind, triggered by all the impressions of the new world crowding in. The task facing me was overwhelming, but fortunately I did not fully appreciate the difficulties I would be faced with. I had finally reached New York, sent by the Israeli Army to resume studies at Columbia University that had been interrupted by the 1947-49 war.

For a while I toyed with the idea of returning to the study of classics. I asked my sponsor, Professor Moshe Schwabe, a prominent classicist, whether I should return to his department. The kind and thoughtful man, who had encouraged me in the pursuit of the study of classics when I arrived at the Hebrew University in 1946, with tears in his eyes discouraged me from returning to his department. The beauty and harmony of classics were eternal and were the foundation of the civilization of Western man, he said. However, we were in a phase in which classics were not appreciated. It was a pity that I could not continue research in this field, but it was a luxury that in my situation I could not afford. My responsibility toward myself was to rebuild a life dislocated by yet another war and acquire a profession. He advised me to identify a field that would be more practical in the new environment, suggesting political science.

The degree taken as Roman Matkowski before leaving Poland in 1945 and the record of graduate studies at the Hebrew University secured admission to Columbia University. I had some difficulty proving that Roman Matkowski and I were the same person. Eventually, all obstacles were overcome and I could address myself to learning English and selecting a subject of academic pursuit.

I had visited a number of large European cities before arriving in this metropolis. However, I was not prepared for the first impressions of New York, which were overwhelming. Its size, the tall skyscrapers, the extraordinary mosaic of people encountered in a constantly changing kaleidoscope are unique and so is the impact it makes on a visitor who is constantly startled by yet another unusual sight. In the early 1950s the city was interesting, people well-dressed and considerate, the streets were clean and safe, patrolled by neat policemen keeping a watchful eye on the neighborhoods. The homeless were not yet a common phenomenon and one could find the "winos" only on Skid Row in the Bowery. The city was full of life twenty-four hours a day, with brightly lit shops always open. The astonishingly efficient subway system transported one rapidly for a dime from one corner of the city to another, and the next day's *New York Times* could be purchased at street corners for a nickel. The first few days were full of extraordinary impressions, and, although I had had a wide range of experiences before arriving in New York, I felt bewildered and overwhelmed.

Slowly gathering courage, I started to explore the tourist sites of the city. The first stop was Rockefeller Center. This architectural complex introduced me to the bold concepts and the breath of vision in the new world. Perhaps it lacks the majesty of the architecture in Rome or the splendor of Paris. Nor does it project, as The City in London does, a blend of tradition with the power of the British Empire at its zenith. Nevertheless, it has a majesty all its own, and it is a testimony to the boldness, innovation, and sense of harmony of previous generations of Americans.

The view from the top of the Empire State Building provided an idea of the enormous size of the city and the uniqueness of Manhattan. A stroll on Fifth Avenue to Central Park and to the museums completed the first effort to get acquainted with New York. Regretfully, the sightseeing had to be left for another day, as I had to settle in at Columbia University.

The registration procedure at Columbia University again brought home the different scale to that which I was accustomed to. The long lines of students, the catalog with the bewildering choice of courses, and the efficient but impersonal process could be dealt with, however, as I was assisted by everybody once they realized I was a foreigner. After this routine was completed, I was assigned an advisor whose responsibility was to approve my program of studies. Fortunately he spoke German, so that we could communicate. He was somewhat puzzled how I proposed to study without knowing the English language.

My reply that I would learn English met with incredulity. He inquired what subjects I wished to study, to which I replied that I was interested in political economy. I was advised that the subject was divided into economics and political science, and I should chose either one or the other. Finally he commented that, as long as I kept out of his classes, he would approve any program I submitted. With time, however, we became good friends, and he guided me through studies at Columbia University. Eventually I was invited to lecture in his department.

My first experience at the university was strange indeed. I enrolled in an elementary course in English for beginners. Next to me was a student somewhat younger than I. I inquired which country he came from. He answered that he was a Brooklynite and wished to study English. This answer startled me, as I discovered that there were native Americans who did not speak English well. Fortunately the teacher, Mrs. Mary Dobbie, who happened to be the wife of the head of the English Department, Prof. Elliott Dobbie, realized that I did not belong in her class and suggested that I enroll at the American Language Center. This center, a part of the university, specialized in an accelerated course of English for foreign students. It also provided a general if superficial introduction to the political system and way of life in the United States. This center was my salvation and made the transition and acclimatization much easier.

The composition of the student body at the center was an extraordinary representation of many nationalities. There were students from Europe, the Middle East, Japan, and quite a few from Latin America. It was an interesting group of individuals who, like myself, were preparing for studies at the university. They brought with them a wide range of experiences and knowledge, occasionally challenging the teachers with questions about U.S. foreign policy, discrimination against blacks, or why native Indians were not given American citizenship until 1924.

Learning American English proved to be a complicated task. The director of the center was a New Englander; the teachers came from Iowa, Georgia, and Texas. They all were highly motivated and well prepared. Nevertheless, they had difficulty realizing that to our ears each spoke a different kind of English. One of the teachers had the brilliant idea of finishing the morning sessions with singing American folk songs like "On Top of Old Smoky," " Blue Tail Fly," and "When Johnny Comes Marching Home." We sang them with great enthusiasm, and it had an interesting impact on the progress made in learning American English and the introduction to proper pronunciation.

Columbia University became the center of my life and the framework through which I explored the United States. The daily routine started at the American Language Center. In the afternoons I attended lectures in a variety of buildings on the old-fashioned campus in the middle of Manhattan. After dinner I went to the movies and sat through two performances. This was an excellent way to get accustomed to the sound of the language and follow the dialogue, broadening my vocabulary. After completing assignments due the next day, I finally could catch some sleep. It was a grueling schedule, but I succeeded in getting through the first semester. The teachers were extremely considerate and helpful. They made allowances for my poor English and graded my papers and tests on the basis of the knowledge demonstrated. It took a great deal of patience and concentration to decode what I wrote in my broken English. Once my effort was recognized, everything within reason was done to facilitate my work. The consideration, the tolerance, and the attention made a strong impression on me.

The first months were difficult, with every minute of the day accounted for and utilized to the maximum. Gradually after my English improved I could relax somewhat and observe my surroundings. The student body was divided into two distinct groups. The war veterans who were subsidized by the government were mature and serious. They came to the university with clear objectives, participated actively in the discussions, and made a significant contribution in the classroom. The second group consisted of young students who either had come directly from high school or had transferred from other universities. These were immature, rather simplistic, and not well prepared. The contrast between the two groups was astonishing. While one could communicate with ease with the veterans, the infantile youngsters were beyond reach. They lived in a world all of their own, basically still playful and with one foot in an extended childhood. The foreign students generally kept to themselves. Most lived on a restricted budget and were primarily interested in getting on with their studies.

The faculty was impressive and distinguished. Regretfully, not everyone was interested in teaching, or had the required skills to be effective in the classroom. It was a departure from what I was accustomed to at the Hebrew University, where most of the faculty members were, in addition to being internationally recognized authorities in their fields, accomplished communicators.

The smaller classes at the Hebrew University, an institution dedicated primarily to graduate studies, facilitated the establishment of personal contacts. At Columbia this was possible only occasionally and only with some members of the faculty. Nevertheless, I was fortunate to be taught by Arthur F. Burns, James Angell, George Stiegler, Ragnar Nurkse, and many other equally accomplished and prominent scholars.

The discussions in the classroom reflected the preoccupations of those days. The depression of the 1930s still cast a shadow on the country, and fear of its recurrence permeated the thinking at the university. The country was fascinated by the FDR era and was basking in the glory of the victory in Europe and in the Pacific. The Cold War was on, with ever-increasing pressure from the Soviet Union experienced throughout the globe. It culminated in the Berlin blockade broken by the decisive action of President Truman. The war in Korea was fought by the troops led by Kim Il Sung, a proxy of the Soviet Union with the assistance of Chinese "volunteers." It was increasingly costly and brought with it the first signs of dissent on the involvement of the United States in Asia. Student knowledge of international affairs and geography was astonishingly limited, and developments were occasionally discussed on the campus with a surprising lack of understanding of the issues involved. These were currents and crosscurrents detected in the midst of dealing with the work load of studies, in a foreign language and in an unfamiliar environment.

The impact of McCarthyism on the campus was very pronounced. There were members of the faculty who had come from California because they refused to sign the declaration of loyalty required by the state university system. Any discussion of Marxism-Leninism or for that matter socialism was suspect, and there was an almost palpable fear permeating the university. A discussion of Marxism was unavoidable in a course on the evolution of economic thought. The lecturer spent one session explaining why she had to present this topic. After discussing Marxism and communism, another session was dedicated to explanation of why these ideas had to be brought up. The preoccupation of the lecturer reflected the "witch hunt" of those days and the hysteria it created. She simply was determined not to get embroiled in a controversy.

It was astonishing to observe the spread of hysteria in the McCarthy period. This stable and sound country was hardly a susceptible target for socialism of the Soviet variety. It was only the extraordinary and inexplicable passivity of the Eisenhower Administration that permitted an obscure and ignorant senator to take apart the fabric of the society and some of its institutions, like the State Department. Eventually after the televised Army hearings, it was the Congress that finally freed the country from this strange scourge.

My primary interest was to learn English, to graduate, and to develop a skill or a profession. Therefore, issues of domestic or international policy were only of peripheral interest. Nevertheless, I had difficulty comprehending the direction of foreign policy conducted by Washington in the 1950s. The Korean war, fought by the United States and its allies under the flag of the United Nations, was won militarily but lost politically after the trip of President Eisenhower to Asia. The vague and inconclusive armistice ended in interminable and meaningless negotiations in Panmunjon.

The support given by Washington to anyone who challenged Great Britain and France and the aggressive pursuit of an anticolonial policy played into the hands of the Soviet Union. It provided the backdrop for the premature dismantling of the colonial system and the destruction of progress achieved through an effort of generations. The spectacle of Roy Cohn, an aid to Senator McCarthy, visiting U.S. embassies abroad, making controversial statements to the press, was embarrassing and damaging. The veiled hostility displayed by John Foster Dulles toward Great Britain and France was hard to comprehend as it was undermining the long-term interests of the United States.

A year and a half quickly passed after my arrival in New York. I completed the requirements for the M.A. degree in the School of Political Science, and all I had to do was to write a thesis to graduate. Shortly after arrival in New York I met Olga in the home of my future in-laws. Her parents were acquaintances of my parents, and as a boy I had sat next to her father in the Temple when my father officiated. We had a great deal in common, our backgrounds were similar, and we could communicate with ease. She was then a law student in her second year. In normal circumstances I would have courted Olga and we would become engaged and then married. My situation, however, was somewhat precarious as I was an army officer on active duty; my future was in the Israeli Army. Olga's father was a man of means, and all I had to offer to this promising young lady was the hardship of a soldier's life. We sorted all this out, however, and we got engaged in the spring of 1953.

A letter arrived from my friend Zaro, who was in charge then of the training of the Israeli Army, warning me that I would be recalled shortly to assume a new assignment. I wrote that in a few weeks I would graduate, and I would appreciate either a prolongation of my stay or a leave of absence. Zaro responded that there was little he could do as the orders were issued by the Chief of Staff. I was disappointed that I would have to leave the United States without graduating.

Olga and I were married in May 1953, and shortly afterward we left for a honeymoon in Europe and Israel. These were happy and carefree days. We were young, full of hope, and everything seemed to point to a bright future. My friends in Israel received Olga with open arms. My assignment was not too demanding and for a while the outlook was rosy.

Gradually, clouds started to appear on the horizon. Olga's rather fragile health started to present problems as the subtropic climate of Israel did not suit her.

It was assumed in the army that I belonged to MAPAI (the party led by Ben Gurion and then in power), while in effect I had no interest in political bickering and had no formal party affiliation. It became clear after my return from the United States that, unless I became politically active, my future in the Israeli Army would be stymied. I no longer had the enthusiasm and desire to lead. It was easy to close my eyes, follow the trends, and, profiting from my record, carve a comfortable niche for myself. However, this I was not prepared to do. I completed my assignment, submitted my resignation from the Israeli Army, and returned to New York to graduate and to start a new life.

Those were difficult days. I was only thirty years old but already worn out and tired by an extraordinary odyssey. It was Olga's support, understanding, and affection that enabled me to go through this difficult time of adjustment. I left the Israeli Army after eight years of dedicated service. My friends were sorry to see me leave but respected my decision and did not ask questions. I on the other hand decided not to explain anything and to keep silent.

During the year and a half of study at Columbia University while still in active service, I had concentrated on subjects that would prepare me for my assignments, either in the Israeli Army or eventually

in the government. Therefore, after completion of the basic requirements of the Department of Economics, I chose macroeconomics,
international trade, and international finance as fields of specialization. As a subject for my thesis I selected capital formation in the
oil-producing countries in the Middle East, because I perceived this
to be a key issue in the years to come. Professor Ragnar Nurkse
agreed to act as my sponsor.

With my military career over, the immediate task facing me was
to find a way to support myself and my family. Therefore, a change
of direction was called for. The pursuit of macroeconomics and
international trade would have led me to a Ph.D. and probably an
academic career. This did not suit me; therefore, I shifted my emphasis to corporate finance, accounting, and statistics, and chose a
different topic for my thesis. The pressure of a deadline previously
imposed by the Israeli Army was lifted, and after my return to New
York I could pursue my studies in a more relaxed fashion.

The contacts made at Columbia University and Olga's friends
provided the first leads to a social life. I found it rather difficult to
communicate as there were very few common interests. Attempts to
answer questions about the war years were beyond comprehension
and bored the listeners. On the other hand I was not too good at the
little chit-chat common at cocktail parties. I naively thought that
politicians active in governing the city and the state would be better
informed, and a common ground could perhaps be found associat-
ing with them.

Olga was active in the reform movement of the Democratic Party
and knew Franklin D. Roosevelt, Jr. and others in the political clubs
of New York. On a number of occasions I met members of the local
establishment socially. I quickly realized that any attempt to explore
international issues in a discussion would be futile. Tension in the
Middle East was on the increase, leading to a confrontation between
Great Britain and France over the Suez Canal. Attempts to alert anyone to the consequences of a loss of the Suez Canal marked me as a
crackpot. After a few attempts to develop interest in these subjects, I
gave up discussing international political issues and concentrated on
my studies.

There was no point in continuing my work with Professor

Nurkse on capital formation in the Middle East. The subject was well-chosen. However, its thrust was of interest to an officer on the general staff of the Israeli Army or a high government official. After some reflection, I chose as a subject for my master's thesis the reorganization of the Missouri Pacific Railroad system. I was warned not to pursue this complex matter. I nevertheless persevered as I had access to a great deal of detailed information on this complicated reorganization that had dragged on for almost twenty years. A brokerage firm with which I was associated at the time was involved in the matter, and its managing partner played a key role in working out a compromise that led to the acceptance of the final plan. My new sponsor, Professor James C. Bonbright, tried to dissuade me from undertaking this project and suggested a number of other topics, but finally gave his consent.

I was given a desk in the stacks of the library of the university and there I set up shop surrounded by books and Moody's railroad manuals. At a certain point I decided to visit Washington and call on the Interstate Commerce Commission. I wrote to a commissioner introducing myself as a graduate student and asked for an appointment. I was received at the ICC by a gracious and distinguished-looking gentleman whose name I recognized from the records of the hearings before the commission. I asked rather naively whether I could copy the docket of the Missouri Pacific Railroad as I was writing a thesis on the subject.

The commissioner with a straight face inquired whether I had brought with me an adequate number of trucks to transport it to New York. Then he took me to the library and showed me rooms full of documents representing records of hearings in courts and before the ICC concerning the Missouri Pacific Railroad's reorganization. I realized that my sponsor, Professor Bonbright, had been right, but there was no way to back out at this stage. The commissioner, seeing my confusion and embarrassment, offered to assist me in the project. He procured the latest plan of reorganization, which employed Professor Bonbright's approach of relative priority in settling the different claims represented by the many classes of debt of the railroad and its subsidiaries, and provided me with an introduction to a law firm in St. Louis representing the trustee.

I left the ICC overwhelmed but also impressed with the ease with which I could meet a senior official of one of the key agencies and the assistance extended to my undertaking. It was the first of many similar experiences, which introduced me to the greatness of the United States and the opportunities it presents. A great deal has changed since. Nevertheless, this and many other incidents demonstrated that the country's brilliantly designed system, not always efficiently managed by politicians, has built-in flexibility and fairness.

After a hot and humid New York summer spent in the stacks of the library of Columbia University, my thesis was ready and I brought it to Professor Bonbright. This completed my studies and I started to look for employment. The placement office of the university proved to be useless. An ad placed in the *Wall Street Journal* produced only one reply from a mutual fund in Philadelphia. An interview with the personnel manager of a major brokerage firm, arranged through a friend of mine from Columbia University, resulted in the advice that I would never succeed on Wall Street.

I erroneously thought that my previous experience and analytical ability could be channeled into a position in a research department of a financial firm on Wall Street. I quickly learned that a degree in economics did not necessarily open doors in the financial community in those days, and a military career was a definite drawback. It was surprising to me that mentioning my military experience invariably ended the interviews. Another aspect of these frustrating days of search for employment was the fact that I had no business experience. My comment that I had just graduated and was prepared to learn was answered by the response that there was no guarantee that after I was trained by the firm I would not leave it.

Finally, I succeeded in getting a job as a research trainee cum assistant mail clerk in one of the wire houses. I did not realize it at once, but it was a lucky break. The firm, Josephthal & Co., was large enough to provide the full line of financial services then available on the Street. It was at the same time reasonably compact so that I was able to comprehend its activities and learn the necessary technical skills. I was assigned an old desk in a large room that served simultaneously as the research department, which housed in addition to the reference library voluminous files and five analysts. In the adjacent room were offices of the partners in charge of research, secretaries, and a ticker tape machine. In a corner an elderly wire clerk sat with a Morse key tapping out signals from messages brought for transmission. These were executed orders, research comments, and other administrative matters transmitted by Morse code to the branches of the firm. Another ticker brought in messages and inquiries to be answered. The extraordinarily efficient and patient wire clerk sat at his desk from 8 A.M. to 5 P.M. with a short period of rest for lunch, which was delivered to his station.

In a large room next door to the research department was a screen with stock quotations projected on it. Salesmen, or, as they were called then, customers' men, sat in rows at their desks with their eyes riveted to the moving tape, like boys in a schoolroom.

Occasionally an announcement was made on a loudspeaker related to a stock split or some important corporate news. The air was thick with cigarette and cigar smoke, the din of the ringing telephones was overwhelming, and the salesmen from time to time ran to a window at the end of the room to place their orders. Occasionally, the analysts were called in to provide information on a security or a company, following an inquiry from the registered representatives.

The rest of the floor was occupied by the order room, the traders, a dividend department with clerks sitting at old-fashioned pulpits entering data and changes in inventories by hand on huge sheets referred to as "blotters." The cage was an enclosed space in one large room where securities were kept during the day. At the end of the working day, after the books of the firm balanced, they were taken to a huge safe in a bank downstairs.

The margin room had another battery of clerks computing by hand the "purchasing power" of the customers, that is, the credit permitted on securities according to margin regulations. Finally the PS (purchases and sales) department, where commissions were computed on old-fashioned comptometers, completed the operations area of the brokerage firm. Most of the calculations were made by hand. Errors were rarely found as these were days when employees took pride in a properly executed task. The firm was in many respects a very unusual one. The operations or the "back office" were run by three Italo-American families. They carefully watched the collection of salesmen, or producers, to make sure that they did not violate the regulations of the New York Stock Exchange or the SEC. The firm was their livelihood, and they jealously guarded its integrity.

This was a dramatic change for me from my previous activities as a general staff officer in the Israeli army. I left my home in the morning for the canyons of Wall Street when it was still dark. I left the firm for the subway to take me uptown after nightfall when the lights in the skyscrapers were already on. Frequently I pondered if I ever would break out of this mold and find my place in this strange and new environment.

The managing partner, after observing me for a while, suggested that I should spend half a year training in every department of the firm. I gratefully accepted this offer, and for the rest of the winter and spring I worked in every department of the firm, familiarizing myself with brokerage procedures. After completion of the training, I was asked to take the examination administered by the Stock Exchange for registered representatives. I failed it miserably because I tried to answer the questions properly and in depth.

The managing partner, learning about it, assigned an order clerk who specialized in preparation of candidates for this examination to prepare me for this ordeal. The sessions with this kind and competent man are well-etched in my memory. He drilled me in answering the questions, stressing repeatedly, "Do not think! Your job is to provide the expected answer. The more you think, the worse off you will be." He finally succeeded in getting through to me, and the next time I took this examination I passed it with flying colors because I refrained from thinking.

Before Thanksgiving and Christmas, a list was prepared in every department stating the size of the family of each employee. This list was shipped to a turkey farm in Vermont, and before the holiday the postman delivered a turkey to each family, a gift from the firm. It was a gesture that probably reflected best the atmosphere prevailing in this old-fashioned firm, run by decent people before greed took hold of Wall Street. Shortly before Christmas each employee was personally invited to call on the managing partner, who had a kind word and a bonus check. Unexpectedly there was also one for me, although I was still only a trainee. This was a slice of old America I had the privilege of encountering in the 1950s when I started my career on Wall Street. It was an old-line brokerage house dedicated to providing service for its customers and protecting their interests. Its management invited loyalty and dedication to work, because it treated its employees decently, with dignity, and was prepared to share the rewards.

In the spring of 1956 I discovered another slice of America. The Supreme Court rejected the appeal of a party opposing the last plan of reorganization of the Missouri Pacific Railroad. I went to Washington to be there when the decision was announced. It was a simple procedure, and after a number of other cases a brief announcement was made. The reorganization that had dragged on for twenty years was over. It had been fascinating to trace the procedures before the commission and the courts, giving everyone a chance to present his case. It was not the most efficient way to settle the issue, but it had a certain fairness and consideration for the position of every party involved.

The Missouri Pacific Railroad arranged an inspection trip for the partners of the investment houses representing an important stake in the railroad. As partners of my firm were unable to participate, I was sent to join the party. I flew to St. Louis on a TWA Super Constellation. This was one of the most beautiful planes designed in the propeller era, and TWA in those days was a leading airline. After Europe and the Middle East it was an elating experience to travel by air in the United States.

At the railroad station in St. Louis a special train was waiting for us consisting of sleepers, restaurant cars, bars, and even a car with showers and a bath. A distinguished group was invited to participate in the inspection trip, consisting of bankers, executives of insurance companies, partners of investment houses, and managers of mutual funds. The group included guests who had arrived from New York, Chicago, Boston, Philadelphia, and Hartford. The hosts were key executives of the railroad and its counsel, Senator Dearmont. This was my first contact with the senior management, partners of financial houses, and politicians from the region served by the Missouri Pacific Railroad.

We left for Little Rock, Arkansas, and from there to Dallas, Houston, Corpus Christi, the Rio Grande Valley, Baton Rouge, Kansas City, and back to St. Louis. The trip took a week, with visits to a variety of places served by this railroad, the size of the French national railway system.

It was an extraordinary introduction to the size of the country and the different states we travelled through. The train stopped at a number of small stations in Mississippi and Louisiana, which provided a glimpse of old America. Farmers in overalls, some smoking cheroots or corn cob pipes, were milling around, and waiting before the station there were old-fashioned wagons pulled by mules. It was a scene that could have been lifted from one of Norman Rockwell's pictures.

A trip on a boat along the Houston channel, with the refineries and petrochemical industry visible for miles on both sides of it almost until San Jacinto, introduced me to the industrial power of the United States. The agriculture of the Rio Grande Valley provided a different view of the wealth of the country. These impressions, combined with the comments made by the well-informed group travelling with me on the train, were an important introduction to the United States, which so far I had seen only from the perspective of New York and Wall Street. It provided a better grasp of the country, the great variety of people, and its wealth. It also made me realize that the United States actually is a continent consisting of many countries united by a political and economic system.

The discussions on the train were interesting and illuminating. It became apparent that the point of view of New Yorkers was not shared by others. It was fascinating for me to listen to the Midwesterners, who represented an entirely different and more balanced approach.

An equally interesting aspect was that international developments were ignored, and the discussions concentrated on domestic issues as if the United States were completely insulated from the rest of the world. During that short period of time, Nasser nationalized the Suez Canal. The joint British-French expeditionary force landed in the Suez Canal Zone and tension in the Middle East was at a high pitch. The Hungarians attempted to free themselves from the yoke of the Soviet Union and wished to introduce communism with a human face. This resulted in Soviet intervention and the treacherous execution of the leaders who had been invited by the Kremlin to negotiate. But we were travelling in a luxurious cocoon—the special train, the famous "Eagle" of the Missouri Pacific, normally serving the St. Louis–Mexico City route, suspended in time. We did not pay any attention to these events, which were hardly mentioned in the local newspapers available on the train. We just discussed the future course of the reorganized railroad.

We arrived in Corpus Christi. After a visit to the town we were driven to a well-appointed country club where the local Chamber of Commerce had arranged a reception and dinner for our party. The guests were seated at tables alternating with members of the local business community. Next to me was the president of an oil company. A large television set, a novelty in those days, in a corner of the lavishly appointed dining room was broadcasting President Eisenhower's address to the nation on the Suez crisis and explaining his decision to side with the USSR against France and Great Britain. To my astonishment my neighbor turned to me and commented "Kurt, why should I care about this ditch?" I was flabbergasted by the statement. It was evident to me that this action by the President ended an era of British and French influence in the Middle East, and its repercussions would be far-reaching, eventually encompassing the Panama Canal. The disinterest and the cavalier attitude displayed by an executive of a petroleum company during an international crisis at the dinner in Corpus Christi was puzzling and disturbing indeed.

We continued the fascinating inspection trip, arriving at the impressive Union Station in Kansas City. From there we visited recently completed classification yards employing IBM computers to weigh the boxcars and redirect them to be assembled into trains on a whole series of tracks. The progress of the boxcars was guided by a system of electronically controlled brakes built into the tracks, which were applied according to the weight, the nature of the shipment, and the speed of the boxcar moving down an elevated hump. The whole procedure was automated and electronically controlled, a harbinger of a yet another technological breakthrough.

A great deal of social activity took place in the bar cars. Alcohol flowed freely but no one was drunk. I was particularly impressed by an elderly partner of Halsey Stuart who was holding court in one of the bar cars, sitting on a table sipping bourbon from a water glass all day long and chasing it with beer. His knowledge of railroad securities was astounding, and the mixture of bourbon and beer apparently provided the right inspiration.

I stuck to Scotch, while others drank martinis, manhattans, and an occasional gin and tonic. On the last day I gathered courage and inquired whether there was French brandy on board the train. The bartender inquired whether I wished to have a Hennessy, Courvoisier, or possibly a Hines. Emboldened I asked for the wine list, and I discovered they had a respectable list of French red and white wines. I was sorry to learn this only on the last day of the trip. It was yet another of many lessons not to underestimate the United States.

I returned full of impressions from the inspection trip of the Missouri Pacific Railroad and the territory it served to my modest desk and the dusty room housing the small research department. It took me a long time to sort out all I had learned. I continued to answer incoming inquiries from the firm's branches, read a great deal, and attended the lunches of the New York Society of Security Analysts.

In those days the NYSSA consisted of a small group that met on the second floor of Schwartz's, a restaurant on Broad Street. The premises were modest and so was the quality of the food. After each meeting the waiters collected the left-over rolls. Judging from the hardness of the rolls served the next day, they were probably "recycled." There we were addressed by the management of corporations who came to present their stories. The meetings were interesting and so were the neighbors at the table. I recall sitting at one of the meetings next to a modest, unassuming gentleman whose comments were perceptive and brilliant. It was Professor Marcus Nadler of New York University, an economic advisor to Manufacturers Trust Company.

One of the old-timers, a tall and nattily dressed individual with neatly trimmed graying hair and a mustache, and always wearing a bow tie, was armed with an impressive Polaroid camera (a novelty in those days), and always took pictures of the visiting executives before the meeting started. It was an interesting and an original business development gimmick. This was almost a ritual. I always pondered what he did with the accumulated photographs of all the visitors.

Time was passing, and it seemed to me that it would not be possible to make further progress in my professional development. Observing my colleagues, I realized that an anylyst's career in a brokerage firm is circumscribed, as in the final analysis his function is to support sales. I was fortunate to work for a brokerage firm that did not exert pressure, and an analyst did not have to compromise his integrity. Nevertheless, I did not wish to spend the rest of my professional career answering wires.

A much older colleague of mine, Richard Burbage, had started as an analyst at this brokerage firm as a young man in the depths of the depression. A kind, soft-spoken and courteous man, he kept to himself. Occasionally at lunchtime we left the firm together, stopped at one of the many little sandwich shops at the end of Broad Street to buy our lunch, and took the ferry to Staten Island and back for a nickel. Dick always had a kind word, always encouraged me, and never complained. In his sixties he still was answering wires and searching manuals for information on obscure securities of long-forgotten companies that were brought to him by the customer's men. One winter afternoon he suffered a heart attack and died at his desk in the corner of the dusty room.

My salary was satisfactory by the standards of the time and I was progressing in the firm. Nevertheless I had difficulty supporting my family on it. In those days it was rather difficult for a woman to get a decent job in a law firm. Olga tried hard and was offered positions only in small firms. She too realized that there was little future for her, as women were discriminated against in those days.

We both became restless and decided to explore other possibilities. We reached the conclusion that I had to return to school. A doctorate in economics did not appeal to me as I did not wish to land on the academic side of my profession. I also realized that in order to break out of the mold I must leave the transportation industry and develop a quantitative approach to financial analysis.

The approaching demise of the railroad industry was apparent, in view of the ICC regulations, labor negotiations, and the expansion of the trucking industry. On one of the trips for the firm I travelled by train from Boston to Providence. I was the only paying passenger on a train with a crew of five running it. The technical expression for it was "featherbedding."

This situation could not go on, and a repetition of the bankruptcies of railroads experienced in the 1920s was only a matter of time. I decided to shift to other industries whose future was brighter. This however required some knowledge of science and technology. Therefore, I opted for a study of industrial engineering, which I expected would provide me with an understanding of methods of production and an introduction to quantitative analysis. My friends at the university tried to dissuade me from the project, pointing out that I would have to return to an undergraduate level of studies. In a way they were right but I again persevered, realizing that the stress on humanities in my education left many areas I had to explore before embarking on a broader career on Wall Street.

One day the managing partner overheard me discussing the Middle East with someone. He suggested that it would be helpful if I briefed him on subjects I thought might be of interest to him. This started me on experimentation with a synthesis of political and economic analysis to be presented in a capsulized form to a busy senior executive. Without realizing it then, I had stumbled into a field I would eventually pursue with considerable success. The changes in the international environment were affecting events in the United States, and with it a demand grew for a flow of information adapted to the requirements of executives with line responsibility.

I again enrolled at Columbia University, this time in the school of engineering, and arranged for a leave of absence from the brokerage firm. I was allowed to keep my desk and come whenever I pleased.

I continued the briefing of the managing partner, not expecting any compensation. Before Christmas, while visiting his office to brief him on developments, he gave me an envelope with his best wishes. I opened it at my desk and to my amazement found a check representing a year's salary and a bonus. A turkey from Vermont with compliments of the brokerage firm was waiting for me at my home.

The studies were a chore as I found myself in a pre-engineering program designed to eliminate students unsuited for this program. My first tour at Columbia had not been easy. This however was a new experience as I had to get through calculus, chemistry, physics and other prerequisites before I was admitted to the engineering program.

The students were a dull and uninteresting group, primarily interested in reaching the promised land of consumerism as soon as possible. It was a rather materialistically oriented group, a far cry from the veterans I had encountered while studying economics. The faculty was equally focused on the subjects taught, with little interest in individual students. It was an assembly-line education process that nevertheless produced competent if uninspired technicians. As I had no intention of becoming an engineer, I rather enjoyed the new disciplines, which gave me broader horizons and a new dimension. These were busy and hard times as mornings were spent at the brokerage firm trading securities to support my family, the afternoons were spent in classes or in the laboratories, and the evenings in the library or learning how to draw blueprints.

At this time Olga was in her last year at the New York University Law School. She graduated in 1956, and I was proud and pleased to see her walk with others in the academic procession to receive her degree. The commencement exercise at the campus of the university in the Bronx remains after so many years still etched in my memory. A retired chairman of a major insurance company addressed the graduates, and in his speech stressed that the previous generation had had to deal with scarcity. It had been a difficult and trying task, he said, and he was proud to belong to the generation that had dealt successfully with this challenge. He pointed out that the current graduates presently would have to deal with affluence. He wished them equal success in dealing with this challenge as his generation had had in dealing with scarcity. His words made a lasting impression, because they addressed the key issue facing American society in the postwar era.

Olga passed the bar examination on her first try and was admitted to the State of New York Bar. She accomplished it while running a house and entertaining our friends. I was somewhat envious because I could not sail with equal ease through my new academic endeavor. Somehow I managed and was now confronted with the task of translating my preparation into professional activity.

I combined undergraduate and graduate studies in economics with an earlier solid academic training in classics, which although interrupted had provided me with an intellectual discipline. The general staff school and military experience provided management and administrative skills and planning techniques. The school of engineering introduced me to methods of quantitative analysis and a broad understanding of technical problems and industrial production. All this had to be forged into a service or a saleable product. In the meantime I returned to my desk as a senior analyst and was given more complex assignments. My interest shifted at this time from the retail end of brokerage activity to the rapidly growing institutional field.

In 1959 after the birth of my oldest son, Andrew, Olga and I travelled abroad. After my testimony in the process of beatification of Metropolitan Andrew Graf Szeptycki, we travelled by car through Europe. I was introduced by my mentor and friend, William C. Schmidt, an executive at the Chase Manhattan Bank, a powerful financial institution then, to leading European bankers. I learned at these meetings that I could communicate with these senior bankers with ease, and my comments seemed to be of interest to them. After a number of successful visits to banks in Rome, the Chase manager provided me with introductions to leading bankers in Switzerland, Germany, Holland, and England.

After my return from Europe I described the visits to the banks to our firm's managing partner, who suggested that I organize a foreign department of the firm. I reflected for a while and decided to accept the assignment. This changed my life and launched me into a whole series of new adventures.

I ventured first into Canada and, armed with an introduction of Chase Manhattan to the Bank of Montreal, I explored my firm's business opportunities in Montreal, Toronto, Winnipeg, and Vancouver. It was extraordinary to observe in Canada the distinct cultural differences and approach to doing business. The links of Canada with the United Kingdom were still strong in those days, giving it a distinct and a separate identity.

Montreal had a definite French character. However, only the English institutions were open to new ideas and to visitors from the United States. The insurance companies like Sun Life, the trust departments of banks, and pension funds of large corporations, like Canadian Pacific and Molson Breweries, offered excellent opportunities for business development. The executives in these organizations were a highly competent if somewhat conservative group.

Toronto, a sleepy town with a distinct English character in those days, was somewhat more interesting, and its brokerage community was given to taking risks and aggressively marketing penny mining stocks. The insurance companies were primarily interested in fixed-interest instruments and real estate. A trip to Western Canada was a fascinating introduction to a still-prevailing pioneer mentality. Central European immigration there was emerging as a major factor, revitalizing the somewhat conservative, well-entrenched Scottish and English establishment.

Winnipeg, extraordinarily cold in the winter, was an interesting financial center. It was the first time I noticed that, whenever a car was parked, its radiator had to be plugged into an electrical circuit to keep the water in the radiator from freezing. The most impressive sight was the legendary Canadian Mounties, wrapped in huge bison coats with the hair outside, regulating the flow of traffic at the major intersections and ignoring the cold wind blowing snow flurries.

The Bank of Montreal opened doors to many sectors of the business community in Manitoba. The most interesting was the Great Western Life Insurance Company, managed by well-informed executives. There for the first time I met an economist who was highly respected and participated in management decisions. Arthur Brown was the first business economist I encountered who employed a broad range of disciplines to economic analysis and forecasting. His work and his approach were a source of encouragement. I introduced him to employing political analysis selectively in forecasting economic trends. Arthur's comments and the role he played at Great Western Life provided insights that guided me in my search for a new approach to economic analysis applied to planning corporate strategy.

Reflecting on my experiments in Canada, I reached the conclusion that there were two areas of activity that would have to be combined in building a successful foreign department of a brokerage firm. A wide network of contacts in financial institutions abroad could provide a flow of commission revenues. An investment policy based on an integrated political and economic analysis utilizing connections abroad could be marketed to institutions in the U.S., providing a competitive advantage. This two-pronged approach could result in breaking into markets previously reserved for the old line investment houses like Lehman Bros., Kuhn Loeb, Eastman Dillon, Kidder Peabody and others.

I launched my project following the Canadian experiment by calling first on the mutual funds industry in Boston. I was somewhat intimidated by the idea of approaching these institutions while representing a brokerage firm known primarily as a wire house. Besides I had resided in the U.S. for only a few years and my English still left a great deal to be desired. The first meeting with Ed Johnson II, the chief executive and founder of the Fidelity Group, was another turning point in my career. Ed, a friendly man with a sharp intellect and deep-seated penetrating blue eyes, made one feel at ease. He recognized the contribution I could make to him and to his associates. Interestingly enough, he never inquired about my background. All he cared about was that I presented an unusual approach to the investment exercise that could make a contribution to his organization.

We engaged in a quick exchange of ideas and compared observations on a variety of subjects, related directly and indirectly to the development of broad investment policy. I was very pleased at the end of the meeting to be invited to visit the Fidelity Group regularly at their modest, cramped, and somewhat old-fashioned offices on Congress Street. This started a long and challenging relationship that continued until the retirement of Ed and his deputy George Sullivan.

My frequent trips to Boston started with a call on the Fidelity Group. I usually arrived on the air shuttle from New York shortly before noon, and, after a brief discussion in Ed's office, we continued over lunch at the dining room where the portfolio managers were assembled. A lively discussion followed with the participation of everyone. The visits to Fidelity and the questions posed by Ed and his associates in the Group honed my approach to an integrated investment strategy.

This activity in Boston was expanded to include other investment institutions like Massachusetts Investors Trust, Loomis Sayles, and Putnam. Eventually I started to call on insurance companies like John Hancock, New England Life, and Massachusetts Life in Springfield, and the trust departments of New England banks. After exploring the opportunities in New England, I ventured to Chicago.

I learned quickly that in most instances every door in the U.S. could be opened once, and a reasonably fair hearing could be expected in this rather open society. It was an exhilarating experience to visit the well-known major financial institutions all over the country and meet captains of industry like Herbert Prochnow of First National Bank of Chicago, William Moses of Massachusetts Investors Trust, and many others. It was a breakthrough that could not be achieved by a new immigrant in any other society.

The meetings in these institutions were unstructured. The host normally opened the discussion by introducing a topic of interest to him. Therefore, I never knew what might be brought up and had to be prepared to cover a broad range of topics. At the early stage of my new activity, the foreign policy of the USSR and the threat it posed to the United States attracted a great deal of attention. The revolution of Fidel Castro and the subsequent Cuban missile crisis caused a great deal of concern in the boardrooms as the Soviet threat was introduced in the Western Hemisphere. Subsequently interest shifted to the balance of payments and balance of trade of the United States, which led to a discussion of the crisis involving the pound sterling and the future of the monetary system. The pressures emanating from Hanoi in South Vietnam and the increasing tension in Southeast Asia redirected focus to Asia. The Middle East and its conflicts were always of interest, as the increasing instability of the region after the unsuccessful intervention of the British and the French posed a potential threat to critical supplies of crude oil. The discussions revolving around these changing topics were concentrated on an interpretation of these developments and their impact on the economy of the United States and on portfolio strategy.

Each meeting was a new challenge, as I was confronting seasoned executives with a great deal of experience and knowledge. It was also a learning experience and an opportunity to perfect my approach to economic analysis and adapt the presentation to the varying and changing interests encountered in different institutions.

An important aspect of my professional activity of building the foreign department were frequent trips to Europe. A trip started usually in Rome where, meeting with friends in the Vatican, I could get an unbiased overview of the situation. The observers in the Curia Romana in those days were extremely well informed and had a farsighted and objective view of the international situation. The visits to the major banks like Banco di Roma and Banca Nazionale del Lavoro were pleasant and interesting but not very productive because these were managed by political appointees. Banca d'Italia provided an excellent overview of the international monetary situation as perceived by a central bank.

Milano was much more interesting as Banca Commerciale Italiana and Credito Italiano were involved in different aspects of international trade. La Centrale, Mediobanca, and RAAS (an insurance company) provided a view of investment banking activity and made me realize that it was an area closed to an outsider. Among the individuals I met in Milano in 1960s were the mysterious Dr. Enrico Cuccia, the gray eminence of Italian finance, and a capable vice president of Banco Ambrosiano, Roberto Calvi. (Calvi was subsequently involved with Archbishop Marcinkus in the strange financial activities of the Vatican's financial institutions and Sindona, the notorious Italian financier. Referred to as God's banker because of his involvement with the Vatican, Calvi was ritualistically hung, his clothes filled with bricks, a variety of currencies, and an address book of the members of the masonic lodge P2, from the Blackfriars Bridge in London by those who had an interest in silencing him.) The practical aspect of all this activity was to pick up leads to securities business in Lugano and Chiasso from where the Italians were investing their assets.

The Swiss banks, at least the large ones, were respectable, conservative, and well run. There were an astonishing number of banks in Zurich, Geneva, and Basel. The problem was to separate the bona fide ones from the variety of adventurers who, behind a facade of respectability of a Swiss financial institution, catered to tax evaders, Latin American dictators, drug dealers, and the Mafia. All were' interested in the U.S. securities markets and in my recommendations of specific securities that were recorded on one's calling card to be reviewed on the next visit. It was difficult to transact business in Switzerland unless a firm maintained an office there. Otherwise one was restricted to dealing only with the Swiss banks, which maintained a representation in New York.

The next stop was Germany. The close relationship of the major banks with industry determined the interests and scope of their operations, which were well beyond those of a brokerage firm. Investment activity was concentrated in smaller private institutions, and I discovered that most of them had a resident partner that had been planted in the major New York Stock Exchange firms in the prewar years. Therefore, a trip to Germany was useful only for collecting information either from the banks or from industry. Eventually the Bundesbank in Frankfurt started to play a key role, particularly in the days when Dr. Otto Emminger was shaping its monetary policy. A visit to it invariably provided insights on the international monetary situation.

On my way to London and Edinburgh I usually stopped in Amsterdam to call on the old line investment houses like Pierson, Heldring & Pierson, Labouchere, Hope and Co., Netherlands Trading Company, and others. The savvy Dutch bankers probably had more international experience than anyone else on the European continent. However, the development of a business relationship with them was a rather difficult undertaking. Their orientation was more toward financing of trade than toward money management activity.

London was a veritable challenge. Visits to Barclays and Midland Banks provided a superb overview of world economic conditions. Westminster Bank was an interesting organization with an excellent foreign exchange trading desk. Bank of London and South America, led by the brilliant Sir George Bolton, was the pioneer in developing the Eurodollar market. Another equally interesting group were the merchant banking houses like Hill Samuel, Warburg, and Montague; however, this sector of the London market had no interest in a New York wire house. The English brokers were in those days a rather snooty and clubby group, and it was a waste of time to call on them.

Edinburgh was a revelation to me. Located in that city were the low-key Scottish trusts guided by extremely well-informed and competent portfolio managers. The old-fashioned and dusty offices on Charlotte Square were misleading, as the Scottish trusts managed substantial portfolios from there. The exchange of ideas with them was always interesting and challenging and led to possibilities of developing meaningful relations. I subsequently found equally interesting investment operations in Dundee and Glasgow. A visit to Scottish trusts was certainly an education in itself.

These trips were fascinating, informative, and exhausting. The real task facing me was to translate all this into meaningful business activity for my firm.

The brokerage firm was oriented primarily toward servicing retail clients. It had neither the required facilities nor research to service large foreign-based institutional accounts. It could execute transactions for U.S. institutions in the days of fixed commissions. These were allocated according to the services provided to institutions by the brokerage house. However, dealing with foreign institutions required a communication set-up and suitable representation abroad. The activities of the foreign department were profitable and could be expanded. However, my projects were too broad and started to divert from the general direction of the firm. I recognized it in time and was confronted with the choice of either scaling down my program or leaving the firm. After discussing it with the managing partner, I decided to leave the firm. It was not an easy decision, as I had spent seven interesting years in this pleasant and friendly environment.

It took some time to wind down my affairs and determine what my next association should be. I explored a number of possibilities and learned that I was still not fully acceptable in the old-line firms, as my background was somewhat too exotic and my approach to professional activity unorthodox. I toyed for a while with joining the international department of a large bank. Having explored a number of openings in Chicago and in New York, I found this direction unappealing.

In Germany I had met executives of Bache & Co., who offered to introduce me to the managing partner of the firm, Harold Bache. An offer was made that I found interesting and I joined this powerful firm. This opened a whole spectrum of new adventures.

The initial encounter with the United States that had started at Columbia University had run its course, and the experience gathered in the seven years had provided a whole variety of insights into this fascinating, dynamic, and always changing country.

It remained elusive and hard to define. I had arrived in New York at a time when the country was basking in the knowledge that it had met the challenge of the war and had led the alliance to victory. It had become aware of its economic power and had succeeded in the transition from depression to a war-driven economy, and then the transformation to the postwar environment and challenges. It was a strong and a virile society permeated with the ideas of fairness and willing to open itself to the outside world. However, it was totally unprepared to deal with the new role it was called to perform.

The Soviet threat, the wars on the periphery of the free world, and the political turmoil in Central Europe could be dealt with. The direction of the society in transition from scarcity to extraordinary affluence was another matter. The values and ideas to which I was introduced as fundamental to the society became a subject of debate and eventually challenge. The mass media and especially television reflected new and disturbing trends. As long as the inequities in the society were challenged within the framework of the law of the land, progress was made. The positive changes and the removal of barriers in the society were encouraging and created hopes that the country would move rapidly toward a better tomorrow.

The occasional hysteria stirred by Senator McCarthy was dealt with by the society and its mechanisms. Admittedly the reaction was slow, and damage was done to individuals whose careers were ruined. The country as a whole emerged from this episode unscathed. The new currents and crosscurrents taking hold of the society were initially a well-meaning reaction of a healthy society bent on improving itself. Gradually, these originally positive and healthy challenges degenerated into widspred social unrest, and a disruption of the society culminating in mindless riots at a number of leading universities. Eventually, all this in the 1960s led to a systematic challenge of existing institutions. The late Herman Kahn coined a phrase to describe this period as the "Drug and Fornication Era."

My contact with these developments was peripheral at best, as I was insulated from these trends not readily apparent in the early stages. I studied and taught at a leading university offering a wide variety of fields to chose from. I worked in a conservative firm managed by honorable and dedicated individuals. I tried to make a place for myself in an industry that after the debacle of 1929 was determined not to repeat the mistakes that had led to its collapse.

The financial industry in those days was tough and ruthless, where an individual was judged by his performance. Nevertheless, there were certain rules followed, and with patience, perseverance, and an occasional break one could succeed. It was hardly a welcoming environment in those days and discrimination was rampant. Nevertheless, at my firm Italo-Americans, Irish, an occasional Protestant, and Jews functioned together reasonably well and in a relatively friendly atmosphere. At the luncheon meetings of NYSSA I encountered a variety of individuals, and gradually I lost the self-consciousness of being a newcomer and outsider. The field trips to the properties of the Missouri Pacific Railroad, Sharon Steel, U.S. Steel, and Stauffer Chemical provided an opportunity to meet professionals from other parts of the country and reconfirmed that I could function successfully in this environment.

It was interesting to observe that it was easy to communicate on issues of mutual interest. The back-slapping and the informality were misleading as relations formed were rather superficial. As long as one did not insist on pursuing complex subjects dealing with broad political or cultural issues, it was easy to fit in and function in this mobile and constantly changing society. There were many individuals like Ed Johnson II who had extraordinary insights and erudition. They were not necessarily an exception; nevertheless an effort had to be made to find them.

I discovered America and made myself at home in it. The task of adapting to a new environment, a new language, and a new profession was a hard one. Having closed the first cycle I was ready to deal with the new challenges confronting me. I still did not understand fully the environment in which I found myself and had a great deal to learn about this enormous and complex country.

CHAPTER 10

The Warfare on Wall Street

EVERY THURSDAY MORNING at eight, the partners and senior executives of Bache & Co. met in the conference room on the sixth floor at 36 Wall Street to discuss the activities of the firm. The meeting was chaired by Harold Bache, who called at random on individuals to make a brief comment. I was aware of the size of the firm and the scope of its activities. However, only after observing the key officials assembled in the conference room did I realize the opportunities and the difficulties my new position represented. I could also sense the complications and the precarious situation in which I found myself. I was no stranger to danger and risks. I had encountered intrigues, evil, jealousy, and callousness in the years of struggle for survival and fighting as a soldier in two armies. The experiences acquired in those turbulent years had served me well. However, the present situation was entirely different and the games were played by quite different rules.

Josephthal & Co., the brokerage firm in which I had spent seven years learning about Wall Street and brokerage procedures, was well-managed, with the tensions, infighting, and petty jealousies kept in check by the managing partner. This gave the firm stability and a sense of direction. Theoretically Harold Bache was the senior managing partner of Bache & Co. He charted the course of the firm, and his imprint on it was clearly felt. However, he did not control it as the managing partner, Ben Pollak, did at Josephthal & Co. It was partially due to the size of the organization, its capitalization, the personalities of individuals in key positions, and the cliques formed to guard jealously their respective interests. It took me some time to sort all this out, to understand the crosscurrents present at the head office, and to plan my own position in it.

The Thursday morning meetings, with the key players gathered in one room, provided a reminder of one's position, allowed assessment of the centers of support, and identified the key antagonists. Harold, sitting at a table facing the assembled executives, opened the session with a brief summary of activities of the week. He was usually followed by Monte Gordon, the director of the research department, who discussed the money supply and FRB figures, and George Weiss, an economist, reporting on comments made at the Wall Street Forum luncheon group of which he was a member. John Roosevelt, the youngest son of FDR, followed with a report on the activities of the institutional department; he was generally succeeded by Harry Jacobs discussing syndication activity. I was called on regularly to comment on the international situation and developments in foreign markets.

It became apparent to me with time that the Thursday meetings were attended primarily by working partners. The money partners, the contributors of substantial capital to the firm who wielded a great deal of power and influence, showed up only occasionally. John Leslie, Gustavo Ajo and a number of others, who manipulated the firm and were scheming unobtrusively to thwart Harold Bache, were generally absent.

John Leslie, an accountant brought in from one of the major accounting firms, played the role of a gray eminence pulling strings discreetly and acting as a legal advisor to Harold. He was an Austrian of Jewish descent, which he did not advertise, and had escaped from Vienna in 1938 after the Anschluss.[1] A quiet and determined man, he had worked his way into a strategically critical position in the firm. He was also an honorary consul of Austria in New York, of which he was immensely proud. He realized that Harold and I shared similar views on the expansion of the firm's international activities and that I was aware he was positioning himself as Harold's eventual successor. We were friendly and prudently kept out of each other's way.

Gustavo Ajo, an assimilated Italian Jew who had escaped from

Italy after the introduction of Nuremberg-type racial laws by Mussolini, was the partner responsible for the International Division. He had started as a salesman of securities in the Chrysler Building office of the firm. During the war he had represented a variety of Italian individual investors who were cut off from New York by world events. This provided him in the postwar years with a significant flow of retail business originating primarily in Italy, which was the source of his power base at Bache & Co. He and his lieutenant, Jack G., were in charge of administration of the International Division, coordinating and supervising the managers of foreign branches, who acted as subcontractors using the franchise and the facilities of Bache & Co. Jack had made money in the film industry in Hollywood and moved on to bigger and better things on Wall Street. He was one of the money partners who employed administrative experience acquired in Hollywood in the International Division. His approach to his task was that of a manager of a group of salesmen. They could have been selling vacuum cleaners or brushes, but all that mattered to Jack was that they produced commissions and kept out of trouble.

I was invited by Harold Bache to organize institutional activity for the firm abroad along professional lines. After studying the offer, I reached the conclusion that the firm was too big, with its activities too diffused and retail-oriented, and the same was true of its International Division. However, Harold convinced me that he intended to shift the stress in foreign markets to institutional activity. Olga suggested that it would be prudent to exchange letters stating the terms of our agreement. She pointed out that such an exchange would constitute a binding contract.

After discussions with Harold were concluded, I wrote a letter to him outlining the terms of our understanding. The key clause was that I would report directly either to Harold or to Charles S., one of the key money partners. Jack G. acknowledged the receipt of my letter and agreed to the terms outlined in it. Thus thanks to Olga I had an ironclad contract in my possession. This setup ultimately created an untenable situation for me, as Gustavo Ajo and Jack G. felt threatened by my activities while John Leslie resented my friendship with Harold. I too was of European origin, and in his mind I was infringing on his control over contacts with foreigners, especially with Austrian and German bankers.

All this became gradually apparent to me with time, as I realized that I was being thwarted in most projects that I had undertaken with the approval of Harold Bache. I persisted in carrying out my work, assuming erroneously that, once the partners realized I was making a contribution to the revenues and the growth of the firm, opposition would eventually abate. To my amazement this was not the case. The more I progressed in developing my program, the greater were the hostility and resentment.

Bache & Co. in those days had 116 offices in the United States and abroad. After settling in the firm and organizing my office, I took off for Europe to get acquainted with the firm's operations abroad. My first stop was Rome where I met Gustavo Ajo and the manager of the Rome office, Count P. B., a member of the black (papal) nobility. Over a pleasant luncheon at the Aqua Santa golf club, we discussed the market, the firm, and my program.

The visit to the office of Bache & Co., was interesting and revealing. The elegant and tastefully decorated premises were in a fashionable and modern building. However, the activity in it seemed to be of a social as well as a business character. I was informed that the son of the former King of Italy was associated with the firm but I was never able to learn what his function was. The few salesmen seemed to concentrate on doing business on the golf course and in social circles over elegant lunches and dinners. It was an effective way to secure a flow of retail business. However, my activities were directed toward different markets and targets.

The Milano office of the firm on the fashionable Monte-napoleone street was somewhat intriguing, as it was located in a commodities firm belonging to the manager's father. An entrance was camouflaged through artful carpentry. Entering a closet, one emerged in an elegant secret private office where Italian clients could be discreetly received. Italian laws made trading in foreign securities and foreign exchange illegal in those days. The office was camouflaged to provide privacy to the clients, who were afraid of the nosey tax officials. I had reservations about whether it was desirable for a leading U.S. firm to get involved in activity violating the laws of a foreign country. The laws were punitive, the country was governed by corrupt politicians, and tax revenues were outright stolen or squandered. However, the revenues were not worth the adverse publicity that might be generated for the firm. My point of view, probably not shared by everyone, I prudently kept to myself.

My next stop was Geneva. Roger Solari, the manager of the firm's office, a cautious and friendly man my age, explained the problems encountered in Switzerland. A broker was limited to dealing with Swiss banks, and individual clients had to be introduced by him to a member of the Swiss Convention, either a bank or an investment institution affiliated with a bank. Then the commissions and fees could be shared. Roger and I hit it off well, and we decided to cooperate as my activities and his were complementary and I was in a position to open a number of doors to him in Switzerland. He explained the working of the international division and the personalities involved. It was a rather disturbing and foreboding picture.

In Roger's office I found the son of the former King of Italy, Umberto, and learned that Gustavo Ajo had obtained for Harold an appointment as an official court broker from Maria José, the former Queen of Italy. Roger's stories were very illuminating and helped me orient myself. I left Geneva increasingly preoccupied with the difficulties that would confront me as I carried out my assignment. I was pleased that so far I had found at least one manager with whom I could communicate and share common interests.

The office of Bache & Co. in Frankfurt was managed by a New Yorker, a competent and able man. He formerly had represented an American bank in Frankfurt and had joined the firm at the same time I did. We had met during his previous association, because his bank had hosted a number of my visits to Frankfurt. His responsibility then, following instructions of the head office of the bank, had been to introduce me to German banks and industrialists. He had been invited by Harold to join Bache & Co. to develop German business as the firm's activities had been limited to serving American personnel in U.S. military installations.

The office in Frankfurt was a retail-oriented branch of the firm, not much different from any of the domestic offices. Its manager was an able and pleasant young man in his early thirties, a Harvard graduate who was progressing rapidly at the bank and could have had a brilliant career. His parents, Germans who had immigrated to the U.S. in the 1920s, had provided him with an excellent education. The expansion of international business had created opportunities in which he could accomplish a great deal in a relatively short time. The offer to join a leading Wall Street firm was very tempting. He had left the bank to become the manager of Bache & Co. in Germany. Harold had great expectations for him and provided him with the required resources and support. Gustavo and Jack were out of their depth in Germany and refrained from interfering with the activities of the manager of the Frankfurt office.

The manager was potentially my ally as he too was aiming to develop an institutional business and link it with the well-developed institutional activity of Bache & Co. in the United States. Sadly, his ability and the opportunities were not accompanied by strength of character. He got involved in a variety of deals and activities that destroyed his credibility in the firm, and he eventually lost his sponsorship. Somehow he got embroiled with Robert Vesco, the individual who looted IOS and became a fugitive to avoid American courts. Vesco still is occasionally heard from in countries where U.S. courts cannot reach him, and the former manager disappeared from the horizon.

My next stop was Amsterdam, where an interesting and experienced Dutchman ran the Bache & Co. office as his personal fief. He resented the occasional visitors from New York and had little use for them. Again Gustavo and Jack were out of their depth and restricted their activities to an occasional pep talk, inviting the well-connected and knowledgeable Dutchman to greater efforts and more commission revenues. Effectively he acted as a subcontractor and kept the visitors from the home office away from his primarily private clients and the Amsterdam banks.

I was well known in key Dutch banks and merchant banks from my prior activities at Josephthal & Co. I succeeded in developing business relations with some and was well received in others. The Amsterdam manager and I were always friendly but he kept a distance. The crafty Dutchman realized that sooner or later Gustavo and I would clash, and he preferred not to get involved.

My next stop was Paris, where the firm's office was headed by Pierre de N., who since the days of World War II had maintained close connections with Americans and, rather unusual for a Frenchman, had a great deal of admiration for everything American. He had been involved in sheltering American pilots shot down over France, and his office was papered with letters of thanks from American military and political personalities for his contributions made during the war. As with many other Frenchmen who found it difficult to progress in the French establishment, he had attached himself to a number of New York brokerage firms, riding on American coat tails. The economic and political conditions in the early 1960s and French fiscal laws prompted Frenchmen to invest in dollar-denominated securities. Pierre and his deputy, Hans Graf Czernin, an Austrian, were ideally placed to serve this activity. The commission business was generated primarily through social contacts, and, as long as French laws were not openly violated, the Paris office was reasonably productive. My visit to the Paris office was a waste of time because Pierre, realizing that I had well-established personal and professional connections in France, was determined to keep me out of what he considered his territory. He wrote a letter to Harold saying that I was discrediting the firm in France and should be forbidden to visit there.

Hans Graf Czernin, the son of the last foreign minister of Austro-Hungary before its collapse in 1918, an elegant and pleasant man who had served in the U.S. forces during the war, was friendly with the Jewish partners of Bache & Co. in New York. However, he had brought with him from Vienna to the United States some of the outlook characteristic of his class. I believe that in his eyes I was an Ost-Jude (Eastern or Central European Jew) and thus had to be kept at a distance. Service in the First Polish Army marching on Berlin in 1945, and a subsequent military career in the Israeli Army freed me from being sensitive on this subject. To me these two gentlemen were just a part of a group of 1,300 securities salesmen at Bache & Co. active from coast to coast in the United States and in a number of foreign countries.

Pierre de N. on one of his periodic visits to New York arranged a cocktail party for representatives of foreign banks and corporations.

The engraved personal invitations to this function informed the invitees that the occasion was the commemoration of the anniversary of the death of one of Pierre's ancestors, who had died in 1415 in the battle of Agincourt. A representative of an English bank invited to attend responded that he could not come because this was the anniversary of the death of an ancestor of his who had been killed by the French in 1815 in Waterloo. The style and approach to business by the French sales team, while entertaining, was not necessarily characteristic of Bache & Co.

My final stop was London, where I found a pleasant Englishman operating on the fringes of the brokerage community of the City and assisted by a young German count, whose Jewish grandmother on an otherwise impeccable family tree had compelled his parents in 1938 to emigrate to the U.K. While both were pleasant, cooperative, and competent, I decided that it would be prudent not to be identified too closely with this rather modest although basically sound retail operation.

A summary of observations made visiting the international operation of the firm led me to the conclusion that Gustavo Ajo, a successful supersalesman in one of the retail offices, had built an impressive production based on European clientele. The social activities—on ships crossing the Atlantic, on selected cruises, and during the summer at fashionable European spas—that were engaged in aggressively by Gustavo and his associates served to expand personal contacts. These combined with the name and the reputation of the firm and subtle but aggressive selling resulted in a satisfactory flow of revenues. Gustavo specialized in collecting less successful sons of European aristocracy, providing them with offices and a variety of services in exchange for introductions, or just the use of their names. The House of Savoia provided a contingent, followed by the Spanish Bourbons, papal "black" aristocracy, and an occasional German princeling. These in turn attracted a following of European "demi monde" and social climbers. This approach to business development was not much different from the activities of some American counterparts who frequented golf courses and country clubs in search of potential clients. This strange collection of personalities and clientele was expanded to include U.S. servicemen stationed all over Europe who were induced to purchasing mutual funds and securities.

My activities since 1959 had been concentrated on the development of contacts with senior management of banks, insurance companies, and Scottish trusts, with some inroads made in Italian, Dutch, and Germany industry. I was alerted in 1962 by a good friend of mine at the Chase Manhattan Bank, Bill Lamneck, an old and experienced Asia hand, that I was only two-dimensional because I was familiar with just the United States and Europe. Introductions were provided by Chase to Japanese government and business leaders, which opened an entirely new horizon. I travelled regularly to Japan, and the encounter with its government officials and business community was a fascinating experience that contributed greatly to my professional development. Eventually these contacts were broadened to the U.S. Treasury, the Federal Reserve Board, the World Bank and the International Monetary Fund, and central banks of France, Germany, Holland, and Italy and the Bank of England.

This had been accomplished before joining Bache & Co. and could have been utilized in expanding its international operations. However, this was not possible with the attitudes and background of individuals operating the international division of the firm. This confronted me with a difficult dilemma to which I did not have an answer at the moment. I was concerned that the new association could jeopardize professional connections developed over the years. In the meantime I continued building administrative support and trading facilities in foreign securities, following the outline of the proposal made to Harold Bache when I joined the firm.

I encountered difficulties and every initiative of mine was interfered with. In 1962 I proposed to organize regular forums in European cities for European institutional investors, at which the firm could present its policies and address topics of interest. This could become a powerful marketing tool for the firm. Roger Solari in Geneva, the manager in Frankfurt, and the manager in Amsterdam were enthusiastic, and so was Harold Bache. The project was killed by Jack G. because of the cost involved. Two years later the *Institutional Investor* magazine took off with the same idea and, without the resources Bache & Co. had at its disposal, built a highly successful operation. Similar business development ideas were always shelved or referred back for further study by Jack G. and others in the International Division. My office was moved, my personnel were harassed, and the atmosphere surrounding my activities became unpleasant. I waited for an appropriate moment to counterattack and expose to the partners the somewhat crude intrigues detrimental to the interest of the firm. Then a personal disaster struck before I could carry out these plans. Olga died while I was on a business trip to Chicago.

I was scheduled to join the resident partner, Robert R., for lunch at the Continental Illinois Bank, where I was expected to make a presentation on the international situation to senior managers. Before leaving the office I was told that there was a phone call for me from New York. I took it in Bob R.'s office. This was the way I learned that Olga had died. I returned to New York to bury my wife and to pick up the pieces of a life shattered once again. My sons were ages two and four. I was fortunate in this tragedy to have an excellent and dedicated housekeeper, originally from St. Martin, and a Belgian nanny, equally kind, competent, and dedicated to the children. There was no time to be sorry for myself. I had to reorganize the household and arrange for a kindergarten for my older son, Andrew. My younger son, Clement, had to undergo minor surgery. I had to take care of the many legal and administrative details following the death of Olga. After the customary period of mourning, I returned to my work at Bache & Co.

Harold was very kind and understanding and so were most of the other partners. Nevertheless, while I was away arrangements had been made to cut my salary in half. My administrative assistant had been given an increase in salary and moved to the International Division, and a whole series of other petty annoying details had been introduced during my absence. It was clear to me that this was an open invitation to hand in my resignation, as for practical purposes I had been turned into an employee without a clear assignment.

A few days later Gustavo Ajo, Jack G., John Roosevelt, and others gathered in Charles S's. office, and I was informed that from now on I would no longer report to him as originally agreed but I would work under the direction of Gustavo and Jack. This was in direct violation of the terms of my contract prepared by Olga before I joined the firm. In a way it was an invitation to resign. I smiled and stated that after observing the international activities of the firm, this was a logical arrangement that I was very pleased with as it would facilitate my work. Charles S., Gustavo A., and Jack G. looked as if they had swallowed a frog. The others were amused. After a week or so Jack G. informed the firm that they did not need my services in the International Division.

There were two alternatives open. I could either sue the firm for breach of contract, or fight it out while changing direction with the assistance of the many friends I had made at Bache. A legal action would result in substantial compensation but it would put in jeopardy my future progress in the industry and the business contacts made in the U.S. and abroad. Equally, personal considerations pointed to the desirability of staying for the time being at Bache & Co. My responsibilities toward my children came first and precluded a new association that would require all the energy and time at my disposal.

I discussed the situation with Harold Bache and asked his advice. Harold was embarrassed and angry with his partners. I inquired why he, a senior managing partner, was unable to have his policies implemented. Harold closed the door to his office, which was generally open, and angrily commented that, although he was nominally in control of the firm, some of his partners did not hesitate to thwart his projects if they felt their interests were not served. This was not done directly and openly but through maneuvering and politicking. He pointed out that he was a minority shareholder and therefore must manipulate personalities and issues in guiding the complex and huge firm. He told me that he was distressed that I had been treated shabbily when I lost my wife and that he would do his utmost to assist me.

I left his office encouraged and perplexed, because I realized the deep malaise permeating the firm. The sabotage of my activities was a result of a perceived threat by Gustavo A. and Jack G. to the little empire they had created, and the other partners had joined in order to attack Harold. I also learned that Harold's support could be a mixed blessing at Bache & Co.

Ed D. and Henry G., partners in charge, respectively, of personnel and public relations, were given the task of unraveling the complicated mess created by the International Division. Ed D., a kind and decent man, who had been a commander of a destroyer in the U.S. Navy during World War II, was distressed by the way I was being treated. He was aware that I was in a position to sue the firm, because I was in possession of an ironclad contract that Jack G. had signed for the firm. Henry G., a competent newspaperman and a former war correspondent, was more interested in the practical aspects of the issue. He appreciated my professional competence but had a hard time understanding an individual who had started as a displaced person and become a recognized professional in the U.S. He had met DPs wandering through Europe after the war, and it was in a way difficult for him to put me in my proper place and to understand my way of thinking. Nevertheless, he was fair and correct in his dealing with me and was equally interested in sorting out the mess in a fair and equitable fashion.

We worked out the broad outline of a new arrangement. It was agreed that I would concentrate on supporting the activities of the Mutual Fund and the Institutional Divisions of the firm by serving domestic institutions. I would be guided by Jack J. and John Roosevelt, the partners in charge. I would be free to travel abroad at my discretion to maintain a liaison for the firm with foreign central banks, private sector banks, and other institutions. The flow of commissions from U.S. institutions on which I would call regularly accompanied by institutional salesmen of the firm would provide the revenue base to finance my project and make it profitable for the firm. This was a satisfactory arrangement, and it freed me from trying to generate business from foreign institutions. As a result, I was doubly welcomed by senior management of institutions abroad because I had nothing to sell. My contacts abroad and in Washington provided a flow of information and insights that were translated into a substantial flow of commission business from U.S. institutions, which were offered a unique and valuable service by Bache & Co.

It was suggested that a new agreement with the firm be signed. I politely declined, stating that the old contract was just fine. The stumbling block was to find a domicile for me in the firm. The Mutual Fund Division was not prepared to take over the cost of running my operation, and the institutional salesmen would refuse to cooperate if they had to share their commissions with my department. Thus I was introduced to the destructive impact of profit centers, which discouraged cooperation within the firm as everyone jealously guarded his revenues, refusing to get involved in activities not directly reflected in the bottom line of the respective departments.

After a series of delicate negotiations and discussions, it was finally decided that the Research Division was the logical place for my activities, and the expense was allocated to its budget. I met with the partners in charge of the Research Division, Adolph W. and Monte Gordon, with whom I worked out a modus vivendi with a great deal of ease. Thus I could embark again on my work. I had the best of both worlds, as I could travel abroad without any restrictions whenever and wherever I thought it necessary and was freed of the responsibility of generating revenues from foreign institutions. My activities from here on concentrated on building relations with institutions in the United States, which opened new horizons and introduced me to many more of the facets of this great country. As a consequence of this arrangement, my activities expanded literally from coast to coast, providing a unique opportunity to meet fascinating people and to get acquainted with the financial community and its activities throughout the United States.

All this was happening while I was still in the shock of having lost my wife. I was trying to get hold of myself, arrange the lives of my two little sons, and at the same time rearrange matters at Bache & Co. Years of military service had trained me to act under pressure, and this served me well in those tragic and hard days. My friends stood by me, and the housekeeper and nanny continued the routine to which my boys were accustomed. I resolved my difficulties at Bache & Co. and resumed my activities. It was only after the dust settled and I had a chance to reflect on all this from a distance in a detached manner that I was able to evaluate these events.

This environment was new to me and differed greatly from other major organizations with which I had been previously associated either abroad or in the United States. The motivation and patterns varied greatly in the broad spectrum of activities in which I had been previously involved. Self-interest, greed, jealousies, and intrigues had always been present to some degree; but the power games at Bache & Co. were somewhat different, because the interests of the firm were frequently sacrificed for the benefit of cliques or individuals. The intense politicking at Bache & Co. originated in a number of quarters with individual partners drifting in and out of respective orbits as circumstances suggested. What bothered me most was the crudeness, the lack of elegance, and the transparency with which these games were played.

The structure of Bache & Co. had developed as a result of the firm's evolution after the death of Jules Bache, the uncle of Harold. Harold controlled the name and had to mobilize outside capital to keep the firm alive. The firm grew and under his stewardship became a veritable gold mine. The core of its business was the retail offices in every major center of the country, with generally respectable salesmen who were carefully supervised by the managers.

Business was good, the economy grew, and fixed commissions precluded domination of the market by institutions. The fledgling institutional business of the firm was developed by John Roosevelt, the youngest son of FDR. The strong commodities division in which Harold was trained as a young man was active in the grain, soybean, and metal markets. The firm was growing and expanding when I joined it, and its International Division was only a minor component of a powerful firm. In 1962 Harold was in his early seventies and his key partners were not much younger. He clearly realized that unless an orderly succession was provided the firm would disintegrate. Several attempts made to invite able and competent men to take over under his guidance were blocked by the influential partners manipulating the firm.

After the sordid episode following Olga's death, I concentrated on the task of building my department and producing revenues essential in a brokerage firm to secure a power base. I had no interest in joining the ongoing infighting and politicking at Bache & Co. I realized that, in addition to encountering competition in the market, I had to be constantly alert to new intrigues and schemes within the firm. It was frustrating to waste time and energy on securing one's flanks that could be employed productively generating revenues in a difficult market environment.

Shortly after my joining Bache & Co., the Mutual Fund Division arranged a luncheon for the presidents of the major mutual funds in New York. We met in a private room at the Broad Street Club, and after lunch was served a lively discussion developed on current affairs. This turned out to be a pilot project, as one of the guests suggested that it would be helpful to meet periodically to discuss the international environment. This suggestion was followed, and a framework was created for an exchange of observations on the economy, the market, the domestic political situation, and the international environment. Each participant managed a large investment organization, which was backed by a research department. Nevertheless, the interpretation of developments debated freely and off the record in a small and restricted forum was greatly appreciated.

These were interesting days. A new direction for the country was introduced by the administration of newly elected President Kennedy. The revolution in Cuba, the emergence of the regime of Fidel Castro, followed by the Bay of Pigs fiasco, brought the cold war nearer to home. Soviet penetration of the Western Hemisphere, the missile crisis, and frequent confrontations with the Eastern bloc and China preoccupied the participants in the round table luncheons. The deteriorating U.S. balance of trade and payments, the expansion of the Eurodollar market, the difficulties of the pound sterling, and the future of the Bretton Woods agreement were discussed. The integration of the European Common Market, the emergence of Japan after the postwar reconstruction, and the economies of Mexico and Canada provided another set of topics. Then the focus of interest shifted to the developing crisis in Southeast Asia and the Middle East.

The changing political and economic panorama also provided interesting topics for the ongoing debate at the lunches. The direction of discussions concentrated on evaluation of the impact of these events on the political situation in the United States, its economy, and conclusions for formulating investment strategy. Connections in Washington and the frequent trips to Europe, the Far East and Latin America provided me with insights that were of great interest to the group and served as a catalyst for a lively exchange of views.

Eventually an invitation was extended by the chief executives of these institutions to visit their offices regularly and brief their research staffs and portfolio managers. This started a program of periodic visits to these investment institutions. Thus a platform was created for me to present a continuing overview of political and economic developments, which generated a substantial flow of commission business for the firm. The countless presentations made at luncheons and meetings provided an opportunity to hone my approach to a synthesis of political, economic, and financial analysis of the situation in the United States and abroad as a backdrop for the development of long-range portfolio strategy.

This activity was gradually expanded to Boston, Chicago, and the West Coast. This was of great interest to me, as I discovered that the interests and the points of view in these cities differed from those found in institutions in New York. With time this provided a better grasp of the crosscurrents shaping the policies of the administration and the Congress. Understanding of the international financial situation, economic developments abroad, and the assessment of political events varied considerably in financial centers throughout the country, and an ongoing exchange of ideas brought a fresh and different perspective.

The administrative details, the organization of the luncheons and the followup were taken care of by the Mutual Fund Division, which freed me to concentrate on my activities. A routine developed with time that contributed to a smooth and profitable operation.

Following the removal of Khrushchev in the Soviet Union and the explosion of an atomic device by China on the same day in 1964, an imaginative executive of the division introduced a new and effective approach. These events happened while I was in Paris travelling with an American delegation visiting European industry. With the assistance of the telephone company, he organized a hookup with the executives participating in the luncheons, and I briefed them from my hotel room in Paris. The conference call was moderated from New York. This procedure also became a regular part of my activities, and similar conference calls were subsequently arranged from London, Switzerland, and Tokyo. These briefings followed by an occasional position paper were a novelty in those days and represented a pioneering effort to combine political science, economics, and financial analysis in support of an investment strategy.

The Institutional Division was managed by John Roosevelt, the youngest son of FDR. John, a tall, gracious, and friendly man, smoked a cigarette in a long holder and the resemblance to his father was uncanny. He was in charge of the division that marketed securities to pension funds, banks, insurance companies, and endowments of universities. It was a pleasure indeed to work with him and the many salesmen of his division in New York and throughout the country. John was intelligent and competent. To my amazement I discovered that in a way his name represented a handicap. Whenever he entered a room the conversation invariably shifted to his illustrious father and his administration. Thus John was rarely permitted to make his own mark.

We travelled to Chicago, San Francisco, Minneapolis, and Washington in addition to speaking at countless meetings with institutional clients of the firm in New York. John was a gracious and entertaining travelling companion with an excellent sense of humor. Somehow he had close personal relations with the leadership of the labor union pension funds. On one of our trips to San Francisco, the Union of Pastry Cooks arranged a dinner in his honor, to which I was invited. After many drinks consumed before, during, and after the dinner, the president of the union made a long and windy speech recalling the splendid days of FDR. Then with tears in his eyes he turned to John with a plea to see the light and join the Democratic Party to uphold family traditions. John happened to be a Republican, and efforts were invariably made to make him see the truth. John graciously thanked them for the advice and elegantly disengaged from this sentimental appeal without offending anyone. I attended a number of other similar functions leading always to the same point. I admired John's patience and the ability to make everyone happy and feel at ease.

John had grown up in the White House and from time to time over a drink shared many anecdotes and stories about his father and his advisors. The stories were interesting, amusing, but never controversial. I remember distinctly one he told when travelling with me to Washington to attend the annual World Bank meeting. FDR had breakfast served on a tray in his bed as he suffered from a cold. The Secretary of the Treasury and someone else whose name I no longer recall came to consult FDR on the price at which gold should be fixed after the "bank holiday" in 1933. FDR reflected a minute and suggested thirty-five dollars per ounce. The suggestion was accepted, and a casual comment made at breakfast provided a yardstick used in international finance for many years and was then incorporated into the Bretton Woods agreement.

During one of my regular visits to Massachusetts Investors Trust in Boston, at a luncheon I met Admiral McCrea, a director of this prestigious mutual fund. He had been a naval aid of FDR and eventually had commanded a ship in the Pacific in the later part of the war. Having learned that I was an executive at Bache & Co., he commented, "I know young John well because I spent the war years fishing him out of the Pacific Ocean." John, a naval officer, had served in the Pacific and had been on one of the carriers sunk by the Japanese navy. Subsequently he had been transferred to another ship, which was sunk in a kamikaze attack. Nevertheless, the label of a socialite stuck to him. One of the last requests made by Harold Bache at a private dinner in his home before his sudden death was to ask me to convince his wife Alice that John was a competent professional and an asset to the firm.

Alice Oddenheimer Bache was a striking woman. Bright, charming, and witty, she kept aloof from the affairs of the firm. A sharp observer, she had very definite opinions that she shared only occasionally with her friends. Alice was from an old and well-known family in the South. Harold had met her as a young man and had fallen in love with her. Somehow she had married someone else and Harold had remained single. After Alice was widowed, Harold again courted her, this time successfully, and theirs was a very happy marriage. It was always a pleasure to be in their home, and Alice and I became good friends. Harold's request to convince Alice that John had a great deal to offer and had depth and knowledge in addition to charm reminded me that it is not easy to be a son of a great and prominent man, as I had learned during my childhood!

The close association with John and his division provided another dimension to my activities. The institutional salesmen of the firm in Chicago, Boston, Pittsburgh, Philadelphia, Detroit, San Francisco, Los Angeles, Houston, and Dallas arranged meetings with key financial executives and money managers. My travelling schedule in those days was very heavy, and every week I visited another city and spoke at meetings, luncheons, and dinners. This activity supported a whole network of institutional salesmen in offices of the firm in major cities in the United States. These were difficult days due to my personal circumstances, but the compensations were the many personal friendships formed and the extraordinary opportunity to see the United States from a unique perspective.

Boston in those days still had its distinct character, somewhat resembling an English city. Its pace was slower than that of New York and more toned down. A short trip from Logan airport brought me to Congress Street and the headquarters of the Fidelity Fund. A luncheon with Ed Johnson II in the simple dining room at which the best pink lamb chops in town were served was always interesting. Ed's questions and comments led into a lively discussion, which prepared me for the other calls in town.

The institutional department at the Boston office of Bache & Co. expanded after I joined the firm. Additional institutional salesman were hired, carefully selected from many applicants. It was a young and well-prepared group, highly motivated but not pushy. Among them were interesting and capable individuals and a retired prominent baseball player from a team that had won the world series. Under my guidance, they prepared an extensive program of visits to insurance companies, mutual funds, trust departments of banks, and corporations. The two days in town provided a cross section of views on a broad variety of subjects. This activity was eventually expanded to include banks in Providence and insurance companies and corporations based in Worcester and Springfield.

I encountered a somewhat different group of executives in the banks, insurance companies, and corporations in Philadelphia. A luncheon arranged by the institutional salesmen either at the Racquet Club or Union League completed the usual program. The proximity of Wall Street had an impact on professional investors in Philadelphia, and ideas espoused on Wall Street were reflected in the discussions. Nevertheless, the views and the approach to investment strategy differed from the one encountered in the institutions in New York.

I always looked forward to a trip to Chicago. The financial community there differed from the one on the East Coast in its approach. Chicago and the Midwest represented to me the heart of America, and I was attracted by the simplicity, low-key approach, and openmindedness of the individuals I met. Intellectually and temperamentally the financial community of Chicago appealed to me most because of a balanced approach and a degree of conservatism without being overly cautious. The process of familiarization with the international environment was in its early stages and it was fascinating to observe the intellectual curiosity and openness to new ideas.

The trips to Chicago were extended to include Cleveland, Milwaukee, Detroit, and eventually Madison. The different characteristics and the distinct economic structure of the cities and regions were a fascinating introduction to the hugeness of the country.

In Chicago, a major industrial, financial, and commercial center, international developments were closely followed and interpreted. Its two major banks, Continental Illinois and First of Chicago, became major players in international markets. Northern Trust attracted investors from abroad interested in professional management of funds in the United States. Industry in Illinois and Ohio was always involved in international trade and had long-established relations in foreign countries. The automotive industry in and around Detroit and the banks serving it were quite experienced in international trade and interested in an interpretation of events in the increasingly complex international situation.

The managers and the personnel in the offices of Bache & Co. were generally a pleasant and interesting group. These hard-working individuals were dedicated to providing a reliable service that made the firm a leading factor in the securities markets in the country. This provided an introduction to a broad spectrum of individuals representing a variety of ethnic groups in the offices of Bache & Co. and in the institutions visited. Each trip was a new experience and discovery. The meetings in the institutions were frequently followed by press conferences with business editors of newspapers and local radio and television networks. I distinctly remember the able business editor of the *Chicago Tribune,* William Clark, who on several occasions wrote excellent reports on my presentations and arranged interviews broadcast live on local radio stations.

Harold Bache was always on the lookout for new ideas and was determined to blaze new trails. He had the rare ability to take a long-range view and, without ever compromising the interests of the U.S., was prepared to engage in controversial activities. The Cold War was at its zenith, and the international situation remained tense after the missile crisis in 1962 and the removal of Khrushchev. The Soviet economy could not produce adequate supplies of food, and the crops were exceptionally bad because of an adverse cycle of weather conditions. Harold reached the conclusion that with accumulating U.S. agricultural surpluses it would serve the interests of both superpowers to arrange sales of grain to the Soviet Union.

He checked the idea discreetly in the State Department and after securing approval sent John Roosevelt and me to Minneapolis to call on Cargill (the largest grain trader in the U.S.) and others to explore the technical questions connected with large shipments of grain to the Soviet Union. Bache & Co. had an active commodities division that could easily handle normal transactions. However, the magnitude of this one was somewhat too large for the firm to deal with without a consortium of others joining in. Bache & Co. pioneered the first major shipments of grain and cattle feed to the Soviet Union, with the assistance of Cargill, Continental Grain, and Dreyfuss.

We also visited Investors Diversified Services, the banks, and the Minnesota Mining and Manufacturing Corporation, broadening the firm's institutional exposure in the State of Minnesota. A trip to Minneapolis introduced me to yet another corner of the Midwest. Agriculture was the foundation of this region and its importance permeated the city. In the days when the railroads dominated the North American continent, Minneapolis was an important junction. The insurance industry grew in St. Paul, adding another dimension. With time the emphasis shifted, and technologically advanced industry expanded in this region. Control Data, Minnesota Mining and Manufacturing Corporation and others gave it a new dimension, with Investors Diversified Services and the lively banks supporting the economy of this corner of the Midwest.

The next project was the West Coast. The Institutional Division prepared for me a program in San Francisco and Los Angeles. This was my first trip to the far west, and I was anxious to get acquainted with this region that was new to me. The scenic beauty of San Francisco was familiar to me from pictures and movies. Nevertheless, I was enthralled by it like everyone else who sees this city for the first time. On arrival at the office of Bache & Co. on Montgomery Street, I asked an institutional salesman to take me on a cable car ride. Somewhat puzzled, he guided me to California Street and we rode up and down on an old fashioned cable car. It was an exhilarating experience, and it reminded me of movies filmed in San Francisco with the cable car ride a part of some of the episodes.

There was not much time left for sightseeing, and we embarked on the program prepared for me. We called on Crocker Citizens, Wells Fargo, and the Bank of Tokyo California. The orientation of executives in these institutions was different from what I had encountered so far on the East Coast and in the Midwest. The East Coast was interested in the Atlantic community, and its international interests were primarily Eurocentric. The Midwest focused on the domestic situation, paying attention only to events abroad that could affect the U.S. economy. The financial community in San Francisco, while following national trends, was interested primarily in the economy of the West Coast, and its international orientation was toward the Pacific Basin.

The highlight of the visit to San Francisco was a luncheon given by Bache & Co. for executives of Bank of America, very appropriately in an excellent Italian restaurant. The bank was still managed primarily by Italo-Americans, mostly second or third generation. It was an interesting and no-nonsense group of executives with special interests in Italy and the European community. At this luncheon I met their new economist, Walter Hoadley, who had just joined the bank. Walter, originally a Californian and a distinguished business economist with a wide range of experience in business and government, shared with me many interests, and we started a rewarding dialogue that has continued for many years. The program of support of institutional sales provided a variety of benefits. However, the most interesting and valuable ones were the opportunities to meet professionals like Walter and many others in my travels throughout the U.S.

The program in Los Angeles demonstrated the limitations of Bache & Co. in certain markets. The firm's office was managed by New Yorkers whose contacts were limited to the film industry and related services. This industry represented a sector of the economy in which I found it difficult to make progress. The mentality and approach of the executives of the entertainment industry were different from those on the East Coast, Midwest, Canada, Europe, or even Japan. A much greater preparation and conditioning was required before I could communicate effectively in Southern California. The dynamism of Los Angeles was much more pronounced than that observed in San Francisco. However, its direction and rhythm escaped me on the first visit. (The limitation was of the Bache managers, who were from New York.) Bache & Co. during my visit was involved in negotiations designed to procure venture capital for a corporation active in the distribution of Japanese consumer electronic products in the U.S. The manager asked Tom W., the regional manager of Bache & Co. who came with me from San Francisco, to join the negotiating team of the firm and the executives of the distributing company for dinner at a popular restaurant, Scandia. Tom and I arrived at the restaurant before the guests. A table was arranged and, while we were having drinks waiting for the others, the headwaiter pointed out a number of well-known film stars sitting at the bar or at tables. He explained that they were non-paying customers because their presence attracted business.

After a while the guests arrived with their wives. The wife of the owner of the distributing firm, a middle-aged American, was a stunning young Japanese. She was placed on my right, and we engaged in a lively conversation. We both were interested in horsemanship, were enthusiastic riders, and compared observations about the different stables on the East Coast. The conversation at the table concentrated on the underwriting and its terms. After a while the owner of the firm turned to me, pointed to his wife, and commented: "I picked her up in Tokyo. She has expensive tastes and likes to spend money." He continued rubbing his thumb and forefinger in a timeless gesture of counting money. The only possible reaction I was able to make was to smile politely. Fortunately he turned back to the Bache executives to continue discussing the terms of the proposed financing. I was embarrassed as the Japanese woman, much younger than her husband, spoke English fluently. We both decided to ignore the comment.

A smorgasbord was ordered, as this was a Scandinavian restaurant. To my surprise a multitiered Lazy Susan was brought to the table with every conceivable kind of smoked and marinated fish. The arrangement looked rather impressive, but our host the industrialist was unhappy with it because there was no smoked salmon. This was quickly remedied, and a platter loaded with it was brought to the table. The host sniffed the fish and commented that indeed it was smoked, whereupon the waiters served it to the guests. The vulgarity finally irked me. When a plate of smoked salmon was brought to me, I looked at it with disdain, which prompted the headwaiter, who had patronized us since we arrived, to inquire whether all was well. I politely stated that I was accustomed to have salmon served with capers and lemon. Capers and lemons were promptly brought by a waiter from the kitchen. The headwaiter solicitously inquired whether I was now satisfied. "No," was my answer, "I am accustomed to have my lemon wrapped in gauze." Gauze was quickly brought, the lemons wrapped in it, and I finally agreed that all was well. Whereupon the manager of Bache & Co. in Los Angeles proudly commented to the guests, "You can see that we at Bache & Co have class." Tom, a Midwesterner, and I left the restaurant after dinner, and he commented "Kurt! This is not an easy way to make a living."

In all fairness, the episode was an amusing one but not at all characteristic of the many meetings and conferences in which I participated. The audiences were varied, the interests concentrated on a broad range of subjects, with emphasis changing from region to region. Los Angeles was an exception and reflected the local personnel of Bache & Co., which catered to a specific market in which neither Tom nor I felt at ease. This brought home the complexity of managing an enormous brokerage firm with a broad range of activities and personalities. The range of activities at Bache & Co. had defined limits that I was unable to cross. It taught to me to be more selective in choosing the market in which I wished to be active. My preparation, my approach, and my style did not suit all, and in some markets like in Los Angeles I found it difficult to adapt and communicate.

Texas was my next stop. I asked my friends at Chase to arrange a briefing for me in the banking division with someone familiar with the Texas business community. The manager of the Brokers and Dealers Division of the bank took me to a lending officer. A youngish tall man with his jacket off was sitting at his desk with his feet resting on it. The size 11 shoes were facing us with the owner slouching in his chair. Bill introduced me and asked the young man to brief me on business conditions in Texas and offer me a few guidelines.

The young banker asked me a few questions about my background and commented that I had better give up the idea of working in Texas because I was not suited for this market. He pointed out that Texans are ignorant and narrowminded, and it would be a waste of time for me to go there. This ended the interview, and Bill and I left the office of the banker shaking our heads. This was the first sign of an invasion of a new generation of managers—arrogant, aggressive, and ignorant. This was in contrast with the many capable, competent, helpful, and impressive executives I met over the years in a variety of banks throughout the country.

This briefing session did not discourage me from travelling to Dallas and Houston. Admittedly I was somewhat ill at ease, not knowing what to expect. I was pleasantly surprised that I was well-received everywhere. While Texans in those days were not excessively interested in the international environment unless it concerned the oil and oil-related industries, they were open-minded, curious, and easy to be with. Dallas had changed enormously from my first visit there after the reorganization of the Missouri Pacific Railroad system. The city had grown, its financial institutions expanded, and the remarkable Stanley Marcus of Neiman-Marcus and others had addressed themselves to the development of a lively cultural life.

Looking out from the dining room of the Republic National Bank or from the Petroleum Club, one could see the flat countryside for miles blending on the horizon with the mostly cloudless blue sky. It was yet another corner of the enormous country with a different rhythm, way of life, and mentality. It added another dimension to my better understanding of the complexity of the United States, its strengths and its weaknesses. The changing society, the changing interests, and the ability to adjust and adapt never cease to amaze me.

Pittsburgh and Atlanta were other centers added to my itinerary. Pittsburgh was home to a number of powerful corporations with a strong imprint of the steel industry and the Mellons. The business community resembled the one encountered in Chicago. It was conservative but not ossified. Its dependence on heavy industry unquestionably tinted its views and outlook. This also limited its maneuverability, which eventually contributed to its being bypassed by technological breakthroughs and the modern Japanese integrated giant steel mills located on the sea. The U.S. steel industry based in Pittsburgh, transporting iron ore and coal to its mills by waterways and rails and shipping steel to the market in the same way, could no longer compete. The power of Pittsburgh could be sensed at the Duquesne Club and the Fort Ligonier retreat of the Mellons. It was nevertheless strength of an era whose time has passed. Travelling regularly to Japan and visiting the new steel mills there, I realized the danger and the dilemma. Regretfully, I was unable to convince the audiences in Pittsburgh of the emerging challenge to their existence in Japan, in Korea, and eventually even in Taiwan.

My first direct encounter with the South was in the Carolinas and in Atlanta. As I completed my formal education in the North, I had acquired a somewhat distorted view of the South—its character, its evolution, the backdrop and the reasons for the Civil War, and a variety of related issues. A direct contact with the South and southerners made me quickly realize that the issues are not as clear-cut as they are occasionally portrayed. It was yet another dimension in the complex mosaic of the United States. Unfortunately my already extensive activities precluded a closer examination of this part of the country, its history, and its culture.

I travelled twice or three times a year to Europe and to the Far East and South Asia. Travelling abroad followed a different routine, as my function was no longer to generate business for the firm. I was responsible for liaison of the firm with the international banking community, central banks, and the Bank for International Settlements in Basel, then a little-known institution, which was to play a key role in the years ahead. A trip started usually in Rome where I could compare observations on a great variety of subjects with distinguished churchmen like Eugene Cardinal Tisserant and many others. Father Michel de Lattre, a good friend of mine from the days of the efforts in the beatification of the Metropolitan Andrew Graf Szeptycki,[2] helped me interpret what I learned during the meetings at the Curia. A visit to Banca di Italia and Banco di Roma completed my program in Rome. In Milano I called on Credito Italiano, Banca Commerciale Italiana, Mediobanca, and RAAS.

In Zurich I called on Schweizerische Ruckversicherung, Union Bank of Switzerland, and the Swiss National Bank. The highlight of my visit to Switzerland was lunch in Basel with Dr. Samuel Schweitzer, the chairman of the Swiss Bank Corporation, and his economic advisor, Dr. F. Aschinger, in a private house belonging to the bank in the old city. At the BIS, Milton Gilbert was invariably sparkling, well informed, and critical of the international monetary policy pursued by Washington. He had an extraordinary ability to put complex problems plaguing the international monetary system in a proper perspective.

In Frankfurt I usually visited with Dr. Otto Emminger at the Bundesbank and the executives of the major German banks, who provided valuable insights into the international monetary situation as seen from their vantage points. Equally interesting was the dean of the private banking community in Germany, Mr. von Metzler. I had not forgotten the war years and consequently I restricted my contacts in Germany to business only. However, I made a few exceptions when I met individuals whom I got to know well, like Dr. Niels Hansen, formerly Ambassador of the Federal Republic of Germany to Israel and to NATO, and Joachim Lenz, formerly of Dresdner Bank in Dusseldorf and subsequently a management consultant and investment banker. Most individuals I encountered in the banks or industry had served in the German armed forces during the war. I could not forget encountering the members of the "master race" either in the ghetto when I was marked for death in a gas chamber, or facing them disguised as a Ukrainian monk. Walking on the streets of Frankfurt, Dusseldorf, or any other city, I could close my eyes and recall the masses, inflamed by Hitler's speeches, screaming *"Sieg Heil."* Observing middle-aged men walking on streets of German cities, I pondered where they had been during the war years.

My next stop was Amsterdam where a discussion in the Netherlandsche Maatschapij, Labouchere and Co., Pierson, Heldring & Pierson, and Hope & Co., old established financial institutions, provided a different perspective on the international financial scene. The Dutch are practical, conservative, and no-nonsense bankers. They possibly did not take advantage of the opportunities offered by the expansion of international trade and capital markets. The experience accumulated over centuries was somehow not utilized.

Nevertheless, the Amsterdam financial community remained sound and solvent while others ran into difficulties over the years. I highly valued their experience in international trade and their balanced and uncluttered view of the international environment. In those days I could encounter individuals who had been trained as young men in Dutch banks in Shanghai, Canton, Singapore, or Indonesia.

My final stop was London, where the City never ceased to fascinate me. A visit to the Bank of England was a unique experience and in particular in my memory are etched the deputy governor of the Bank of England, Sir Maurice Parsons, and his low-key, highly competent advisor for North America, John Kirbyshire. Barclays Bank and its impressive group of executives were another favorite stop of mine as was the Westminster Bank and the International Division of the Midland Bank. Time permitting, I called on merchant banks like Warburg, Barings, and others. At the end of my stay I would give a small dinner party at the Savoy in a private dining room for my friends, at which over cigars and brandy or Calvados we compared observations and debated issues that attracted our attention.

Representing Bache & Co. at the annual World Bank meetings as a special guest was another interesting exercise. In the 1960s these meetings were attended by the governors of the central banks and ministers of finance of the member countries, accompanied by their staffs. A small and select group of internationally recognized experts was invited to participate as observers. I was privileged to be included and attend meetings over many years. It was a congenial and friendly gathering in those days, as most participants and guests knew each other, and the World Bank meeting provided a platform for a pleasant get-together. On the day before the meeting started, Roy Reierson, the distinguished economist of the Bankers Trust Company, would arrange a dinner party for his friends at the Cosmos Club. The invited guests consisted of a relatively small number of Americans and foreign guests, like Dr. Otto Emminger of the Bundesbank, Guido Carli of the Banca d'Italia, chairmen of international banks, Treasury officials, and prominent economists. These dinners became the highlight of the World Bank meeting, and the discussions and comments were helpful in sorting out the maze of problems getting more complicated with each year.

A dichotomy developed gradually in my professional activity. My activities in Europe and in the Far East were concentrated on broad corporate strategy and evaluation of the impact of international developments on corporate planning. I was consulted by central banks and key executives in the international banking community, who recognized a unique approach combining political, economic, and financial analysis that I was able to provide. On my return to the United States, my activities concentrated on generating business for the Institutional and Mutual Fund Division, speaking at luncheons and dinners primarily on investment strategy and allocation of portfolio resources. This activity was productive, interesting, and pleasant. However, it turned me increasingly into a professional public speaker with an element of entertainment invariably connected with it.

It was probably a time for a change. I had once again outgrown the brokerage firm. While Bache & Co. offered many opportunities, I had become too specialized. Nevertheless, I was comfortable working with Harold Bache, Monte Gordon, John Roosevelt and many others. My contacts with the International Division were limited, and the intrigues of the money partners were of little interest to me. Besides I felt an obligation to Harold Bache, who had stood by me in difficult days. Therefore, I did not look actively for a new association.

The 1960s were on the surface relatively tranquil. A storm was brewing in the Middle East. The growing fatal involvement of the United States in Southeast Asia was not yet fully recognized. The deteriorating balance of payments and trade, the difficulties of the pound sterling, and the turmoil in the newly created states following the collapse of the colonial systems were ominous indeed. Soviet foreign policy and the generous assistance extended to every disruptive movement throughout the world stoked the fires of discord, conflict, and terrorism.

Bache & Co. navigated rather well through the business cycles and the gyrations of the market, expanding and consolidating its position in the industry under the guidance of Harold Bache. The issue of his succession remained unresolved. Another attempt to introduce a chief executive was torpedoed, compelling Harold to return and continue to manage the firm. The chief executive was in his seventies; the partner in charge of the firm's banking relations, Bill Reed, was in his early eighties; Charles S. was in his late seventies. Consulting firms were invited from time to time to make recommendations that would streamline and improve the management of this enormous organization. Their intervention produced more politicking, created more cliques, and laid the foundation for the future demise of the firm.

I managed to keep out of all this and attended to my activities. The Arab-Israeli war in 1967 and the approaching collapse of the Bretton Woods agreement kept me busy. The impact of international developments on the markets and the movement of investments and portfolio management were of greater interest than the internal affairs of Bache. The institutional clients of Bache & Co. throughout the country were eager to hear an interpretation of events and guidance on how to draw investment conclusions. I travelled more extensively than ever and was called upon to make presentations more frequently.

The war in Vietnam exerted ever-increasing pressure on public opinion in the United States and divided the nation. The involvement of the United States in Vietnam expanded dramatically after the Kennedy Administration took over. Eventually the U.S. committed itself to supporting the regime of Ngo Dinh Diem, while the Soviet Union amplified its support of North Vietnam.

Confusion in Washington combined with a lack of understanding of Southeast Asia produced statements emanating from the White House that were misinterpreted in Saigon and resulted in the assassination of Diem and his brother. The disintegration of what was left of Vietnam's political infrastructure followed. The country was taken over by a corrupt and incompetent military while the war was directed from Washington, employing methods applicable to automotive production lines. Computer "whiz kids" were in charge of designing military strategy. It became apparent to me travelling in Europe and in the Far East that the U.S. was headed toward a political disaster, with the nation torn apart by a war it neither understood nor supported. After completing my visit in the Far East in the autumn of 1967 I decided to go to Vietnam to observe the situation there first hand.

Before leaving Tokyo I obtained personal introductions from the Bank of Tokyo, Banque De l'Indochine, Hong Kong and Shanghai Bank, and Shell Petroleum Company. My trip was hosted by the Chase Manhattan Bank, which had a rather important operation in South Vietnam.

I stopped over in Bangkok before continuing to Saigon. Chase Manhattan Bank had arranged a whole series of meetings for me with government officials and bankers. Mr. Pisud, the governor of the Bank of Thailand, the central bank, suggested that I meet his subgovernor. I was ushered into a large office where I was received by a gracious and beautiful woman. I was somewhat surprised as I was not accustomed to meeting a woman in a high government position in Asia. Khunying (lady, a title) Suparb Yassundara was a competent economist and well known and respected in international banking circles. The conversation was lively and interesting, and we decided to continue in the afternoon while visiting the klongs (waterways crisscrossing Bangkok) and then have dinner together.

At dinner we were joined by the managers of Chase Manhattan Bank. We discussed the pound sterling and its future. The pound was then still employed extensively in clearing international trade, and the Bank of Thailand maintained a substantial position in it. Khunying Suparb in the course of the evening inquired what I would advise her to do with holdings of pounds. I suggested that they be sold and dollars purchased with the proceeds, because the pound's devaluation was imminent. (Before departure for the Far East I had learned in Basel that the industrial nations were not prepared to renew the revolving credit lines to continue to defend the pound.) We agreed that, after my return from Vietnam, we would meet again. The next day I took off for Saigon.

At Tan Son Nhat, the airport of Saigon, I was met by a driver of the Chase Manhattan Bank who took me to the Hotel Astor on a quiet side street. The driver indicated to me that this hotel was chosen because its owner paid taxes to the Thieu regime and also to the Viet Cong. Therefore, it was not harassed or attacked by the insurgents. At the hotel in the bathroom I found a bottle of Scotch with the compliments of the Chase Manhattan Bank, with a note recommending it for brushing my teeth. This was the start of a fascinating and illuminating visit that opened my eyes to the issues facing the United States and the far-reaching consequences of its military intervention in Southeast Asia.

I was advised by my host not to leave the hotel after dark. In the evenings I settled at the bar to have a drink before retiring. The hotel was a favorite of newspapermen and war correspondents, who gathered there to compare their experiences of the day. Many Americans were among them. However, the majority came from Europe and other parts of the world like Australia and Latin America. I was taken aback by the critical and contemptuous attitude of the newsmen toward the policies pursued by the United States in Vietnam. The most surprising aspect to me was that the destructive criticism was shared by the American contingent. I listened and kept to myself, reserving judgment for later.

The views expressed at the bar were not much different from the ones disseminated by TASS, the Soviet news agency. The war was fought by brave men facing a difficult enemy in unfamiliar terrain. They were led in the field by competent NCOs and officers. The intervention in South Vietnam was politically mismanaged, and strategic decisions were made by U.S. military bureaucrats and not soldiers. The real damage was inflicted not by the North Vietnamese and the Vietcong but by newspapermen whose reporting was one-sided and hostile. They eventually undermined popular support at home for the fighting men who had been sent to Vietnam by the nation.

In the dining room of the hotel in the morning, the radio was blaring news from the United States. In the restaurant were many soldiers who had come to Saigon for rest and recreation. These were average youngsters, black and white, from every nook and corner of the United States. The radio was reporting demonstrations taking place on campuses of American universities against the war in Vietnam. (A few weeks earlier while riding a horse in Central Park in New York I had encountered such a demonstration of students carrying Vietcong flags and yelling, "Ho Chi Minh, we shall win!") It was strange and eerie to sit with soldiers who had come for a day or two of rest from the battlefields and listen to a description of such a demonstration. It was a sad and most disturbing spectacle to watch the impassive faces of the youngsters listening to reports from home.

I met with Japanese, Chinese, Dutch, British, and others and gathered their views and impressions. I even met a Vietnamese, a graduate of the Harvard Business School, who enthusiastically spoke about an industrial park planned for the outskirts of Saigon. The same night the windows of my room were shattered by a blast of air. I ran down to the hall to be told by the owner that there was nothing to worry about—B52s were bombing the positions of Vietcong on the outskirts of Saigon.

The first week in Vietnam was exciting and disturbing, as it did not take too much time to recognize that matters could not go on as they were. The conduct of the war was not left to competent military commanders, yet it had to be won because the United States was politically fully committed. The existing situation would inevitably lead to defeat and humiliation. The meetings with a broad representation of businessmen, newspapermen, and individuals to whom I was introduced raised many questions without providing answers.

I was looking forward to the weekend and some relaxation after an exhausting schedule. A French banker and his Vietnamese wife kindly invited me to join them on an outing to a country club located a few miles up the Saigon River. It was a beautiful Saturday morning, and I joined my hosts at the landing where a motorboat was tied up. We took off and passed under a well-guarded bridge, continuing to the country club. It was a lazy Saturday morning and I enjoyed daydreaming in the sun. Children were playing in the sand nearby, and my hosts were engaged in a conversation with another couple. Suddenly someone tapped me on the shoulder, interrupting my pleasant drifting in and out of a nap watching the passing clouds in the sky. It was the representative of the International Monetary Fund attached to the National Bank of Vietnam, who told me that he had received a wire this morning from Washington with the news that the pound sterling had been devalued.

My outing was over. I thought that I should be available to New York for comments on the consequences of the devaluation of the pound, and not at the country club in Saigon. Fortunately before leaving for Asia I had advised the Commodities Division and Bill Reed, the partner in charge of banking, to shorten outstanding positions of pound sterling. Here I was in Saigon without access to a telephone and to reliable information.

At four o'clock everybody rushed to the boats to return to Saigon. I was told that after five o'clock in the afternoon the premises were taken over by the Vietcong, and it was advisable to leave beforehand. Rather depressed, I returned to the hotel, helped myself to a good slug of Scotch, and reflected on what to do. It was Saturday evening in Saigon and it dawned on me that as I had crossed the dateline it was Friday evening in New York. This gave me time to reflect, to prepare a cable, and find a way to send it out.

Relying only on what I had learned over the years observing the international monetary situation, I composed the text of a comment. As I was for practical purposes cut off from the outside world, I had to rely on myself and the inspiration of an ample supply of Scotch provided thoughtfully by Chase Manhattan Bank. I prepared a sharply focused cable addressed to Harold Bache. A more difficult task was to find a way to get it to New York. This was accomplished with the assistance of the well-connected hotel manager who bribed post office officials. The cable went out Sunday morning Saigon time. It arrived at Harold's desk Monday morning in three parts. The last part was delivered first and the rest had to be retrieved from the wire services with some effort during the morning hours.

The final few days in Vietnam were spent in a series of interviews

with U.S. military and the embassy staff. These discussions reconfirmed that the U.S. forces in the field were displaying the same
courage and determination as the soldiers and marines had during
World War II. The logistic support was impressive and lavish. The
senior command and the political leadership guiding it were another
matter. A definite lack of clear-cut strategic objectives was obvious to
a professional observer. Somehow Washington, with the exception of
President Johnson, did not project a determination to win the war.
The hostile press and politicians were eroding public support for a
war fought far away and not understood. The many knowledgeable
French, Japanese, and British observers active in business, or representing their governments in Saigon, with previous military experience in the region, pointed out that unless the policies of Washington
changed, the war would end in a political disaster similar to the one
experienced by the French fighting the Vietminh in North Vietnam.

I walked through the wide avenues of Saigon with old leafy trees
providing protection from the searing sun. The streets were full of
vendors, sellers of food prepared in the middle of the sidewalks, with
motorcycles, bicycles, and rickshas creating a complex pattern of traffic that a policeman clad in a white uniform was trying to sort out.
Shops in which one could find every conceivable American,
European, or Japanese product were inviting and interesting, each
sort of a minisupermarket with a department store and souvenir shop
combined. Turning a corner one faced a large Roman Catholic cathedral resembling a structure in a French provincial town. Saigon was
humming with life, business was conducted everywhere, and the
Vietnamese were friendly and pleasant. Only the occasional thud of
an exploding grenade, or a bomb dropped from a motor scooter,
reminded one of the ever-present Vietcong and North Vietnamese
and the war. It was disturbing to see the young, somewhat bewildered
American soldiers wandering around, enticed by girls wearing tight-
fitting silk dresses with a characteristic high cut up the thigh, pulling
them in by their sleeves to enter the myriad bars. I left Saigon for
Bangkok greatly disturbed and pondered where all this would eventually lead. This was November 1967, only a few weeks before the
start of the Tet offensive, which resulted in a massive military defeat
for the Vietcong and a political defeat of the United States.

On my way to New York I stopped in Bangkok. Khunying Suparb of the Bank of Thailand was pleased to see me and grateful for the advice given to sell out the bank's positions of pound sterling. Thanks to her introduction I could get a view of the war in Vietnam as seen from Bangkok and an unbiased assessment of the situation. Observers there were of the opinion that Washington was vacillating, unable to determine whether to win the war militarily or to search for a political solution.

On the evening before my departure, after dinner I was taken by Khunying Suparb and the commander of the police to visit Petchbouri Road, a long avenue crossing Bangkok. On both sides of the rather broad thoroughfare for more than a mile were "bathing establishments" with names like Colorado, Texas, Oklahoma, Cowboy, and so forth, displayed in garish neon signs. We entered a prominent one and observed the proceedings. In the middle of a large hall was a wooden structure with enormous show windows. Behind them young Thai girls were sitting on benches, each with a disk with a large number attached to the front of her dress. Soldiers entered from time to time, enticed by the garish neon sign. Drinks were brought and a girl selected by a soldier by the number came out from the brightly lit glass enclosure.

Khunying Suparb and the chief of police commented that these were young peasant girls brought from the North to Bangkok, enticed by promises of a well-paying job. They ended as prostitutes and prisoners of these establishments. The crime-ridden prostitution industry was protected by politicians, and therefore little could be done about it. It was pointed out to me that easily available drugs smuggled from Burma were sold in these establishments, thus spreading the use of heroin and addicting thousands.

I left for New York deeply disturbed by the visit to Vietnam and equally perturbed by what I was shown in Bangkok. A few days after my return I was invited to Harold's home for dinner. It was as always an elegant affair, and there were twelve of us at the table. After dinner Harold asked me to share with his guests what I had learned during my trip to Asia. I commented briefly on my observations and concern. The next morning Harold called me and asked me to express the same ideas in a letter to him. My letter was forwarded with a covering letter from Harold to many chief executives and members of the Congress.

I subsequently received a number of favorable comments on my observations, and among them was a short note from a lawyer, Clark Clifford. I asked Harold who this individual was. Harold told me that he had forwarded my letter to President Johnson, who had shown it to Clark Clifford, a Washington lawyer and an influential advisor of Presidents since the days of President Truman. Clark Clifford wrote a gracious note congratulating me on an excellent analysis of the situation in Vietnam and said he agreed with my conclusions.

A few weeks later I was pleased and encouraged to read in the *New York Times* that Clark Clifford had been appointed by Mr. Johnson as his new Secretary of Defense. I was somewhat surprised to learn later that he was instrumental in convincing President Johnson to suspend the bombing. I never fathomed what changed his mind and made him recommend a sudden and drastic departure from a course that had been pursued for a number of years.

The firm had reached the outer limits of its possibilities and an overhaul of the management at the head office was imperative before the firm could resume its growth. However, this was not possible in the existing power structure at the head office. I discovered, visiting offices of the firm in the U.S., that not all had the potential for institutional activity because of the orientation of the managers and the personnel. This was demonstrated to me at the Los Angeles office, which catered to a specific and limited segment of the market. Minor management changes were introduced from time to time but by and large the firm was drifting. At one of the Thursday morning management meetings a Florida-based partner commented that the firm must make preparations to process transactions when the volume would reach 50 million shares daily. His comment was dismissed by others as ridiculous.

One autumn morning in 1968 I arrived at 36 Wall Street and noticed that the door to Harold's office was closed, which was unusual as he normally arrived before everyone else. Harold had died during the night. The news spread quickly in the offices of the firm. A notice was circulated informing us that John Leslie would act as an interim chief executive.

Harold's funeral was held at the Temple Emanuel to which Harold had belonged. The simple dignified service was followed by a brief eulogy made by one of his personal friends. The casket was lifted by the pallbearers with the partners of the firm accompanying it. John Leslie and Gustavo Ajo led the procession, followed by others. It was a group of old and tired men who remained in charge of this enormous and profitable empire built by Harold. It also represented an end of an era on Wall Street, as Harold was one of the last self-made tycoons who had dominated it for a long time.

Nothing on the surface changed, and the firm continued as before. It took almost a year before the void left by Harold's death was fully comprehended. The firm proceeded for a while, propelled by existing momentum. Then it started to lose money and was gradually gutted to maintain the positions and the benefits of the managers. They benefitted personally by eventually selling out the firm to Prudential Insurance Company, thus destroying in the process careers of many fine and capable individuals loyal to the firm who had invested many years of their lives serving Bache & Co. Prudential Insurance acquired a troublesome shell that caused it many a headache and enormous losses. After years of costly and futile efforts and changes in the management, Prudential decided finally to take it over. Thus the Bache name disappeared from the roster of firms on Wall Street.

A new generation was taking over the Street, market conditions were changing, new imaginatively led firms were emerging from practically nowhere and expanding rapidly. Wall Street had embarked on a dramatic transformation, and within a decade most of the well-established and well-known firms had disappeared, preparing the ground for the aggressive, greedy, and ruthless men who eventually spawned the corporate raiders, the inventors of junk bonds, and their ilk.

~

After a brief period of preparation and training I had embarked on a discovery of America. It was a fascinating adventure which permitted me to find my place in this complex and always changing society. Eventually, I succeeded in creating a unique professional niche with which I experimented first at Josephthal & Co., the brokerage firm that had trained me, and then at Bache & Co. Now it was time to move on and explore new horizons. In 1969 I opened my consulting firm and was on my own. A journey of that sort could be completed only in America.

After finishing my training at Josephthal & Co., a seasoned back office clerk, Eddie Begley, an old timer, sent me to the New York Federal Reserve Bank to certify a Treasury check and to make a delivery to Graves & Churches at 125 Broadway. At the Federal Reserve Bank I was told that there was no need to certify a Treasury check. Graves & Churches at 125 Broadway proved to be Trinity Church. This practical joke was my initiation to Wall Street and it indicated acceptance by peers. The many kind individuals in the "front" and in the "back" offices whom I had the privilege to encounter at the start of my career prepared me and taught me the skills that made it possible for me to survive all my years on Wall Street.

CHAPTER 11

The Discovery of Japan

STORIES TOLD BY Konrad Sztykgold, a friend of Olga's parents, over an excellent cigar and a brandy provided my first introduction to Japan. He was a colorful and hard-to-define individual. Born in Warsaw, he had served in World War I as an ensign in the Imperial Russian Army. Captured by the Germans in 1914 in the battle of Tannenberg in Prussia and interned in a POW camp near Berlin, he somehow managed to complete engineering studies at the School of Mining in Berlin.

Konrad returned to Warsaw after the war and married the daughter of one of the richest industrialists in Poland. His father-in-law, who did not much care for his new son-in-law, provided a generous dowry for his beautiful daughter. He informed Konrad that an equal sum was on deposit with a lawyer with instructions to release the funds to Konrad the day he decided to terminate this unsuitable marriage. Konrad's and Elizabeth's marriage, if at times somewhat unorthodox, proved to be a very good one. She once told Olga that, while it was not easy to be married to Konrad, she was never bored. It was the greatest compliment a wife could pay her husband after thirty years of marriage.

In a few short years, Konrad Sztykgold became a successful banker and a millionaire in the Free City of Danzig. After the crash of the New York stock market in 1929, Konrad was penniless and bankrupt. He left his wife and daughter in Warsaw in the care of his in-laws and went to Berlin. There he managed to rebuild his fortune and was eventually sent by the Weimar Republic to the United

States to repurchase the so-called Young bonds. (These were securities representing debt incurred by Germany for the payment of reparations after World War I.) After the crash of 1929 these bonds could be purchased in New York at a fraction of their face value. Konrad lived in the United States while Elizabeth and Stephanie, their daughter, lived in Warsaw. They met every summer on the French Riviera for a long, leisurely vacation.

In 1932 the astute Konrad disengaged from the German government and in partnership with Serge Rubinstein, a young Russian emigre and a graduate of Oxford, purchased gold mines in the Chosen Valley in Korea. Konrad travelled frequently to the Far East and for a while resided in Tokyo at the old Imperial Hotel built by Frank Lloyd Wright. He was wheeling and dealing from there throughout the Far East, importing machinery and weapons from the United States and Europe.

Konrad represented English, French, and Belgian armament manufacturers and had excellent contacts with the Chinese warlords. In 1936 Konrad and Serge Rubinstein sold the gold mines in Korea to a *zaibatsu*,[1] realizing that the Japanese would make it difficult for foreigners to manage a business in a strategically sensitive region. This transaction was completed in Tokyo, and Konrad and his partner were paid in blocked yen. The enterprising Konrad had excellent relations with government officials, who somehow obtained for him a permit to keep the blocked yen in a hotel safe. He explained that he needed ready cash to assemble a collection of obis (elaborate sashes worn by Japanese women) and netsukes (elaborate miniature ivory, stone, or wooden carvings used to fasten the medicine and tobacco boxes worn by men in the old days, veritable works of art).

Eventually, he told the inquisitive officials that he wished to arrange an exhibition of these objects in the United States and Europe to introduce foreigners to the beauty and intricacy of Japanese arts and customs. The collection of the most elaborate and expensive obis he could find were kept in his suite at the Imperial Hotel until he was ready to leave for the United States. An obi is rolled on a cardboard drum to prevent the delicate material from being creased. He stuffed the inside of the cardboard drums on which the obis were rolled with the blocked yen and left with his superb collection by ship to Hawaii. On arrival in Honolulu, the smuggled yen were placed on the open market, playing havoc with its rate of exchange. The Japanese government was compelled to support its currency and the enraged Diet (Parliament) passed a law that forbade Sztykgold, or his descendants, ever to enter the country again.

After the German attack on Poland in 1939, Konrad succeeded with the assistance of the U.S. Embassy in getting his wife and daughter out from burning Warsaw via Wilno to Moscow and from there through Mongolia, China, and India to the United States. The lex (law) Sztykgold passed by the Diet in Japan prevented them from taking the more direct route via the Transiberian railroad to Vladivostok, Yokohama, and San Francisco.

Konrad's interests during the war shifted to natural gas and petroleum, and he became a wildcatter in the Texas Panhandle. He resided for a while in Wichita Falls, and after a series of successes expanded his activities to a search for natural gas in Alberta, in Western Canada.

I met Konrad and Elizabeth while courting Olga at the home of my future in-laws. They were much older than I, which did not prevent us from becoming close friends. Shortly after my return to Israel in 1953 to complete my military service, I was surprised to find Konrad there with a crew of Texan roughnecks and two rigs, drilling oil wells on the Carmel near Zichron Yaakov. Olga and I were delighted with the reunion, and we spent many a pleasant weekend touring Israel with them.

His Southern Baptist friends in Wichita Falls, learning that Konrad was drilling in Israel, asked him to bring home pictures of Ein Karim, the birthplace of John the Baptist. On one of our excursions we drove to this charming place near Jerusalem. The pictures shown to his friends and neighbors in Texas during one of his frequent visits to the United States created a problem. When the slides were projected in Wichita Falls, his guests commented that he had not been shown the right place. They commented that, "John the Baptist could not have been born in a place where there were so many Catholic churches."

One day Konrad came to see me in despair because the Texan crews had informed him that they were quitting and going home.

Without ketchup they could not tolerate the awful Israeli food. A case of ketchup procured by a friend of mine, a manager of a food processing plant, saved the day.

Olga and I returned to New York from Israel in 1955 and shortly afterwards so did the Sztykgolds. Olga and I would visit the Sztykgold's frequently. Olga and Elizabeth often chatted in the living room while Konrad and I enjoyed a Havana cigar, his favorite H. Upmann Naturales, and a brandy in his library. Konrad spent many an evening relating stories of his exploits in Japan and Korea and his trips to Hong Kong, Shanghai, Canton, and Saigon. I was fascinated and never tired of listening to him describing these exotic, far-away places. In a way he tried to transfer the experience accumulated in the Far East to me, then a young man, while reliving this fascinating phase of his life.

Elizabeth, a delightful, bright, and elegant lady, had to tolerate and compete all her married life with the streak of adventure in this fine and unusual man. She was pleased that this phase of their life was over. Konrad's daughter and son-in-law loved him dearly, but their interests were elsewhere, and these exploits were too remote from them. Sensing that I too had a streak of an adventurer in me, and that I would not remain filed away for the rest of my days in a brokerage firm on Wall Street, he generously shared his experiences. I listened and learned, hoping that one day I would have the opportunity to explore this fascinating part of the world.

Konrad became ill. I visited him frequently during his stay in a hospital and was with him when he died. Shortly before his death he took out his beloved collection of netsukes. He selected three miniature carvings by a famous artist and offered them to me. One represents Oishi Kuranosuke, the leader of the forty-seven ronin of the Asano clan, brooding at Ichiriki, a tea house in Kyoto. Another represents Oishi Kuranosuke, disguised as a travelling merchant, on his way to Tokyo to lead an attack on a snowy December night on the mansion of Lord Kira. The third one represents a jovial Chinese gambler. They remind me of my friend Konrad and the stories of his exploits in the Far East.

My professional activities in my early years on Wall Street had concentrated on the United States and Canada. My background and experience were conducive to following developments in Europe and the Middle East, and my orientation was toward the Atlantic. The Chase Manhattan Bank, a powerful institution in those days, was helpful in broadening my contacts and provided me with support during my frequent trips abroad. I often lunched at the bank's executive dining room, sharing my observations with senior managers of its international division to reciprocate for the courtesies extended. At one of these small lunches I met William Lamneck, who was then in charge of Japan and Southeast Asia at the head office of the bank.

Before the war Bill had managed the office of the Chase National Bank in Shanghai. In November 1941 he had left for a home leave, which spared him the bitter experience of Japanese internment camps. After the war in the Pacific, Bill had been selected to join a team of bankers sent to Tokyo to assist the administration of General Douglas MacArthur in reorganizing Japanese financial institutions. His contribution to the reconstruction of the devastated country was acknowledged by the government of Japan, which had decorated him with the Order of the Sacred Treasure, the highest decoration offered to foreigners.

Bill, an old China hand, listening to my comments on the international situation, remarked that my views and interpretation of events were interesting but two-dimensional. "You are familiar with the United States and Europe," he said. "An introduction to the Far East and Southeast Asia will provide you with the missing dimension. I have to get you there one of these days." This comment intrigued me and reminded me of the stories told by my friend Konrad Sztykgold. It reaffirmed my wish to visit Japan and learn more about this mysterious country.

The performance of the Kodo drummers of Sado Island is one of the many ways a westerner can get acquainted with Japan and its people. In a way their performance personifies the spirit of this old and complex culture, which generally remains an enigma to an outsider. Sado Island, a desolate speck of land off Honshu, was a favorite place of exile for political undesirables employed by the Shoguns, the military leaders of Japan. Chikamatsu, the great playwright of Japan, has written a drama performed in the Bunraku theater telling the story of Nichiren, a monk exiled to this island. The story unfolds, conveyed by movements of dolls brought to life by the artful manipulation of black-clad and hooded artists with only a suggestion of scenery. The narrator recites the story, accompanied by musicians in heavily starched black kimonos mournfully playing shamisens. The music and the narration create an atmosphere of desolation and sadness and provide a backdrop for the drama that is conveyed by the movements of the manipulated dolls.

Sado Island, whose ruggedness and climate somewhat resemble the coast of Maine, was chosen as their home by the very unusual fraternity of the Kodo drummers. There they live in modest circumstances, keeping fit by jogging and exercising every morning regardless of the weather. The study of music and mastery of the assortment of drums occupies their time whenever they are on the island back from tours.

The Kodo musicians perform intricate compositions on a variety of drums, from small ones to the giant Taiko-san. The performance appears at first as a simple and possibly primitive exercise. Then gradually the audience is captivated by the intricate rhythms and the discipline with which the volume of the sound of the drums is controlled. A transition occurs from a delicate, almost imperceptible throbbing produced by drumsticks hardly touching the tightly stretched skins, to a powerful hammering with larger sticks accompanied by the sound of a percussion instrument that measures the phrases of the composition and signals the changes in the rhythm. The drummers, dressed only in loincloths and white bands of linen wrapped around their heads with butterfly-like ties above their foreheads, perform as a perfectly synchronized team. They follow in utmost concentration a score and an imaginary conductor, with every muscle and sinew engaged in performing an intricate composition.

The finale of this extraordinary and captivating performance is a performer making the giant Taiko-san drum come alive. The drummer, standing motionless in front of the giant drum, is accompanied by two musicians sitting on the floor in front of drums somewhat smaller than the Taiko-san, resting on wooden easels flanking the giant drum in the center of the stage. The Taiko drummer has two baseball bat-like drumsticks balanced in his hands. The two drummers sitting on both sides of the giant drum with their feet firmly planted on the easels hammer at their instruments at an increasing volume and speed.

When they reach a crescendo, the Taiko-san drummer joins in, bringing the giant drum to life. The rhythm accelerates as he pounds the giant instrument with ever-increasing intensity and power. The other drummers gradually reduce their pounding and fade out, falling silent and motionless in front of their instruments. The huge Taiko-san responds to the drummer with a deep reverberating sound. The accelerating rhythm and controlled force of the drummer, totally absorbed in his task, generates a hypnotizing sound that fills the hall. Every muscle and sinew on his back is brought into play, with sweat streaming down his body in total concentration on beating the tightly stretched skin of Taiko-san with the intertwined symbols of ying and yang painted on it in black and white. He almost attacks the giant drum, with the sticks dancing in his hands to the rhythm indicated by a female musician using a metal triangle.

The audience is hypnotized by the rhythm and the power of the performance. All eyes are riveted on the Taiko-san drummer, who appears as if he were an extension of the giant instrument. Suddenly the rhythm changes, the drumming shifts from powerful strokes to a slower beat and gradually lowered volume. The exhausted and hard-breathing drummer suddenly stops. The two musicians on his left and right take over, and the throbbing sound of their instruments continues for a while and finally it too fades out.

The discipline, the dedication, the team effort, the constant striving for improvement and perfection in this magnificent performance points to the secret of success of Japan and its people. Whether this spirit of dedication, referred to as *Yamato Damashii,* can be transmitted to the next generation of Japanese brought up in the affluent atmosphere of a successful economic superpower remains to be seen.

There are many facets to this fascinating country and it takes a lifetime of study to get acquainted with its characteristics and nuances. It is also an always-changing, fascinating, perplexing, and, in the final analysis, mysterious world not easily understood by an outsider.

When I first began my visits to institutions in Europe and the

U.S., Japan came up from time to time in discussions, because it was a significant borrower of short-term funds in international capital markets. Its credit standing had been restored because, after signing the peace treaty, the Japanese government retired its prewar debt and paid interest due that had accumulated during the war. Therefore, when I learned that the New York Society of Security Analysts (NYSSA) was organizing a trip to Japan, I decided to join the delegation.

In 1962, the NYSSA delegation was a guest of the Japanese Association of Securities Dealers. It was a well-planned and carefully arranged visit with the objective of introducing the analysts to the structure of the Japanese economy, its capital markets, its corporations, and opportunities to invest. The group consisted of fifty rather senior members of the Society, and a number of wives accompanied the delegation. We left New York on a chartered Boeing 707 for Tokyo with a stopover in Anchorage. It was one of the first organized tours of that sort to Japan, and great expectations were attached to it by the Japanese and by the investment community on Wall Street.

We arrived in Tokyo on a pleasant April evening and were greeted at Haneda Airport by our hosts and the press with television cameras. Tired but excited by the unfamiliar sights and the impressive reception, we boarded buses that took us to the old Imperial Hotel. We travelled through Tokyo, still a city of small, primarily wooden structures, with numerous shops lining the streets. The inscriptions in unfamiliar and exotic characters describing the nature of the businesses were intriguing and indicated how illiterate we were in Japan. Paper lanterns in front of the restaurants, shops and drinking places and the carbide lamps lighting the food and fruit stalls along the streets gave Tokyo at night a dreamy and mysterious character. Men in kimonos on elevated *getas* (wooden platforms with a thong for a toe) were purposefully strolling on the sidewalks, with an occasional woman passing by in a kimono and obi carrying an old-fashioned oiled paper umbrella.

We arrived at the Imperial Hotel after passing through Ginza with its many blinking multicolored vertical neon signs extending an invitation to the many bars, restaurants, and cabarets. My arrival

in Tokyo brought back memories of the fascinating stories told by
Konrad Sztykgold. In the hotel room we found folders with the program of activities, literature introducing Japan and its culture, and
small gifts. The excitement, the jet lag, and the new environment
made it difficult to go to sleep.

The program started with a briefing of the delegation by senior
government officials and industrialists. Dr. Saburo Okita, the chief of
the Economic Planning Agency, Mr. Haruo Mayekawa and Dr.
Toshihiko Yoshino of the Bank of Japan addressed the analysts, setting the stage for an introduction to the economy of Japan. Dr. Okita
and Dr. Yoshino, both internationally recognized economists, outlined the plan of Prime Minister Ikeda to double national income.
They were followed by Mr. Mayekawa, a distinguished and brilliant
central banker, who explained monetary policy. The witty managing
director of Yawata Iron & Steel Corporation, Mr. Tadayoshi Yamada,
explained the workings of Japanese industry and problems encountered in the expansion of the industrial base. Mr. Shigeo Horie, the
chief executive of the Bank of Tokyo (the successor of the Yokohama
Specie Bank), spoke about the banking system. Mr. Kazuo Tsukuno,
of Yamaichi Securities Company, one of the hosts and organizers of
the trip, spoke about the securities industry in Japan.

It was a most impressive tour de force as all the speakers were
leading experts in their fields and spoke impeccable English. Mr.
Mayekawa, at an early stage of his distinguished career, had been the
representative of the Bank of Japan in the United States. Mr.
Yamada had been an aide on the staff of General Douglas McArthur,
and Mr. Tsukuno, born on the West Coast, had attended schools
there before returning to Japan shortly before the outbreak of the
war with the United States. Subsequently, I learned that these had
been the architects of the postwar reconstruction of Japan and had
laid the foundation for its becoming an economic superpower. The
overview presented in these briefings provided insights into a long-
range strategic plan based on an assessment of the position of Japan
in the world, its markets, and where the thrust of its expansion
should be directed.

The formal sessions took place at the Daichi Insurance Building.
The organization of the meetings, the displays, and the audio and

visual support were superb. In two rather full days we were introduced to the economy of Japan and the problems it faced. Following the formal sessions, we visited a number of corporations in the Tokyo area. Among them was a unique and aggressively led electronics company named Sony, where at the gate of the plant the buses carrying the guests were greeted by an orchestra consisting of the employees of the company playing classical music. We were guided through the factory and laboratories by its chief executive, Mr. Akio Morita.

The display of transistor radios, tape recorders, television sets, and other related equipment manufactured by Sony was indeed impressive. In the laboratories we were shown experimental products that introduced miniaturization and integrated circuits to consumer electronics. The enthusiasm and the youth of the managers and the employees engaged in a search for new products and improvements of existing ones made a strong impression on our group. Sony, in the early stages of its development, was bustling with energy and purposeful activity.

Canon was another company where we were introduced to the progress made in optics and precision instrumentation. We were shown an unbelievable array of photographic lenses that had become legendary during the Korean War. These were lenses of an extraordinary quality and innovative optical engineering that soon swept the markets, replacing products made in the U.S., U.K., and Germany. In the laboratories we were shown experiments with copying machines and calculators, indicating a new direction in an attempt to diversify and to reduce the dependence of Canon on photographic equipment. We were shown the factory and laboratories by the founder of the company, Dr. Mitarai, a gynecologist, who in his seventies was still guiding this innovative company.

The visit to Honda Motors was yet another surprise. The motorcycles of Honda, a little-known company, had appeared as if out of nowhere in a number of international races and competitions and had taken most of the first prizes. Astounded motorcyclists were starting to switch to the machines, which were revolutionary in design and performance. We were guided through the plant by the founder of the company, Mr. Honda, an unassuming engineer who had turned a small bicycle repair shop into a thriving manufacturer of motorcycles and eventually cars. The spirit prevailing at Honda somewhat resembled the one encountered at Sony.

A trip to the facilities of Hitachi Company in the Ibaraki prefecture was a change of pace. We left Tokyo in comfortable air-conditioned buses and travelled on excellent but narrow roads through a countryside with flooded, carefully tended rice paddies glistening in the sun. A cluster of farm buildings with thatched roofs gave the landscape its unique character, with the green and yellow colors of the fields accentuated by the variety of brown hues of the peasant houses and villages on the horizon. Precious and scarce land was carefully cultivated, with an occasional peasant at work using a miniature power plow or tractor to weed the fields.

Sitting next to me on the bus was a managing director of Hitachi, an elderly gentleman who spoke the King's English without a trace of an accent. His impeccably tailored suit and general appearance indicated that he had spent many years in England. We struck up an interesting conversation, and Mr. Haraguchi invited me to visit him at the head office of Hitachi in Tokyo.

The visit to the Hitachi plant in the Ibaraki prefecture again was a surprise. The expertise of this large and well-established company in electrical engineering was well-known. However, we were shown advanced electron microscopes, medical equipment, and facilities engaged in the manufacturing of components for atomic power plants. Again we encountered a tour de force in all facets of the most advanced electrical engineering. We returned to the Imperial Hotel from Ibaraki City accompanied by Hitachi managers who provided brief explanations and answered questions.

At the hotel an invitation was waiting for me to a dinner party extended by Mr. Konosuke Koike, the chairman of Yamaichi Securities Company, and his wife. In the hotel lobby I joined a small group of other members selected from our delegation, and we were driven in limousines to Kanetanaka, a restaurant in Shimbashi. We entered what appeared like the doorway of a spacious private home. We were ushered in by waitresses through a miniature garden over an artfully laid path made from large smooth stones sprinkled with water. They were glistening in the dark and reflected the light of the stone lanterns and the brightly lit entrance hall. An elderly lady was waiting for us in an exquisite brownish kimono. Her obi with an intricate design in a shade of dark blue curiously blended with the brown hand-printed silk of the kimono.

We were advised to take off our shoes and an old man servant with a clean-shaven head dressed in a traditional gray jacket, baggy pants, and getas helped us into slippers. There were seven of us in the party, three analysts accompanied by their wives and I. Everything was new to us, and we were wondering whether the man servant would be able to return the right shoes to their owners. We were led upstairs to a spacious room with bare walls plastered with a yellowish brown clay and wooden pillars that were more a decoration than a support. They were highly polished with an occasional patch of bark left on the exposed trunk. New tatami mats, tightly woven from straw, covered the floor. Their scent filled the room, pleasantly lit with bright but indirect lighting. In a corner of the room in a place of honor called *tokonoma,* on a slightly elevated shelf, a deceptively simple flower arrangement was displayed, over which hung a scroll.

Our hosts were waiting for us in the spacious room. We were seated on cushions on the floor at a long low table made of polished dark mahogany. Kamakura-bori (hand carved wooden plates lacquered red), little plates with cups of green tea, were served by waitresses with tiny colored cookies elegantly wrapped in tissue papers with the kanji (Chinese) characters of the name of the restaurant printed on them. O-shibori, steaming hot small towels, were offered so we could refresh ourselves.

On my right was a Japanese lady in a western evening dress, Taeko-san, or Mrs. Yamanouchi, the sister-in-law of Mrs. Koike, the wife of our host. She smiled, and in perfect English told me that she was equally ill at ease as this was her first experience at a geisha party. Looking around I noticed that the Japanese ladies were new to the experience and as tense as the western contingent. Gradually everybody relaxed, and the westerners were provided with additional pillows by the solicitous waitresses. Nevertheless, we were still not very comfortable and were trying hard not to squirm.

Waitresses arrived with trays on which were artistically displayed delicate hors d'oeuvres appropriate to the season and little china flasks of hot sake. The waitresses poured the sake into tiny cups, each different and chosen from a collection on a tray presented to the guests. We drank *kampai* (bottoms up), and a lively conversation started, sharing the impressions of our first visit to Japan with our hosts.

From my neighbor Taeko-san I learned that she had grown up in England, where her father had been a managing director of the Yokohama Specie Bank's branch before the war. Her husband, also a banker, had been a manager of the Shanghai office of the bank. There the family lived for a number of years. Her husband had been arrested after the communist takeover and had spent a number of years in a Chinese prison. He had been released in the 1950s, but he had died shortly after their return to Japan. We discussed our children and the direction of postwar Japan. Individual trays were brought for each guest with the first course, which consisted of sashimi (sliced raw fish), grated daikon (Japanese radish) with a hint of shiso (an herb), and a few tiny dishes with Japanese vegetables and crab meat in vinegar. Somehow we managed to eat with chopsticks with the discreet assistance of the waitresses.

We hardly noticed the entrance of the geishas in exquisite kimonos, traditional wigs, and heavy makeup, who joined us at the table, refilling our sake cups. They frequently changed places so that we could converse and admire each of them. Most of them were middle-aged ladies accompanied by younger geishas. Taeko-san, my neighbor, told me that the most accomplished geishas in Shimbashi had been invited to entertain the guests on this special occasion.

In a corner of the room a screen was set up serving as a backdrop for a geisha playing a shamisen (a string instrument resembling a banjo). Another one was performing a highly stylized dance telling a story that escaped us altogether. Later a koto (a traditional string instrument probably originating in China) was brought in and a composition was played for us by another geisha, including the song "Sakura" popularized by a movie about Japan with Marlon Brando. The geishas appeared discreetly and left equally unnoticed, with new ones joining us in the course of the evening. A tray with broiled fish and ginger root was served, followed by miso soup and rice with pickles. Artistically arranged peeled mandarin oranges, *mikam,* served on a silver plate completed the meal. A variety of green teas was served throughout the evening, with the geishas and waitresses refilling the tiny sake cups whenever they noticed that they were half empty.

It was a lovely and relaxed evening, brought to an end by the tune "Auld Lang Syne" played on a record player, signaling that the party was over. We returned to the entrance hall where our shoes, polished while we were upstairs, were waiting for us.

The hostess and the waitresses assembled, helping the guests with shoe horns to get back into their shoes. Bowing deeply they invited us to come again soon. We left through the tiny garden, accompanied by servant girls carrying umbrellas to protect us from the drizzling rain, to the waiting limousines.

In the morning we left the Imperial Hotel with young girls wearing uniforms, neat little hats, and white gloves helping us to board waiting buses. After closing the doors, they stood throughout the trip next to the drivers, assisting them in negotiating narrow passages on the roads twisting through the residential quarters of Tokyo. We stopped in Kamakura to visit the shrine of Hachi-mangu (the god of war) and admired the large Daibutsu (a large statue of Buddha) standing in a garden after a *taifun* (hurricane) centuries ago had swept away the wooden temple in which it was originally housed.

After the grueling program arranged for us in Tokyo, we were looking forward to a rest and some sightseeing. Our next stop was Hakone at the foot of Mount Fuji, where we stayed in a western style hotel, using it as a base to visit the beautiful Hakone National Park. The weekend in the countryside restored our strength, and we were ready to continue to Odawara, where we boarded the Shinkansen train to Nagoya.

The trip by bus to Hakone provided time to reflect on the events of the week and sort out the barrage of impressions that left one somewhat disoriented. Some of us fell back on financial analysis and took out slide rules (pocket calculators were not yet invented), studying the annual reports and looking for answers in figures. Others enjoyed the sightseeing and the introduction to a new and mysterious world.

I was daydreaming and thinking about the stories told by Konrad Sztykgold during the long winter evenings over cigars and brandy.

The image of the little netsuke representing the brooding Oishi Kuranosuke at Ichiriki displayed in an étagère in my living room came to my mind. It reminded me of my unusual friend and his adventures. I had always been intrigued to find out what the netsukes represented since I received them from Konrad. In the material assembled for us by our hosts I found a brief outline of Japanese history. There I encountered the story of the forty-seven ronin and their leader, Oishi Kuranosuke.

A *daimyo* (the head of a clan, a feudal lord), Asano Naganori, lord of Akko, failed to offer suitable gifts to the master of ceremonies, Lord Kira, when his turn came to serve at the court of the shogun in Edo (the old name for Tokyo). The disappointed official taunted and humiliated Asano to a point that the enraged daimyo attacked his tormentor in the presence of the shogun. Asano Naganori was ordered at once to commit *seppuku* (ritual suicide) for breaking the rules, the clan was dispersed, and the Asano samurai became *ronin* (masterless samurai). The story became known throughout Japan, and the population awaited the reaction of the dispersed clan.

Oishi Kuranosuke, the leader of the clan's samurai, divorced his wife, left his children, and, perpetually drunk, consorted with geishas and entertainers at Ichiriki, a famous tea house in Kyoto. His behavior invited contempt, as Oishi Kuranosuke apparently had forgotten his allegiance to the clan and the family of his dead lord.

While brooding and drinking at Ichiriki, he signed up forty-seven faithful ronin, former samurai of the Asano clan, who joined him in his plan to take revenge on Lord Kira. The oldest participant was in his eighties; the youngest was Oishi's sixteen-year-old son, who insisted on accompanying his father. They assembled secretly in Edo and on a snowy cold December night attacked the heavily defended mansion of Lord Kira. The forty-seven ronin prevailed, captured the despised master of ceremonies, and cut his head off. They washed it ceremonially and carried it wrapped in white cloth through the streets of Edo to Sengakuji temple, where they deposited it with the chief priest against receipt. At this temple one can still see the original document signed by the forty-seven ronin swearing to avenge their lord and the formal receipt that was issued by the temple for the head of Lord Kira, which is displayed with their armor and weapons.

The shogunate was perturbed by the act of defiance and protest. However, it did not dare to punish the forty-seven ronin, who were admired by the whole country for their dedication to duty and their allegiance to their dead master. They were placed in the mansions of the leading daimyos and as honored guests waited for the shogun's decision. After consulting with the Emperor in Kyoto, the shogunate ordered them to commit seppuku, because after this splendid deed they were so pure that, if allowed to go on with their lives, they could only blemish their perfect record.

Their graves, marked with crossed swords indicating that they committed ritual suicide, and those of Lord Asano and his wife, can be seen in the small cemetery at the Sengakuji. To this day visitors to the temple burn incense sticks on the graves of the ronin and the wife of Lord Asano. Asano Naganori lost his temper and contributed to the ruin of his family and his clan, however, and no incense is lit at his grave.

This complicated story, somewhat strange to a westerner, still fires the imagination of the Japanese. Plays inspired by the story were written for the Kabuki theater and are a popular part of its annual repertoire. Bunraku performances retell this moving story, with the narrator accompanying the dolls that come alive in the hands of skilled manipulators. Several movies were made of this tale, of which the Japanese never seem to tire.

It was difficult to reconcile this tale glorifying *bushido,* the code of the warrior, with what we had seen at Sony, Canon, and Honda. This bustling, energetic, and modern society seemed to be in conflict with the cherished old traditions and ways deeply rooted in the psyche of these remarkable people. There are no easy and simple answers to this question. Books have been written by observers explaining Japan, advising how to deal with the Japanese, and how the Japanese mind works. Most of these books are only partially correct and usually only scratch the surface of the issues. After a quarter of a century of advising the Japanese, I consider myself a beginner and still have a great deal to learn. The Japanese are racially and culturally a homogeneous people representing an old civilization and are the product of a complex and rich history. They are changing, as is everybody else. However, they still seem to remain anchored in their culture and traditions, even though modern times and internationalization have had an increasing impact on this fascinating society.

While visiting companies I noticed that everyone wore in his buttonhole a trademark of the enterprise. It is in a way a coat of arms, like the one displayed on the kimonos of the retainers in the Tokugawa period. It identifies its wearer as a member of a group, a clan. Instead of a *mon*—the coat of arms of the Satsuma, Choshu, Tosa, or Bizen clans—the modern Japanese displays the three red diamonds of Mitsubishi, the symbol of the well of Sumitomo, or the insignia of Hitachi that resemble an electrical motor. Mr. Yamada had drawn my attention to the flower arrangements displayed in a visible place in every factory and office. He pointed out to me that a Japanese, to refresh his spirit, has from time to time to rest his eyes on a small, symbolic part of Japan, which the flower arrangement represents.

Travelling on the new speedy Shinkansen train from Odawara to Nagoya we could see in the distance Mount Fuji towering over the landscape. The unique shape of the snow-covered conic volcano has always fascinated the Japanese. Looking at the landscape, I reflected on what I had seen and heard.

In Nagoya we visited Toyota Motors, the Mitsubishi Heavy Industries plant in Komaki, and Noritake, a manufacturer of china. The stay in Nagoya followed the routine established in Tokyo, and we continued to Osaka. In both cities we were introduced to the economy of the region and its industry. Gradually the boldness and the scope of Prime Minister Ikeda's program to double the national income, explained to us in Tokyo by Dr. Saburo Okita and Dr. Toshihiko Yoshino, emerged. The industrial complexes erected along the Tokaido road were evidence of an industrial revolution taking place in Japan that would change its character and its position in the world.

The program was interspersed with imaginative entertainment and visits to the famous tourist sights. Kyoto and Nara were the highlight of this part of our trip. The visits to the many temples and gardens were accentuated by the cherry blossoms at their peak. We returned to Tokyo, where a concluding session summarized this extraordinary and unique opportunity to be introduced to Japan.

I called on Mr. Haraguchi at Hitachi headquarters, who invited me to a restaurant named Tsujitome for lunch. We were driven to a modern multi-storied building in Ginza and took the elevator to emerge in a country style courtyard with a well in the middle of the hall and decor recreating the atmosphere of an authentic old restaurant in Kyoto. It was a surprise and an unusual experience to have lunch in an authentic country inn recreated on a floor of a modern high-rise building in the Ginza. Mr. Haraguchi introduced me formally to the owner, and for years I had an account at Tsujitome, a privilege reserved for senior executives of Japanese banks and enterprises.

I left Tokyo fascinated by Japan and simultaneously unnerved. It was the first time in my life that I had experienced total dependence on others, as I was illiterate and unable to move freely to explore this world, fascinating but closed to an outsider.

A few months later I returned to continue my exploration of Japan. This time I came on my own with Chase Manhattan Bank acting as my host and a program suggested by Bill Lamneck. The bank's Tokyo manager recommended that I meet their advisor, Mr. Sakimura, who would assist me in making appointments. Mr. Sakimura, formerly a managing director of the Yokohama Specie Bank, had been blacklisted by General MacArthur's administration. Someone had had the brilliant idea that the bank as an institution should be added to the list of war criminals as it had abetted the war effort by providing financial support for arming Japan. Thus most of its managing directors had been blacklisted, among them Mr. Sakimura.

The highly respected banker, an elderly gentleman with a drooping mustache fashionable in the latter phase of the Meiji era, had been hired by Chase Manhattan Bank as an advisor and a liaison with the Bank of Japan and the Ministry of Finance. His office was in a room outside the bank's premises, and there I was offered the customary cup of green tea. Mr. Sakimura asked me a few questions and engaged me in a conversation on a variety of topics. Before I had a chance to tell him what I was interested in, the interview was over. Mr. Sakimura asked me to return the next day at nine o'clock. I arrived punctually at the bank and was told that Mr. Sakimura was waiting in his office. I was offered a cup of green tea and a list of appointments made for me for the rest of the week.

This kind and unassuming man, after the brief interview, had reached the conclusion that I should be introduced to key officials in the government, banking, and industry. He had prepared a program that included Dr. Okita, Dr. Yoshino, Mr. Mayekawa, Mr. Shigeo Horie and many others whom I had met while travelling with the NYSSA delegation. These introductions could be arranged only by Mr. Sakimura because of the respect he enjoyed among the Japanese. They ignored altogether that he had been blacklisted by the administration of General MacArthur and were not impressed that he had become an advisor to a powerful American bank.

In Tokyo I met Leo Martinuzzi, an executive of Chase Manhattan Bank who was preparing a visit of David Rockefeller to Japan. Comparing observations, we both agreed that we had not made much headway in advancing our respective objectives. The reception in the offices we visited and the ceremonial cup of green tea were accompanied by polite conversation on generalities and was frustrating to both of us. I suggested that we invite a few key officials to a traditional *kaiseki* (formal Kyoto-style dinner) dinner at Tsujitome.

The introduction of Mr. Haraguchi of Hitachi proved helpful, and our reservations were accepted at this exclusive restaurant. We invited Mr. Mayekawa of the Bank of Japan, Mr. Murakami, director of the International Division of the Ministry of Finance, and Dr. Saburo Okita of the Planning Agency. Leo Martinuzzi and I arrived at the restaurant early and were ushered to the private room reserved for the party. Our guests arrived and were surprised to find themselves in an exclusive *kaiseki* Kyoto restaurant. They took off their jackets, sat down on the tatami mats at the low table, and relaxed. It was the first occasion for both of us to spend an informal evening frankly discussing a broad range of topics with high government officials.

Before leaving Tokyo I made some inquiries and was told that Mr. Sakimura was partial to old-style *yokan* (sweet bean paste cake). At Toraya (Tiger), a traditional old yokan confectioner that had moved from Kyoto to Tokyo with Emperor Meiji, I bought an elaborately packaged bean cake with the tiger trademark displayed on the wrapping. I called on Mr. Sakimura to thank him for his efforts on my behalf. The elderly gentleman smiled and stated that not too many Americans called on him to thank him before leaving Japan. From then on he treated me as his protégé and as such I was introduced in Japan to leaders in industry and finance.

The Industrial Bank of Japan arranged visits to the heavy industry installations in the Tokyo area. The Yamaichi Securities Company guided me through the intricate relations between the ministries and agencies involved in planning and regulating the economy. I was fortunate to have the assistance and the counsel of the many friends I made while exploring Japan.

Mr. Konosuke Koike, the chairman of Yamaichi Securities, a distinguished and highly respected man whose father had founded the company, was among them. His counsel and introductions opened many a door. At his home I was introduced to members of his family and Taeko-san, whom I had met at the geisha party at Kanetanaka. This became a personal friendship with a family that continued for many years. Mr. Shigeo Kurebayashi, the economist of the Fuji Bank, made a point of combining a review of the economy with an excursion to a temple or a garden. Mr. Tohru Shimamoto, the chairman of the Hokkaido Bank, to whom I was introduced by his son who was an executive of the Bank of Japan, took me to corners of Japan not easily accessible to a foreigner. He travelled with me to Mashiko to visit his friend Hamada Shoji, the famous potter who was appointed a living national treasure (an official designation). We explored a number of Buddhist Temples in the countryside. He also introduced me to modern woodblock artists like Kitaoka Fumio and Munekata, and another national living treasure, Yuki Tsumogi, a weaver of silk for men's kimonos.

There were many interesting foreigners living in Tokyo who helped me a great deal by explaining various aspects of Japanese culture and the functioning of its society. Manfred Rasche, the representative of the Commerzbank, was one of them. He was a German who had lived for many years in the Far East and had acquired unique insights into Japan and China, where he travelled regularly for his bank. He and his wife Thea were gracious hosts and in their home I could relax after the strenuous days submerged in a Japanese environment. Their lovely children, a boy then five years old and a girl age nine, spoke German haltingly but preferred to converse in fluent Japanese.

Iwao Hoshii, a prominent Japanese economist, was equally helpful in unraveling the mysteries of Japan. A German from Aachen and a member of the Society of Jesus, after completing studies in Holland and France he had joined the Jesuit Province in Japan. There he had been active in a variety of areas, finally settling at Sophia University. After World War II he had left the Society of Jesus, had married and become a Japanese citizen. He worked for many years as an economist with Mr. Kurebayashi at the Fuji Bank. His counsel and guidance were very helpful over the years.

The westerners living in Japan were an unusual, varied, and intriguing community that had fascinated the Japanese from the days of the Meiji restoration. There were those who, sent by corporations and banks, concentrated on their assignments and paid attention to the environment only as it related to their work. Others were inclined to take an interest in the culture and made some not-very-successful efforts to socialize with the Japanese. There were other expatriates who arrived either as members of the allied military personnel, as teachers, or as missionaries. Fascinated by the Orient, they were no longer able to return to their own environment. Even their home leaves were spent travelling in Southeast Asia. Over the years I met representatives of practically all European nations, and also quite a number of Americans, who had become enthralled by the Orient. Most of them were intelligent, well-informed, and competent individuals. Nevertheless, after a while their vision of Japan became myopic and tended to develop a bias. Only a handful of individuals like Dr. Iwao Hoshii acquired a unique and full understanding of this complex country and its people.

I made a point during my stay in Japan of concentrating on getting acquainted with the Japanese, their institutions, and their culture. Submerged in a Japanese environment for three or four weeks at a time, I gradually acquired an ability to move freely in the country and feel comfortable among Japanese. I also designed a methodical program to get acquainted with the functioning of the Japanese economy. A series of meetings at the Bank of Japan and the Ministry of Finance provided an introduction to the developments in the economy and the policies of the government. At the banks and the securities companies, I could obtain an assessment of the trends in the economy and identification of its problems.

Following these visits I made a point of inspecting industrial plants, with the assistance of the management of the corporations. They were pleased to reciprocate for courtesies extended in Tokyo and New York and arranged visits to plants and laboratories I was interested in seeing. I concentrated at first on public utilities and heavy industry. Visits to Tokyo Electric and Kansai Electric demonstrated the emphasis of the planners of the Japanese economy on the supply of adequate electric power to satisfy the requirements of rapidly expanding industry. The enormous modern power plants had no counterparts in the United States or in Europe. Bold and innovative design followed the newest available technology in this field. The power plants fired with either coal or crude oil presented a pollution problem in the densely populated industrial regions. The design of the tall steel chimneys and the introduction of scrubbers reduced the pollution.

The heavy use of steel in construction and the requirements of the manufacturing sector led me to an exploration of integrated steel mills. Mr. Tadayoshi Yamada, a managing director of Yawata Iron & Steel (subsequently merged with Fuji Iron & Steel to form Nippon Seitetsu), arranged for me to visit the newest plant of the company in Yawata, on the island of Kyushu. I flew to Fukuoka and there at the airport I was met by an elderly gentlemen, a retired professor from the University of Kyushu, where he had taught English literature. His explanations and his translation of comments made by the plant managers contributed greatly to the success of the visit. The steel mill was new and was built on land reclaimed from the sea. Iron ore, coal, and other supplies were brought in ships docking at the mill's harbor. The finished coil and steel plates for the shipbuilding industry were loaded on ships and were transported either to the plants on the island of Honshu or exported abroad. This was a most interesting application of industrial planning.

The kindly host thoughtfully provided by Yawata Iron & Steel

Co. did not restrict his comments to the production of steel. He showed me the living quarters of the managers and workers of the plant on a hill outside Yawata. There on top of the hill were spacious homes surrounded by small gardens assigned to the general managers. Below were smaller houses inhabited by middle management. At the foot of the hill were multi-storied apartment houses of the workers and their families. Recreation facilities, schools, a hospital, and a store were provided and subsidized by the corporation.

We were driven to a guest house and after an *o-furo*, a Japanese-style bath, we relaxed over sake. The formal dinner as always was beautifully arranged on assorted dishes to match the color and the texture of the food served, including a specialty of the Hakata region, chicken sashimi. These were very thin slices of raw chicken breast that, dipped in *shoju*, tasted like raw fish.

To my surprise I learned that my host, who spoke excellent English, had never been outside Japan. We compared observations made during the day and discussed a broad range of subjects. My host made a comment still etched in my memory. He pointed out that a Japanese must learn thousands of characters to be literate. A knowledge of at least eight hundred characters is required to be able to read and write. A well-educated Japanese knows at least three to five thousand characters. Among them are *kanji* (the Chinese characters), *hiragana*, and *katakana* (both abbreviations of Chinese characters, with *katakana* used to transcribe foreign words). An Asian thinks in pictures, and it takes a great deal of time and effort to assimilate the knowledge of the required amount of characters to accomplish this. A Westerner constructs words and expresses his ideas from a limited number of letters or building blocks that simplify the process. Therefore, he has more time to explore and learn and can think with ease in abstract terms. My host suggested that I watch a Japanese listening to a foreigner. The Japanese generally will draw characters in the air with his hand to assist him in understanding the statements made.

At Fukuoka Airport waiting for my plane to return to Tokyo, I could see U.S. Air Force jets taking off into the night with the exhausts of the jet engines emitting an eerie bluish-reddish light as they gained speed on the runway. The cold war was on in 1962, and

the planes were patrolling the skies, discouraging the constant testing of the Japanese airspace by Soviet long-range bombers flying
from the airfields in Siberia. The Japanese economic empire was
comfortably and without cost constructed behind a strategic
umbrella provided through the courtesy of the American taxpayer.

On the way to Tokyo I reflected on my visit to Yawata. The layout of the steel plant, the enormous furnaces, the blooming, slabbing, and cold-rolling mills controlled by efficient crews presented a
remarkable sight. This installation was a dramatic departure from
the layout of steel mills I had seen at Hoesch, Krupp, or Thyssen in
Germany, and the most modern steel plant in the United States, the
huge installation of U.S. Steel in Fairless, Pennsylvania.

I visited the Yawata plant in 1962. Fifteen years later I inquired
in a casual conversation with Mr. Tadayoshi Yamada over a dinner at
a Japanese guest house *(o-zashiki)* how the Yawata plant was doing.
He responded that the obsolete pilot plant had been scrapped and
had been replaced with a larger and more modern installation, the
Kimitsu Works in Chiba prefecture.

I have visited many steel mills in Japan. However, the most
astounding sight was presented by the Kakegawa plant of Kobe Steel
in Kansai prefecture. This integrated facility was designed to produce annually after its completion 15 million tons of steel. When I
visited it, one-third of the plant with furnaces and hot and cold
rolling mills was fully operational, producing 5 million tons annually. Parallel to it another production line was under construction,
with the land for the third and final production line still being
reclaimed from the sea. This was an extraordinary feat of engineering and management, as the whole complex operation functioned
efficiently, with finished products shipped at one end of the mill,
while at the other end pumps were removing seawater from enclo-
sures built to reclaim land for the final stage of construction.

In 1982 Mr. Yamada insisted that I visit the new integrated steel
mill of the merged steel companies, now called Nippon Seitetsu, in
Oita, near Beppu on the island of Kyushu. I flew in from Tokyo and
was greeted at the airport by the deputy plant manager, an engineer
trained in metallurgy at MIT in the United States. After a short visit
to the popular resort city, Beppu, we proceeded to nearby Oita

where I stayed at a hotel belonging to the corporation. From my window I could see an enormous integrated steel mill. To my astonishment there was no visible smoke, or signs of any activity. The appearance of the plant was that of a huge installation mothballed in the midst of a lush garden.

My host, one of the managers of the Oita plant, picked me up at the hotel in the morning and we drove to the plant. The visit started at the monitoring installation. Large maps of the region displayed on the walls indicated a complex setup connected to the monitoring stations strategically in place around Oita, Beppu, and the bay.

The prefecture permitted the construction of the huge integrated mill with an annual capacity of 15 million tons of coil and plate under the condition that it would not pollute the environment in the resort region. All gas, smoke, or any other form of pollution was trapped and disposed of. A monitoring system sounded an alarm if pollution was discovered anywhere in the region. As a consequence, there was no outward visible activity, and the installation was surrounded by lush vegetation characteristic of this southern region of Japan.

The mill was completely automated, with crews walking around monitoring the equipment and occasionally servicing a component. A computer center controlled the whole operation. The mainframe and the electronic equipment in steel mills previously visited had been installed by IBM. At the Oita plant, all electronic installations had been already manufactured by Japanese electronic firms, with IBM providing only typewriters for the supervisors at the stations monitoring activities throughout the plant.

Bulk carriers were docked in a huge harbor, where they were unloaded by a remote electronically controlled system of conveyor belts operated from a tower similar to a control tower at an airport. Continuous casting of steel eliminated the blooming and slabbing process. The product emerged at the other end of the immense plant, to be loaded at the second harbor onto waiting carriers. The total operation was controlled by three thousand workers.

After an interesting but exhausting day, we drove to Beppu, where at a guest house the general manager of the plant and his deputy were waiting for us. As is customary in Japan, after a cup of tea served in a guest room we took off our clothes and put on comfortable cotton yukatas (kimonos) and then went to the communal bath. There we undressed, washed sitting on little wooden stools, and then entered a pool filled with hot mineral water and soaked away the tiredness of the day. Refreshed, we entered a pool of cold water and in yukatas proceeded to the private dining room where the waitresses were waiting with beer and sake and little tidbits.

The general manager had been in Oita only a few months, having returned from Bao-Shan in China where he had supervised the construction of a steel mill. The tales of his experience were fascinating and provided insights into developments in China. The lively discussion continued over a formal Japanese dinner. The next day I took off from the airport of Oita for Tokyo. I could see the Oita plant underneath at the bay of Beppu submerged in vegetation with no smoke in sight.

On a number of occasions I encountered in annual reports of corporations pictures of ships built in Japanese shipyards. I was intrigued by the naval architecture and its departure from conventional designs. These were primarily tankers and bulk carriers and occasional specialized vessels—ferries, fishing boats, and research ships. My next project after visiting steel mills was shipyards. I approached Mr. Konosuke Koike, inquiring whether Yamaichi Securities Co. could assist me in my efforts. Mr. Koike, Mr. Tsukuno and I went to the offices of Mitsubishi Heavy Industries, where we were greeted by the president.

After an exchange of salutations, we all proceeded to a modest office on an upper floor somewhere in a corner of the building. The president and others bowed deeply with more than the usual reverence to a man in his sixties with an impassive face standing next to an old-fashioned roll-top desk. It became apparent that the man wielded power and influence in contrast with his modest office. He was a retired admiral of the Imperial Navy who was officially a senior advisor of Mitsubishi Heavy Industries. I was introduced to him by Mr. Koike, and the purpose of my visit was explained. After a few questions, our hosts made a few phone calls, and again bowing unusually low my Japanese friends left the office.

Accompanied by an official of Yamaichi Securities, I left the next day by plane for Fukuoka and Nagasaki. It was November 1962 and the autumn in Japan is very beautiful. The trees turn yellow and red almost as in Vermont. Somehow the hues are somewhat more subdued. We stayed in Nagasaki at Yataro, formerly a mansion of the Iwasaki family, which before the war had controlled the giant Mitsubishi Zaibatsu. The view of the Nagasaki bay from the hotel was splendid, and at night the brightly lit slopes of the hills surrounding the city and the harbor remotely resembled Hong Kong.

We were received in a very friendly way at the Mitsubishi shipyards in Nagasaki. Our introduction had opened the doors, and an interesting program had been prepared for me and my escort, the official of Yamaichi Securities. We were joined by an impressive man with an air of authority about him. He had been a vice admiral in the Imperial Navy and after the war had been employed at the Mitsubishi shipyards in Nagasaki.

First we visited the laboratories where, in special pools constructed to reproduce all possible weather conditions a ship might encounter at sea, balsa models of tankers with the characteristic bulbous noses were tested. A 100,000- to 150,000-ton tanker was common at that time. The models being tested were in preparation for building tankers displacing then mind-boggling 500,000 tons and 1,000,000 tons. The program of tests in the laboratory indicated that the architects were in an advanced stage of designing larger tankers and bulk carriers.

At the shipyard I was introduced to the modular method of building ships. It probably originated in the United States, following the destruction of the Pacific fleet in Pearl Harbor and the submarine attacks on shipping in the Atlantic. Ships had to be built rapidly and efficiently in the shortest possible time. A module was completed on the ground, with steel plates properly bent and bulkheads, steam pipes, electrical wiring, and other equipment installed on the ground. Subsequently the completed module weighing from 200 to 400 tons, depending on the capacity of the special moving cranes over the dry dock, was lifted into place and welded together. Riveting was eliminated altogether.

Equally interesting was the ingenious solution to simplify the creation of blueprints. Steel plates were covered with a chemical sensitive to light and rolled under a enormous camera-like structure that projected the blueprints onto them. The chemical solution was treated, which removed the substance, leaving only the blueprint with all the required processing instructions on the steel plates for the shipyard workers to follow.

A few days later visiting the shipyards of Ishikawajima Harima in Yokohama, I learned that this process was already obsolete. There the blueprints were entered into a sophisticated specially designed computer mainframe, which controlled machine tools employed in cutting, shaping, and welding the components. Large steel plates were placed on huge platforms travelling slowly through the yard on enormous wheels, with a battery of electronically guided machines performing the required tasks. At the end of the hall the ready components were lifted by a system of cranes and deposited at the dry dock to be assembled into a finished module. There the fitters installed the variety of pipes and electrical cables into the modules, readying them to be lifted and deposited onto the ship in the dry dock by an enormous crane. Thus production was simplified with a number of time-consuming processes eliminated. I had seen experiments with electronically controlled machine tools years earlier at the Olivetti laboratories in Rho near Milano. The Japanese had developed the concept and employed it in their shipyards, controlling cutting, shaping, and a revolutionary joining of steel plates welding them simultaneously together on both sides.

The visit to Nagasaki shipyards was an eye-opening experience. My host, the former vice admiral, guided me through the facility, providing explanations I could comprehend, thanks to my engineering studies at Columbia University.

The program in Nagasaki included the obligatory visit to the site of the explosion of the atomic bomb and a museum housing exhibits explaining the tragedy. We were guided through it by a high official of the city and the explanations given were designed to make Americans feel guilty and contrite.

As a survivor of the Holocaust, a legally condoned and industrially carried out genocide of a people, I was not impressed. The carnage I had seen as a soldier at the end of the war and the brutal and cruel treatment of the civilian non-Jewish population in Poland and the Ukraine by the German troops provided me with a somewhat different perspective on this human tragedy.

President Truman, confronted with the choice of either invading Japan or using an atomic device, made the right if difficult decision. It saved thousands of Japanese and American lives that would have been lost if the battles fought in the Pacific had continued on to the Japanese islands. The mass suicides of Japanese military and civilians on Okinawa and elsewhere provided an indication of what would have happened had the war been brought to the shores of Japan. The carnage created by desperate people led by fanatics would have exceeded by far the tragic casualties caused by the two atomic bombs. General Tojo's regime had experimented with biological warfare and other non-conventional weapons. Unspeakable atrocities had been perpetrated against POWs and civilians by Japanese troops. Therefore, I found the moralizing somewhat excessive.

At dinner the vice admiral and I discussed a broad range of subjects. The impressive former naval officer told me that he had been stationed in Jakarta during the war and had supervised shipments of cobalt, molybdenum, and other rare metals to Germany. I learned to my amazement that German submarines had called regularly in Jakarta, arriving after a long voyage from Bordeaux, St. Nazaire, and other French harbors in the Atlantic, carrying badly needed optical devices and precision instruments for the Japanese. They returned to Europe loaded with rare metals and other strategic materials Germany was short of. They were secretly resupplied and refueled during the long cruise by ships under a neutral flag. This activity ended with the landing of the Allies in Normandy in 1944.

This interesting detail threw light on the determination of the Japanese to develop their own optical engineering and manufacturing facilities and explained the emphasis given to this field by MITI, which I observed when visiting Nikon and Cannon. Equal attention was given to the precision instrumentation essential in research and development.

The visit to Mitsubishi shipyards in Nagasaki was indeed fascinating, and my host made a considerable contribution to my understanding of the growing technological and engineering capabilities of Japan. The visit ended showing me a detailed scaled-down model of the huge battleship *Musashi*, the pride of the Imperial Navy, built in the Mitsubishi Shipyards in Nagasaki, and sunk in the last sortie of the Imperial Navy into the Pacific. The strategically critical Mitsubishi shipyards in Nagasaki were the real target of the atomic bomb.

Before leaving Nagasaki I had a little time for sightseeing. I was led by the Yamaichi official to the legendary home of Madame Butterfly overlooking the harbor. The house and its furnishings were from the early Meiji era and authentic. I could recall the haunting music of Giacomo Puccini, who had never been to Japan but had captured its mood. The perception of Puccini conveys a tragic story that was probably repeated many times in similar circumstances and ended tragically when the two cultures met and clashed.

The mementos of the Dutch trading station that was for a long time on Deshima, an artificial island off Nagasaki, were fascinating as were the scrolls portraying the Namban—the southern barbarians that were strangers to the Japanese. The Tokugawa shogunate appreciated this useful but potentially dangerous contact with the outside world. Therefore, everything either brought to or leaving Japan had to pass through a bridge linking the artificial island Deshima with Nagasaki. The annual visit of the Dutch traders to bring gifts to the shogun and renew the charter was a complicated undertaking as they had to be prevented from sightseeing on their way to Edo. It was feared that they might learn too much about the inner workings of Japan. Something of this mentality has carried through to modern times.

Nagasaki was the center of Jesuit activity in Japan, which was terminated with the Christian Edict after it was discovered by the rulers that in addition to spiritual activities the Jesuits were meddling in local politics. When they persisted and stayed on after being asked to leave, thirty-six of them were executed in Nagasaki.[2]

I was shown scrolls used by the Jesuit fathers in the late sixteenth century to teach the catechism. One scroll depicted a dying Japanese lying on a futon (a Japanese sort of mattress) with his soul descending downward to be greeted by Han-ya, a Buddhist deity, traditionally represented with horns and large eyeteeth, which the Jesuits understood to be the devil. Another scroll represented the same dying Japanese with his soul ascending to heaven to be greeted by angels with a baroque western look, smiling and surrounded by other Christian symbols. I could not help but reflect on the intellectual arrogance of well-meaning missionaries who, after arriving from far-off Europe or the Jesuit province in Goa in the sixteenth century, were telling the Japanese that their beliefs and values were wrong and must be changed.

I had many opportunities to discuss this subject with Taeko-san, the daughter of the governor of Chiba prefecture, former Viscount Kano. Taeko-san was a Quaker and for a number of years had served on the governing Council of the Society of Friends in London. From Taeko-san I learned that the chasm between Japan and the West can be reconciled provided that it is carried out tactfully and in the spirit of mutual respect.

Nevertheless, the scrolls remained etched in my memory. Over the years I have seen many expressions of a similar condescending attitude displayed by Europeans and Americans in their dealings with the Japanese.

On the way to Tokyo we stopped in Nagoya and visited the Komaki plant of Mitsubishi Heavy Industries. There I was shown production lines under license from Lockheed for the F-104 manufactured for the Japanese Defense Forces, and assembly of sophisticated rocketry. I was also shown work on an experimental executive airplane. The metallurgy, and the ability to manufacture serially advanced air frames and fit them out with Japanese-made jet engines and advanced electronics, were impressive indeed and demonstrated the progress made by Japan toward becoming an economic superpower. The management, the engineers, the foremen, and the workers on the assembly lines were purposeful, well-prepared, and motivated. The housekeeping in the numerous industrial installations I visited was excellent and represented an outward expression of the motivation and the dedication of the teams working in them. I made a point of having my lunches in the factory dining rooms. They were very simple but neat, and the food served was carefully prepared, tasty, and adequate. Equally impressive were the recreation facilities allowing the workers to exercise, bath, or watch television in their free time.

The concept, the magnitude, and the design of the doubling of national income of Prime Minister Ikeda, to which I was introduced during my first visit to Japan, emerged as I visited industrial installations after completing my work in Tokyo and in Osaka. It was a carefully planned strategic design, executed with almost military precision, and guided and supported by the Ministry of Finance and MITI.

The first massive investment in the postwar era was concentrated on building a modern utilities industry and manufacturing heavy electrical equipment. Subsequently the emphasis shifted to manufacturing heavy earth-moving equipment and erecting large integrated steel mills, and replacing U.S.-made machinery with Japanese products. This was followed by an expansion of consumer electronics, optical equipment, and communications. Simultaneously, shipbuilding was encouraged in order to import raw materials in Japanese hulls and export manufactured products abroad in cargo and specialized vessels. After completion of the first phase, efforts were redirected to consolidation and expansion of the automotive industry. The computer industry and the development of software were left to a later stage.

The high level of saving in Japan was not sufficient to supply the huge amounts of capital required for these ambitious programs. Japanese banks borrowed wherever they could, eventually exhausting long-term and medium-term credit lines.

Japanese bankers could be found knocking on the doors of small regional banks like Frost National Bank in San Antonio, borrowing amounts as small as $500,000 for thirty days. These funds were then lent on a long-term basis to finance massive industrial investment. It took an extraordinary degree of cooperation between the banks and the Japanese government and an imagination to juggle these loans. The restored credit standing of Japan, which recognized the obligations undertaken by the militarists, and an interest rate carrying a premium made this possible. In those days one of the vice ministers of finance for international affairs complained to me that he had reserves of foreign exchange to cover only two months of payments for the purchases of raw materials.

My introduction to Japanese culture and custom, thanks to the personal friendships I developed over the years, made an equally important contribution to my learning about Japan and its people.

The study of the Japanese economy and the identification of investment opportunities were frustrating exercises because the commonly
employed yardsticks of analysis did not apply. A review of balance
sheets pointed to an extraordinary fragile and heavily leveraged corporate structure. The unique relationships existing between the government, management, and labor resulted in a functioning society
that followed its own set of rules. The national character of this
unique ethnic group provided strength and motivation to a degree
rarely found elsewhere.

The Tokugawa era (1612-1868) of relative peace allowing the
formation of an orderly and regulated society left an imprint that
carried through the Meiji restoration and well into modern times.
The resulting characteristics of this well-defined society produced
results that could not be duplicated in any other environment. The
Japanese are successful in adopting improvements and techniques
brought from the United States and Europe. However, it is difficult
to duplicate their innovative methods of management and production because these are effective only in a society that is cohesive,
homogenous, and evolved over a long period time.

There are unquestionably drawbacks and limitations in Japan
resulting from a certain rigidity and resistance to change always present in a highly structured society. The reconstruction of the country devastated by the war could be accomplished because of the presence of a high degree of motivation, discipline, and national pride.
Admittedly the Korean and the Vietnam Wars turned Japan into a
logistic base for the U.S. forces engaged in Asia and provided a powerful stimulus for the growth of its economy. The practically unlim-
ited access to the U.S. market provided the additional impetus for
the expanding economy of Japan. American management abetted
their efforts, as whole sectors of industry in the United States preferred to concentrate on supplying the defense sector rather than pay
attention to the requirements of the domestic market. An excellent
example was the neglected sectors of consumer electronics and photographic equipment, which were practically taken over by Japanese
imports.

Nevertheless, the extraordinary achievements of Japanese
industry could not have been accomplished had it not been for the

national character molded during the long span of the Tokugawa rule. Realizing this, I addressed myself to a study of this period and made every effort to learn as much as I could about the characteristics of this unique society.

While crisscrossing Japan visiting industrial plants and financial institutions, I utilized every available free moment to explore its culture. The thoughtful assistance of my many friends made it possible. My primary objective was to understand the functioning of the society and to develop an ability to discern trends within it. As the Japanese economy expanded and gained momentum, its impact on international trade and payments was unfolding long before it became visible and recognized. This was the area that interested me most, as it became clear that Japan with time would emerge as an economic superpower.

The strategic design of its planners emerged after a few visits to industrial installations and the explanations provided by my friends in the government and industry. The introduction to laboratories and the experimental new products alerted me that the arrogant and inaccurate notion that the Japanese are able only to copy Western technology was completely wrong. Equally curious and misleading was the comment made early in the days of the occupation by a highly positioned American official to Mr. Konosuke Koike that the Japanese were intellectually only twelve years old.

A powerful and complex structure was overlooked because only a few took the time and effort to understand the historical and cultural background of the Japanese people and relate it to current economic and financial activity. There were and are many brilliant and competent scholars in the United States with a deep knowledge of Japan and the Japanese. Among them was the highly regarded ambassador Dr. Reischauer. Another example of brilliant and intuitive scholarship can be found in the book *The Chrysanthemum and the Sword* by Ruth Benedict. But their collective and valuable contribution could not provide guidelines for forecasting the future direction of Japan and its place in the changing international environment.

During my frequent trips to Japan I did not miss an opportunity to get acquainted with every facet accessible to me of its culture and its life. Therefore, I was very pleased to be invited to attend the finals of a sumo tournament in Tokyo. An uncle of a friend of mine, a connoisseur and a supporter of the sport, owned a superb seat next to the ring, the equivalent of a box at the world series. This was my introduction to this ancient and ceremonial sport.

On arrival at the stadium we were greeted by attendants who accompanied us to our seats on a small elevated platform covered with tatami mats. Shortly afterwards they returned with cushions, a huge bottle of sake, *o-sembei* (a variety of Japanese rice tidbits, nuts, dried fish), and *mikan* (mandarin oranges).

Settled comfortably on the tatami-covered platform with our shoes off, we relaxed, sipped sake and nibbled on the o-sembe. In this fashion we spent the afternoon and the early evening watching the last matches of the tournament, which decided who would be the victor. The hall was filled to capacity with a public representing every walk of life and age group. Opening the last day of the tournament was a procession of huge, obese-appearing, almost naked men wearing richly embroidered colorful aprons tied in the back with elaborate knots of white rope. They were led by their attendants displaying tablets with the names of the sponsors on them. They walked around the elevated ring in which the referees, dressed in gaudy kimonos and headgear of bygone days tied under their chins, were waiting under a canopy hanging from the ceiling, which resembled a cover of a shrine carried in a religious procession during a festival. The judges, retired yokozunas wearing black kimonos with white sashes, sat impassively around the ring.

Then the contest commenced. The names of the two competing sumo wrestlers were called out in a formal, stilted fashion. They entered the ring and bowed, flexing their legs and arms, turning now and then to a container of salt in the corner, picking up a handful and throwing it with gusto into the air to ward away evil spirits and purify the environment. This exercise went on for a while and, on a signal of the referee given with a fan, the encounter took place. It was over in hardly more than a few seconds. The victor's name was announced by the referee, who handed him an envelope with the prize. Both sumo wrestlers bowed to each other and to the public and walked away with dignity from the hall, while two new contestants entered the ring and followed the same routine.

At the outset the spectacle appeared grotesque to the uninitiated and the contest no more than huge fat men pushing and shoving one another to get an opponent out of the ring. Gradually the extraordinary concentration and skill became apparent, as did the stylized and ritualistic character of the contest. What came to mind were the sketches of Hokusai Katsuhika (a famous woodblock artist in the Edo era, 1760–1849) portraying sumo wrestlers in preparation for the creation of his well-known woodblock prints. The final contest ended, the winner was presented with a silver trophy, and with a long bow performed the highly stylized exercises that ended the tournament.

This too was part of the many aspects of Japan I was discovering, which eventually led to a better understanding of the country and its people. The ritual, the precision, the attention to detail, the drive for perfection, the dignified acceptance of defeat, and the concentration were a reflection of the many factors that over the centuries have shaped the Japanese.

The evolution of the Japanese economic, financial, and technological empire was due to the careful strategic planning and the determination and skills of the managers. However, the character of this nation shaped over many centuries has greatly contributed to the success of the process. The sumo wrestlers, the kabuki theater, the pilgrimages to the many Buddhist temples and Shinto shrines, the Kodo drummers—all added to a bewildering kaleidoscope of impressions gathered by an occasional visitor. They indirectly provided keys to an understanding of the postwar evolution of Japan.

The highlight of every visit to Japan was an evening at the Koikes. They all were cosmopolitan in their outlook, were familiar with the United States and Europe, spoke excellent English, and had attended western schools. It was only the elegant and beautiful Mrs. Koike senior whose traditional manner and ways reminded me that I was in Japan.

Interesting and lively conversation, the witty comments and broad range of interests of the guests, usually members of the family, made a visit to the Koikes a memorable occasion. At the end of the lunch or dinner Mrs. Koike performed the tea ceremony, offering everyone green tea in beautiful old tea bowls. When the utensils of the ceremony were brought in everyone fell silent, paying attention to the highly stylized and measured movements of Mrs. Koike's hands performing this simple and at the same time elaborate ceremony with an extraordinary elegance. This was invariably the highlight of each visit to the Koike's home.

Taeko-san's eldest daughter got married during my stay in Japan. I was invited to the wedding, which took place in one of the new hotels in Tokyo. The guests gathered in a spacious room outside the chapel. The women were wearing formal black kimonos decorated with little white *mon* (coat of arms) and beautiful obis. The men arrived in dark suits, the family members in morning coats. They bowed and exchanged greetings as they arrived. It was the only time that I saw Taeko-san wearing a kimono, gracious and smiling as always, greeting the arriving guests. I had always assumed that Taeko-san was entirely westernized after spending her childhood and her youth in London.

Observing her at the wedding of her daughter, I realized that, while familiar with western ways and western culture, this extraordinary lady was at her core a Japanese. A deeply believing Christian, she combined the outlook and the practices of a western religion and the deep knowledge of western civilization with her roots, that of a scion of an old and prominent family, which has produced leaders for Japan over centuries.

The guests moved to the chapel, where a Protestant ceremony was conducted in Japanese by a minister. This ability to blend ideas and cultures while always remaining oneself is the secret of the strength of Japan. Taeko-san and other members of the Koike family introduced me to this facet of Japan.

I also learned a great deal from another friend of mine, a prominent economist. He, a highly respected professional, on a number of occasions mentioned that he was a practicing Christian. His wife was a Buddhist and, while my friend appeared westernized and spoke excellent English, she always wore a kimono and an obi and was attached to the old traditions of Japan.

Her features, those of a classical Japanese beauty, reminded me of the delicate faces portrayed in the woodblock prints of Utamaro. We spent many a weekend exploring nooks and corners of old Japan of which she was so fond. The last time I saw her was after I remarried and brought my wife Donatella to Japan to meet my many friends. Our friends invited us for dinner in a splendid private room at the Fukuda-Ya inn in Tokyo. Mrs. K. was frail and terminally ill but cheerful and gracious as always. It was a memorable and relaxed evening with *ma-cha* (powdered green tea used in the tea ceremony) served in splendid precious chawans. Before saying goodby my friend's wife turned to Donatella and said that she had wanted to meet her first before offering her a wedding present. Before we left Tokyo, delicate and beautiful silver spoons were left at our hotel. This was the last time we saw my friend's wife. We were sorry to learn that she died a few months later.

On my next visit to Japan my friend, his daughter, an accomplished concert pianist, and I went to Hakone where the bank maintained a guest house. We roamed through the area during the day, visiting all kinds of interesting places like the famous Hakone barrier. In the evening before returning to the guest house we stopped at the Hakone Jinja shrine on the shores of Lake Ashi.

The last rays of the setting sun brightened the path leading to the shrine, hidden by enormous cedar trees. At the shrine my friend asked a priest to perform a memorial service for his wife. It was a simple ceremony, which took place outdoors with rays of the setting sun providing a little light shining through the branches of the huge cedars. I was somewhat surprised to see my friend participating actively in the service.

After the brief memorial service, his daughter picked up a wooden box at a little stand where a young girl in a traditional attire was accepting offerings. She brought it to me, asked me to shake it well, pick up a stick with a number on it, and hand it to the shrine's attendant. I was given a folded piece of paper with a message in Japanese. She read the message and, displeased with the content, tied the carefully folded piece of paper on a nearby tree full of similar pieces of paper. We left the shrine for the guest house, took a bath and dressed in kimonos. We then took a short nap before dinner, stretched on tatami mats.

After we had some sake and relaxed, I asked my friend's daughter what it was that she did not like in the message I had picked up from the attendant. She explained that by shaking the wooden sticks in the box and picking one I had selected a number with which the attendant chose the paper predicting my future. As she did not like its content, it was best not to accept it but leave it to the gods in the shrine. Therefore, she folded it and left it on a tree with the other fortunes that were not accepted.

I gathered courage and asked my friend about his participation in the memorial service. I mentioned that I was very pleased to be present. However, my religion did not permit me to participate in another cult. He responded that westerners have a different concept of religion than the Japanese. He is a professed Christian, but this however does not prevent him from adopting the best from other religions. Therefore, he participated in the memorial service in a cult different from the one he observes.

Japan, its history, its culture, and its people are a subject of a lifetime study. I, like many other westerners who have come in contact with the Far East, developed an interest in this unique country. My objective was to focus on the postwar reconstruction of the Japanese economy and understand the role it would play in international relations.

I concentrated on learning about the functioning of its political system, the sectors of government responsible for economic planning, its financial institutions and markets, its industry, management practices, and labor relations. The personal contact and the friendships formed over the twenty-five years of activity in Japan provided insights without which Japan would remain an enigma, as it generally is to a westerner. My introduction to it was almost over and a new phase commenced in which I could utilize the years of effort and the occasional scholarly pursuit to get better acquainted with Japan and its people.

CHAPTER 12

The Rise of an Economic Superpower

Y AMAICHI SECURITIES CO., the host of the first delegation of securities analysts that visited Japan in 1962, was the firm that best suited my objectives of further exploration of Japan. The executives of Nomura Securities Co. were interested in immediate business results. Nikko Securities Co. had a very close relationship with Bache & Co., and I wanted to remain independent in my survey of Japan. Daiwa Securities Co. was a pleasant and competent firm, but somehow, I preferred the style of Yamaichi Securities Co. and found them easier to deal with.

I became friendly with the firm's managers in New York and assisted them in the development of business in the United States. They in turn reciprocated by arranging my trips to Japan and also made suggestions for the itinerary and the topics to pursue. The managers in Tokyo, among them Mr. Kazuo Tsukuno, were helpful in arranging visits to industrial plants in Japan. The assistance and the guidance of Mr. Sakimura of Chase, and Mr. Mayekawa and Dr. Yoshino of the Bank of Japan, added another dimension and together with the Yamaichi Securities Co. made each visit to Japan productive and pleasant.

My friends arranged sightseeing programs on weekends, always introducing new and an interesting facets of Japan. A performance of Kabuki was one of them. The Kabukiza, a Kabuki theater in the Ginza district, is an interesting building somewhat resembling a shrine. Brightly lit at night and decorated with colorful paper flowers and lanterns, it beckons with a promise of drama and excitement. The large, interesting curtain is made of an unusual combination of huge silk stripes in black, green, blue, and brown. The *hanamichi* is a platform on which actors arrive and depart; it stretches throughout the hall to the stage. The audience consists primarily of middle-age Japanese. Occasionally a group of women would arrive, probably from out of town, travelling together, as is the custom of the Japanese.

An attendant dressed in a black starched kimono appears before the curtain and hitting wooden clappers announces the beginning of the performance. At the sides of the stage the narrators and the shamisen players sit on elevated platforms in kimonos with heavily starched exaggerated shoulders. The curtain lifts and a beautifully designed, brightly lit backdrop sets the mood, indicating what will happen. The narrator introduces the story and the procession of actors walks on the *hanamichi* to the stage. Their bright almost gaudy costumes and their heavy makeup exaggerate their features. The theme of the lengthy performance, which starts in the afternoon and ends late in the evening, is a perennial favorite, the story of the forty-seven ronin—Chushingura.

The title appearing on the program is somewhat different, as in the days of the Tokugawa regime the story was considered controversial and represented a challenge to the authorities. Therefore, the play's title was tactfully changed, and both the public and the shogunate were satisfied.

Observing this and many other performances, I realized that underneath the mask of imperturbability the Japanese are a highly emotional people. This feeling finds its expression in the emotions displayed freely on the stage in the Kabuki dramas. The highly stylized performance of the Kabuki actors, the voice of the narrators, and the shamisen accompaniment are an emotional display the audience thoroughly enjoys. There is an intermission, allowing the audience to disperse to have dinner in the many sushi shops and restaurants at the theater, or purchase an o-bento (a box with tidbits, an equivalent of a sandwich) to be enjoyed with hot tea sitting at one of the many tables.

The attendant with a wooden clapper, curiously reminding me of the one used by the Studite monk waking up the community for prayers, announces the beginning of the second part of the performance. After two hours I usually left, as this was my limit. However, over the years I returned to the Kabukiza many a time and found the performance and the audience equally fascinating.

In those days my friends avoided discussion of their service in the Imperial Army or the Navy during the war. The exceptions were the vice-admiral at Mitsubishi Heavy Industries Shipyard in Nagasaki and Mr. Shomura, a managing director of Yamaichi Securities Co.

Shomura-san (a proper way to address a Japanese) was a graduate of Etajima, the Imperial Naval Academy, the equivalent of Annapolis. He suggested that I accompany him on a lovely Saturday morning during the cherry blossom season to the Yasukuni shrine. The cherry trees were in full blossom and were covered with a cloud-like veil of flowers, looking from the distance like snow. Occasionally a gust of wind caused the white petals to fall, adding to the illusion of snow.

Before entering the shrine, Shomura-san approached a fountain and, with a wooden cup attached to a bamboo stick that was filled with water from the fountain, rinsed his mouth and washed his hands, following the Shinto custom of purification. Then we proceeded to the inner shrine, where in front of it he clapped his hands and bowed deeply three times. He was paying respect to the souls of his comrades who had fallen in the Pacific during the war. Shomura-san had been wounded on the island of Truk and evacuated back to Japan. By the time he recovered, the war was over.

We proceeded to a museum in which mementos of the wars fought by Japan are kept, together with pictures of fallen soldiers and sailors and decorations of famous heroes like Admiral Togo and General Nogi. I observed all this with mixed feelings, remembering the massacre of Nanking, the attack on Pearl Harbor, and the brutal treatment of POWs and civilians. The Yasukuni shrine was a symbol of extreme nationalism, worship of the Emperor, and the idealization of death in the service of the nation. It was also a depository, in the belief of Japanese, of the souls of the many who had died in wars that were fought by most of them with little choice in the matter.

Regardless of their views and beliefs, they did their best as they understood their duty and responsibilities. The sense of community, the nation, and a link with the past were conveyed with equal emphasis, as was militarism and extreme nationalism. This visit was almost twenty-five years ago, and the question is frequently posed whether the new generation perceives these ideas in the same way.

The northernmost island in the archipelago of Japan, Hokkaido, somewhat resembles New England. The autumn there is a lovely time for a visit, with the weather relatively pleasant and the leaves turning yellow and brown-red. Sapporo, the major city, is decorated with daikon, enormous elongated radishes, drying in the air to be pickled and turned into *O-shinko.*

Mr. Shimamoto Tohru, the chairman of the Hokkaido Bank, invited me to come to Sapporo. I spent two pleasant days visiting the bank, addressing a gathering of businessmen and industrialists, with a little time thoughtfully left for sightseeing.

During the World War II, Mr. Shimamoto had been the representative of the Ministry of Finance attached to the Japanese Embassies in Berlin and Rome. With him had been posted a young and promising central banker, Mr. Haruo Mayekawa, subsequently the Governor of the Bank of Japan. The war years spent in the Third Reich had provided both men with a unique perspective that had served them well in the postwar years. It was always a great pleasure and challenge to discuss the international monetary situation with either of them. Both in different ways greatly contributed to my better understanding of Japan and the problems it faces in the international environment.

Mr. Shimamoto arranged a visit for me to the Muroran steel mill of Fuji Iron and Steel, the Oji Paper Company, and an Ainu village. The trip to Hokkaido concluded with a stay in Noboribetsu, a popular hot springs resort.

The Muroran steel works were the oldest ones I had seen in Japan, having survived the systematic bombing that leveled other industrial centers. It was interesting to visit and compare this facility with the Yawata and other steel mills built after the war. The contrast was striking, as Muroran works resembled Hoesch and other German steel mills in the Ruhr that had been rehabilitated and rebuilt to restore them to what they had been before the destruction by American and British bombs. Consequently they were of old design and not very efficient. The American mills at that time were in not much better shape, and their only advantage was their size.

The new Japanese mills introduced the most advanced technological breakthroughs in steelmaking, from oxygen-injected furnaces to continuous casting. Only the new Dutch mill, Staalfabriken Hoogoven, resembled the recently constructed mills of Japan.

A visit to Oji Paper Company introduced me to the issue of trade between the Soviet Union and Japan. In exchange for purchasing lumber in Siberia for its paper mills, Oji Paper was permitted more extensive fishing rights off Hokkaido, important to this company because of its large production of an excellent smoked salmon. However, the cold war and the foreign policy of the Soviet Union precluded the development of substantial trade. The issue of the Northern islands (Kurile Islands) Etorofu, Shikotan, Habomai, and Kunashiri blocked progress, because in those days an expansionary Soviet foreign policy dismissed any claim registered by the Japanese to have these islands returned. It became an issue of national importance, and there was tacit agreement that no normalization of relations between Japan and the Soviet Union would take place until this issue was resolved.

The discussions at Oji Paper Co. on this subject were followed years later by comments from Mr. Haruo Mayekawa, who subsequently served as a deputy governor of the Import Export Bank of Japan. He pointed out that the development of natural gas fields in Sakhalin provided an interesting insight on the relations between Japan and the USSR. There is unquestionably a mutual interest in the development of resources in the Soviet Pacific by the Japanese. The raw materials have a ready market, and the capital equipment and the know-how of the Japanese are badly needed to develop the rich resources in Siberia.

Nevertheless, the animosity lingering since the Russo-Japanese war at the beginning of the century, the numerous conflicts in Manchuria in the 1930s, and finally the treachery of Stalin violating the nonaggression treaty in 1945 preclude progress in the negotiations. Japan, respecting the terms of the agreement signed by its foreign minister Mr. Matsuoka in 1940, refused to join the Germans and attack the USSR in 1941. Through the Soviet spy planted in

Tokyo, the German journalist Richard Sorge, and his collaborator Ozeki Hatsumi, an advisor to Prince Konoye (Prime Minister of Japan), information was passed on to Moscow that the powerful Kwantung army would not violate the nonaggression treaty and attack Siberia. This allowed Stalin to move Siberian divisions of the Red Army to stop the German assault on Moscow.

The treachery of Stalin in 1945, declaring war on Japan in the last few days of the war, resulted in the death of thousands of Japanese soldiers and civilians in Siberian labor camps. The situation has changed, and the disintegration of the Soviet Union has created new circumstances. Nevertheless, the Japanese remain cautious and distrustful and are waiting for further developments in Russia.

Before leaving Oji Paper Company, I was offered a beautiful pottery plate with a real maple leave embossed and glazed over on it. My hosts explained that their primary responsibility is to provide satisfactory financial results. However, they are also interested in supporting artists in Hokkaido, who are invited to express the unique character of this island and its natural beauty in painting, sculpture, and pottery.

On the way back to the airport of Sapporo we stopped to visit an Ainu village. At the entrance to it was a modest souvenir shop belonging to a Japanese. It was late autumn and there were no visitors except the official of the Hokkaido Bank, the driver, and myself. The shop displayed the usual Ainu wood carvings representing a bear with a salmon in his snout—small, medium, and enormous carvings of a never-changing design.

My eye was caught by a unique carving, done with more precision and different from the others, displayed in the shop. It represented a bear sitting and holding a salmon in his paws. I pointed to the carving and asked my host to tell the shopkeeper that I wished to purchase it. The shopkeeper refused, explaining that he had carved it himself; it was the mascot of his shop and not for sale. I chose another bear, had it wrapped, and paid for it. The shopkeeper then picked up his mascot and handed it to me, stating that while it was not for sale, he was offering it to me as a gift because I admired his work. I still remember the lesson I was taught. The bear holding the salmon is displayed on a shelf in my library, reminding me of the poor shopkeeper at the entrance to an Ainu village. He was unimpressed by the important visitor from far away who was accompanied by a Japanese banker. Money was unquestionably important to him. However, it was secondary to his dignity. His mascot had no price, but he was pleased to offer it to a foreigner who admired his work.

I returned to Tokyo with Mr. Shimamoto, and during the flight we discussed my visit. He pointed out that Hokkaido is the only region permitting expansion and growth in this small overcrowded country. Hokkaido offered the greatest luxury in Japan, space.

On arrival in Tokyo I learned that the Japanese stock market had crashed. It was 1965 and the sharp drop in the prices of securities at the Kabuto-cho, the Japanese equivalent of Wall Street, resembled in its magnitude and impact the crash of 1929. The collapse of the market caught the securities firms unprepared and overextended, as was the whole financial structure of Japan. The debacle was triggered by a sudden and unexpected liquidity preference on the part of investors, which had caused a massive redemption of mutual funds. This in turn had had a snowballing effect on the market.

The decline gained momentum, bankrupting three large securities companies, Yamaichi, Nikko, and Daiwa. Only Nomura, the largest, escaped the debacle, having sold its positions in equities before the crash. A dichotomy developed between the increasingly unrealistic prices of equities in a market overheated by speculative fever and a sound expanding economy ready to embark on a major expansion of exports of technologically sophisticated manufacturing products.

The position of Japan, a heavy borrower of short-term funds in international capital markets, was a precarious one as there was a real danger that lines of credit might not be extended by commercial banks. The lenders were primarily American and Canadian banks, with British, German, Dutch and French banks concentrating on servicing trade of their countries with Japan.

The debacle faced by the securities industry and the overextended lines of credit maintained by the Japanese banks required a imaginative and swift intervention. The Bank of Japan, the central bank, stepped in and made available half a billion dollars to a newly formed Joint Securities Company for the purchase of equities in support of the market. Apparently this was the first instance when a central bank intervened directly to assist a floundering securities industry.

I was invited to lunch at the Bank of Japan with Mr. Mayekawa, Mr. Inoue, and Dr. Yoshino while this rather unorthodox operation was going on. We discussed the debacle of the securities industry, and I was asked to comment on this operation, which was unusual for a central bank. I pointed out that in view of the large outstanding short-term debt in the United States and in London, it was essential to maintain the credit standing of Japan. The short-term borrowing had been employed to finance long-term investment in plant and equipment. The debacle of the Tokyo stock market and the bankruptcy of the leading securities companies could result in a refusal to roll over the outstanding short-term debt by American and British financial institutions. In those days Japan had balance of payments problems, and its meager reserves would not permit a repayment of outstanding short-term foreign debt.

The funds committed to the Joint Securities Company were practically exhausted. While the free fall of prices in the stock market was arrested, a recovery was not in sight. I was told that the Bank of Japan was preparing a second tranche of funds to inject into the securities industry to support the market. I pointed out that the sharp drop of prices of securities and the bankruptcy of securities companies could lead to the conclusion among foreign bankers that the highly leveraged Japanese economy was on the verge of a collapse. Therefore, an explanation was called for to stress that the Japanese economy continued to grow, inflation was contained, and the technical correction of the stock market was fueled by unfounded fears. A number of suggestions were made how to accomplish this, among them to have the Minister of Finance and the Governor of the Bank of Japan issue a joint formal statement.

My proposal was that a personal letter written by a prominent and well-known commercial banker to presidents of major banks in the United States and in Europe probably would be more effective. I recommended Mr. Iwasa, the president of the Fuji Bank, whom I had met on several occasions at the annual meetings of the World Bank. This well-known commercial banker was highly respected and trusted. His personal letter that was subsequently used allayed the fears of the foreign bankers, and the financial storm generated by Kabuto-cho, not the first and not the last, subsided.

Bold and unorthodox intervention of the Bank of Japan in 1965 rescued the securities industry. The method of intervention was ingenious. Each bankrupt investment company was divided into two. A new company under the same name was formed free from the commitments of the old one and able to continue to operate. Even a new company symbol was created for it. The old and bankrupt company was provided with loans at a low interest rate from the Joint Securities Company to finance the carrying of portfolios of securities that could not be liquidated. It was expected that the loans would be repaid by the bankrupt companies in eighteen years. Thus the Bank of Japan became indirectly one of the largest holders of Japanese equities. This ingenious intervention proved effective, the equities market recovered, and the loans were repaid by the bankrupt companies in three years. These were then dissolved, leaving the new operating companies free to continue unencumbered by the debacle.

I was distressed to observe the embarrassment and the difficulties faced by my friends at Yamaichi Securities Co., which was threatened with bankruptcy. The Industrial Bank of Japan, heavily involved with the securities industry, appointed one of its executives, Mr. Hidaka Teru, as the new chief executive of this securities firm.

Hidaka-san was a remarkable man, with a gift for instinctive leadership and a cheerful disposition. I made every effort to assist him in his task. My responsibilities at Bache & Co., a powerful and well-connected company in 1965, provided me with a platform and maneuverability that I utilized to assist Mr. Hidaka. John Roosevelt helped greatly with arrangements made for Mr. Hidaka to visit chief executives of institutions in Boston and in New York.

This remarkable banker with an excellent sense of humor quickly gained the acceptance and the loyalty of the executives of Yamaichi Securities Co. Under his leadership and with the support of the powerful Industrial Bank of Japan, the troubled investment company gradually regained its position in the market. Shortly after the crisis, it resumed the implementation of an imaginative program mapped out by Mr. Konosuke Koike that involved expansion of the firm's activities to Hong Kong, London, Amsterdam, and Zurich.

Mr. Hidaka appreciated the assistance extended to him and his associates in those difficult days. Whenever in Tokyo I was invited to join him at the Matsumuro, a favorite after-hours watering place of senior executives of the Industrial Bank of Japan, followed by a dinner at the excellent traditional restaurants in Shimbashi or in Akasaka. We were usually accompanied by Mr. Tsukuno. Mr. Hidaka's favorite was a fugu (blow fish that must be properly prepared as it can be poisonous) restaurant, Fuku-den. At one of these dinners he invited me to become a senior economic advisor of the firm and assist in the development of the Yamaichi Research Institute. I regretfully was unable to accept this interesting invitation, because I was already committed to a consulting arrangement with the Bank of Tokyo.

After the debacle of the Yamaichi Securities Co. was over, Mr. Hidaka arranged a garden party with entertainment provided by geishas and maikos (apprentice geishas) at Chinzan-so, a popular restaurant in the midst of a beautiful traditional garden. It was a lovely evening spent with my friends, at which I was presented with the insignia of the new Yamaichi Co. This was an elegant way to express thanks for the assistance extended and to make me an honorary member of the team.

The debacle of the securities industry introduced me to the inner workings of Japanese society. Closely knit personal relations are central to understanding its functioning. The clearly delineated nature of relations can be oppressive and there is little tolerance for the unusual and the unorthodox. Rare exceptions are made, as in the case of Mr. Hidaka, Mr. Nobutane Kiuchi, and others whom I encountered. This privileged position was earned by a series of extraordinary accomplishments. Japanese society is generally a conforming one and functions by consensus. Dissent is permitted, and there are vigorous arguments before a decision is reached. However, once a course is decided on, everyone joins in regardless of his views.

The opportunity to study the functioning of a Japanese organization at close quarters developed after I left Bache & Co. to open my own management consulting firm. Over the years of activity in

Japan, I became friendly with the senior management of the Bank of Tokyo, formerly the Yokohama Specie Bank, a unique financial institution with a long and distinguished history and its own traditions. It was formed during the early Meiji era to assist trade with the outside world. The bank had always close if complicated relations with the Ministry of Finance and the Bank of Japan. It acted also as a bank of the Imperial Household and was for a long time the sole bank authorized to handle foreign exchange. This prestigious institution attracted able and well-educated young men who were privileged to work at a bank that offered an opportunity to be stationed in foreign countries, rare in those days.

Among its highly professional personnel were linguists with an excellent knowledge of English, German, French, and many other languages. A great deal of attention was paid to getting acquainted with foreign cultures. During the many years that I advised the bank's management, I met cultivated and erudite individuals with a wide range of interests. It was a challenge to assist the bank in planning its activities. It was an equally rewarding experience to spend many an evening socially with the executives of the Bank of Tokyo in Japan, in the United States, and in every major financial center throughout the world.

The perspective of its managers added an interesting and a different dimension to the analysis of the international financial situation, based on a first-hand knowledge of the countries in which they were stationed. The London office of the bank provided insights into the European scene. The offices in Seoul, Singapore, Hong Kong, Bangkok, and Saigon made it possible for me in a relatively short time to familiarize myself with conditions in these markets.

Shortly after opening my consulting firm, I was invited by my friend, Mr. Soichi Yokoyama, the president of the Bank of Tokyo, to consult with the bank. I had met him while still at Bache & Co. during his tenure as an agent of the bank in New York. We had always enjoyed an exchange of views on international developments and how they affected policies of the bank. He inquired whether I would be interested in briefing his associates on a regular basis.

Mr. Yokoyama was a quiet, soft-spoken, gracious man with a ready smile. His hair had turned prematurely white in contrast with his young face. His banking career spanned many years and included Hanoi, London, and New York. His leadership, following the equally impressive Mr. Hara, formerly an official of the Ministry of Finance, was reflected in the strengthening of the bank's international position and the rapid expansion of its activities in the United States and in Europe.

Mr. Yokoyama suggested that on my return to New York I get in touch with Mr. Kozawa, then the agent and resident manager of the Bank of Tokyo in the United States. This was the start of a unique phase in my professional career. I was privileged to participate for almost a decade in the decision-making process of this unique Japanese institution. Mr. Kozawa tactfully guided me through the complex process of establishing a consulting relationship with the bank and we both experimented with ways to make the relationship productive and meaningful.

Mr. Kozawa, Mr. Yokoyama's key associate, was an equally quiet, soft-spoken individual with a ready smile and a sharp intellect. This relaxed baldish man, wearing glasses with thick lenses, projected the impression of a scholar. This appearance was misleading as he was a born leader of men, decisive, innovative, and able to inspire and motivate his associates. Mr. Yokoyama and Mr. Kozawa during their tenure at the bank were responsible for a whole series of bold decisions that guided it through a difficult transition in the postwar years and positioned it to meet the requirements of the expansion of the Japanese economy in the 1970s.

A routine was established in New York with Mr. Kozawa's assistance that consisted at first of regular briefing sessions of the executives of the bank. Subsequently these were extended to the executives in the U.K. and in Europe. This provided an opportunity to get acquainted with the middle management of the bank, an interesting and challenging team that was well-prepared for their respective assignments. After graduating from prestigious universities in Japan, most of them had attended schools in the United States and Europe. Mr. Kozawa eventually extended these regular briefing sessions to managers of Japanese trading companies in New York, and later expanded them to Japanese companies in London and Dusseldorf.

These briefings were provided as a courtesy extended to the key customers of the Bank of Tokyo. The lunches were held in the conference room of the Bank of Tokyo Trust Co. at the Waldorf Astoria, with Nippon Restaurant delivering an elegant o-bento box lunch. Guests, usually eight or ten senior managers representing the major trading companies, identified themselves, and the ones newly arrived in New York exchanged calling cards. The comments made by the guests indicated the interests of the trading firms. After the o-bento boxes were removed and green tea was served, I presented an overview, followed by a discussion.

A close relationship developed with Mr. Kozawa, and in time we became good friends. I was invited to come to his office whenever he encountered a problem, and there over a cup of tea we discussed issues of interest to him. On occasion I was asked to join a team of executives of the Bank of Tokyo in negotiating business deals with investment banking firms in New York, or with the management of corporations. Mr. Kozawa always found new ways to explore additional consulting activities, which greatly broadened the range of services I provided the bank.

Mr. Kozawa's tenure in New York probably can be characterized by two decisions made as agent of the Bank of Tokyo. The New York real estate market collapsed in 1971-72. The bank's activities had expanded and more space was required to accommodate its existing operations and allow for future growth. A long-term lease was offered to Mr. Kozawa at 100 Broadway, an old prewar building in a choice location in the financial district. The old and dilapidated facilities required a great deal of renovation, which the landlord offered to carry out.

Mr. Kozawa concluded that the headquarters of the bank's operations should remain in the Wall Street area and that New York would weather any financial difficulties. He signed a long-term lease while major banks embarked on building elaborate and costly premises in midtown. Twenty years later the Bank of Tokyo still maintains its headquarters at 100 Broadway at a fraction of the cost incurred by major U.S. and some foreign banks.

The acquisition of a bank in San Diego was the second decision during his tenure that demonstrated the far-sightedness of Mr.

Yokoyama and Mr. Kozawa. They realized the importance of the West Coast in U.S.-Japan relations and the desirability of Americanization of the Bank of Tokyo California, a well-managed compact operation based in San Francisco with a regional office in Los Angeles. This fully owned subsidiary of the bank concentrated on business originating in Japan and the servicing of the Nissei community on the West Coast. The acquisition and the mapping out of the transition, balancing between the Japanese and Nissei management of the Bank of Tokyo of California and the American management of the newly acquired bank in San Diego, was carried out flawlessly, thanks to the guidelines provided by Mr. Kozawa and the support of the president, Mr. Yokoyama, and his team.

Mr. Kozawa was promoted and left New York for Tokyo in the late autumn of 1973. His stewardship had laid the foundation for the extraordinary growth of the bank's activities in the United States, which was carried out through the fully owned subsidiaries California First, the renamed bank on the West coast, and the Bank of Tokyo Trust Co., a bank operating under a charter of the State of New York.

The fair in Osaka in 1972 was a watershed in the postwar evolution of Japan. The devastated and impoverished country had recovered fully from the shock of the defeat. It had painstakingly rebuilt its economy and reorganized its government, adapting a series of reforms introduced by the staff of the farsighted General Douglas MacArthur. The bold planning, the introduction of advanced technological innovations, and the judicious employment of scarce capital paid off handsomely. At the end of the 1960s the extraordinary national effort started to bear fruit and was reflected in an improved standard of living.

The outbreak of the Arab-Israeli war in 1973 led to two oil price shocks, which profoundly changed the international environment. This presented Japan with a formidable and unexpected challenge.

The first oil shock was administered following the Arab-Israeli war in the Middle East in 1973. The subsequent defeat of the United States in Vietnam brought into sharp focus the vulnerability of Japan. Its power generating plants, transportation, shipping, and industry could function only if there was an uninterrupted flow of crude. Over 70 percent of Japan's requirements was supplied by the Middle East, and the balance was provided by imports from Indonesia and China or purchases in the world markets. A quintupling of the price of crude oil administered a shock not unlike a massive earthquake.

A large percentage of crude was supplied on long-term contracts by American international oil companies. The Japanese, accustomed to relying on the United States, which provided a strategic umbrella and dominated the world monetary system, were taken by surprise. The whole painstakingly erected structure was suddenly threatened by the massive increase in the cost of a key element—energy.

It was inconceivable to the policy-makers in Tokyo that the United States would accept this form of taxation without representation and would not react to protect its own and Japan's interests. In some circles it was hinted that this was a conspiracy to cripple the economy of Japan and to curb its success in the international markets. This seemed to be confirmed when it was recognized that the sharp increase in the price of crude oil was meekly accepted by Washington and was administered by the major oil companies.

The expansion of exports in the world economic system based on a free trade doctrine preached by the United States was the keystone of the planning of the Japanese national economy. Free access to markets secured the flow of foreign exchange for the purchase of raw materials, food, and fuel. All this was thrown out of balance by the oil embargo. The Japanese could not believe that U.S. foreign policy during the Administration of Mr. Nixon would be engineered by Dr. Henry Kissinger, a political scientist with limited understanding of the functioning of the world economy and its monetary system. Therefore, the far-fetched conspiracy theory found supporters in Japan.

The collapse of the international monetary system agreed on in Bretton Woods in 1944 by the U.S. and the U.K. was followed by a whole series of experiments and "agreements," which after a few months either proved impractical or were circumvented by the forces unleashed in the markets. The flow of funds from and to Japan, based on an orderly foreign exchange performance of the pound sterling and the U.S. dollar, was buffeted by fluctuations in foreign exchange rates, threatening the functioning of the delicately balanced Japanese economic structure. All these changes and realignments were taking place in the 1960s in international forums, with the Japanese hardly ever consulted.

While attending the annual meetings of the World Bank and the International Monetary Fund as a special guest, I noticed that the Japanese delegation played only a peripheral role in the deliberations, which was out of proportion to the increasing importance of Japan's growing economy. The key decisions were made in a clubby atmosphere dominated by the U.S. and the U.K., with some European central banks playing an increasingly important role as did the Bank for International Settlements in Basel. At the private dinners and lunches, at which critical issues were discussed and decided on, it was rather unusual to see a member of the Japanese official delegation or a Japanese banker. This changed with time, as in the mid-1970s the impact of redirected international flows of funds finally registered.

The inconclusive end of the Korean War in 1952, following the introduction of Chinese "volunteers," the endless negotiations in Panmunjom, and the occasional humiliation of Americans by the North Koreans, were ignored by the Japanese, who appreciated the power of the United States. The conduct of the war in Vietnam, the turmoil in the Middle East, and the trip of President Nixon to China subtly shifted the attitude of the Japanese, who recognized the changed political balances in the Far East and South East Asia.

The Japanese believed that they enjoyed a special relationship with the United States. They meticulously followed American foreign policy, assuming that they would be consulted, or at least informed, before major changes in direction were introduced. Consequently, the foreign policy of Japan in the Far East was anchored on the premise that the People's Republic of China was to be kept at arm's length. Therefore, the official relations of Japan were directed toward the Republic of China in Formosa or Taiwan, and the dealings with the mainland, "occupied temporarily by the communists," were discreetly conducted by intermediaries. For example, Japan Airlines maintained a regular service to Taipei, and only an obscure, little-known subsidiary of the carrier operating under a different name flew to Peking and other Chinese cities from Tokyo. This and many other similar examples demonstrated the extraordinary adherence of Tokyo to the official line pursued by Washington, even if it did not serve the long-term interests of Japan. At one of the dinners given for me by Chase Manhattan Bank, Nobutane Kiuchi, a prominent economist and chairman of the Mitsubishi Research Institute, mocked the government officials who joined us with his comment that he expected to see Chiang Kai Shek ride into Peking on a white horse in the not-too-distant future.

The spectacle of President Nixon's visit to Peking that had been arranged by Dr. Kissinger was perceived differently in Asia than in the United States and Europe. There it was seen as a breakthrough and a bold opening to an intriguing giant, who, after a few unsuccessful leaps forward and a short-lived experiment with liberalization referred to as "let a thousand flowers blossom," had been plunged by Mao Tse Tung into the chaos of the cultural revolution.

The political somersault of Mr. Nixon's administration evoked a different reaction in Asia. I was in Tokyo during the visit of President Nixon to China, which could be followed on Japanese television networks. The American delegation flew to Peking without stopping in Japan to pay a courtesy visit to consult its key ally in the Far East.

The American party arrived in Peking to be greeted in a low-key fashion by a delegation of government officials. The cars carrying President Nixon and his entourage travelled through the eerily empty and silent streets of Peking. Only after the American guests were received by a smiling Mao Tse Tung did a sudden change take place. The streets were filled with friendly people greeting the Americans with flags, flowers were displayed everywhere, and Peking assumed a festive appearance.

The West perceived this welcome as a major shift in the policies of the People's Republic of China and an extraordinary opening that promised an expansion of profitable trade with the mainland. Asia perceived it as homage paid by Mr. Nixon to the old and feeble "Helmsman." It was observed that only after Mao Tse Tung gave the signal did the real reception start, with flags and slogans appearing on the streets filled with crowds greeting the American guests.

The view of the world as seen from Peking differed from the one seen in Washington and in Tokyo. The occasional pilgrimages made by prominent westerners like Malraux and writers like Han Suyin to pay homage encouraged the megalomania of Mao Tse Tung and contributed to an even greater arrogance of his entourage. It might be helpful to remember that the last Empress of China was firmly convinced that her vassal, Queen Victoria, was paying an annual tribute to her. No one dared to explain the real state of affairs in the world. The clique ruling in Peking was better informed and better versed in the ways of the West than the last Manchu Empress. Nonetheless, while recognizing the still-great power of the United States, the Chinese concluded that the U.S. was following Great Britain in its decline, and its role in the Far East and Southeast Asia with time would be reduced if not eliminated. In the meantime the gullible Americans could be used to provide capital, transfer technology, and assist in ending the isolation of China.

After the visit to Peking, the American delegation returned home, again omitting a stopover in Japan or even a ceremonial handshake with the Prime Minister, Mr. Eisaku Sato, at the Haneda Airport for the benefit of the television cameras. Shortly afterwards Japan reversed its foreign policy and resumed contacts with the People's Republic of China. Japan Airlines closed its offices in Taipei and started a regular service to Peking, while its obscure subsidiary serving routes to mainland China took over handling the air traffic to Taiwan. This maneuver was repeated by corporations and trading companies, who had dealt quietly for years with the People's Republic of China.

These were difficult days for Japan, and the premises underlying its policies were reevaluated in government, in industry, and in the complex and carefully balanced political establishment of the Liberal Democratic Party. I had to travel more frequently to Japan to assist my clients.

Informal discussions at the Bank of Japan and the Ministry of Finance concentrated on the reassessment of the changing political landscape in the United States, culminating in the embarrassing resignation of President Nixon, which was hard for the Japanese to comprehend. Again what was perceived in the United States as the greatness and resilience of the political system surprised Asia and was viewed as self-destructive and possibly a silly washing of dirty linen in public.

The oil shock and the "peace with honor" in Vietnam, followed by the humiliating departure of the last Americans from Saigon who were lifted from the roof of the U.S. Embassy, was a watershed that started the process of global realignment, with massive changes occurring in the international environment. The second oil shock a few years later followed by the mindless recycling of "petrodollars" accelerated it and added yet another dimension to an amazing voluntary transfer of wealth.

In the spring of 1974, I was invited to brief the management of the Bank of Tokyo and its corporate clients on the likely impact of the oil embargo and the sharp increase in the price of crude. The embargo and the quintupling of the price of crude imposed by OPEC was considered a political measure in response to the war in the Middle East. The Egyptian forces had crossed the Suez canal in October 1973 and successfully engaged the surprised Israelis in the Sinai Peninsula. Simultaneously massed Syrian tanks had attacked the Golan Heights and were on the verge of breaking into Israel proper while Soviet-made anti-aircraft missiles reduced the effectiveness of the Israeli Air Force.

A bold Israeli counter-attack across the Suez canal cut off the Egyptian forces in the Sinai, which was followed by the destruction of the Syrian armored spearhead in the Golan Heights, bringing the Israelis within shelling distance of Damascus. This changed the military equation of the conflict and could have led to a confrontation between the United States and the Soviet Union.

At the time of my visit to Japan, delicate negotiations were being conducted under the auspices of the United States to arrange a disengagement of the armies that were poised for another battle. Interpretating the developments in the Middle East and their impact on the economy of Japan was the task given to me by Mr. Yokoyama and Mr. Kozawa.

A formal program consisted of two lunches arranged at the Nagasaka-so, the guest house of the Bank of Tokyo in the city. One lunch was arranged to brief chief executives of Japanese corporations, the other was arranged for presidents of subsidiaries of

American corporations in Japan. After a brief introduction by Mr. Yusuke Kashiwagi, formerly Vice Minister of Finance and the future president of the bank, I commented on the developments in the Middle East and the impact of the oil crisis on Japan. The thrust of my presentation was that the flow of oil would resume, albeit at a higher price, because international oil companies were cooperating with OPEC in administering the imposed increase. I pointed out that Japan had completed the expansion of its industrial plant, which was now efficient and highly competitive. Therefore, it was less vulnerable and probably better positioned to absorb the oil shock than those of other industrial nations.

My comments were based on the assumptions that: (1) the political vacuum in the Middle East existing since the departure of the British from the region could not be filled by the United States; (2) the Soviet Union, through shipments of modern weapons, its activity in the United Nations, and support of international terrorism could cause difficulties and greatly complicate the existing debacle, but could not establish a permanent presence in this region; and (3) the spectacular military defeat of the Egyptians and the Syrians, the fourth since the creation of the State of Israel, would not advance a political solution in this region.

The quintupling of the price of crude oil introduced by OPEC was planned long before the Yom Kippur war. I pointed out that, once Occidental Petroleum and Exxon accepted without protest contractual revisions introduced by Moamar Qaddaffi after the overthrow of the Senussi regime in 1969, it was only matter of time before other OPEC nations followed suit. The cooperation of international oil companies in administering the increase in the prices of crude and their powerful lobby in Washington blocked attempts of political or military intervention.

Therefore, under these circumstances I suggested that the best course of action was to observe developments, adjust Japan's economic policy, and introduce countermeasures only after the impact of the increase of the price of crude could be evaluated. My recommendation was to introduce swiftly conservation of energy but not at the expense of industrial activity. I believed that the flow of oil would be restored sooner or later. I suggested a reevaluation of the yen upward because the competitiveness of Japanese industry and its technological advanced products would permit absorbing the impact.

The Japanese audience at the guest house of the Bank of Tokyo *Nagasaka-so* listened attentively to this interpretation and asked questions to clarify my statements. There was a great deal of apprehension and a feeling of frustration, because their carefully laid plans had been annulled by developments that had little to do with Japan. The Japanese managers had difficulty in understanding why the United States had accepted the imposed increase in price without a reaction. They were fearful that the flow of oil would be eventually interrupted again, causing a collapse of the carefully balanced Japanese economy. I pointed out that the flow of oil must resume as the objective of OPEC was to increase its revenues; the embargo was used to exert pressure on the industrialized nations to accept the change in the price of crude oil.

I was fascinated to discover that the Japanese had no knowledge of the Middle East despite their heavy reliance on the supplies of crude oil from this historically turbulent region. I had great difficulty in conveying that the United States and Great Britain no longer controlled the Middle East, and that the Soviet Union's meddling and generous supplying of weapons to Syria, Iraq, and Egypt were adding fuel to the fire. The American guests invited by the Bank of Tokyo to the second lunch represented primarily major oil companies. They seemed to have accepted in their stride the increase in the price of crude and the recycling of petrodollars.

After completing the briefing of the bank's management and its guests at the Nagasaka-so, I left for Osaka where I addressed the Kankeiren, an influential organization of key industrialists and bankers in the Kansai region, and at a small dinner a select audience gathered by the Bank of Tokyo at the exclusive Osaka Club. From Kansai I went to Nagoya where I addressed a meeting of the Doyukai (an organization of corporate managers—a powerful and influential pressure group) on behalf of the Bank of Tokyo.

The meetings in Osaka and Nagoya were less formal and a lively discussion developed after my presentations. The degree of concern was equally as great in Kansai as it had been in Tokyo. However, the industrialists in Kansai area were concentrating on the practical aspects of the "oil shock."

The initial reaction to the oil shock of surprise, disappointment, frustration, and apprehension wore off. The sense of crisis spurred the government, industry, and the financial institutions into action. The general thrust of the adjustment process emerged in the discussions at the Ministry of Finance, the Bank of Japan, the Economic Planning Agency, and the management of industrial corporations and trading companies.

Emergency measures called for maintaining an adequate reserve of crude oil at all times in tank farms and in a fleet of supertankers travelling at low speed from the loading facilities in the Gulf to Japan. Thus, in addition to the inventory in the tank farms, a floating inventory was added, determined by the tonnage of tankers available and the speed of the vessels. Most of the crude was delivered on long-term contracts by the major oil companies, and only a fraction was available in the open market.

There was no choice but to accept the sharp increase in the dollar price of oil. The yen, fixed at ¥360 per U.S. dollar by the Japanese in the days of General MacArthur, started to drift upward, eventually ending in the 120-160 range. With time, this reduced the impact of the increase in the price of crude. This maneuver required careful calibration of the rate of exchange to enable industry to maintain a critical level of exports.

The rapid shift of capital movements resulting from the voluntary transfer of wealth from the industrialized and developing countries to OPEC redirected the activities of Japanese banks and securities companies to the newly affluent countries. The oil-producing countries in turn became the providers of capital for the last phase of the expansion of Japanese plant and equipment. "Petrodollars" accumulated at a dizzying rate in the statelets of the Gulf, in Iran, in Libya, Nigeria, and others.

American banks "recycled" these dollars by unfortunate loans to governments of Latin America and Central Europe. Much of this money ended in numbered accounts in Swiss banks or were reinvested in the United States. However, a certain percentage was invested in plant and equipment of the borrowing countries, which in turn generated demand for Japanese capital equipment and other products.

The gradual revaluation of the yen kept inflationary pressures in check while this enormous adjustment of the Japanese economy took place. The conservation of energy in heavy industry, disciplined consumption of electricity, and a shift to more efficient internal combustion engines made their contribution. The lights of the brightly lit Japanese cities were dimmed, and once again Tokyo at night acquired for a while a dreamy look with lanterns replacing the gaudy, colorful, and striking neon signs.

Industry doubled its efforts to introduce the most advanced technological innovations in metallurgy, electronics, electrical equipment, communications, and shipbuilding, as well as in optical and medical instrumentation. At the same time unprofitable industries and weak companies were either phased out altogether or were absorbed through mergers. The once-powerful textile industry of Kansai was gradually phased out, to be replaced by technologically advanced industries that absorbed the thus-released labor supply.

The introduction of integrated circuits and miniaturization contributed to the development of a whole array of technologically advanced and innovative products that revolutionized the consumer electronics market. As there were no substitutes for Japanese cameras, tape recorders, high-quality color television sets, high performance audio equipment, copying machines, and many other products, the re-evaluation of the yen had little impact on the expansion of exports. The shipbuilding industry, utilizing innovative production methods, enjoyed a boom that lasted for a long time, aided by the availability of easy credits to the shipbuilders and the shipping industry. The automotive industry was ready with economical cars that started to replace the gasoline guzzling, shoddily built, overdecorated cars manufactured in Detroit. The stress on quality control from the supplier of components to the end product paid off handsomely as reliability, performance, and advanced technology became a common feature of Japanese-made products.

The methods of quality control introduced by Prof. Edward Deming, well-known in Japan and meticulously followed, produced the expected results and contributed greatly to the successful expansion of Japanese exports. Prof. Deming's approach to quality control was ignored by management in the United States, which persisted with disastrous results in following antiquated methods based on statistical sampling.

Inventions like transistors at Bell Laboratories and VCRs at Texas Instruments, and innovation in the steel-making process and continuous casting techniques at MIT were adapted and translated into products in Japan. The stress on technological innovation and quality control gave the expansion a momentum that still continues. Eventually, Japan's remarkable economic growth contributed to the emergence of newly industrialized countries referred to as NICs. I introduced this term in the discussions of Korea, Taiwan, Hong Kong, and eventually Malaysia and Thailand in a variety of professional forums in the United State, Europe, and the U.K.

Two incidents come to my mind that in a way help to illustrate this phase in the evolution of the Japanese economy. I was invited by Mr. Honda to spend a day with him at the Honda Motors plant in the outskirts of Tokyo. I arrived there in the morning, and Mr. Honda and his chief engineers proudly showed me the laboratories in which experiments were made with improved internal combustion engines, suspensions, coating of bodies, noise level, and other related activity. Mr. Honda and his associates, wearing overalls, were clearly taking an active part in these experiments.

At lunch in a simple dining hall we were served sandwiches, sodas, and coffee. I gathered my courage and asked Mr. Honda what had motivated him to compete with Detroit and for practical purposes reinvent the automobile. The extraordinary success of his company with motorcycles had been recognized and admired. Why then shift from a successful and profitable operation into a risky activity of competing with the major manufacturers of cars in the United States and Europe? Mr. Honda, who had started as an owner of a bicycle repair shop after the war, smiled and replied that one can always improve on an existing product. Honda Motors' success with motorcycles was due precisely to this philosophy. An existing and well-established product was revolutionized by utilizing technological innovation and perseverance in the continuous effort to perfect it, keeping the competition in check. He hoped for a similar result with cars.

On a visit to the production lines of Hayakawa Electric, better known by its new name of Sharp Electronics, in Nara, I noticed that the finished products, in this case calculators and cash registers, were installed on shelves of slowly moving platforms to be tested before being shipped to markets. Each unit was plugged in and activated to run through a program. The platforms moved slowly through hot and humid chambers with temperatures and humidity resembling a turkish bath. From there the platforms continued to a refrigerated chamber, and finally were exposed to vibration and shaking. Malfunctioning units were identified and removed. I inquired about the objective of this rather costly procedure. The managers told me that a product that can survive the passage through the "torture chambers" can be shipped to the market with the knowledge that its rather generous guarantee will rarely if ever need to be honored. It is cheaper, he said, to assure that the product leaving the assembly line functions properly than to be confronted later with costly servicing and repairs. I was led to the packaging department, where specially engineered packaging for each product assured that it would reach the market in a pristine condition.

These were the "secrets" of success I discovered during my numerous visits to manufacturing installations in Japan. The meticulous training of the labor force and a paternalistic attitude of the management resulted in a dedication and loyalty of employees difficult to match in the West.

Visiting the personnel manager of the Hitachi Corporation in Tokyo, I was surprised to see in an adjacent large conference room young women taught the art of flower arrangement. I asked the manager who had organized this cultural activity. He replied that this was the responsibility of his department, because these young women had to be prepared for marriage. Flower arrangement and performing the tea ceremony are an essential part of the proper preparation of a young Japanese woman for marriage.

I discussed the process of adjustment to the oil shocks with Dr. Toshihiko Yoshino at the Bank of Japan, and I inquired about the limits to this extraordinary expansion of industrial capacity. Dr.

Yoshino suggested that he arrange a program of visits when I came to Japan again.

On my next visit he arranged a program that included the Kimitsu works of Nippon Seitetsu (steel company), a shipyard of Hitachi Zosen, and a petrochemical plant, all in Chiba prefecture. The traffic jams on the way to Chiba were of monumental proportions. During the visit to these installations the level of pollution was such that I could not breathe, I developed a headache, and my eyes watered. The workers in the plants were lethargic and pale, and special stations were set up with oxygen tents for those overcome by the pollution and the smog. The working conditions in the shipyards and at the Kimitsu works and in other installations in the Chiba prefecture could no longer be tolerated and presented a veritable health hazard. Similar catastrophic pollution of the environment caused by ever-increasing industrial activity in the Kanto (Tokyo plain) and Kansai regions reached a degree that became a threat to the well-being of the population and a political problem. The Minamata tragedy (mercury poisoning of a bay that crippled inhabitants of the area) was a symptom of the danger facing the industrialized regions of Japan, forcing the government to introduce emergency measures to deal with the threat to the environment.

The message was loud and clear. The visit arranged by Dr. Yoshino and the Bank of Japan demonstrated succinctly that the industrialization of Japan had reached a limit. Massive resources had to be committed by the government and industry to clean up the environment, improve the infrastructure, and pay more attention to the standard of living. Since then the conditions have improved and impressive progress has been made in dealing with the congestion on the roads, cleaning the air, and eliminating existing sources of pollution.

Rapid capital accumulation in the oil-producing countries contributed to a sharp increase of imports of manufactured products from Japan. Eventually massive petrochemical installations, power plants, water desalinization, construction of infrastructure and housing were undertaken with the readily available capital from oil revenues in OPEC. Japanese industry and trading companies became major beneficiaries of this activity, which added a renewed impetus to the expansion of Japan's economy.

Some of these funds lent to Latin America, Africa, and Central Europe were squandered. Nevertheless, a substantial amount of over $300 billion borrowed was spent in Japan and in Southeast Asia, importing machinery, earthmoving equipment, consumer electronics, and a large variety of other products. This created a secondary stimulus for the economy, preparing Japan and the newly industrialized nations of Southeast Asia for a second oil shock administered jointly by OPEC and the major oil companies. The strong yen provided a flow of raw materials and food acquired at attractive prices, as most of these were paid for in U.S. dollars. A calibrated monetary policy and rapidly growing financial institutions to service this new global activity laid the foundation for massive Japanese investments in the United States, Canada, Western Europe, and Australia while increasingly attracting foreign capital to Japan. Professional portfolio managers started to invest aggressively in Japan to a point that Scottish trusts committed up to 50 percent of the funds they managed to Japanese equities.

The oil "shocks" of the 1970s were eventually absorbed. Japan regrouped, redirected its efforts, and emerged as an industrial, technological, and financial superpower. Tokyo's capital market joined London and New York, emerging as a major financial center.

The representatives of Japan, once virtually ignored in international forums, increasingly exerted influence and their counsel was invited. Japanese capital formation with time replaced that of the Middle East, and Japanese investments were invited by the governments of the states in the U.S., by the U.K., Spain, Ireland and a long list of others. The "globalization" of Japan commenced with a more assertive posture displayed as evidence of affluence. Japan embarked on yet another "restoration," adapting to the new international environment, as challenging as the Meiji Restoration had been.

Mr. Tadayoshi Yamada, the retired managing director of Nippon Seitetsu and the chairman of the World Trade Centers sprouting all over the globe, invited me for lunch at a club on a high floor of the newest addition to the network of the Trade Center in the Hamamatsu district of Tokyo. He pointed to the landscape as seen from the top floor of the building. We walked around, observing the skyline and identifying sights of the city. Suddenly, it dawned on me that a wooden city had been replaced by modern skyscrapers visible as far as the eye could see. The massive complexes of Kasumigaseki and Marounuchi, and on the horizon the towering blocks of the new buildings in Shinjuku reflected a city changed since my first visit in 1962 to Japan.

ço

My years of work in Japan provided an exciting adventure and an introduction to the Far East. They opened a new and fascinating world. All this was possible thanks to the many friends who guided me through the difficult task of exploring this complex society.

The introduction to Japan completed my professional education, which had commenced with an involuntary exposure to Marxism-Leninism, direct contact with the concept of the new Europe introduced by the Third Reich, and service in two armies fighting two wars before continuing my education studying economics and industrial engineering. The study of Japan and the preparation for my work there required curiously more effort and diligence than many other endeavors. Yet, after all these years, Japan still remains elusive and as full of contradictions as ever.

EPILOGUE

MY SEARCH for a harbor that started in 1945 in Italy is still going on. The departure of the survivors of the Holocaust on the *Fede* from the pier at La Spezia was supposed to bring a new and peaceful existence. Instead, after a brief respite I was again involved with other young men and women in a war and a struggle for survival.

The dreams of a new country, Israel, woven by the young students in the clandestine commanders school of the Haganah in Juara in October 1947 have only partially materialized. These young people were the "silver platter" on which the State of Israel was brought as a gift to long-suffering Jewry. This was the way the poet Nathan Alterman described them in his moving poem, "The Silver Platter."

Nevertheless, reality did not necessarily correspond to the dreams woven in the cold autumn nights in the hills of Ephraim sitting around a fire and sipping coffee from a *finjan*. A few weeks later the graduates were leading troops in a cruel and bloody battle. The survivors of the War of Liberation returned to their homes, expecting a peace that is still eluding that tormented land a half century later.

A different struggle awaited me in the canyons of Wall Street. There was no physical danger involved, but the task of carving a place for myself in the new world was difficult and at times harsh. My professional activities concentrated on the international aspects of finance and investments. This resulted in countless encounters in the boardrooms of banks and corporations in London, Paris, Dusseldorf, Frankfurt, Milano, Edinburgh, Tokyo, and from coast to coast in the United States. Each represented a challenge that had to be met alone, relying on all the resources I was able to marshall. And so I became a witness to the evolution of international events from a strange and unique vantage point.

I observed the decline of the United Kingdom, the disintegration of the Bretton Woods Agreement, the reemergence of the real victors of World War II—Germany and Japan—and a long series of events that set the stage for the present cycle. The international environment remains turbulent and perilous, presenting ever new challenges and dangers.

The support and the assistance extended in unexpected quarters by many friends made the strange journey possible. Most of them are gone, and all that remains are memories. Memories are still vivid of the feeling of helplessness and despair of innocent people condemned to death, milling on the streets of the crowded ghetto in Lwów and in Rawa Ruska, waiting for execution. One can still hear in one's mind the din of the battles and the horrifying whining of falling bombs, followed by explosions.

The visit to the pier in La Spezia almost half a century after the drama of the hunger strike reminded me of the young people assembled on it, hopeful and optimistic, before sailing in the two small fragile fishing vessels into the unknown.

Somehow reflections change direction and bring into focus again the dining room in the commanders school of the Haganah in Juara in 1947 and the sound of the verses from the Bible read solemnly at the head table. I still remember after so many years the faces of the young men who gave their lives to defend the Jewish settlements and the new State of Israel.

Attending the graduation of one of my sons from Dartmouth College and the other from the University of London, I was reminded of the young students at the Hebrew University in 1947, torn away from their books and entrusted with the defense of Jerusalem. They too were hoping and dreaming of a better tomorrow. Many of them fell in battle and are buried at the military cemetery on Mount Herzl.

Somehow above all that, I can still discern the soothing sound of the Byzantine liturgical chant of the Studite monks who saved my life. A strange kaleidoscope of memories and reflections, a result of a strange journey.

The struggle goes on. New challenges have to be met and the harbor beyond the horizon for which I yearned all my life remains an unattainable illusion. Perhaps it does not exist, and the struggle and the battles won and lost are the only meaning of our existence.

The compass that guided me all these years was the memory of the encounter with Metropolitan Andrew Graf Szeptycki and his brother Clement, the two spiritual giants who by their example charted a course for many. The efforts of their lifetimes seemed to be destroyed at the end of their journey through life. Time has shown that the seeds they sowed resulted in a rich and rewarding harvest. The church they led survived years of oppression and martyrdom to emerge from the catacombs after the disintegration of the Soviet Union to thrive once again.

Homer, the immortal bard of antiquity, described in *The Iliad* and *The Odyssey* the deeds of Ulysses, one of the principal protagonists of the saga. The ethos of *The Odyssey*, after the dramatic return of the hero to Ithaca having survived all the trials of his long journey, ends with the slaying of the arrogant suitors who were pursuing Penelope his wife during his absence. This closes the tale that for millenniums has fascinated Western civilization.

Reflecting on the tale of Ulysses, one can imagine the hero, a king-shepherd, relaxing at a fire with Penelope after a hard and long day in the fields. His life is now preoccupied with crops, weather, the flock of sheep, and the settling of petty arguments that erupt from time to time among his subjects.

The aging hero, observing the dancing flames licking the logs in the fireplace, is perhaps thinking that the years of the siege of Troy and the perilous journey home represented the most interesting part and probably the very essence of his life. Therefore, possibly, the wise bard of antiquity ended the saga at the high point of the drama of *The Odyssey*. Perhaps the peaceful existence of the king-shepherd on the rocky island Ithaca in the fold of his family was an anticlimax to years of heroic deeds and adventures.

Tyotomi Hideyoshi, the military leader who united Japan, sensing his approaching death, wrote a poem, as was customary in those times. In it he stated:

> My Life
> Came Like Dew
> Disappears Like Dew
> All of Naniwa*
> Is Dream after Dream.

In a free interpretation, the poem states that life is perhaps an illusion, and great accomplishments are only an illusion within an illusion. The search for the meaning of life that has preoccupied humanity throughout recorded history goes on. Its significance remains an enigma and an unanswered question.

The long journey, at times tragic, painful, and perilous, was and remains interesting. The stories told cover an extraordinary panorama. They provide a glimpse of almost forgotten events and offer insights gathered in unusual circumstances on a broad spectrum of issues. They were written as a tribute to the many splendid individuals I was privileged to encounter, who made the journey possible and to whom I owe so much.

New York
July 1992

---

*Naniwa—ancient name for Osaka and the Kinki district, center of power of Hideyoshi

NOTES

CHAPTER 1

1. Katowice, in Upper Silesia, was an industrial town in the midst of a large steel, coal mining, and machine building complex. It had been a part of the Commonwealth of Poland, but after the partition of Poland it became a part of Prussia. Following the unification of Germany in 1870, Silesia developed into an important industrial center thanks to English, French, German, and Belgian investments. The terms of the Treaty of Versailles were somewhat ambiguous about the borders of Silesia, which became a subject of a bitter dispute between Germany and the resurrected Poland. This dispute, like many similar ones in Central Europe, was resolved in a bloody struggle between the Polish miners and steel workers and the Germans who settled in the region after the partition. The Poles prevailed in Upper Silesia, which was a province of Poland when my family resided there.

2. In 1965 I was invited to address a convention of public utilities executives in Chicago. After my presentation, one of the hosts, a consulting engineer, intrigued by my slight accent, inquired where I originally had come from. When I replied that I had lived for a while in Katowice, he asked whether I was related to Dr. Ezekiel Lewin, the rabbi of the city in the 1920s. Learning this was my father, he related the story. The engineer, originally from Katowice, witnessed this amusing incident as a young man.

3. Lwów was founded in thirteenth century. Ruins of the first castle still can be seen on a hill dominating the old city. Lwów received its charter under the Magdeburg law in 1340. It granted the city the right to self-government in exchange for services rendered, financing, and taxes paid to the crown. Trading routes leading to the Hanseatic cities on the Baltic and to Scandinavia from Venice and Northern Italy passed through the city. Traders travelling from Turkey and the Middle East on the way to Moscovy, Scandinavia, and Germany utilized the city as a transit station. Traders arriving form Nuremberg, Amsterdam, and Antwerp stopped before continuing to Kiev and the Black Sea.

The city was governed by a council elected by the guilds and merchants. Its population represented a complex ethnic and religious mosaic consisting of Roman Catholic Poles, Greek Catholic Ruthenians (Ukrainians), Jews, Greeks, Armenians, and Volochs (an ethnic group of Latin origin inhabiting present-day Rumania). Lwów was a seat of three Catholic archbishops—the Roman, the Greek, and the Armenian—each with its own cathedral, gems of Gothic, Renaissance, and Baroque architecture. The city had a significant presence of Christians of the Eastern Rite (Orthodox), Moslems (Tartars), and, after the Reformation,

443

Protestants. The importance of the city and its close ties with Italy were reflected in embassies maintained by the Republic of Venice, Florence, and Genoa, whose palaces can still be seen in the old city.

The presence of Jews in Lwów can be traced to the thirteenth century. Following the massacre of communities by the Crusaders in the Rhein Valley, an eastward migration of Jews gained momentum. The persecution of Jews in Western Europe instigated from time to time by the Roman Catholic Church prompted the search for a more tolerant environment. The Commonwealth of Poland under the Jagiellon dynasty and subsequent rulers was relatively tolerant and provided a favorable environment for Jews escaping from the West. Jews lived in their own quarters (there were no ghettos), were the king's wards, and enjoyed a considerable autonomy.

The Jews were established in the strategically important city with excellent connections to Jewish communities in Amsterdam and Venice. Thus they provided merchants with access to these early capital markets. The city's fortifications protected it from the frequent raids of Tartars and Cossacks. Its defense was entrusted to its citizens, including the Jews, who were responsible for one of the key towers (the Jewish tower was still standing in 1939; it was used as a storage facility for the city's sanitation department). In 1648 the rebelling Cossacks led by Bohdan Chmielnitzky demanded a ransom and the delivery of the city's Jews for lifting the siege. The city council flatly refused to comply and successfully defended Lwów.

The wars in the seventeenth and eighteenth centuries and the political changes in Central Europe reduced and eventually stopped the free flow of trade responsible for the city's prosperity. It remained an important administrative, cultural, and religious center. However, a decline set in that was reversed only after the partition of Poland. Lwów was selected by the Austrians as the administrative center for Galizia and Lodomeria (Southern Poland, referred to as Malopolska). Linked with Vienna and Budapest, it became again a trading, industrial, and financial center.

The collapse of the Austro-Hungarian Empire in 1918 turned the city into a battleground between Poles and Ukrainians. During the battle for the city both Poles and Ukrainians attacked the Jewish community, each accusing it of supporting the other side. The pogrom of 1918 was a foretaste of what was to come. The years 1919-39 were relatively quiet, with occasional anti-Semitic outbursts occurring more frequently after the death of the dictator Jozef Pilsudski, who appreciated the enormous contribution Jews were making to Poland's culture and its economy.

In 1939, following the Ribbentrop-Molotov agreement, Lwów was occupied by the USSR and annexed to the Ukrainian Socialist Soviet Republic. The invasion of the USSR in 1941 brought Germans to Lwów. They incorporated the city and the region into the Generalgouvernement (the designation given to occupied

Poland, which was governed from Krakow). The Soviet army in turn reoccupied Lwów in 1944 and restored the political status imposed in the autumn of 1939.

The entire Jewish population of the city was murdered by the Germans with the assistance of the Ukrainian police. After the arrival of the Soviet troops in 1944, out of a prewar Jewish population of over 135,000 about fifty Jews registered with the Jewish Committee.

In 1945 Stalin ordered the deportation of the entire Polish population to Western Poland. The Ukrainian inhabitants were exiled to Siberia. All that remains from the old splendor are monuments and churches, still majestic and beautiful although poorly maintained and neglected. Lwów is inhabited by new-comers, Ukrainians and Russians who settled there in postwar years following the industrialization of the region.

4. Haskala was a movement in the Jewish community in Germany, which after the French Revolution and the Napoleonic wars propagated emancipation from the impact of centuries of restrictions imposed by the surroundings. The move-ment eventually led to the founding of Conservative Judaism and indirectly con-tributed to assimilation. This movement spread eastward to the Jewish communi-ties in the partitioned Poland of the second half of the nineteenth century.

5. Rawa Ruska was before World War II a town with a population of approxi-mately 15,000 inhabitants on the main highway connecting Lwów with Warsaw.

After the partition of Poland in the eighteenth century among Russia, Austria, and Prussia, it became an important administrative center. The administrator of the region, the court, the archives, and a high school (gymnasium) were domiciled there. The territory administered from Rawa Ruska during the Austro-Hungarian rule after World War I included a number of smaller towns like Narol, Lubycza Krolewska, Hrubieszow, and others.

In the nineteenth century it became an important railroad hub, with lines from west to east and from south to north crossing in Rawa Ruska. The town, a service center for a primarily agricultural region, declined after the fall of the Austro-Hungarian Empire in 1918. Its population, mostly Jewish (approximately 12,000, according to a census held in 1938), was poor and subsisted from trading with local peasants and from processing scraps of Persian lambskins left after the production of fur coats then fashionable in Central Europe. These scraps were imported from Leipzig in Germany, an important center of the fur industry, and were painstakingly sewn together and exported back to Leipzig, allowing the Jews to eke out a meager income.

In 1939 the region was annexed to the USSR and Rawa Ruska became again an important military garrison town as it had been under Austrian and Polish regimes. The Germans captured the town in 1941 and utilized the enormous Soviet military installation erected outside the town as POW camp. Incarcerated there from September 1940 to January 1941 were Soviet prisoners of war without food or water. They all perished, to be replaced by French, Belgian, and Dutch prisoners of war in the winter of 1941. They too disappeared without a trace.

The Jewish population was left alone until the winter of 1941. After the Wannsee conference in Berlin, at which it was decided to kill all European Jews (euphemistically referred to as the "final solution"), one of the first death camps was erected in Belzec near Rawa Ruska. In January 1941 a few hundred Rawa Jews were rounded up and shipped to Belzec to test the newly erected gas chambers and crematoria. This was repeated again in February 1942. Jews from all over the region were gathered in Rawa Ruska by the Ukrainian police in the summer of 1942. The ghetto was closed, and all its inhabitants were deported to be gassed in nearby Belzec. Hardly more than twenty Jews hidden by Poles survived. After the return of the Soviets in 1944 the depopulated town became a minor administrative center and today it is hardly more than a large village.

6. The conflict between the Poles and the Ukrainian minority intensified in the 1930s. Ukrainian extremists were supported by Berlin in its "Drang Nach Osten" policy pursued secretly in the days of the Weimar Republic and more openly by the Third Reich. The Organization of Ukrainian Nationalists carried out a series of terrorist acts culminating in the assassination of Minister of Interior Boleslaw Pieracki. This prompted the Polish government to resort to the policy of "pacification." Cavalry regiments were stationed in Ukrainian villages, destroying crops, brutalizing peasants, and burning Greek Catholic Churches. A protest registered with Pope Pius XI by the incensed Metropolitan Andrew Graf Szeptycki and his request for intervention earned him an unrelenting hostility of the Poles and the Polish Roman Church. The "pacification" destroyed any possibility of a compromise between the Poles and Ukrainians.

7. Jews represented 10 percent of the population. They lived in their communities, followed their customs, practiced their religion, and spoke Yiddish, a form of an old German dialect. There were no closed ghettos; nonetheless, the social contact with the local population was limited. The Jews supported themselves primarily as tailors, carpenters, coppersmiths, tinsmiths, locksmiths, and cobblers. They were merchants, innkeepers, and since the early nineteenth century an increasing number had entered free professions and become lawyers, physicians, architects, and teachers.

Jews originally were invited to settle in Poland in the thirteenth century because their skills were in demand. The massacres of Jewish communities in the Rhein Valley by the Crusaders prompted a search for more friendly places. Jews settled in Poland in increasing numbers, became wards of the kings, and were given a charter defining their rights and responsibilities. The Jewish communities prospered and enjoyed a considerable autonomy. As the Commonwealth of Poland expanded eastward Jews moved on and settled in Lithuania, the Baltic lands, Russia, and the Ukraine.

The Commonwealth of Poland, a union of Poles, Lithuanians, and Ruthenians (subsequently Ukrainians), was under the Jagiellon dynasty a dominant political and military power in Central Europe. It evolved in its early days into a kingdom governed by laws. After the death of the last Jagiellon, the kings elected by the nobility followed these policies and Poland remained a country that accorded protection to all—Jews, Armenians, Greeks, Tartars, Moldavians, and, after the Reformation, even Protestants.

The Cossack revolt in 1648 led by Bohdan Chmielnitzky in the Ukraine resulted in massacres of the Polish and Jewish population inhabiting the Kresy (borderland). Subsequent wars fought by Poland with Sweden and Moscovy sapped the strength of the country, and excessive liberalism made it ungovernable. Its last moment of greatness led by their king Jan Sobieski, before the final decline set in, was the defeat of Turks in 1683 before Vienna. A hundred years later the once great country was partitioned between Russia, Prussia, and Austria.

The new rulers of the partitioned Poland differed in their attitudes toward Jews. The Germans, who were discriminating and rigid, believed that keeping the Jews in quasi ghettos at least provided legal protection. The Austrians were more liberal and appreciated the contribution of the Jewish community. The emancipated and well-educated Jews reached positions of importance in the Austro-Hungarian Empire and, like Poles and some Ukrainians, were knighted (given the title "von," the equivalent of knighthood). Jews were generally oppressed in Tzarist Russia with occasional violence encouraged by the government and the Russian Orthodox Church in the Ukraine and Moldavia.

The once vibrant and thriving Jewish community was divided into three components, each of which evolved somewhat differently under the three powers ruling the partitioned country. However, the protection of the Crown and the Polish nobility disappeared, to be replaced by new and not always friendly and accommodating regimes. The Jews, treated reasonably well over the centuries, saw themselves as an integral part of the Polish community. Some spoke excellent Polish and sympathized with the yearning of Poles to overthrow the yoke of the foreign rulers, in particular the oppressive Russian rule. A Jew, Colonel Berek Joselevich, commanded a Polish cavalry regiment in the Napoleonic wars. His son, Josele Berkowicz, led a Jewish detachment in the 1831 revolt of Poles against Russia. The orthodox rabbi of Warsaw, Maisels, was implicated in the 1863 uprising against the Russians and almost ended on the gallows with other leaders of this tragic episode. A large number of Jews fought in the Legions of Pilsudski in World War I. The list of Polish officers murdered in 1940 in Katyn by the NKVD included a disproportionate number of Jews.

After World War I, Poland was resurrected practically in its pre-partition borders. After the initial elation, difficulties emerged. The Polish elite had been decimated in the Napoleonic wars and the revolts against Russia in 1831, 1863, and

1905 as these were fought primarily by the upper classes. A great number of the participants were exiled to Siberia or emigrated to France. Standards were lowered and intolerance, bellicosity, and anti-Semitism exacerbated ethnic conflicts. The lot of Ukrainians, Byelorussians, Lithuanians, and Jews was equally difficult and was aggravated by poverty and a poorly managed national economy.

This took its toll on the newly established state, which was glued together under the terms of the Treaty of Versailles. After the assassination of President Narutowicz in 1926, Marshal Pilsudski, the legendary leader of the Polish Legions in the World War I, took over and ruled the complex country intelligently and effectively. He appreciated the contribution of the Jews and their role as traders, industrialists, and financiers to be critical to the development of a backward and primarily agricultural country.

After his death in 1935 a political vacuum developed with corruption and inefficiency undermining the very foundation of the State. The new rulers, an incompetent military clique, had no sense of direction and were foundering in a deteriorating European situation. The Jews of Poland found themselves submerged in a sea of hostility, with nowhere to go, and no future to look forward to. This was the backdrop of the subsequent destruction of Polish Jewry in the Holocaust during World War II.

8. Andrew Graf Szeptycki, Archbishop of Lwów and Metropolitan of Halicz, was born in 1865. He was a scion of a noble family that originally followed the Eastern Rite before becoming assimilated. Andrew was born a Roman Catholic and was raised in a traditional Polish home. His grandfather, Alexander Fredro, was a prominent Polish playwright. The deeply religious young man joined a monastic order and became a priest. He was entrusted by Pope Leo XIII with the task of revitalizing the Uniate or Greek Catholic Church. He unrelentingly pursued this path until his death in November 1944.

Before World War I he accomplished a great deal. In 1914 Lwów was occupied by Russian troops and the Metropolitan was arrested and imprisoned in a Russian Orthodox monastery. There he came in contact with the hierarchy of the Russian Orthodox Church and laid the foundation for an agreement to be signed with Rome. The outbreak of the Bolshevik revolution ended these efforts.

The Metropolitan was freed and returned to Lwów to resume his pastoral activity. He was appointed Apostolic Exarch for the East while imprisoned in Russia, and subsequently was reconfirmed in this post by Popes Pius XI and Pius XII.

During his long tenure he organized the spiritual life of the Greek Catholic migrants in Germany, France, Belgium, and Holland, and extended this activity to the Ukrainian communities in the United States and in Canada.

The deteriorating relations between the Poles and the Ukrainians after World War I complicated his life. He was accused by Poles of being a traitor, while the

Ukrainians distrusted him as a Pole. The greatness of the man and his sanctity overcame this and to the end of his days he was highly respected by most and hated by some. The process of beatification of the Metropolitan, initiated in 1956, is still taking place in Rome.

9. Lord Curzon shortly after World War I was involved in negotiations to define the borders of the newly resurrected Poland. He attempted to address the conflict between the Poles and the Ukrainians by identifying a demarcation line separating the two feuding ethnic groups. This was referred to as the Curzon Line. The demarcation line agreed on by the Third Reich and the USSR in the Ribbentrop-Molotov agreement roughly followed the Curzon Line.

10. The Polish army defeated by the Germans in 1939 retreated eastward. The Soviet army crossed the Polish border and disarmed the retreating units. The officers and the NCOs were sent to POW camps in Starobielsk, Kozielsk in Byelorussia. There they were joined by reserve officers who after registration were arrested in the territory occupied by the USSR. They represented the intellectual elite of Poland—lawyers, physicians, teachers, newspapermen, and engineers who were mobilized in 1939. They were all executed by the NKVD in the spring of 1940 on Stalin's order. This was finally admitted by Moscow after the disintegration of the Soviet Union.

11. Stakhanov was a coal miner selected by Stalin's propaganda machinery who had exceeded his assigned norm six times. The artificially created circumstances permitted this "heroic" achievement. The propaganda machinery introduced a campaign to emulate the achievement of Stakhanov, resulting in pressure to produce that exceeded the exploitation of workers that had prevailed under the worst conditions existing in Western Europe after the industrial revolution.

12. Ihumen Clement Szeptycki (Clement Graf Szeptycki, the brother of the Metropolitan) and Father Hrycaj, the Metropolitan's secretary, were present during my father's visit to the Metropolitan after the arrival of the Germans.

13. The barracks of St. Brigitte, referred to commonly as Brygidki, were built by the Austrians to house a large garrison. Adjacent to it was a section of the compound that served as a military prison. The complex occupied a whole block in the center of the city. The Poles turned the huge compound into a prison. The NKVD took it over and used it as a transit point for prisoners shipped to camps in the USSR. The prison was always filled to capacity, with an occasional transport of prisoners moved at night in trucks covered by canvas to the railroad station to make room for the newly arrested. During the day in front of the gates there was always a long line of people waiting with packages of food and clothing for the prisoners.

14. Fifty years later in 1991 while in Paris visiting Msgr. Michael Hrynchyshyn, Apostolic Visitator to Ukrainians in France, I was invited to attend a preview of a

documentary made by a French television crew on the Greek Catholic Church in Western Ukraine.

The preview started with shots of Lwów, an ancient and a beautiful city, and towering over it the cathedral of St. George. The narrator briefly outlined the history of the city and the Greek Catholic Church. He commented on the persecution suffered by the Ukrainians and their Church at the hands of the oppressive Soviet regime. Suddenly to my astonishment the courtyard of the Brygidki prison appeared on the television screen—the smoldering ruins, and the Jews carrying decomposed bodies. In one of the shots I could see a blurred group in a corner of the courtyard, myself among them.

The narrator commented that these were Ukrainian prisoners executed by the NKVD extricated from the cellars and carried by the grieving families to be identified. In reality most of the prisoners executed by the NKVD in Brygidki were Poles and Jews. There were also a few Ukrainians among them.

The horror in the ruins of the Brygidki prison on July 1, 1941, was photographed by German officers. Apparently there were among them crews of newsmen filming the event. The photographing and filming were described in my book published in Israel in 1947 by Am Oved, *Aliti miSpezia*. The newsreel remained buried in some forgotten archive to be discovered by the French television crew preparing the documentary on the Greek Catholic Church. It was incorporated in the program with suitable if inaccurate captions.

The Ukrainian tormentors on the streets and in Brygidki were easily identified because they wore blue-yellow armbands. The local population was abetting the outrage taking place on the streets. The atrocities in Brygidki were committed by SS men, easily identifiable by skulls with crossed bones on their caps, German military police (with brown cuffs on the their blue-gray field jackets), German soldiers, members of the Ukrainian battalion "Nachtigall" in German uniforms with yellow-blue shoulder patches, and Ukrainian "milicja."

The killing in Brygidki occurred on the second day of the occupation of the city by German troops. The "Petlura Days" organized by the newly formed Ukrainian Police (Hilfspolizei) resulted in additional thousands of Jews killed in August 1941. The "final solution of the Jewish question" was decided on at the Wannsee conference much later, in December 1941. The liquidation of the Jewish communities in Galizia (Western Ukraine) occurred in the years 1942-43.

Brygidki, a minor episode in the Holocaust, was the start of an all-out assault on the values of the Western man, his beliefs, the concept of law and justice, and the dignity of human life. Western civilization still has to recover from the horror perpetrated during World War II with the assistance of Ukrainians, Lithuanians, Croats, and other collaborators throughout Europe occupied by the Third Reich.

The documentary is an illustration of how truth can be twisted and manipulated knowingly or through ignorance. The records documenting the Holocaust and other horrors perpetrated are challenged by "revisionists." Therefore, the careful documentation and painstakingly assembled evidence since the end of World War II will prevent distortions of the truth as evidenced in the illustration of a newsreel woven into the documentary in 1990 on the Greek Catholic Church.

15. The Ukrainian battalions of volunteers were formed after 1939 in preparation for an assault on the USSR. Their task was to cut lines of transportation and communication and incite local population to an insurrection. Their excellent choirs prompted the German commanders to give them the nickname "nightingale." The volunteers wore German uniforms with blue and yellow arm patches and were led by the future minister of social welfare of the Federal German Republic, Dr. Theodor Oberlander, who was responsible among others for the atrocities perpetrated in Brygidki. The batallions "Nachtingall" and "Roland" were disbanded after the Germans crossed the prewar border between Poland and the Soviet Union.

16. A complete set of identity and working papers issued by the German authorities in Lwów and in Rawa Ruska commencing with the words "der Jude Kurt Lewin" is still in my possession.

CHAPTER 2

1. The Hutzuls, Bojkos, and Lemkos are mountaineers dwelling in the Carpathian mountain range. They are Eastern Slavs related to the Ukrainians living on the plains. Isolated in mountain valleys, they maintain a distinct dialect, customs, and garb. Most of them are Greek Catholic although there are many Orthodox communities. They are shepherds and lumberjacks and descend in the summer into the lowlands to work as seasonal workers on farms. Metropolitan Andrew arranged for dismantling one of these ancient mountain churches and transporting it to Lyczakiw where it was restored and left in the care of the Studites.

The skyt (retreat) in Luzky was located near the treeline close to the Hungarian border. This part of the Carpathian range was populated by Bojkos who subsisted working as lumberjacks in the extensive forests.

Large tracts of forest in this sector of the Carpathian mountain range, primarily cedar and pine, were the property of the Greek Catholic Church and represented the endowment of the diocese of Lwów. Pidlute (the summer residence of Metropolitan Andrew), Luzky, Osmoloda, and Czorna Rika were small settlements in which the foresters and administrators of the property resided. The narrow-gauge railroad was built to transport logs to a sawmill in Broshniw at the base of the mountain range.

2. Old Slavonic was the original language spoken by the Eastern Slavs from which the Byelorussian, Bulgarian, Russian, and Ukrainian languages evolved. The two brothers, Cyril and Methodius, who converted Eastern Slavs to Christianity trans-

lated the Scriptures and the Liturgy from Greek into Old Slavonic in the ninth century and developed the Cyrillic alphabet still in use today.

3. A separation consisting of icons dividing the altar from the nave in churches of the Byzantine Rite. The central door, referred to as the royal door, remains open during the Liturgy except during the consecration. The side doors are used for the entrance of the celebrant carrying the Gospels and later the chalice and the diskos.

4. The Vikings in the eighth and ninth centuries sailed south on the rivers of Eastern Europe, explored the region and some became rulers of the indigenous population. Their influence can be traced in the design of the traditional apparel, embroidery, pottery and the architecture of the wooden churches. The trident, a common emblem of the vikings, became the Ukrainian coat of arms. Prince Valdemar (Volodymy) and his mother Olga invited the Byzantines to baptize Ukraine in the tenth century.

5. Halyczyna was a name frequently used to describe Western Ukraine ruled by Austria after the partition of Poland. It is derived from the name Galizien in German describing this administrative district of the Austro-Hungarian Empire.

6. A partisan division was formed in Byelorussia's forests by Major General Kowpak, which operated behind German lines destroying supplies, blowing up bridges, and attacking small German garrisons guarding railroad hubs. Starting in Byelorussia in the winter of 1942 the partisan units progressed through Pidlasha, Volyn into Western Ukraine, and from there to the Carpathian range where they remained until the arrival of the Red Army in 1944. The partisan raid penetrated deep into the rear of the German Army then fighting in Russia and the Ukraine to test the vulnerability of the logistic system supporting the German military machinery.

7. The Red Army marched into Poland in September 1939 and following the notorious Molotov-Ribbentrop agreement occupied its eastern provinces. Western Ukraine was promptly annexed to the Ukrainian Socialist Republic. The Germans attacked the USSR in June 1941, and its forces occupied Byelorussia, Ukraine, approached Moscow, the Volga, and the Caucasus. After lifting the siege of Stalingrad (Volgograd) the Red Army launched a series of offensives that brought it back to Western Ukraine in June 1944.

CHAPTER 3

1. Odilo Globocnik in the District of Lublin and Katzmann in District Galizien were lesser-known war criminals. Both were Generals der SS und Polizei, the highest rank in the police in the Third Reich. Both common criminals joined the NSDAP and advanced in the 1930s with others like Sepp Dietrich and Bach-Zelewski in the ranks of the SS.

Katzmann and Globocnik were the administrators of the "final solution" in

Poland. Belzec, Sobibor, Treblinka, and some minor death camps were in their jurisdiction, as was the training camp Trawniki for Ukrainian personnel serving in them as guards.

Odilo Globocnik, an Austrian of Slovenian origin, was transferred in the winter of 1943-44 with the approach of the Soviet troops from Lublin to Trieste as gauleiter (administrator) of the region. In May 1945 he shot himself before the Allied troops arrived.

2. The designation of the sectors of the Eastern Front was made in the early stages of the war. There were three Byelorussian Fronts and four Ukrainian Fronts (theaters). As the front lines moved, the designations were no longer applicable. Nonetheless, the Soviet General Staff retained them until the end of the war. The First Polish Army fought in the First Byelorussian Front commanded by Marshall Zhukov. The Second Polish Army formed in Lublin fought in the First Ukrainian Front commanded by Marshall Konev.

3. A Polish government in exile had been formed after the fall of Poland in Toulouse and was headed by General Wladyslaw Sikorski. After the fall of France it was transferred to London where it functioned until the return of Prime Minister Mikolajczyk to Poland in 1945. The PKWN was formed in June 1944 in Lublin as a parallel Polish government controlled by Moscow.

4. The Polish Special Battalion was originally a paratrooper unit. The carefully selected personnel were trained to form and lead partisan units operating behind German lines in the forests of Russia and Byelorossia. Team officers, demolition experts, and wireless operators were dropped behind German lines and were coordinated and supplied by the Partisan Headquarters (The Polish Special Battalion). Subsequently it became an elite combat unit of the First Polish Army until it was incorporated into the Fourth Infantry Division of the First Polish Army.

5. NKVD (Narodny Komissariat Vnutrennych Diel-Komisariat of Internal Affairs) was the renamed dreaded GPU which evolved from the Czeka (Czerezwyczjna Komisja) formed after the revolution by the Pole Feliks Dzierzynski. Its activities, the terror, and the atrocities committed are well documented. NKVD evolved from this instrument of terror after the purges of the 1930s. It was a complex organization controlling prisons, labor camps, and mining for gold and diamonds. It had its tentacles everywhere and became a state within the state. It guarded the borders and maintained a separate army and air force employed to control the population.

CHAPTER 4

1. Italy immediately after World War II was occupied by the Allies, with Great Britain playing a predominant role in governing it.

2. The mayor of La Spezia spent some time in a British jail for permitting the construction of the water pipeline and other assistance extended to us.

3. Captain Charles Orde Wingate was assigned by the British authorities governing Palestine to the fledgling Haganah organization during the Arab terror of 1936-39 to train its members. The "Special Night Squads" (Plugor Sade) trained and led by him eliminated Arab bands infiltrated from French-controlled Syria and restored order.

He gained fame during World War II as a commanding officer of the expeditionary force that reconquered Ethiopia from the Italians, and subsequently as the brilliant architect of the daring raids behind the Japanese lines in Burma carried out by the Chindits (brigades operating behind enemy's lines and supplied by air). Israeli volunteers accompanied him during the reconquest of Ethiopia and served under him in Burma.

4. The latter were fringe organizations given to terrorist activities.

5. The less fortunate Italian units that survived the Soviet offensive in the winter of 1942 in the region of Stalingrad and retreated with the German troops were disarmed by their former comrades in arms near Lwów and executed after the fall of Mussolini's regime.

6. The first Jewish units were formed in 1940 and served with distinction in North Africa as a part of the Eighth Army. Subsequently additional Jewish units were created and functioned in the framework of RASC (Royal Army Service Corps) and women units serving in hospitals, driving ambulances, and working in the areas of communications and logistics. Finally a Jewish Brigade was formed that fought with distinction in the Eighth British Army in Italy. It consisted primarily of Haganah members and was commanded by officers trained by the British. It was a cohesive group and became an important component of the future army of the State of Israel.

7. There was a clandestine command of the Haganah in Europe, which organized the transports of survivors of the Holocaust from Poland, Hungary, Rumania, and Germany to France and Italy. There they waited like the Shaar Yashuv group for an opportunity to continue legally or illegally to Eretz Israel (Palestine). The command of the Haganah was in charge of acquiring ships and organizing illegal transports to Palestine referred to as Alija B. It was assisted in its clandestine operations by the Jewish units of the Eighth British Army stationed then in Italy.

8. The couple eventually settled in a kibbutz in the Sharon Valley, where he was killed in the war of 1948, leaving a widow and a small child.

CHAPTER 5

1. A district (*machoz* in Hebrew) represented a cluster of settlements organized to defend themselves in the event of an attack. Each settlement was responsible for its own defense perimeter, and its weapons were stored by the armorers in camouflaged hiding places. When needed, the district could mobilize field units of the Haganah (volunteers with advanced training organized in sections and platoons).

These could be employed in an emergency to rescue a convoy or a settlement in the district under attack. A fully armed platoon of the Palmach was generally stationed in a district.

2. The British Police divided the country into districts. The headquarters of the Northern District responsible for the Galilee and Jordan Valley were in Haifa.

3. The Jewish Agency represented the Yishuv. Its members were elected and reflected the composition of the political parties in the Yishuv. The key positions in the Jewish Agency were in the hands of the Labor movement (Mapai and the more leftist Mapam). The Diaspora before World War II was represented by General Zionists, the mainstream of the Zionist movement in Central Europe. After World War II the Jewish Agency was dominated by the Labor movement.

It acted for practical purposes as the unofficial government of the Yishuv. It controlled a network of institutions and was responsible for dealings with the British government in London, contact with other governments, and contacts with the Diaspora. The Haganah and the Palmach were controlled by it and acted only if instructed by the Jewish Agency.

The IZL led by Menachem Begin and LECHI, referred to as the Stern Group, did not recognize the authority of the Jewish Agency and acted independently.

4. The text of the oath of the Haganah: "I hereby declare that I wish to join voluntarily out of conviction and sense of duty toward my people the ranks of the Haganah, an organization to defend Eretz Israel.

"I hereby swear to be faithful to the Haganah, to obey its rules and follow its objectives all my life as decreed by its high command complying with the principles outlined by the elected leadership of the Yishuv.

"I hereby swear to remain for the rest of my days at the disposal of the Haganah, to accept without reservation its rules, and without any hesitation to respond if called to active service at any time and at any place and to obey all orders and fulfill faithfully all instructions.

"I swear to devote all my efforts, all my strength, and sacrifice my life in the defense of my people and my land, for the freedom of Israel and the redemption of Zion."

5. Possession of weapons was prohibited by law. If attacked, the settlements had to defend themselves, as the British could not be relied on. (From the early days the leadership determined that each settlement had to defend itself.)

Therefore, weapons for self-defense were accumulated over the years. These were primarily infantry weapons consisting of rifles, pistols, hand grenades, light machine guns, and mortars. The armorer's responsibility was to store and maintain the equipment in safe, well-hidden places, "slicks" in the slang of the Haganah.

The armorers (*nashak* in Hebrew) supplied the weapons and ammunition before an operation. After completion of the assignment, the equipment was returned to them to be stored. It was a rather secretive group of innocuous-looking individuals. Only the Palmach units were armed and were responsible for hiding their own equipment.

6. Operation Ten Plagues was designed to open a corridor to the Negev, which was cut off from the rest of the country by Egyptian forces. The Israeli attack was carried out by a relatively large force (15,000 men consisting of IDF and Palmach brigades). It removed the Egyptian threat to Tel Aviv and freed the Negev.

The Faluja pocket resulted from this operation, in which the Israeli forces trapped an Egyptian division. Among its officers were Major Gamal Abdel Nasser, Captain Anwar Sadat and others who eventually overthrew the regime of King Farouk.

7. The Palmach was a separate clandestine military component of the Haganah. It consisted of volunteers who, after graduating from high school, served two years in the Palmach. On completion of regular service they remained in the reserves of the Palmach.

Units of the Palmach, usually in platoon strength, were strategically placed in the kibbutzim throughout the country, providing an ever-ready military force if and when needed.

In 1947 the Palmach was mobilized with its operational headquarters in Tel Aviv. The three Palmach brigades, Harel, Jiftach, and Negev, absorbed the full impact of the 1947-49 war. They fought in the Galilee, on the Jerusalem front, and in the desert. They lost a disproportionate number of commanders and soldiers. (From approximately 7,000 members of the Palmach mobilized in 1947, over 1,000 fell in the War of Liberation 1947-49.)

Israel probably survived the first phase of the 1947-49 war thanks to its heroism and self-sacrifice. My battalion was attached to the Tenth Palmach Brigade Harel (The Mountain of the Lord) through most of the siege of the Jerusalem. Subsequently I was attached to the Southern Command (consisting primarily of Palmach units). I learned to respect and function with them. I was greatly disturbed to see the Palmach abruptly dismantled in 1949 because of internal political considerations.

They unquestionably had their shortcomings and their limitations. Nonetheless, their courage, self-sacrifice, and dedication saved the new State of Israel when it was attacked by regular armies of the neighboring Arab states in May 1948.

8. Barclays Bank DCO (Dominion Colonial and Overseas) and its managers were always correct and rather friendly toward the Yishuv. One of them, Stephen Mogford, subsequently a general manager of the bank and a director of Barclays Bank Plc, was a great supporter of Zionism. If anything, the bank's premises

would have been protected by the Haganah if some mischief had been planned by the IZL.

9. "The Silver Platter" by Nathan Alterman (translated into English from Hebrew by Ada Aharoni) tells of a people (the Jews) waiting at daybreak (after the night of struggle) for a miracle (the State of Israel). Into the crowd come an exhausted young couple, a girl and a boy, who represent Hebrew Youth. These young heroes fall at the feet of their people, having given their all in the struggle. "We are the silver platter / On which lies / The Jewish Homeland," they say. "The rest will be told / In the history of Israel."

CHAPTER 6

1. Meir Zorea (Zaro), a captain in the Jewish Brigade in World War II, was decorated with a Military Cross for influencing the course of a battle fought by the Eighth British Army in northern Italy in 1945. He served with distinction in the Israeli Defense Forces in a wide range of key positions. He is a member of the kibbutz Maagan Michael.

After Moshe Dayan left the Israeli Army, Zaro agreed to return to active service. As a general he served with distinction in a variety of key posts before retiring as Inspector General of the Israeli defense system.

2. A battle was fought in the days of Judah Maccabi in Beit Choron, today an Arab village. Hence the name given to the Sixty-second Battalion.

3. The Haganah and its elite Palmach units were transferred after the proclamation of the State of Israel on May 15, 1948, to the Israeli Defense Forces—the regular army of the newly established state.

4. Colonel Michael David Marcus, a graduate of West Point and a veteran of World War II, was a staunch supporter of Zionism. After discovering the horror of the concentration camps after the fall of the Third Reich, he dedicated himself to the creation of a home for the survivors of the Holocaust. He joined the command of the Haganah in the winter of 1948 and was instrumental in forging its units into a regular army. He was killed accidentally in Abu Gosh in May 1948 by a sentry.

5. The Arab Legion was formed by Brigadier John Bagot Glubb, a British advisor of Abdallah, the Emir of Transjordan. In the aftermath of the World War I, Ibn Saud heading his tribe of Wahabi Ikhwan Bedouins in 1924 occupied Mecca and Medina, ending the long rule of the Hashemites. The sons of Sherif Hussein of the Arab Revolt were installed by the British, Feisal as King of Iraq and Abdallah as Emir of Transjordan. Each was given a stipend and advisors in order to stabilize the region and protect the oil fields in Iraq, which were critical to the Royal Navy. Brigadier John Bagot Glubb was attached to Emir Abdallah and was given the task of organizing a camel corps whose responsibility was to guard the pipeline

from the oil fields of the Iraq Petroleum Company to the refinery in Haifa. This Bedouin force was commanded by British officers and NCOs and was gradually expanded into the Arab Legion. The well-trained and equipped Brigades of the Arab Legion presented in 1948 a major threat to the newly proclaimed State of Israel. The Haganah and subsequently the Israeli Defense Forces faced the Arab Legion in the Jerusalem sector, in Latrun, and in the settlements south of Bethlehem.

6. Itzhak Sade as a young man was a pupil of Captain Charles Orde Wingate and served under him in the Special Night Squads fighting to neutralize Arab bands terrorizing the Yishuv and the British. Itzhak Sade was the founder of the Palmach and with Yigal Alon and others forged it into an efficient permanently mobilized arm of the Haganah. He eventually commanded the Eighth Brigade, the nucleus of the future Israeli Armored Corps.

7. A brigade commander cannot issue orders directly to a field unit. The established chain of command must be observed to prevent conflict with the overall plan of a battalion commander, whose responsibility is to coordinate all units. Otherwise "friendly fire" will cause casualties.

The elite Sixty-first and Sixty-second battalions of the Sixth Brigade were originally formed from Haganah members. After May 1948, conscripts were included to replace the killed and the wounded. The positions separating the Jewish sector from the Arab sector were defended by reserve units formed from middle-aged and elderly individuals who were not suited for combat field units. These reserve units were formed to free the Sixty-first and Sixty-second battalions for combat and were commanded by officers practically without any formal training. A transfer of a MM (Haganah commander graduate of a school) to these units was humiliating as it indicated incompetence, cowardice, or both.

8. "The Lavon affair," the culmination of a long-standing feud between David Ben Gurion and Pinchas Lavon, briefly the Israeli Minister of Defense, was triggered by an intelligence mishap in Egypt. Moshe Dayan, then the Chief of Staff of the Israeli Army, forced subordinates to forge documents, which were employed to incriminate the innocent Lavon in the mishap. "Evidence" was fabricated that Lavon had ordered these hare-brained activities. The scheme to implicate Lavon misfired, as his lawyers exposed the forgery, and its perpetrators were punished. The details of the affair, a matter of public knowledge in Israel, were hushed up and to this day the "Lavon affair" is referred to in Israel as "the messy business." The political careers of Lavon and others embroiled in it by Moshe Dayan (acting on whose behalf?) were destroyed. Moshe Dayan managed as always to keep out of direct involvement in this mess.

CHAPTER 7

1. The Slavs, among them Ukrainians, were considered an inferior race by the Germans and therefore did not qualify for the rapidly forming units of Waffen SS (combat units sponsored by the Reichsministerium of Heinrich Himmler). It was only in 1943 that Dr. Otto Wachter, the governor of District Galizien, and Colonel Bisanz, a German agent planted before the war in Lwów, who cultivated contacts with the Ukrainian community, finally convinced Himmler that Ukrainians could be trusted as allies. Attempts to secure the support of the Metropolitan Andrew to this belated venture were unsuccessful despite persuasion and threats. Only chaplains were delegated to the newly forming SS Division Galizien.

The division was formed from the Ukrainian Police, other auxiliary units, and volunteers who preferred to join the division rather than be shipped to munitions factories in Germany. A combat unit of the SS Division Galizien, thrown into the front line near Brody to stem the advancing Red Army, was annihilated. Units in training were assembled in Rimini, Italy, after the war ended. The intervention of Msgr. Ivan Bucko at the Curia Romana prevented their repatriation to the USSR.

2. Regretfully, Olga was a very fragile individual. The pressures of life in Israel and its climate, the return to New York with all the frustrations and the struggle to establish a stable economic base, and adapting to new circumstances took their toll. Olga died in 1963, leaving our two little boys, ages two and four. She made a critical contribution to my ability to adjust to a new country and a new profession. She made an equally important contribution to advancing the cause of beatification of the Metropolitan Andrew Szeptycki.

3. Dr. Hans Frank headed the Generalgouvernement, an administrative unit established by the Third Reich for the occupied districts of Poland not annexed to the Third Reich after the fall of Poland in September 1939. Western Ukraine or the so-called District Galizien was incorporated into the Generalgouvernement in 1941 after the attack of the Third Reich on the USSR.

Dr. Frank, one of the war criminals tried in Nuremberg, was executed. Dr. Otto Wachter, another war criminal, was sheltered by Msgr. Bucko and the then Roman Catholic Bishop of Innsbruck. The involvement of Msgr. Bucko with Dr. Otto Wachter was exposed by Hans Jakob Stehle, a German free-lance journalist close to the Curia Romana, who wrote a number of articles dealing with the cause of beatification of Metropolitan Szeptycki.

4. Joseph Cardinal Slipyj, archbishop of Lwów and Metropolitan of Halicz, succeeded Metropolitan Andrew Graf Szeptycki in 1944. He was arrested by the Soviets and spent eighteen years in prisons and labor camps. He was released from prison by Khrushchev as a gesture of good will and arrived in Rome during the

Second Vatican Council. His release signalled a change in the Soviet policy toward the Vatican. Shortly after arrival in Rome he was given a Cardinal's hat.

CHAPTER 8

1. The Tatars since the days of Genghis Khan occupied the shores of the Black Sea and Crimea. The once-powerful Golden Horde that threatened Central Europe and in the annual raids reached Lower Silesia had dwindled with time. Nevertheless, the Cossack and Tatar raids continued until the end of the seventeeth century. Hence, a network of fortresses and fortified churches had been built to provide refuge and protect the population.

The objective of these raids was loot and yassyr. Young men and women were captured by the raiders to be sold in the slave markets in the towns on the shore of the Black Sea and in Istanbul. Polish and Ukrainian slaves were highly prized—women for the harems, men to row in the galleys of the Ottoman fleet. Young boys were especially valuable as they were raised as Moslems and incorporated into Janissar Corps, the guard of the Sultan and the elite unit of the army of the Ottoman empire.

2. See Chapter 3.

3. See Chapter 2.

4. This was disclosed by a freelance journalist residing in Rome, Hans Jakob Stehle. He mentioned it in a paper submitted at the Symposium on Metropolitan Szeptycki organized by the University of Toronto in 1984. It is also mentioned in the memoirs of an Austrian archbishop of Innsbruck who apparently was sheltering the war criminal, Dr. Otto Wachter, jointly with Archbishop Bucko.

CHAPTER 10

1. Anschluss refers to the incorporation of the Republic of Austria into the Third Reich. There was some opposition to it. Nevertheless, the carefully cultivated myth that the Austrians were victims of the Nazis is not true. The population greeted the arriving German troops with enthusiasm; the primate of Austria, Cardinal Innitzer, decorated the St. Stephen's cathedral with Nazi flags and issued a pastoral letter concluded with the greeting "Heil Hitler."

2. See Chapter 7.

CHAPTER 11

1. The term *zaibatsu* was applied to the large industrial complexes in prewar Japan. A considerable economic and political power was concentrated in the hands of the managers in the years between the wars. These industrial complexes

differed in composition and activity. Therefore, the term represents an oversimplication describing a broad range of industrial enterprises with varied characteristics.

2. The Christian Edict was issued by Toyotomi Hideyoshi in 1595(?) after the discovery of Jesuit meddling in internal political affairs. It was enforced first by Tokugawa Ieyasu and finally by Iemitsu, the third shogun. After the Shimabara Rebellion (a Christian Jesuit-led rebellion in 1637-39) Japan was closed to the outside world; with the exception of the Dutch trading post on an artificial island off Nagasaki, the Christian Edict was ruthlessly enforced until 1858.